GENDER IN ANCIENT CYPRUS

GENDER AND ARCHAEOLOGY SERIES

Series Editor
Sarah Milledge Nelson
University of Denver

This series focuses on ways to understand gender in the past through archaeology. This is a topic poised for significant advances in both method and theory, which in turn can improve all archaeology. The possibilities of new methodological rigor as well as new insights into past cultures are what make gendered archaeology a vigorous and thriving subfield.

The series welcomes single authored books on themes in this topical area, particularly ones with a comparative focus. Edited collections with a strong theoretical or methodological orientation will also be considered. Audiences are practicing archaeologists and advanced students in the field.

EDITORIAL BOARD

Philip Duke, Fort Lewis College
Alice Kehoe, Marquette University
Janet Levy, University of North Carolina, Charlotte
Margaret Nelson, Arizona State University
Thomas Patterson, University of California, Riverside
K. Anne Pyburn, Indiana University
Ruth Whitehouse, University College London

BOOKS IN THE SERIES

SUBMISSION GUIDELINES

Prospective authors of single or co-authored books and editors of anthologies should submit a letter of introduction, the manuscript or a four to ten page proposal, a book outline, and a curriculum vitae. Please send your book manuscript/proposal packet to: Gender and Archaeology Series, AltaMira Press, 1630 North Main Street # 367, Walnut Creek, CA 94596, (925) 938-7243, www.altamirapress.com

GENDER IN ANCIENT CYPRUS

Narratives of Social Change on a Mediterranean Island

DIANE BOLGER

ALTAMIRA PRESS
A Division of Rowman & Littlefield Publishers, Inc.
Walnut Creek • Lanham • New York • Oxford

AltaMira Press
A Division of Rowman & Littlefield Publishers, Inc.
A Member of the Rowman & Littlefield Publishing Group
1630 North Main Street, #367
Walnut Creek, CA 94596
www.altamirapress.com

Rowman & Littlefield Publishers, Inc.
4501 Forbes Boulevard, Suite 200
Lanham, MD 20706

PO Box 317
Oxford
OX2 9RU, UK

Copyright © 2003 by AltaMira Press

British Library Cataloguing in Publication Information Available

Library of Congress Cataloging-in-Publication Data

Bolger, Diane R.
    Gender in ancient Cyprus : narratives of social change on a Mediterranean
island / Diane Bolger.
Includes bibliographical references and index.
        p. cm. — (Gender and archaeology series ; v. 6)
    ISBN 0-7591-0429-8 — ISBN 0-7591-0430-1 (pbk.)
  1. Gender indentity—Cyprus. 2. Sex role—Cyprus. 3. Cyprus—Antiquities. I.
Title. II. Series.
    HQ1075.5.C93B65 2003
    305.3'0939'37—dc21

                                                                    2003007524

Printed in the United States of America

♾™ The paper used in this publication meets the minimum requirements of American
National Standard for Information Sciences—Permanence of Paper for Printed Library
Materials, ANSI/NISO Z39.48-1992.

Contents

List of Figures and Tables

Figures

Tables

Abbreviations

ACD	artificial cranial deformation
B.C.	calibrated date B.C.
CGI	Cypro-Geometric I period
EB, EBA	Early Bronze Age
EC	Early Cypriot period
EChal	Early Chalcolithic period
GB	Glossy Burnished Ware
LChal	Late Chalcolithic period
LB, LBA	Late Bronze Age
LC	Late Cypriot period
LNeo	Late Neolithic period
MB, MBA	Middle Bronze Age
MC	Middle Cypriot period
MChal	Middle Chalcolithic period
PPNB	Pre-pottery Neolithic B period
RP	Red Polished pottery
RW	Red-on-White pottery

Series Editor's Foreword

I AM VERY PLEASED TO INTRODUCE Diane Bolger's in-depth study of gender in the archaeology of Cyprus. This book models an important method for considering the archaeology of a region using gendered themes. Her method of inquiry is tailored to discoveries on the island of Cyprus but could be adapted as a template for the archaeologies of many other areas. Her creative methodology includes the careful examination of various aspects of the archaeological record through time for insights into gender relations, roles, and ideology, before weaving all the strands together into an explanation of social change, including, but not limited to, changes in gender.

Using the latest theory in gender and in archaeology, Bolger considers in separate chapters the main strategies that have been used to analyze gender from archaeological sites. These include the use of space, gendered labor, figurines, evidence of children, and mortuary data. In each of these chapters, she grounds the topic in a theoretical discussion while presenting and explaining the relevant data. Next, she pulls the previous chapters together into a narrative of social change through time in Cyprus, revisiting sites and regions as necessary. In a final chapter, Bolger considers the impact of the gender of archaeologists on the archaeology of Cyprus, both past and present. Appendices include a sketch of Cypriot archaeology through the Bronze Age, which will assist the reader not grounded in the archaeology of this region, and a gazetteer of the sites to help put the sites in context for those who work in other parts of the world. Therefore, this is many volumes in one.

Altogether, this volume is a tour de force of gender archaeology. Bolger controls the latest literature and discusses the application of old and new theories to the sites at hand. The book is written for the practicing archaeologist, but students can benefit from its transparent structure and detailed exposition of archaeological data. Courses in gender and archaeology will profit from its use, regardless of the region that is most familiar to the instructor. The volume will also provide an excellent addition to courses on

Mediterranean, Near Eastern, or European archaeology. Because the book includes all the relevant data, students can understand the application of theories to the sites. As it is free of jargon and clearly written, students will be able to comprehend how data can be used to understand not only changes in the construction of gender roles, but also social change in general.

Sarah Milledge Nelson, Series Editor

Preface and Acknowledgments

MY PURPOSE IN WRITING a book on gender is both personal and professional. In the first place, it represents the application to archaeological material of a long-standing engagement with feminist theory that grew out of my involvement with the women's movement during the 1970s and that has continued to shape my views about society. At the same time, I have been impelled to undertake this project by what I consider to be a blatant gap in the archaeological research of the ancient Near East that, despite the adoption of more theoretically based approaches over the last few decades, continues to marginalize gender in its treatment of the past.

It is my hope, therefore, that this book will make a positive contribution to the prehistory of the eastern Mediterranean region by examining at close range some of the fundamental aspects of gender and their correlations with the dynamics of social, political, and economic change in Cyprus over the course of more than eight thousand years. Its scope ranges from the earliest traces of human habitation on the island to the ultimate phases of the Bronze Age, when Cypriot society began to experience profound social changes resulting from advances in social complexity and a more intensive involvement in extrinsic cultural, economic, and geographical spheres.

Due to teaching obligations in Germany and annual fieldwork commitments in Cyprus and Syria, this book has been several years in the making, and I would like to acknowledge the support of those who have helped me maintain the momentum necessary for seeing it to fruition. First, I thank the participants in the international conference "Engendering Aphrodite: Women and Society in Ancient Cyprus" that I co-organized in Nicosia in 1998, at a time when I was just beginning this book. The positive response and enthusiasm for a conference on gender, a topic that had never before been the focal point of in-depth research in Cypriot archaeology, was extremely encouraging for my project, and the presentations and discussions that took place during that long weekend in March were instrumental in reconsidering and revising some of my own ideas. I am particularly grateful to Joanne Clarke, Tracey Cullen, Carole McCartney, Elinor Ribeiro, Joanna Smith, Laurie Talalay, and Jennifer Webb, whose papers (published in Bolger and Serwint 2002) have been included for discussion in various chapters of this book. In addition, I would like to thank Nancy Serwint who, as director of the Cyprus American Archaeological Research Institute (CAARI) and fellow organizer of the conference, became a trusted friend and colleague during my stay in Nicosia; Diana Constantinides and Vathoulla Moustouki, permanent staff of the CAARI, for their unstinting friendship and support (as well as steady streams of Cypriot coffee); and Sarah Nelson, editor of the Gender and Archaeology Series, whose encouragement and support during the final stages of writing was instrumental to the book's completion.

I am indebted to many others in Cyprus, without whose help the writing of this book would have been a far more onerous task. Thanks are due to the administrative staff of the Department of Antiquities in Nicosia, particularly its director, Sophocles Hadjisavvas, for granting permission to study material in the Cyprus Museum and the Paphos District Museum, and to the staff of the District Archaeological Museum in Paphos, whose hospitality and unfailing good humor have always made my visits there a positive and pleasurable experience. In addition, Walter Fasnacht kindly allowed me to reprint the cover illustration from the promotional brochure of the Almyras project, and Alison South supplied important information on skeletal material from *Ayios Dhimitrios* and gave me permission to publish a plan of Tomb 11 prior to the final publication of the site. Finally, I owe a debt of gratitude to a number of my colleagues of the Lemba Archaeological Project for valuable research that, in one way or another, has been incorporated into the present work; particular thanks are due to Elizabeth Goring, Dorothy Lunt, and Eddie Peltenburg.

This book could not have been completed without the assistance and support of colleagues in Germany and the U.K. In particular, I would like to thank Paula Harbecke, former director of the University of Maryland European Division, for facilitating study leave in Cyprus during the 1997–1998 academic year, and Jane McHan, head of Social Sciences, who consistently encouraged my research in the Near East during my fifteen years with the university. Since much of this book has been written in my post as research fellow at the University of Edinburgh, I would also like to express my thanks to the Department of Archaeology and especially to Eddie Peltenburg, who has been an unfailing source of emotional and intellectual support for this project and who has taken the time to read and comment on an earlier draft of the work.

Finally, I thank the Institute of Aegean Prehistory (INSTAP), which helped fund my study leave from the University of Maryland so that I could carry out research for this book. I am particularly appreciative of INSTAP's willingness to support a topic that normally encounters obstacles from traditional funding sources on the grounds that gender is too "political."

I could not in good conscience end this introductory note without expressing a great debt of gratitude to the growing body of scholars who have had the courage and tenacity to pursue research programs and teaching curricula on the archaeology of gender over the last few decades; although most of them are not personally known to me, their intellectual efforts have furnished a wealth of detailed information and insights into "gendered ways of knowing" the societies of the ancient Near East, Europe, and regions more remote. Unfortunately, the manuscript was completed before the appearance of *Sex and Gender in the Ancient Near East* (Parpola and Whiting 2003), the publication of a special session on gender held in 2001 at the 47th Annual Meeting of the International Congress of Assyriology and Near Eastern Archaeology, which should serve as a significant addition to the growing bodies of evidence on gender in the ancient world.

It is my hope that gender will continue to gain ground in the coming years as a focal point of archaeological research of the ancient Near East. This book has been written with that longer-term research agenda in mind in order to demonstrate the rich possibilities afforded to gender studies by the archaeological record in the "cradle of civilization" and to reiterate the continuing need for others to follow suit.

Introduction: Facing the Cypriot Past I

> Why have archaeologists produced a prehistory of genderless,
> faceless blobs?
>
> —TRINGHAM, "HOUSEHOLDS WITH FACES: THE CHALLENGE
OF GENDER IN PREHISTORIC ARCHITECTURAL REMAINS"

ARCHAEOLOGY IS A SOCIAL SCIENCE, yet people are rarely identified in archaeological writing, either in general excavation reports or in more thematically based
investigations of the remote past. While we manage to fill many pages with detailed accounts of the material remains of human activities—architecture, art, pottery
and stone tool production, subsistence strategies, and ceremonial rituals, to name but a
few—and while we closely scrutinize the evidence through careful observations, metic-
ulous recording methods, detailed classifications, and up-to-date methods of scientific
analysis, in the end we seem to have little to say about people themselves.

To what extent did changes in technology, economy, and environment influence the
ways in which individuals shaped and reconstructed their social relationships? In what
ways did they interact, compete, and collaborate, and how did they negotiate social identities? How do we envision their private, domestic, and public lives? How did they view
themselves and each other? By examining prehistory from a gendered perspective, we can
begin to answer these questions. At the same time, we can begin to humanize the social
structures of the past, filling in some of the missing faces of the individuals and groups
who comprised its various cultures and exploring the impact of various trajectories of
social and economic developments on the dynamics of personal relations. As part of
this process, we are encouraged to confront our own unmediated assumptions about the
ways in which the world should work.

Before we can begin to investigate issues of gender in ancient Cyprus, it is necessary to consider the material evidence that forms the basis for any archaeological

analysis and to construct provisional models that can serve as frameworks for discussion. Although theoretically based approaches constitute a small proportion of research on prehistoric Cyprus, the recent adoption of post-processual models has begun to open up the field to new ways of examining the evidence that challenge more traditional, descriptive approaches. The evolution of society from egalitarian farming communities to hierarchical polities during the Cypriot Bronze Age, for example, which has been the focal point of a number of recent papers, provides a useful framework for interpreting changes in material culture throughout its various phases. Some archaeologists also believe that ethnicity and acculturation have played a formative role in the introduction of Bronze Age culture to the island and the development of an ethnically mixed population during its later phases (Frankel, Webb, and Eslick 1995; Frankel 2000).

Yet, even in these more theoretical investigations, gender remains a largely unexplored landscape, and Cypriot archaeology today is in the same critical state that other areas of the discipline faced over a decade ago when studies of gender and archaeology first began to appear in print. There are signs that this situation is beginning to change, but focal points adopted thus far have been limited until recently to discussions of figurines (Bolger 1992, 1996; Hamilton 1994), the documentation of differential participation by men and women in the field of Cypriot archaeology (Webb and Frankel 1995), and the analysis of gender roles in early prehistory within a binary analytical framework (Bolger 1993; Frankel 1993b). While the recent publication of an international conference in 1998 on women in ancient Cyprus will undoubtedly have an impact (Bolger and Serwint 2002), there is still a long way to go to catch up with gender studies undertaken in other areas of the ancient world such as prehistoric Europe and the Americas.

Why has gender been excluded from traditional archaeological accounts of the Cypriot past, and why do current post-processual models continue to ignore gender as a principal factor? Why, amid a growing body of literature on the archaeology of gender, have archaeologists in Cyprus been unwilling or unable to interpret the material they excavate from the point of view of changing gender constructs?

To see where Cyprus fits (or does not fit) into broader research agendas currently being undertaken in other regions of the Mediterranean, we need to consider some of the traditional narratives of archaeological inquiry that have deliberately or inadvertently left gender out of the picture. I will begin to address this question by considering excerpts from several publication reports from the last century that typify traditional scholarly approaches to social interpretation in Cypriot prehistory. As we shall see, the failure of traditional archaeological narratives to deal explicitly with gender, as revealed by the use of the passive voice, obscures the issue of agency and leaves the door open for unmediated assumptions concerning men's and women's roles as social agents.

In the Passive Voice:
Essentialist Narratives of the Cypriot Past

One way of analyzing traditional narratives of the past is to examine the language archaeologists used in writing excavation reports. Often, the particular words and gram-
matical structures we incorporate into our writing reflect underlying assumptions or patterns of thought that we may not be consciously aware of. A common example is the
frequent use of the passive voice, which allows the writer to speak about actions and activities without having to identify the subjects who performed them, thereby giving an
appearance of dispassionate, scholarly objectivity. Passive constructions create a depersonalized view of the past, emphasizing actions rather than agents and resulting in the
nameless, faceless blobs Tringham has so aptly described (1991). The following is a typical example of the use of the passive voice in the archaeological literature of Cyprus,
an excerpt from Catling's summary of the cultures of Neolithic and Chalcolithic
Cyprus:

> Sotira's plan suggests that much domestic work *was performed* within the individual houses.
> These have no courtyards, and few domestic installations *were built* outdoors. Cooking
> *was done* in the houses for, while there were no hearths or ovens outside, at least one
> hearth was standard equipment in every house. Parts of some houses *were partitioned* off
> by flimsy walls to form small subsidiary rooms, some of them used as working areas;
> there is evidence of flint-knapping and the preparation of ground stone tools in such
> contexts. Others contained troughs, or pits in the floor, for the preparation or storage of
> foodstuffs. On every house floor querns and corn-grinders *were found*, evidence both for
> crop husbandry and food preparation. The picture of the house as the main working unit
> *is given* further emphasis by the presence in every one of vessels of pottery and stone, flint
> blades, stone grinders, pestles, hammers and polishers, and bone tools. (Catling 1966:
> 14–15; emphasis mine)

This passage is replete with details about architecture, furnishings, artifacts, and
tools; yet in no instance are particular people associated with them. Activities "are carried out" by nameless, faceless agents. The repeated use of the passive voice (six times
in this paragraph alone) underscores the impersonal nature of the activities under discussion and assumes that subjects are unknown, unknowable, or unimportant. The absence of subjects does not preclude their existence, however, since they may be implied
or presumed, even unconsciously, by the author. To make subjects explicit, both to ourselves and to others, we must "translate" these passive constructions into the active voice.
In doing so, we restore human agency to the interpretation of the archaeological record
and are compelled to link particular individuals or groups of people with specific actions.

It is an interesting prospect to imagine what subjects archaeologists would supply if
pressed to rewrite that passage in the active voice or, indeed, what nouns and pronouns

we would choose as subjects if we had to translate the passage into the active voice. How would our choices reflect our own views of the past? The following is a "translation" of Catling's passage on Sotira into the active voice with multiple subjects (in italics) provided for selection (of course, there are many other possible subjects):

> Sotira's plan suggests that *men/women/children* performed much work within the individual houses. These have no courtyards, and *men/women* built few domestic installations outdoors. *Men/women* cooked inside the houses . . . parts of some houses were partitioned off by *men/women* to form small subsidiary rooms . . . there is evidence that *men/women/children* manufactured flint and ground stone tools in such contexts. Others contained troughs, or pits in the floor, where men/women prepared or stored foodstuffs. On every house floor querns and corn-grinders were found, evidence that *men/women/children* had been involved in both crop husbandry and food preparation. The picture of the house as the main working unit of *men/women/children* is given further emphasis by the presence in every one of vessels of pottery and stone, flint blades, stone grinders, pestles, hammers and polishers, and bone tools.

Passive writing does more than convey a false impression of scientific objectivity: it also obscures the issue of agency and cloaks the adoption of presentist norms. In the passive voice, the stage has no actors or, at best, the actors are gender neutral (Baker 1997). But gender neutrality, rather than being truly unbiased or objective, disguises assumptions about "appropriate" male and female tasks. In the above passage, did the author or we assume that women cooked and that men made and used stone tools? That men built houses and women tidied them up? That men cultivated crops, while women processed, cooked, and stored foodstuffs? And what about children—were they involved in any or all of these activities? Since children normally contribute significantly to economic production in pre-industrial societies, we can imagine that they participated in domestic activities, but in passive writing, children, like women, remain invisible. The interstitial narrative that emerges from the use of the passive voice is that men were largely responsible for the "significant" achievements of the prehistoric past, while women and children played only marginal roles.

Alternative, less impersonal narratives of the past, though few and far between, indicate that presentist assumptions and gender stereotyping have continued to inform much scholarly work in Cypriot archaeology. One of the boldest and lengthiest attempts to people the Cypriot past was written forty years ago by J. R. Stewart in a summary of daily life in Cyprus during the Bronze Age:

> There is some slight evidence for monogamy and children appear to have been tenderly cared for. Certainly man and woman slept together in one bed . . . the household chores were much as they are today . . . these were performed by groups of people, whether the women of a single household or an association of neighbors (probably the former). . . . Ploughing also seems to have been a communal operation, perhaps employing all the males of the family to manage the oxen, steer the plough and carry the bins of seed. . . . The [pottery] industry

seems to have been delegated to the women of the household and it is legitimate to visualise potters' shops. . . . Metal working was also probably a specialized craft, sometimes in the hands of itinerant men. . . . The men of Vasilia carried formidable swords. . . . Basketry and weaving were probably feminine occupations. . . . *The general view which we get of Early Cypriot life is a remarkably modern one, and the excavator who knew Cyprus before the War can people the age with village friends of to-day; kindly, domestic, courteous and yet passionate.* (Stewart 1962:290–92; emphasis mine)

In this passage, Stewart has effectively "read backward" from his own view of the present and has assumed that society has remained virtually static over the course of thousands of years. The implicit assumption is that life has not changed since the Bronze Age and that stereotypical gender roles of the present can serve as effective models for understanding the behavior of women and men in the past: men are engaged in "active" tasks, such as metalworking, warfare, and plowing, while women pursued more "passive" endeavors, such as child rearing, basketry, pottery making, and household chores.

The active nature of male labor is further reflected in the use of transitive verbs and colorful adjectives to characterize men's tasks: men "manage" oxen, "steer" the plow, and "carry" seed bins and "formidable" swords. Women's activities, in contrast, are couched in passive, intransitive terms: children "are cared for," chores "were performed," pottery "was delegated," and weaving and basketry "were" feminine occupations. The use of the passive voice in conjunction with essentialist views on gender roles in the division of labor has, therefore, resulted in a narrative of the past in which men participate as active agents, gainfully employed in important economic tasks, whereas women are relegated to the roles typical of a middle-class housewife of twentieth-century Europe.

In spite of its obvious gender biases, Stewart's discussion is a rare example of a scholarly attempt to people the prehistoric Cypriot landscape. What is particularly interesting is that it has attempted a social interpretation of the living rather than the dead. Most archaeologists, then and now, are more likely to discuss the roles and statuses of individuals in mortuary contexts since the presence of skeletal material and associated grave goods makes it easier to do so. Indeed, descriptions of burial remains can provide important insights into the writer's implicit assumptions about gender, as can be seen in the following passage from Gjerstad's *Studies in Prehistoric Cyprus*:

This reveals a belief in a future life similar to that before death, and therefore the tomb equipment of the dead furnishes us with an excellent index to the customs and living conditions of the life on earth . . . the peasant was given his axe, his dagger, his spearhead, and his arrows . . . the woman retained her spindle whorls, needles, pestle and cornrubber, scrapers to scrape the dough from the baking trough, and the most important pieces of jewellery . . . also the idols of the great fertilizing goddess seem to be exclusively associated with women. This may be attributed to the important part which the women played in the rites concerning generation and vegetation in primitive life. (Gjerstad 1926:86–87)

The polarized pictures of women and men presented here are typical of much archaeological writing and reflect essentialist notions associating women with life and nature and men with cultural involvement in the wider public sphere. Regrettably, these views permeate the traditional narrative accounts of the past and persist in much archaeological reporting in Cyprus today. However, they are gradually being challenged and supplanted by more critical, gendered perspectives on the past.

A final example of androcentric bias in the reconstruction of the Cypriot past is not a text but rather an illustration from the cover of a promotional brochure for the copper-smelting site of Ayia Varvara-*Almyras* in the Sia Valley (fig. 1.1). Men are shown standing in the rear, in front of fires, engaged in copper-smelting activities. Women and children are depicted in the foreground in seated positions; they are making stone tools and engaging in other preparatory work for the men. Although busily engaged in work, they appear to be working at a more leisurely pace than the men at the furnaces behind them. This visual narrative of Iron Age life (which the brochure's text assures us is "reconstructed by archaeological finds") is extremely interesting since it represents a rare attempt by an archaeologist to give faces to ancient Cypriot populations. By the same token, however, it conveys a stereotypical division of labor, with task allocation occurring along gendered lines and with women portrayed in relatively ancillary roles.

In reality, of course, there is little or no archaeological evidence to support such a gendered division of labor. It has simply been assumed by most archaeologists that metalworking was male business and that women and children were better suited to tasks

Figure 1.1   Cover design from a brochure on the copper-smelting site of Ayia Varvara-*Almyras* (courtesy of the Almyras excavations, Cyprus).

that required less technological expertise and physical labor; men and women were not only separate, but apparently also not equal. Because this illustration appears in a commercial brochure rather than in the pages of a scholarly journal and has been distributed across the island by tourist agencies, a powerful image of the past has been widely broadcast to an audience that includes Cypriots, tourists, and resident foreigners. As most of those individuals will probably never read scholarly books or articles on Cypriot archaeology, this stereotypical image furnishes them with what little "evidence" they will ever encounter for the roles of men, women, and children in prehistory. To avoid these pitfalls, archaeologists must become aware of their own attitudes toward gender and exercise greater responsibility in their use of archaeological knowledge in reconstructing past societies, not only in the publication of scholarly books and articles, but in the dissemination of information to the public at large.

Narratives of Complexity: The Ambiguity of Social "Elites"

So far I have cited examples of archaeological writing from earlier in the twentieth century. For more recent examples of language that obscures the role of gender in Cypriot prehistory, I now turn to a consideration of narratives of social complexity on Cyprus during the third and second millennia B.C. I will say more later in this chapter about the content of these and related approaches to the past, particularly with regard to their failure to incorporate gender into evolutionary models of early society. Here, though, I will simply concentrate on the language of the several relevant passages:

> By the beginning of the ProBA (=Late Cypriot) period, Cypriot society and the economy underwent major transformations. The newly built port cities of the 17th–14th centuries B.C. rapidly developed into trade emporia with concentrated populations and specialized artisans and producers. The production of copper had increased and the political economy had matured: material indicators of intensification and expansion suggest the emergence of new social and political roles which themselves necessitated new types of insignia, information and ideology. . . . As the economic and social rift between elites and non-elites widened, some of the earliest known ashlar structures were built. To organize and secure control over an island where authority had been strongly localized in scope, developing elites established unequal access to essential resources and prestige goods, and adopted legitimizing symbols that enabled them to co-opt goods and labor for their own political and economic ends. Mortuary ritual was used to reaffirm elite status, and perhaps to establish links with ancestral power groups. (Knapp 1996:90)

In this passage, the economy is likened to an organism that expands, increases, and matures, and economic growth is ultimately responsible for divisions within formerly egalitarian social groups and for the production and trade of commodities such as precious metals and other prestige items by which emerging elites established and maintained power. But precisely which individuals or groups comprise the elites referred to here? Are "power groups," ancestral or otherwise, presumed to be composed primarily of powerful men? Did emerging male-dominated elites exclude female kin? If so, what contributions did women make to this process, and what are the relationships between changing gender constructs and social complexity? Within this broad, unilinear model of socioeconomic change, society appears to move inexorably toward a predetermined goal (i.e., a higher level of complexity, hierarchical rule by elites), and, because gender is not made explicit, we are left to speculate on the particular gendered identities of the "powerful social elites."

Critical of approaches such as Knapp's, which he finds "too formal and economic," Manning has attempted to account for socioeconomic complexity in "explicitly social terms" (1993:35). However, the continual references in the following passage (and indeed throughout the entire article) to "emergent elites" as agents of change further obscures and reifies social groups. Neither the language used, however, nor its implicit structural meaning, brings us any closer to the people of the Bronze Age, and the relationship between gender and social status remains elusive:

> The emergent elite may also seek to produce their own valued resources, or prestige goods, with which to trade, or for immediate display of status and wealth. Their agricultural surplus thus allows their support and sponsorship of specialised production. The evidence for the first significant exploitation of Cypriot copper in the Early Bronze Age, and the rapid development of Cypriot metallurgy in the course of the Early Bronze Age, in apparent emulation of foreign metallurgy and its influence, may be seen to be a case of such specialised surplus production sponsored and supported by the (pre-existing) emergent elite in the context of a prestige goods economy and foreign stimulus. (Manning 1993:47–48)

Once again, we are left to puzzle over the identity of elites and non-elites. Who, in particular, created the necessary "agricultural surplus" that "allowed their support and sponsorship of specialized production"? Who, in economic and political terms, benefited from those new productive strategies? Who was responsible for the development of metallurgy, for the emulation of foreign pottery and metal types, and for their display? Should Manning's earlier reference in this article to the "prominent male" in the center of a well-known figure scene inside a Red Polished pottery (RP) bowl from Vounous (Manning 1993;fig. 2.7) be taken to mean that emerging elites were headed exclusively by powerful males and that women's participation was only marginal?

In addition to the potential biases inherent in paradigms of social complexity, its preoccupation with large-scale phenomena such as metallurgical production and foreign trade marginalizes the role of *habitus* (Bordieu 1977) as a mechanism of social expression, despite Manning's intention (1993:35) to "structure the argument in purely social terms." Similar criticisms could be applied to many post-processual treatments of social complexity in other areas of the ancient Near East. The general assumption that "big events" function as "prime movers" in prehistory, in conjunction with a "gender neutral" narrative of the past, creates a theoretical vacuum that opens the door for the introduction of essentialist views, such as the association of women with private domestic spheres and men with the cosmopolitan sphere of trade, politics, and public life (Gero 2000). Although this is probably not the result that Manning intended, the reader is left with an unmediated view of the past in which men played prominent and instrumental roles in the transformation of societies from simple egalitarian villages to complex urban polities, while women, restricted largely to the domestic social sphere, contributed only marginally to those developments.

Evolutionary models of social complexity obscure this picture further by implying that advances in technology were generally and uniformly beneficial to Cypriot society as a whole and that emergent or advanced states of complexity were the inevitable and desired goals of socioeconomic change (on the dangers of unlineal models, see Kingsnorth 1993). Such teleological paradigms of social change privilege the role of elites in this process and, in conjunction with essentialist views, further circumscribe women's roles in the evolution of complex societies. Peltenburg (1993) cautions against the use of unilinear models of social change and discusses specific examples in the archaeological record of prehistoric Cyprus of the recursive character of social change.

Archaeological evidence suggests that models of punctuated equilibrium may be more appropriate for the archaeological record of prehistoric Cyprus. The failure of Cypriot society to keep pace with its mainland counterparts in the advance from egalitarian to hierarchical social structures should not be viewed ethnocentrically as "cultural lag" or the persistence of a state of inert backwardness; instead, it should be integrated into a more nuanced view of social complexity that acknowledges recursive modes of social change and embraces the possibility of heterarchical as well as hierarchal modes of sociopolitical organization. I will explore these ideas more extensively in chapter 7.

In the end, unilinear narratives of social complexity that focus only on broad trajectories of socioeconomic change tend to underplay the importance of the dynamics of everyday human experience, Bordieu's *habitus*. Narratives of complexity that fail to give a central place to gender are not capable of measuring the impact on the dynamics of social relations of changing social, economic, and political structures and therefore continue to project the genderless, faceless images of the past so highly criticized by Tringham (1991) and others. While feminist and post-processual archaeology have succeeded in delivering increasingly gendered approaches into the mainstream of archaeological research over the last twenty years, the impact of gender is only just beginning to be felt in Cypriot archaeology. Consequently, before turning to particular aspects of gender in ancient Cyprus, it will be useful to summarize the research that has taken place over the last decades within the wider framework of research on the archaeology of gender.

Gender and Archaeology

The first substantial scholarly publication to address issues of gender within the field of archaeology was an article written by Conkey and Spector (1984) that examined some of the reasons for archaeology's overall lack of interest in the subject of gender. Among the main contributing factors cited by the authors were pervasive androcentric bias and Western ethnocentrism with regard to interpretation of male and female roles in the past and their application to non-Western pre-industrial societies. Moreover, the failure to incorporate gender as a central factor in archaeological interpretations of the past was linked to static views about men's and women's roles in society. Placing gender at the center of the discussion forces us to come to grips with those assumptions and enables us to understand the social dynamics of past societies in their own terms. By engendering the past, we are obliged to question our own views of human relationships and to formulate explicit theories based on conscious social perspectives rather than unmediated presentist norms.

In an essay written in 1991, Wylie returned to these themes by documenting the continued lack of scholarly attention to gender in archaeology throughout the 1980s. Noting the presence of socially based approaches in other aspects of the discipline, she concluded that the failure to develop an archaeology of gender contradicted the general trend toward socially based theoretical models:

> It is clear, then, that the failure to develop an archaeology of gender cannot be considered wholly or exclusively a matter of constraint unique to archaeology . . . the real question is why archaeologists have not taken steps to overcome the methodological limitations with which they inevitably deal, *in this particular problem area*. (Wylie 1991:33; emphasis hers)

This passage was part of an essay published in what can now be regarded as a landmark volume on the archaeology of gender, *Engendering Archaeology: Women and Prehistory* (Gero and Conkey 1991). Contributors were selected for their expertise in particular aspects of the archaeological record—pottery, architecture, paleobotany, and the like—and asked to interpret that evidence from the point of view of gender. Accounts from those attending the conference indicate that many participants were intellectually challenged and personally affected by the process of engendering the past. Their published contributions, which in many cases were radical revisions of the papers they had originally presented, are testimony to the editors' claim that "an engendered past addresses many longstanding concerns of archaeology . . . but throws them into new relief"(Gero and Conkey 1991:15).

The impact of this volume, the first of its kind, was considerable, and its success accounts in large part for the numerous books and articles on gender and archaeology published during the last decade. Only a portion of these can be mentioned here; therefore, I include works that readers interested in prehistoric Cyprus will find most useful and interesting. Anthologies that, like *Engendering Archaeology*, cover a broad geographical area and address a wide range of issues and themes, include: *The Archaeology of Gender* (Walde and Willows 1991), *Women in Archaeology* (du Cros and Smith 1993), *Women in Human Evolution* (Hager 1997), *Gender and Archaeology* (Wright 1996), *Reader in Gender Archaeology* (Hays-Gilpin and Whitley 1998), and *Gender and Material Culture* (Hurcombe and Donald 2000).

Anthologies with a particular thematic and/or areal focus include: *Women in Archaeology* (Claassen 1994), which covers the lives of little-known women archaeologists of the nineteenth–early twentieth centuries; *Women in Prehistory* (Claassen and Joyce 1997) and *Manifesting Power* (Sweeley 1999), both of which focus on the archaeology of the Americas; *Gender and the Body in the Ancient Mediterranean* (Wyke 1998), *Reading the Body* (Rautman 2000), and *Engendering Aphrodite* (Bolger and Serwint 2002), which address gender issues in Cyprus from the Neolithic through Medieval periods; and, finally, *Invisible People and Processes* (Moore and Scott 1997), which is the first book to specifically problematize the role of children in the past in relation to gender constructs.

Works by single authors that address particular themes and/or geographical areas include: *Women in Prehistory* (Ehrenberg 1989), which has been used widely as a textbook in courses on women in European prehistory; *The Creation of Patriarchy* (Lerner 1986), a largely historical book with a focus on ancient Mesopotamia; *Daughters of Isis* (Tyldesley 1995) and *Women in Ancient Egypt* (Robins 1993), both of which examine the roles of women in ancient Egypt; *Gender in Archaeology* (Nelson 1997), which deals with the relations of power; *Women's Work* (Barber 1994); and *What This Awl Means* (Spector 1991 and 1994) and "Archaeological Practice and Gendered Encounters with Field Data" (Gero 1996), both of which examine issues of gender in relation to archaeological field techniques.

In addition to the works cited above, women in other anthologies and journals, now at the forefront of research on the archaeology of gender, have made a wide range of contributions. These women include E. M. Brumfiel, J. Collier, M. Conkey, L. Fedigan, J. M. Gero, R. Gilchrist, C. Hastorf, R. Joyce, A. Kehoe, S. M. Nelson, I. Silverblatt, J. Spector, M. L. Stig Sorenson, R. E. Tringham, R. P. Wright, A. Wylie, M. Yanagisako, and A. Zihlman. These authors cover a diversity of themes, among them issues of status; prestige; the relations of power; gendered views of the body; women's biology and health; feminine technologies; subsistence and food systems; differential roles of men and women in production, reproduction, exchange, and trade; gender identities as expressed through representational art; gender and the household; questions of gendered identities as attested by mortuary evidence; and the effects of sociopolitical change, especially the emergence of state-level society, on gender constructs. There have also been several important contributions concerning the introduction of courses on gender into university curricula since many researchers have noted that pedagogical processes help to establish research programs and to transmit concepts of gender to younger generations of scholars (e.g., Conkey and Tringham 1996; Morgen 1989; Romanowicz and Wright 1996; Spector and Whelan 1989).

No single approach or school of thought has emerged from the studies listed above. Nelson (1997) has characterized this as "multivocality," while Wright (1996:16) likewise observes the wide range of interdisciplinary techniques now being applied to gender and archaeology. Despite their differences, however, there is a common belief that there is more to the process of engendering the past than merely identifying and documenting the activities and identities of women and men. Recent approaches to gender engage in the investigation of cross-cutting aspects that reveal its complexity, such as the ways in which past cultures constructed gender differences, not only between men and women, but among women of differing classes, ages, and ethnicities; many have attempted to move beyond binary divisions of gender to consider aspects of gender ambiguity and multiplicity. Through all of these recent approaches to gender runs the importance of archaeological "deep time" for charting long-term trajectories of social change. Equally important is the acknowledgment of contextual evidence in the interpretation of gender constructs of the past. Considerations of context (spatial relations of material culture) and time (whether the relatively short-term span of the life cycle, or longer-term diachronic changes) are crucial themes in this study as well.

Due to the tremendous output on the archaeology of gender during the 1990s, most archaeologists have, at the very least, come to accept gender as a legitimate subject of academic research, even if they do not engage in it themselves. While this more positive attitude has not yet succeeded in propelling gender studies fully into the mainstream of archaeological research, it has begun to transform the ways in which many archaeologists view the past and the ways in which those views are transmitted in the classroom (see Wright 1996:chaps. 7–9). Many archaeologists today are consciously abandoning traditional approaches that interpreted the past through the distorting "lenses of gender" (androcentrism, gender polarization, and biological essentialism, as defined by Bem 1993) and are developing new theories and methods for investigating the ways in which past cultures defined gender roles, constructed social identities, and naturalized or legitimized gender differences. It is this great diversity of approaches that most fundamentally characterizes gender studies today, with more emphasis being put on diversity within the monolithic category "woman" than on differences between conventional binary gender categories of "men" and "women."

Within the considerably narrower framework of Cypriot prehistory, it is somewhat frustrating to observe that we are still in the first stages of this critical process. Indicative of the slow pace of change is that a major international conference, "Early Society in Cyprus," held at a time when gender was beginning to be introduced into other areas of the discipline, failed to include a single paper on gender or even on the roles of women in the island's ancient cultures (Peltenburg 1989), and a "call for papers" on gender topics issued at a meeting of Cypriot archaeologists in Sweden (Åström 1992) has elicited a very weak response. Although this can be attributed in part to a traditional lack of scholarly interest among Cypriot archaeologists in social theory, the situation has not changed with the introduction of postprocessual models by some archaeologists during the last decade, as we have seen earlier in this chapter. With few exceptions, in fact, the treatment of women in Cypriot archaeology has largely been confined to the study and interpretation of anthropomorphic figurines (e.g., Bolger 1992, 1996; Hamilton 1994, 2000).

In order to demonstrate the contributions made by women to the development of complex society in Cyprus, however, we need to consider a wide variety of evidence that encompasses the more mundane activities of day-to-day existence, rather than just the images of women in artistic representations, since the latter are often refracted, not reflected, by women's actual political, economic, and social positions. I hope that the recent publication of an international conference on gender and Cypriot archaeology (Bolger and Serwint 2002) will help rectify this situation. Given the rich store of material evidence available for prehistoric Cyprus, however, much more work needs to be done.

I wrote this book as an in-depth introduction to some of the key issues and problems of gender in Cyprus from prehistoric to early historical times and to integrate patterns of gender with other social and economic developments. The contextual approach I have adopted here necessitates treatment of archaeological evidence in greater detail than would be required for a shorter, more general analysis. For those unfamiliar with the archaeology of Cyprus from the tenth–late second millennium B.C., there is an outline of major phases and developments in the prehistory of Cyprus, including principal sites, major artifact groups, and key socioeconomic developments, in Appendix 1. Appendix 2 includes a map and gazetteer of major prehistoric sites.

Narratives of Social Change

One of my main objectives in writing this book is to try to interpret changing patterns of gender relations within the larger framework of emerging socioeconomic complexity as Cypriot societies were transformed from small relatively egalitarian villages to larger and more complex urban centers. Diachronic models of culture change that aim to account for long-term patterns of gender hierarchy, in particular the differential statuses of women and men, are by no means new, having occupied various sociologists, biologists, and anthropologists since Darwin. Nevertheless, it is important at the outset to clarify the methodological framework that distinguishes this work from earlier approaches to gender and the *longue durée* (long-term development). The latter are numerous and wide ranging, but most tend to fall into one of three general categories: sociobiological narratives, unilinear narratives based on Marxian models of the emergence of the state, and gynecentric narratives arguing for the existence in the remote past of matriarchies. I briefly summarize and critique these in the following paragraphs.

Sociobiological Narratives

Sociobiological narratives attribute differences and inequalities between women and men to biological factors such as differences in physical strength and reproductive capacity. Gender roles are viewed as essentially static and unchanging, biologically fixed since the time of the emergence of the earliest H. sapiens, if not earlier. Although biologically based accounts of social behavior can be traced back to the nineteenth century, they have been given renewed impetus by the work of Harvard entomologist E. O. Wilson (1975) and others, who have attempted to explain the evolution of social behavior according to Darwinian principles of natural selection.

While granting greater complexity and flexibility to human groups, Wilson maintains that adaptability itself is a genetically determined trait that was selected for. Critics of Wilson's book, in particular, and sociobiological models, in general, argue that the large and complex human brain has, to a large extent, freed humanity from its genes (Gould 1977). Just as human beings are not programmed to speak a particular language, neither are they compelled by their genes to assimilate and perform predetermined social roles. The ability of humans to observe, evaluate, and consciously transform their environments is one of the key characteristics that set us apart from the rest of the animal kingdom.

In addition to a lack of scientific evidence linking behavioral traits to particular genes (the mapping of the human genome has failed to identify genes for such behaviors as "dominance," "passivity," and "aggression"), many sociobiological approaches have been sharply criticized for their dangerous social and political implications, including the justification of status quo inequalities between social groups and the apparent futility of movements opposing racial, political, and economic oppression. With regard to gender, sociobiological models emphasize the differences between women and men that evolved hundreds of thousands of years ago as the result of natural selection. Biological factors, such as physical strength of males for protection/provisioning of females and infants and successful mating and reproductive strategies among females, are seen as the underlying causes of male-linked behaviors such as dominance and aggression and female behaviors of passivity and nurturance. In its most extreme form, sociobiology maintains that inequalities between the sexes, and even the domination, subjugation, and rape of women by men (Thornhill and Palmer 2000) are the inevitable (albeit "regrettable") results of the human need to survive; in other words, they are part of the "natural order" of things. In the face of such strong and long-evolving biological forces, which even shaped the ways in which we act and think, gender becomes a biological rather than a social construct. Recent gender research, however, has demonstrated the ways in which "scientific" attempts to dichotomize sex into polar opposites ("male vs. female"), both now and in previous generations, have been heavily influenced by cultural biases and essentialist thinking (Fausto-Sterling 2000).

Gender and the Patriarchal State

These narratives of gender hierarchy are based heavily on conflict theory as developed by Karl Marx and applied by Engels (via Morgan) to the origin of the family and the status of women. Unlike sociobiological models, which view gender roles as relatively static entities, Marxian narratives view gender as a variable construct linked explicitly to the economic and political relationships of particular cultures (Sacks 1979). According to Engels, primitive societies were egalitarian due to the lack of economic surplus and private property, and women played important economic roles. With the emergence of private property, however, power became concentrated in the hands of elite groups of men (Lindsey 1997:7), and, in conjunction with the rise of the organized state, female labor was largely confined to the domestic sphere, leading to a decline in female status relative to that of males.

Although versions of the Marxian model can be applied generally to many societies around the world that have undergone the transition to modern statehood, they are far too broad and schematic to be universally applicable, and they provide few details of the processes by which such changes are thought to have occurred in particular geographical and temporal settings. Anthropological field research, particularly fieldwork involving long-term residence and participant observation, had not yet begun at the time of Engels's writings, nor was there much known about the structures of non-state societies of the remote past. General categories such as bands, tribes, chiefdoms, and states, which lump societies into large monolithic groups, are inadequate for classifying the wide range and complexity of human behaviors demonstrated in the ethnographic record today (Yoffee and Sherratt 1993). Moreover, the assertion that changes in (previously egalitarian) gender constructs always occur subsequent to, or contemporaneously with, changes in the economic sphere needs to be demonstrated rather than assumed.

Archaeological approaches to the *longue durée* have the potential to test these models by interpreting material evidence within a contextual framework, making it possible to deduce small-scale temporal and spatial variations in cultural behavior. By identifying and observing cultural patterns that occurred over the course of many centuries, archaeologists can chart trajectories of changing gender constructs in a more highly refined and detailed manner; the patterns that emerge in the process tend to oppose the unlinear trajectories of change inherent in general evolutionary paradigms such as those proposed by Marx and Engels.

Gynecentric Narratives

Gynecentric narratives postulate high female status, usually centered on some form of matriarchal rule, among pre-state societies of the remote past; one of the main bodies of evidence used in these discussions are figurines which are presumed to be female and are interpreted as deities (Lesure 2002). These idealistic narratives, aptly labeled "new age" archaeology by Meskell (1995), draw heavily on the research of European archaeologist

Marija Gimbutas, whose books on Neolithic Europe paint a utopian image of the past in which society was presided over by peaceful, artistic, and religiously inclined women (e.g., Gimbutas 1974, 1989, 1991). Gimbutas used evidence of upper Paleolithic cave art, especially the so-called Venus figurines, as well as female figurines found at Neolithic sites in Europe, to reconstruct the origins and development of a matrifocal society extending back to c. 40,000 B.C. and continuing to the mid-fourth millennium B.C., when more aggressive social structures ruled by males are thought to have brought an end to the worship of female deities and matriarchal rule.

The weaknesses of Gimbutas's arguments should be largely transparent to those familiar with modern archaeological methods, and, as they have been documented extensively by others (see, in particular, Chapman 1998; Lesure 2002; Meskell 1995; and Tringham and Conkey 1998), there is no need to repeat them here. But the common thread of criticism that emerges in all serious archaeological critiques of "goddess theories" is their overt lack of attention to contextual detail. There is a strong tendency to conflate figurines of all types together over long stretches of time (e.g., upper Paloelithic–Neolithic, a period of 40,000 years) and across wide geographical regions; in addition, variation in size, shape, design, and context of figurines is underplayed or ignored in Gimbutas's studies.

For earlier periods (i.e., the upper Paleolithic), where much of the figurative material was discovered prior to modern excavation methods, there is little contextual evidence on which to draw. But this cannot be said of the sites excavated by Gimbutas who, although she had the means to do so, failed to record contextual details and to incorporate them in her interpretation of the material culture. In recent years, increasing emphasis has been given to the importance of archaeological context in the study of prehistoric figurines (e.g., Bailey 1994; Bolger 1996; Conkey 1991; Hamilton 2000; Meskell 1995; Talalay 1987, 1993, 2000; Talalay and Cullen 2002; Tringham and Conkey 1998). Out of these concerted efforts, new narratives of social change are likely to emerge that will be informed by contextual details and that will differentiate the symbolic and practical meanings of figurines according to their particular spatial and temporal locations.

The Importance of Context

While the models of social change summarized above could conceivably be used to provide testable hypotheses concerning patterns of gender relations over long temporal spans, they share the common fault of being deductive and exclusively theory driven, with evidence drawn on selectively to prove a predetermined outcome. Of course, much recent work in the archaeology of gender has rejected all of these models and has sought to explain gender through a variety of theoretical and methodological means. However, the focus of much of this research on particular circumscribed geographical regions in restricted temporal frameworks has not dealt systematically with long-term changes in gender relations and has contributed to the persistence of essentialist models of gender differences up to the present. Archaeological inquiry has the capacity to undermine these models by examining evidence contextually and differentiating gender constructs through time and across space. Moreover, it renders untenable universal theories of culture change based on monolithic categories such as "state," "pre-state," "women," and "men" in its attempt to distill patterns of social relations as they are likely to have actually occurred in the past (to the extent, of course, that this is objectively possible).

Links between gender constructs and other aspects of socioeconomic development must be demonstrated rather than assumed; in contrast to evolutionary models in which social trajectories are seen to emerge gradually from one century to another, contextual models are far more likely to be nonlinear and recursive. It is possible that these methods can be integrated with the concept of *différence* by "third wave" feminists in which gender divisions within a given population are not treated as monolithic groups but as affiliated members of differing economic groups and social identities. Factors such as status, class, ethnicity, and identity must be integrated into investigations of gender differentiation to explore the ways in which gender cuts across other social and economic categories (Moore 1994).

Through contextual analysis of material remains, archaeology has the potential to overcome and replace evolutionary and essentialist models of gender through time. The present narrative aims to instill gender into the genderless account of Cypriot prehistory outlined above. It is largely on the basis of detailed contextual evidence that I will attempt to chart the changes in gender constructs on the island over the course of approximately 8,000 years. Within this broad chronological framework, the theme of gender is broken down into discrete but interrelated chapters that address issues of gender from the perspective of short-term changes associated with the temporal rhythms of the human life cycle. Although the study focuses on a single island in the Mediterranean, I hope that the overall approach to gender and the *longue durée* developed here has relevance for an understanding of gender in other regions as well.

Gender, Time, and the Life Course

Archaeology has the potential to refine and redefine generalizing narratives of long-term social change, but, as we have seen, traditional chronologically based approaches within the discipline do not necessarily get us any closer to engendering the past. Archaeologists, like other social scientists, have tended too often to paint the past in broad brush strokes, with major economic advances regarded as being "prime movers" in the development of society from a small-scale egalitarian isolated one to a large one in which wealthy elites are engaged in international sphere. This faceless portrait has neglected issues of identity and agency and has completely ignored the equally fundamental issues of daily life and human relations.

As a remedy to the relative anonymity of much archaeological research, current approaches in the archaeology of gender, influenced in part by the work of Braudel of the

Annales School (Bintliff 1991, Foxhall 2000), have moved away from definitions of prehistory as a series of major events and have begun to focus on smaller time scales and the small-scale activities of individuals in everyday life. Moreover, a change in attitude with regard to time scales of the life cycle has begun to take place as the result of recent work on life cycles of primates, both human and nonhuman, all of whom appear to plan and strategize for their survival according to immediate, short-term needs (Morbeck, Galloway, and Zihlman 1997:xviii). By approaching human behavior from the point of view of the events and processes of the life cycle, we can succeed in shifting interpretations of the past from broad to shorter-scale episodes and begin to examine the impact of socioeconomic change on the role of human agency in social change and the politics of personal relations. This allows us not only to appreciate the complexity of human behavior but also the changing patterns and performances of identities such as gendered behavior that individuals engage in throughout their life course (Butler 1990; Gilchrist 1999; McLeod 1997).

Central to this research has been Bordieu's concept of *habitus*, which Gilchrist (1999) has characterized as "practical logic and sense of order learned unconsciously through enactment of everyday life." This is complemented by his notion of *hexis*, or "knowledge acquired during childhood," which is "built upon throughout the life course, reinforced by physical movement through cultural spaces and public endorsement through rites and ceremonies" (Gilchrist 1999:81). Gilchrist observes, further, that the life course emphasizes the "contextual process in which the biological life cycle is culturally segmented and marked materially and symbolically" (Gilchrist 2000:325). Material culture provides important evidence of life-cycle processes since, as Foxhall states, "the lifecycles of artifacts, structures and spaces are entwined with the lifecycles of humans"(Foxhall 2000:485).

Equally important, and closely associated with Bordieu's emphasis on experience, is the role of agency in the construction of gendered individuals (Dobres and Robb 2000) and Butler's concept of gender performance (1990:24–25, 134–41). Together, these approaches enable us to identify individuals and groups as active participants in social constructions of gender as well as measure the ability of elite and/or gender groups to circumscribe the participation of non-elites of different genders in different phases of the life cycle. In the process, faces and flesh can be imparted to an otherwise anonymous and skeletal narrative of the past, and monolithic gender groupings based on binary oppositions can be diversified according to cultural, political, and economic variables.

Gender in Ancient Cyprus

All human societies attach great significance and symbolic meaning to life history features that mark important social and biological developments among all animals, such as birth, sexual maturity, reproduction, and death (van Gennep 1960). This book is the first in-depth attempt to engender the material remains of prehistoric societies in

Cyprus by examining some of the ways in which different social groups experienced and shaped important life-cycle processes and by exploring the extent to which those experiences, in turn, helped construct and redefine gender identities over the course of approximately 8,000 years.

Chapter 2 (Setting the Scene: Gender and Domestic Space) sets the scene by exploring evidence for gender and the built environment, focusing in particular on the emergence of the household as a bounded unit of social interaction and the changes in kinship structures that very likely accompanied it. This is used to investigate long-term trajectories in the design, use, and function of domestic structures and their correlations to gender constructs.

Chapter 3 (Working Actors: Gender, Technology, and Labor) selectively examines evidence from the Neolithic, Chalcolithic, and Bronze Ages for the economic activities of daily life with a view to assessing the interfaces between gender, technology, and economic production. After critically assessing various models of task differentiation, I consider evidence for the relationship between gender and economy in three key areas of Cypriot prehistory: food production, pottery production, and textile manufacture.

Chapter 4 (Performing Gender: Figurines, Ritual, and Social Identity) considers the evidence of a wide range of anthropomorphic figurines for which the island's prehistoric cultures are well known. Made first in limestone, then in pottery and bronze, they furnish rich evidence for issues of gender and identity in the Cypriot past. The lack of a contextual basis in most studies of figurative material has generated a wide range of conflicting interpretations, but recent studies reviewed here attempt to develop new approaches based on contextual considerations and the function of the figurines in the performance of gender.

Chapter 5 (Invisible Characters: Children and Adolescents) focuses on the role of sub-adult members of society who, like women, have remained invisible in traditional archaeological accounts of Cypriot prehistory. Three particular sets of evidence are considered in this chapter: clay models attached to vessels portraying scenes of daily life that may suggest the representations of adolescents as a third gender category; data concerning the mortality rates and burial practices according to infants and children during the Neolithic and Chalcolithic periods; and skeletal evidence for the practice of artificial cranial deformation, a custom known in Cypriot prehistory from the Cyprot-Pre-pottery Neolithic B period (PPNB) onward that may have been intended to signify elite status during the Late Bronze Age (LBA).

In chapter 6 (Endings: Gender and Mortuary Ritual), mortuary remains are used to establish connections between individual identity and group affiliation, which, in turn, shed light on the means by which past cultures in Cyprus defined and negotiated gender. By correlating change in burial practices and kinship structures to advances in socioeconomic complexity, we can gain insight into the ways in which the roles of men, women, and children may have been fundamentally transformed. Further evidence points to the existence during the LBA of nonbinary gender constructs and differential treatment of women according to group affiliation and economic status.

While the analysis of gender into chapters based on discrete categories of evidence is logical and utilitarian, it has the potential to mask overlapping themes that connect them. Consequently, chapter 7 (Denouement: Themes and Threads) addresses particular gender-related themes that cut across the evidence presented in the previous chapters. These include gender and agency, gender and the life cycle, the gendered body, gender ambiguity, and multiple genders; in addition, it explores some of the effects on gender constructs of advances in socioeconomic complexity from the Neolithic through the Bronze Age.

In the final chapter of the book (Cypriot Archaeology: Who Tells the Story?), I examine issues of gender equity in archaeology, giving particular emphasis to the differential roles of women and men in the field of Cypriot archaeology over the last thirty years. The relatively circumscribed role of women in archaeological research on the island, and, in particular, the low numbers of women who have served as directors of field projects, is linked historically to the low priority given to gender research until recently. The situation is rapidly changing today, and, as women become more involved in fieldwork and publication, the archaeology of gender should ultimately be granted a more central place in studies of the Cypriot past. I hope that this book will make a positive and substantial contribution toward that goal.

Setting the Scene: Gender and Domestic Space   2

> A whole history needs to be written of spaces—which at the same
> time would be the history of powers . . . from the great strategies of
> geopolitics to the little tactics of the habitat.
>
> —FOUCAULT, "THE EYE OF POWER"

SPACE HAS BEEN CHARACTERIZED as a "morphic language" used by societies to communicate and interpret the relationships between groups (Hillier and Hansen 1984). The spatial configurations that humans construct reflect, create, and reinforce social tensions, with the organization of space functioning as both "product and producer" of existing social and economic relationships (Moore 1986:89). As walls and the spaces within and around them serve as tangible and concrete boundaries around and between people, the reorganization of the built environment is inextricably linked to the dynamics of social interaction, in particular those involving gender (Price 1999).

This chapter explores the interfaces between gender and domestic space in Cyprus from the Neolithic period to the Late Bronze Age, a long chronological span stretching from the ninth to second millennium B.C. Particular emphasis will be placed in this discussion on the emergence of households as bounded units of social interaction; I will use that important development, and the changes in kinship structures that very likely accompanied it, to investigate long-term trajectories in the design, construction, use, and function of domestic architecture, developments that can then be correlated to gender constructs. Ethnographic evidence from traditional pre-state societies can also help to elucidate the reconstruction of gender roles accompanying processes of sedentarization as societies shifted from nomadic strategies of hunter-gatherers to those of agriculturalists living in permanent villages and urban centers (Draper 1997; Kent 1995; Moore 1986).

Sedentism and Society in Prehistoric Cyprus

Excavations of prehistoric settlements in various areas of the island have shown that early sedentary society in Cyprus was composed of relatively small, egalitarian groups of village-based subsistence-level cultivators. The first known evidence for sedentary habitation in semi-permanent or permanent structures occurred during the Aceramic Neolithic period, a long period in Cyprus dating roughly from 8500–5500 B.C. While the earliest phases of the Aceramic Neolithic are only beginning to be understood (see Appendix I), the later Aceramic or Khirokitian phase has been the subject of archaeological investigation for many years (Dikaios 1953; Le Brun 1984, 1989, 1994).

During the Chalcolithic period (c. 4000–2500 B.C.), social and economic factors such as population growth, agricultural intensification, surplus storage, and accelerated exploitation of copper resources contributed to greater degrees of sedentism and the first signs of social hierarchy. Toward the end of the third millennium B.C., and continuing into the second, Cyprus began to take part in larger geographical and economic spheres, developments that can be inferred from changing demographic patterns, accelerated rates of craft specialization, trade in prestige items, and the production of metal ornaments and tools (Knapp 1993; Manning 1993; Muhly 1985).

Excavations at a number of large settlement sites of the LBA situated on or near the coast (especially Enkomi, Kition, Kalavasos, and Hala Sultan Tekke) have provided evidence of increased levels of population, trade, militarism, and craft specialization and of the advent of a market economy based on the production and distribution of copper and prestige goods. In all likelihood, the concentration of surplus wealth into the hands of powerful groups of elites was instrumental in shaping new social constructs and in contributing to the breakdown of corporate kin groups and their gradual fusion under increasingly centralized political authorities during the course of the LBA (Keswani 1996b; Peltenburg 1996). At the same time, the earliest evidence appears on the island of the construction of impressive urban administrative centers, sometimes referred to as "palaces," which clearly have a public rather than purely domestic function.

In attempting to investigate the dynamic interrelationships among sedentary society, domestic space, and gender constructs in Cyprus during the Neolithic, Chalcolithic, and Bronze Age periods, it is useful to keep in mind the following transformations in the built environment taking place on the island between the seventh and second millennia B.C. that form the basis for the subsequent discussion:

1. A gradual shift in the location of domestic activities from extra-mural zones during the Aceramic Neolithic to interior space during the Late Neolithic period (LNeo), Chalcolithic, and Bronze Ages

2. The expansion of storage capacities over time, as well as the increasing tendency to "protect" stored goods inside buildings rather than in extramural storage facilities

3. The abandonment of traditional roundhouse architecture at the end of the Chalcolithic, and the shift during the Bronze Age from one- or two-roomed structures to multi-room complexes with party walls and functionally discrete workspaces

4. The initial appearance during the Middle Bronze Age (MBA) of detached multi-room structures that might be regarded as "houses"

5. The construction during the Late Bronze Age (LBA) of independent special-function buildings of nondomestic character, often interpreted as "palaces" or administrative centers

In the following sections, I will consider these changes in the use of the built environment in greater detail in order to explore the ways in which they might be linked to kinship structures, systems of economic production, and modes of exchange—developments that are likely to have contributed to a fundamental restructuring of gender roles and the dynamics of personal relations within the domestic environment.

From Hunter-Gatherer to Sedentary Farmer

Little is known of the earliest cultures of Cyprus. The most substantial evidence for hunter-gatherer existence on the island is the collapsed rock shelter site of Akrotiri-*Aetokremnos* on the southern tip of the Akrotiri peninsula (see fig. 3.1 in this book), where large deposits of Pleistocene fauna, including pygmy hippos, have been interpreted as possible evidence for a hunter-gatherer butchering/processing site (Simmons et al. 1999). Radiocarbon dating places the site early within the tenth millennium B.C., about a millennium earlier than the earliest known site of the Neolithic (see table App I.1). Although over 98 percent of the excavated faunal remains comprised the bones of pygmy hippo, the interpretation of the site as a butchering/processing locale for hippos and other fauna appears unlikely (see ch. 3).

In their final site report (Simmons et al. 1999:ch. 13), the authors argue for the use and processing of entire hippo carcasses for food, clothing, and other purposes. The presence of stone tools and burnt patches interpreted as hearths attests to the presence of humans at the site. However, the lack of any clear evidence for microliths, projectile points, butchery marks, or seasonal occupation is troublesome and, together with the absence of parallels in Cyprus or in the mainland Levant, makes it difficult to come to firm conclusions regarding the site's precise function(s). The authors link the abandonment of the site later in the millennium to the extinction, perhaps through overkill, of *Phanourios*. Whatever the reason for its abandonment, the Akrotiri site demonstrates an early attempt at colonization of the island. That effort ultimately proved unsuccessful, for there is no evidence for cultural continuity between the Akrotiri phase and the settlements of the succeeding Neolithic period.

The earliest known sites of the Aceramic Neolithic for which there are radiocarbon dates, Parekklisha-*Shillourokambos* and Kissonerga-*Mylouthkia*, have cultural components dating to the ninth millennium B.C. Parallels to mainland developments have prompted some archaeologists to adopt the term "Cypro-PPNB" to characterize this phase of the Aceramic Neolithic of Cyprus (Peltenburg et al. 2000, 2001a, 2001b). With a gap of almost a millennium between settlements of the Cypro-PPNB date and the Akrotiri site, this phase apparently constitutes a fresh wave of colonizing activity on the island during which a variety of plants and animals (including sheep, goat, pig, cattle, wheat, and barley) were introduced for the first time. This time, colonizing efforts appear to have met with greater success, establishing a secure economic basis for subsequent settlement throughout the island.

Excavations by a French team at Parekklisha-*Shillourokambos*, under the direction of Jean Guilaine, are still in progress. Preliminary reports on the excavated features show them to be different from those at sites of the later Neolithic (see below), including a triangular enclosure with no known parallels (Guilaine et al. 1995:fig. 7). Its timber structure, shape, size (76 sq. m), and features suggest that it may have been a stockade used to pen animals brought by colonizers from the mainland (see Peltenburg et al. 2001a:39). While earlier excavations at the site suggested that none of the buildings from the Early Phase at *Shillourokambos* were domestic in character (Guilaine et al. 1995:19-23), recent campaigns have yielded traces of upstanding curvilinear architecture that may constitute the earliest domestic structures on the island (Guilaine et al. 1998). The interpretation of these structures, however, awaits further study and publication.

Excavations by the Lemba Project of Aceramic Neolithic features at Kissonerga-*Mylouthkia* near Paphos have yielded an abundance of PPNB features, most importantly a series of water wells that are the oldest-known examples in the world. In addition, they have revealed what appear to be traces of a Cypro-PPNB curvilinear building. Here, a plaster floor containing a hearth with fire-cracked stones was laid over the top of a pit; although the remains of this building are fragmentary and poorly preserved, it serves as tantalizing evidence of the ways in which pits were modified to form rudimentary buildings. Further analysis of these structures awaits the publication of the final site report (Peltenburg 2003). Unfortunately, these early sites, important though they are for establishing the processes by which the island was first colonized, have not furnished much evidence for the use of architectural space. For that we must turn to sites of the later Aceramic Neolithic period, in particular the settlements at Cape Andreas-*Kastros*, Kalavasos-*Tenta*, and Khirokitia-*Vounoi*, which have yielded more substantial evidence for evolving domestic architectural and social structures during the seventh and sixth millennia B.C.

Domestic Architecture of the Late Aceramic Period

The Neolithic settlement at Cape Andreas, excavated in the early 1970s by a French team under the direction of Alain Le Brun, lies at the tip of the island's panhandle, the closest point on the island to the Levantine mainland. Radiocarbon dates place the site in the late seventh–early sixth millennium B.C. Although excavations were curtailed by the political upheavals of 1974, much valuable evidence has been published (Le Brun 1981). The best-preserved architectural remains derive from Levels V and VI, and, in both strata, it was determined that higher levels of domestic activity took place outside of the structures than inside them. In Level V, for example, 70 percent of the flint cores, 68 percent of the grinding implements, 75 percent of the axes, and 81 percent of the bone tools were recovered from extramural contexts. Percentages in Level VI were nearly identical, with the majority of cores, flakes, stone vessels, and grinding implements found in extramural areas.

The emphasis on extramural activity indicated by the spatial patterning of tool types is further reinforced by the frequent location of hearths outside buildings. Level V provides the best evidence here, with three of its four hearths located extramurally (Le Brun 1981:fig. 6). With regard to activities that may have been performed in non-built zones, the spatial patterning of artifacts points to the existence of specialized activity areas. In contrast, deposits within buildings show little discernible spatial patterning, and floors are not subdivided into separate activity zones. A similar pattern was noted at Kalavasos-*Tenta*, a site located near the coast between Larnaca and Limassol that is probably somewhat earlier than Cape Andreas and is now thought to have had a substantial Cypro-PPNB component (see Peltenburg et al. 2000, 2001a, 2001b). Here, as at Cape Andreas, excavations revealed few hearths inside structures, while a variety of extramural pits contained burnt material (Todd et al. 1987:50). The pits occur in pairs or clusters, indicating that certain extramural areas were used consistently for cooking. Among modern hunter-gatherers, hearths serve as focal points for communal activities, and the settling of nomadic or semi-nomadic foragers into permanent villages is frequently accompanied by the relocation of hearths into private, interior spaces. This phenomenon appears to have social ramifications, with camp design shifting from "close" to "distant" as hearths and their associated activities move indoors.

Organizational principles involving the use of extramural space for domestic activities began to shift to interior locations during the later phases of the Aceramic Neolithic, a phenomenon best observed at the sixth millennium B.C. site of Khirokitia-*Vounoi*, the largest Neolithic site known on the island. Extensive architectural remains at this site were exposed by the Department of Antiquities under the direction of Porphyrios Dikaios in the 1930s and 1940s (Dikaios 1953) and by Le Brun since 1977 (Le Brun 1984, 1989, 1994). In his most recent report, Le Brun (1994:133–38) has noted the considerable degree of care and attention given to divisions of interior space in architecture from Levels I to III. Although a few of the buildings are single room units lacking internal divisions, like those at Cape Andreas, most have their floors divided into multiple segments (Le Brun 1994:figs. 47–49). The partitioning of interior space was accomplished by a number of methods, including division by leveling, the use of platforms, and the construction of partition walls.

Although there is no clear chronological pattern in the adoption of particular construction methods, the most common building type was composed of five internal zones formed by a combination of all of the aforementioned techniques. Hearths at Khirokitia, in contrast to those at Cape Andreas and *Tenta*, were regularly positioned inside buildings, and, in general, there appears to be greater focus on interior space. Settlement density, moreover, differs considerably from that of Cape Andreas, where a far greater proportion of communal space was devoted to extramural activities. This pattern, once established, seems to have taken hold, for it continued into the LNeo and Chalcolithic period as well at a number of well-documented sites around the island, as we shall soon see.

A typical spatial arrangement of buildings at Khirokitia consisted of several small circular structures positioned around an open area interpreted as a courtyard and used, among other things, for grinding grains (fig. 2.1). The structures are 2–3 m in diameter and were equipped with identical internal features, including partitions and hearths. In a recent article, Le Brun has interpreted these structures as residential units housing nuclear families, while the clustering of structures around a common work space is regarded as a reflection of an aggregate social structure involving the linking of small residential groups (Le Brun 2002:25). However, the proposal that nuclear families resided in the small structures at Khirokitia is not explored or substantiated, and it is hard to conceptualize given the miniscule (2–3 m) diameter of many of the buildings. Moreover, burial evidence of individuals buried underneath the floors of structures suggests that adults may have lived separately, either alone or with their children, but not in nuclear family arrangements (see ch. 5).

The Segmentation of Space in the Late (Ceramic) Neolithic

Excavations at the LNeo site of Ayios Epiktitos-*Vrysi* were interrupted, as at Cape Andreas, by the events of the 1974 war, but sufficient evidence had been recorded to publish an overall account of settlement practices in the north of the island during the latter half of the fifth millennium B.C. (Peltenburg 1982a). Most of the buildings at this site were functionally identical multi-purpose buildings. The paucity of evidence for industrial activity in extramural areas, while perhaps attributable to the subterranean position of the buildings and constraints of the surrounding landscape, nonetheless attests to the continuation of spatial patterns noted at Khirokitia and Kalavasos-*Tenta*.

In contrast to those sites, however, it is interesting to note that artifact types recur in each of the excavated structures, with little of the functional variation between buildings noted elsewhere and a high degree of standardization of internal space. The shift in building function to a multi-purpose facility may be associated with the introduction

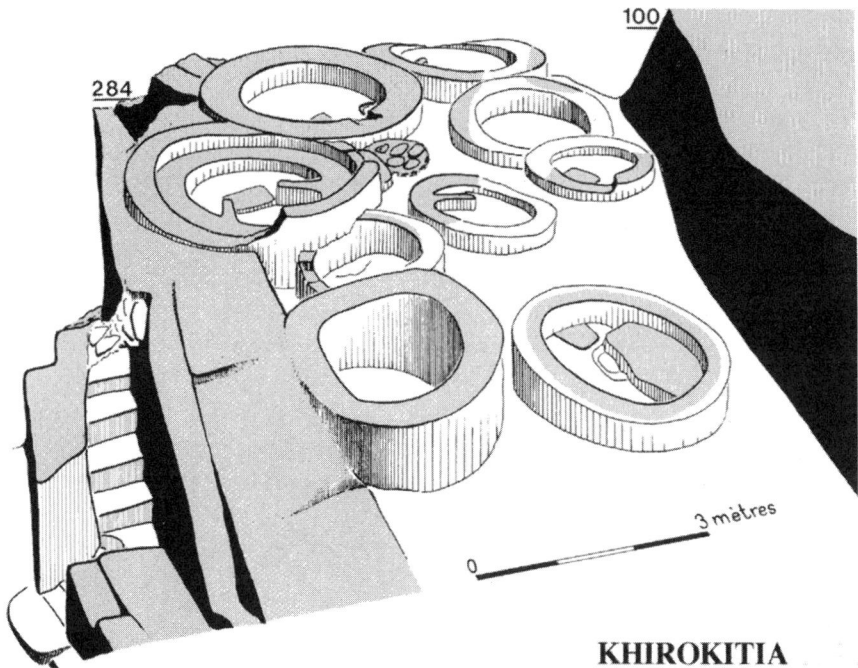

100

284

3 mètres

0

KHIROKITIA

Figure 2.1.   Isometric drawing of entrance and buildings at Khirokitia (after Le Brun 1994:fig. 11, from drawing by O. Daune-Le Brun).

of a variety of ceramic vessels at this time and suggests that industrial activities may have been performed by small, household groups. This hypothesis draws additional support from the overall settlement plan in which spatial divisions between distinct clusters of houses may possibly represent divisions among corporate kinship groups (Peltenburg 1982a:97).

A similar segmented settlement plan seems to have been adopted at the contemporary site of Sotira-*Teppes* near the south coast (fig. 2.2). In the Phase I settlement, a cluster of four structures forms a distinct complex along the NW edge of the plateau; two additional structures in this also appear to form a discrete architectural unit. In Phase 3, three separate clusters of buildings were uncovered, and a number of other structures indicate the addition of subsidiary rooms. Unfortunately, Dikaios's discussion of extramural areas at Sotira is brief and the treatment of finds from these areas lack sufficient contextual details (Dikaios 1961:168–71). As a result, it is difficult to assess the nature and degree of extramural activity at the site.

In other respects, however, the spatial variations at the site suggest a somewhat different use of domestic space from that of *Vrysi*. The persistence of differential patterns of artifact distribution in the majority of excavated structures at Sotira, for example, suggests that the adoption of standardized, multifunctional structures did not take place

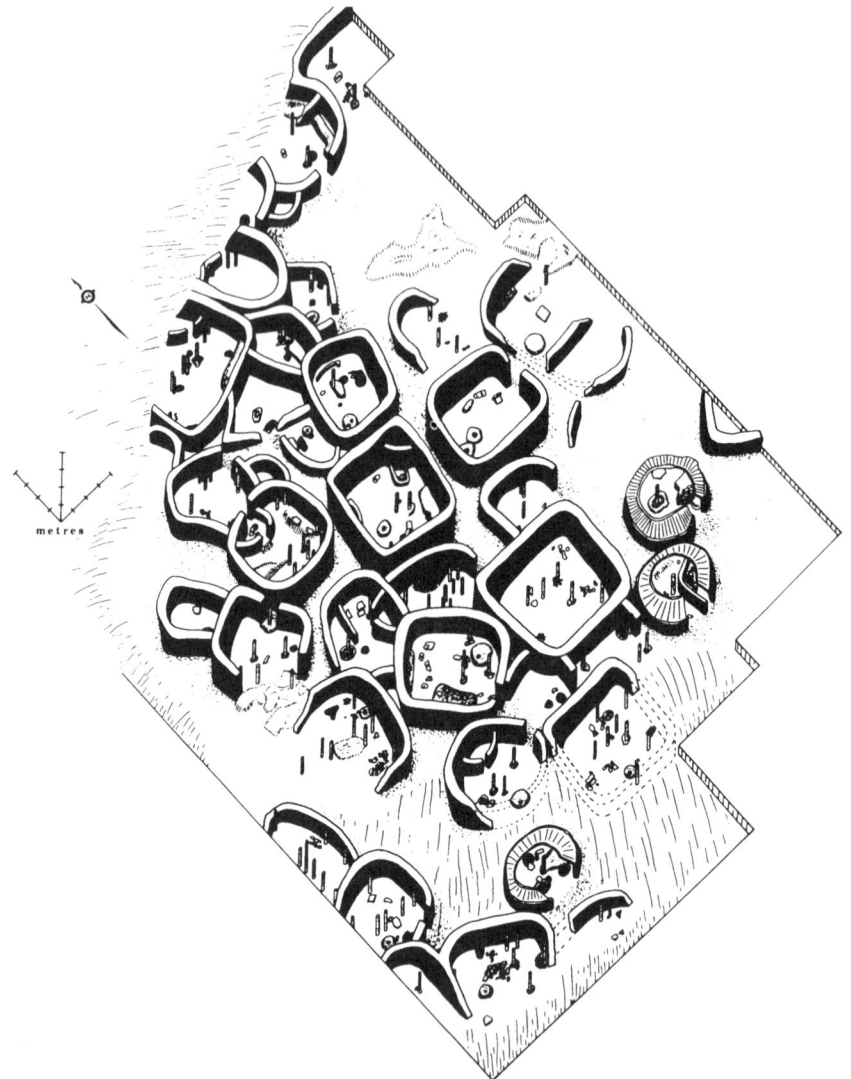

Figure 2.2.   Isometric drawing of the settlement at Sotira-*Teppes* (after Peltenburg 1978:fig. 1).

simultaneously at every site on the island and underscores the regional character of culture during the LNeo. Several structures in the Phase 2 settlement were multi-purpose
in character; these contained hearths and were significantly larger than other contemporary buildings with less varied activity levels (Stanley Price 1979a). The latter lack
hearths or have their hearths located in ancillary annexes. The absence of hearths in
many of the smaller structures has led some archaeologists to interpret them as

dwellings or ceremonial structures, but there is no direct evidence for this. Their presence can be seen instead as part of an increasing compartmentalization of interior space, as can the frequent occurrence of segmented floor space through construction of narrow stone-built walls, a phenomenon observed in all three phases of settlement (Dikaios 1961:160–61).

Domestic Space in the Chalcolithic Period

Sites of the Early Chalcolithic period (EChal) (c. 4000–3500 B.C.) are different in character from those of the LNeo, with activity and perhaps even habitation in large ashy hollows (Kissonerga-*Mylouthkia*, Kalavasos-*Ayious*) and some evidence for flimsy timber-posthole constructions (Maa-*Paleokastro*, Kissonerga-*Mylouthkia*). Additional evidence for a timber phase of construction, as well as a successive phase of more substantial stone and pisé structures, comes from Kissonerga-*Mylouthkia* near Paphos (Peltenburg 2003:ch. 13). However, the limited occurrence of this type of building as well as its flimsy, ephemeral structural elements and patchy floor plans, makes it difficult to draw conclusions about their spatial arrangements. Better evidence for the latter comes from two other sites in the Paphos District—Lemba-*Lakkous* and Kissonerga-*Mosphilia*.

Excavations by the Lemba Project at Kissonerga and Lemba under the direction of Edgar Peltenburg have yielded substantial evidence of domestic structures for the MChal (Peltenburg et al. 1985, 1998). Although occupation is attested to at Kissonerga as early as the Aceramic Neolithic period, the first architectural remains at these sites occur during the Middle Chalcolithic period (MChal). The traditional roundhouse plan still predominates, and a number of buildings have floors partitioned by low radial ridges running from the hearth to the wall (fig. 2.3). These demarcate activity zones associated with work platforms and stone implements from storage areas, effectively dividing the room into discrete functional areas.

The replication of previously existing segments during refurbishment and renovation underscores the deliberate patterning of spatial divisions. In addition to evidence of the buildings themselves, the discovery at Kissonerga of a building model complete with a door, a platform hearth, and radial partition ridges segmenting the floor (fig. 2.4) adds a new dimension to our understanding of actual structures at the site, since it was found in direct association with a group of anthropomorphic figurines depicting women in various stages of pregnancy and childbirth (see Peltenburg et al. 1991 and Bolger 1992, 1996). Together with the female limestone figurine from a MChal building at Lemba (Peltenburg et al. 1985:fig. 81), these constitute the earliest firm evidence we have from Cyprus linking females to domestic space and suggest that already by the early third millennium B.C. some domestic structures had come to be regarded as a focal point of female activity, perhaps in association with particular stages and/or events within the life cycle.

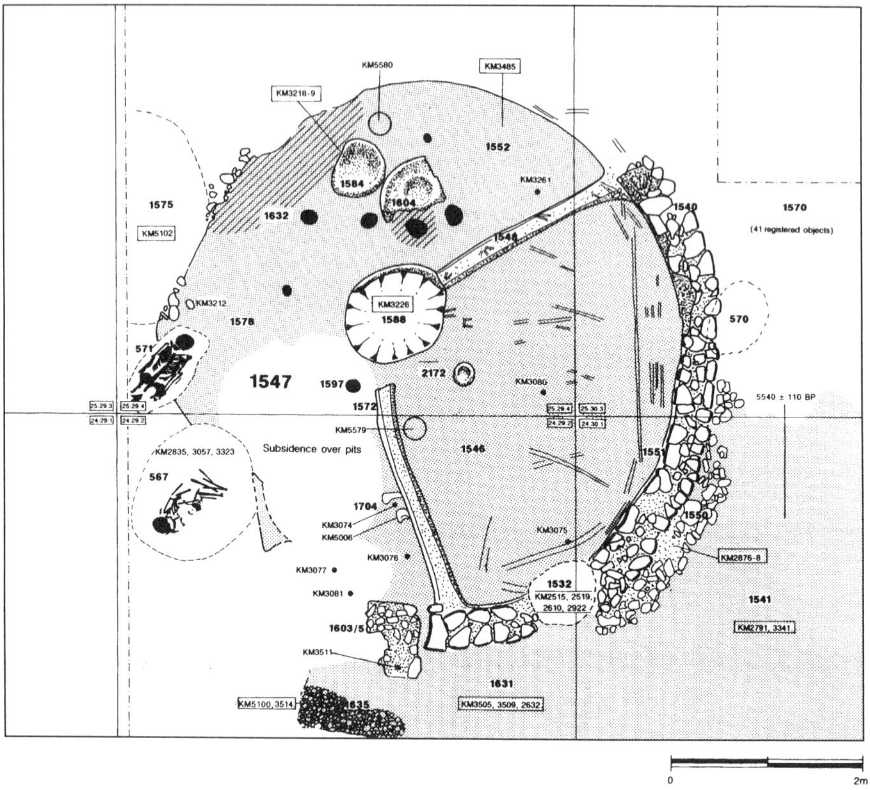

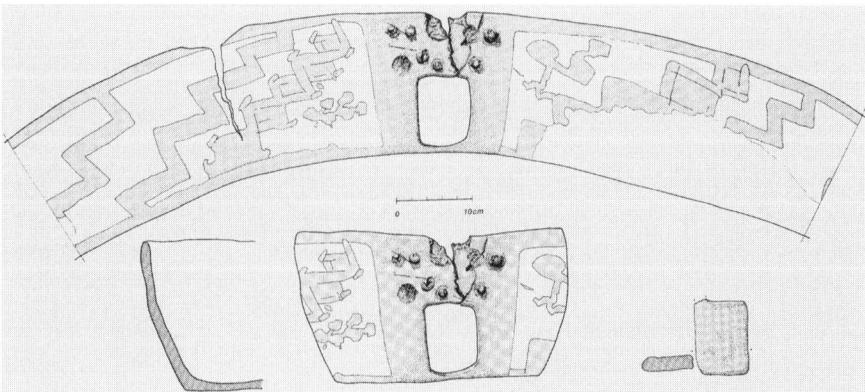

Figure 2.3. Plan of radial building 1547 at Kissonerga (after Peltenburg et al. 1998:fig. 28).

Figure 2.4. Kissonerga building model KM 1446 with external decoration and door (after Peltenburg et al. 1991:fig. 15).

Increasing degrees of sedentism are also reflected in the amount of space allotted to storage during the Chalcolithic period. At Lemba, extramural storage areas were excavated, dating to both the MChal and LChal (Peltenburg et al. 1985:129–33). During Period 2 (MChal), two such areas were found. The first comprised a series of eleven pits containing large storage vessels; grains of barley associated with these pits suggest storage of dry comestibles. Additional evidence for storage derived from the "Timbered Store Area" below Building 10 (Peltenburg et al. 1985:130–31), a large extramural surface full of pits and demarcated by stake and postholes in a plan suggesting that the area had been roofed over. Approximately half of the pits uncovered here contained fragmentary remains of large storage vessels.

The trend toward extramural storage continued at Lemba during the LChal, where evidence of an underground storage complex was uncovered in a large open space south of Building 3 (Peltenburg et al. 1985:133). Here, a central cavity was connected to three radial pit-shaped niches, two of which retained fragments of storage vessels. Although storage vessels at Lemba were often situated extramurally, the tendency over time was to "protect" storage by installing large vessels or constructing permanent storage amenities inside buildings. Intramural storage at Lemba increased significantly during the LChal, with a total of eighteen storage vessels recovered from buildings (Peltenburg et al. 1985:326–28). This contrasts sharply with Periods 1 and 2, which together yielded fewer than ten such vessels.

An even more profound example of the shift to intramural storage is the Pithos House at Kissonerga (see fig. 3.5 in ch. 3), an LChal roundhouse that contained a minimum of forty large *in situ* storage vessels (Peltenburg et al. 1998:ch. 5). Eleven of these were permanent or semi-permanent installations, as indicated by the special platforms and stone settings built adjacent to the wall to secure them. Although it is not clear whether the contents of this building represent communal wealth as part of a redistributive economic system or the holdings of a single household, the vast capacity for storage here (an estimated total of more than 5,000 l) attests to the increasing importance of domestic structures for containing and protecting surplus wealth. Similar developments have been observed in many of the early communities of the neighboring Levant, where increasingly elaborate and capacious storage facilities have been linked to intensified production of prepared food during the Late PPNB (Wright 2000). Here, as in Cyprus, the growth of "privatized" storage reinforces increasing social divisions between "public" and "private" space as well as changes in communally based kinship structures and the development of nuclear family groups (Banning 1996; Banning and Byrd 1987; Bender 1967; Blanton 1994; Byrd 1994).

The Emergence of Complex Space:
Early–Middle Bronze Ages

During the Early and Middle Bronze Ages, the continued importance of storage is attested to by the use of large *pithoi* and by the practice of storing comestibles in permanent facilities such as plastered bins and installations. These renewed efforts to secure surpluses inside buildings are likely to be associated with increasing levels of social complexity and competition as society began to move away from the kinship-based structures associated with less sedentary modes of economic production. Moreover, it is likely that the adoption of new architectural practices based on rectangular plans facilitated the addition of new architectural elements that would have been required to accommodate growing populations and new types of social organization (Swiny 1989:21). Until quite recently, there was little settlement evidence in Cyprus from the Early Cypriot–Middle Cypriot periods (EC–MC), but excavations over the last several decades at sites such as Sotira-*Kaminoudhia* (Philia facies, EC), Marki-*Alonia* (Philia facies, EC–MC), and Alambra-*Mouttes* (MC) have begun to provide us with a clearer picture of the ways in which earlier Chalcolithic traditions were supplanted by new architectural designs.

Marki-Alonia

Recent excavations at the site of Marki-*Alonia* in central Cyprus have begun to shed important light on society of the Early Bronze Age (EB)–MBA (Frankel and Webb 1993, 1994, 1996a, 1996b, 1999, 2000, 2001). The settlement is typical of the agglomerative architecture seen at other sites of the period (fig. 2.5), but in contrast with other settlements such as Sotira-*Kaminoudhia* where complete units were not identified (Swiny 1989:20), the architectural remains at Marki have made it possible to isolate a number of architectural units that the excavators believe can be associated with behavioral households, a difficult task given the Bronze Age practice of continually adding, demolishing, and rebuilding walls. Careful work over a number of lengthy seasons, however, has enabled the excavators to delineate the complex processes of building and rebuilding that transformed simple two-roomed structures into larger multiroomed complexes (see, most recently, Frankel and Webb 2000, 2001).

Excavation during the 1998–1999 seasons brought to light a complex of rooms that illustrate the growth of smaller to larger household units during the EC. During ECI–II, a two-roomed structure or duplex was constructed at the site (Rooms CII and CV; see Frankel and Webb 1999:fig. 4). This consisted of a large rectangular space unevenly partitioned by a short crosswall, resulting in one larger and one smaller room. The larger room (CII) contained grinding surfaces, pot emplacements, a mortar, and a hearth, while the smaller room (CV) contained a clay-lined structure interpreted provisionally as an oven and a plaster bench. It would thus appear that household activities were divided spatially, with grinding and cooking taking place in the larger of the rooms and baking in the smaller room; both rooms had storage facilities. As the excavators point out, this freestanding duplex represents the best evidence for EC architecture known on the island and is important for establishing a break at the very start of the Bronze Age with earlier roundhouse traditions.

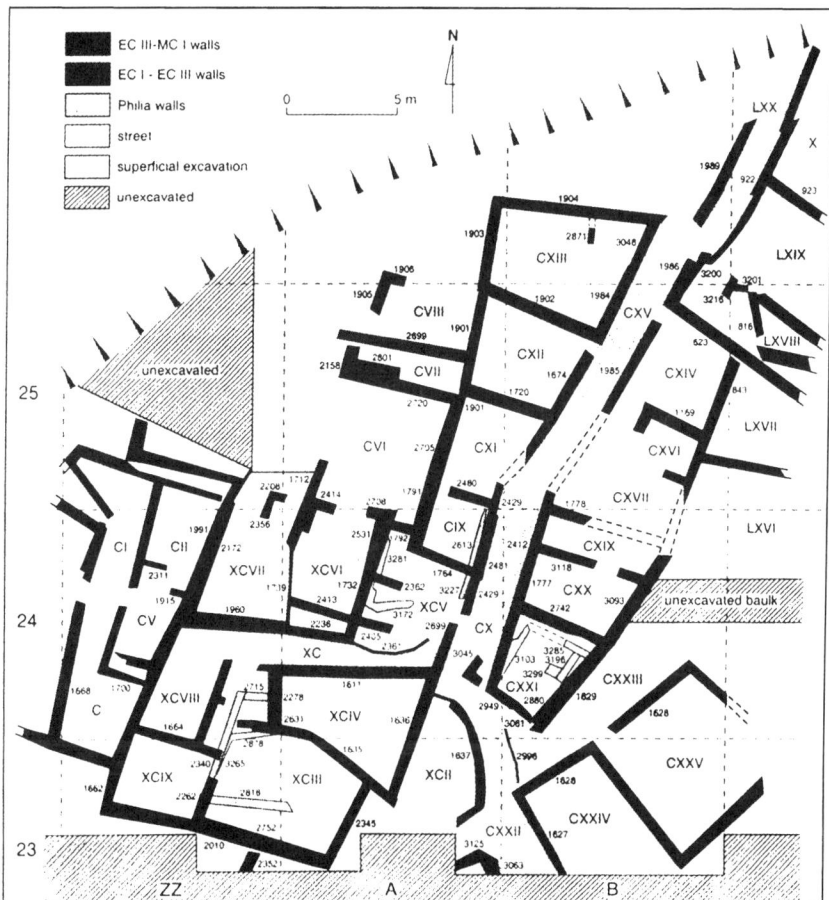

Figure 2.5.   Plan of the settlement at Marki-*Alonia* (after Frankel and Webb 2001:fig. 1).

In later phases at the site (ECIII/early MCI), smaller units such as the duplex described immediately above were incorporated into larger multi-roomed domestic structures. Rooms CII and CV, for example, form part of a six-room unit during ECIII (see Frankel and Webb 1999:fig. 2, rooms C–CV). During the MC, three separate, noncommunicating suites have been discovered: Units LI–LII, Units LXV–LXVI, and Units L–LX–LXI. The lack of finds on the floors of these structures, however, as well as the difficulty in separating use and abandonment episodes, pose problems for interpretation, and the excavators believe that a larger exposure is needed to determine the function of rooms and to define the limits of individual households (Frankel and Webb 1996a:50; Webb 2002). In general, though, the adoption of complex architectural plans comprising rectangular or subrectangular units marks a departure from earlier architectural traditions based largely on circular plans and may have been adopted in part to accommodate an expanding range of domestic activities.

Although the dearth of finds from the floors of the buildings makes it difficult to determine whether rooms were functionally differentiated, the advent of larger architectural units can undoubtedly be linked to the intensification of agriculture, the Secondary Products Revolution (Sherratt 1983), and the introduction of new social structures. In their various preliminary reports, Webb and Frankel have given particular attention to the variety of innovations within the domestic sphere at Marki (in pottery production, textile manufacture, cooking and storage facilities, etc.). They have argued convincingly that this complex package of technological innovations, as well as the social and behavioral transformations they represent, can only have resulted from the arrival on the island of cultural groups from the Anatolian mainland (Frankel 2000; Frankel, Webb, and Eslick 1995).

Sotira-Kaminoudhia

While the final publication of *Kaminoudhia* had not yet appeared at the time of this writing, it is possible to glean something of its architectural layout from preliminary reports. Swiny (1985:119) has observed that in Area A, dating to the EC, larger units were subdivided by partition walls to form multicellular structures (e.g., rooms 1/3 and rooms 4/19/20; see Swiny 1985:fig. 1). There was apparently no standardized or preconceived plan for the arrangement of the rooms within the buildings since rooms vary in shape, some with curvilinear and others with rectilinear walls. Functional analysis of the Area A complex led him to conclude that domestic activities took place in all rooms and that some of them may have had special functions (e.g., spinning/weaving [rooms 7a, 14, 15], storage [room 7], flint knapping [room 8], and food preparation [room 17]). But here, as at other sites, the scarcity of *in situ* finds on the floors of the buildings make firm conclusions difficult (Swiny 1989:21).

Alambra-Mouttes

The settlement of Alambra-*Mouttes*, located near Marki and roughly its contemporary, shows a more regular arrangement of rooms, with structural units aligned adjacently as "row houses" (Coleman et al. 1996:fig. 11). They are roughly similar in plan, with a front porch or courtyard in front and smaller rooms for storage and industry behind created by subdividing a large room by building L-shaped partitions. Finds from floor levels were more numerous here than at Marki, and patterns of artifact distribution, showing reduplication of types between structures, suggest the existence of small independent social groups engaged in similar activities involving food preparation, cooking, storage, textile production, and occasional metalworking. Benches, platforms, plastered bins, and supports for storage vessels are permanent features within the buildings and again point to an increasingly sedentary existence. Although part of larger agglomerative networks, the domestic structures at Alambra to a large degree anticipate a final type of domestic architecture to be considered here, the detached house.

Gjerstad's "Houses": Homes for Nuclear Families?

With the ECIII and MB in Cyprus come the first candidates for detached multi-roomed domestic structures, which contrast sharply with the customary agglomerative arrangements described above. Two such examples exist, one from Alambra and one from Kalopsidha, both of which were excavated by Gjerstad earlier in the century. The Kalopsidha house (MCIII) consists of eleven rooms around a central courtyard (fig. 2.6). It was not fully excavated and may in fact have been part of a larger complex, but the rooms as published appear to form an integral unit. According to Gjerstad (1926:27–37), the courtyard (Room 5) had been used for food preparation and cooking; the other rooms were used for storage, lounging, sleeping, food preparation, cooking, and perhaps even ritual activity. The use of an unroofed space for cooking, however, has not been found at other sites of the period and warrants a reevaluation of Gjerstad's interpretations (see Frankel and Webb 1996a:54). Whatever its particular function, the existence of a central courtyard within a building marks a change in domestic spatial arrangements that constitutes a new stage in the privatization of labor and the use of interior space.

A similar, somewhat earlier possible example of a house was found at Alambra on the southwest slope of the *Mouttes* hill (Gjerstad 1926:22–24). It has been dated to ECIII (c. 2000 B.C.) and consisted of two rooms adjoining a large courtyard. In

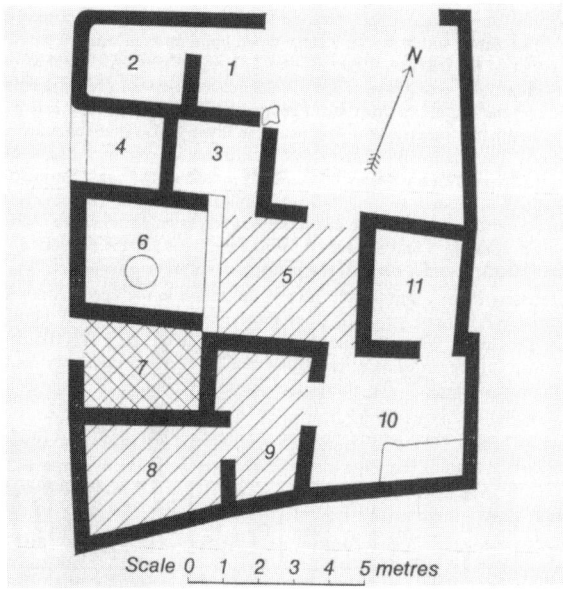

Figure 2.6.   Plan of Gjerstad's house at Kalopsidha (after Gjerstad 1926).

contrast to the later house at Kalopsidha, the courtyard here adjoins the rooms rather than being enclosed by them. In the north room were found a possible olive press, benches used as shelves for vessels, a hearth, a mortar, and cooking pots. The south room had a similar bench, querns and grinding stones, and several loom weights. There are problems with the interpretation of these structures, however. In their final site report, the excavators of Alambra noted difficulties of separating *in situ* floor material from underlying material on account of the patchy nature of floor preservation (Coleman et al. 1996:31). A similar problem exists at Marki in separating use from abandonment phases (Frankel and Webb 1996a:2–3, 25–26). Modern techniques of excavating and recording have brought to light many of the problems involved in interpreting the stratigraphy of domestic structures and thus we must treat earlier excavations such as Gjerstad's with extreme caution (Barlow 1985).

These difficulties notwithstanding, the similarities between the permanent features of freestanding structures and those of the contemporary agglomerative complexes are numerous (room size, wall thickness, the use of clay benches and plaster bins, etc.), suggesting a unilinear development from one to the other. Moreover, the freestanding domicile serves as an appropriate metaphor for the social changes that had been set in motion a millennium before and would appear to represent a further stage in the emergence of nuclear family structures from the earlier kin-based networks of hunter-gatherers and simple farmers.

Episkopi-Phaneromeni

Preliminary reports on the site of Episkopi-*Phaneromeni* indicate continuity of settlement plan, at least in some parts of the island, from the end of MC through to the early stages of the Late Cypriot period (LC) (Carpenter 1981). Although little is known of the MBA settlement in Area G, fragmentary architectural remains reveal basic similarities to the agglomerative settlement plans characteristic of Marki and Sotira-*Kaminoudhia*. More is known of the extensive Late Cypriot IA (LCIA) settlement at *Phaneromeni*, and similarities to Marki are seen in such common features as plaster bins and unlined pits, both of which were probably used for storage. Analysis of the various structures at the site provides evidence of traditional techniques of demolition and reconstruction, such the removal of external walls, the introduction of partition walls, and the blocking of doorways. As at other sites of the late third– and early second millennia B.C., there is little evidence for functional differentiation of building space. Elsewhere on the island, however, the traditional patterns of construction were beginning to be abandoned in favor of large-scale construction in which domestic space began to be sharply segregated from other specialized functional components such as areas for copper working, textile manufacture, olive oil production, and large-scale storage. These changes coincide with greater levels of socioeconomic complexity, including the advent of urbanism, social hierarchy, and regionally differentiated political organization.

Gender and the Fragmentation of Space

In the preceding pages, I have reviewed the evidence for changing spatial constructs in Cyprus from the Neolithic through LCI, a period of roughly 6,000 years. In that discussion, I have tried to emphasize how space and place were transformed from exterior to interior, open to closed, and public to private spheres, and I have proposed that changes in spatial configurations of domestic structures both reflected and shaped the social structures that produced them.

Ethnographic evidence suggests strong correlations between the segmentation of space and the differentiation of gender roles within society. In a cross-cultural study of segmentation, architecture, and the use of space, Kent has provided a useful framework for interpreting long-term changes in architectural practices by linking them to increasing levels of socioeconomic complexity (1990). Cultures included in the study were divided into five categories (four of them pre-state groups) based on degrees of complexity. The least complex (Kent's Category I) consisted of groups with little or no sociopolitical stratification or economic specialization and no apparent division of labor; the use of space in these societies is freely defined, multi-purpose, and not gender specific. With increased levels of complexity come changes in the segmentation of space. In Category II, for example, the division of labor is more sharply defined, there is limited political stratification, and gender divisions are more pronounced. Accordingly, architecture is more segmented, and spatial divisions reflect functional and gender-specific distinctions. In Categories III and IV, social ranking is more prevalent, and there is evidence of class divisions and gender-based divisions of labor; buildings in these groups show internal partitioning, functional specialization, and gender segregation.

Archaeological evidence from prehistoric cultures of the ancient Mediterranean regions corroborates the view provided by ethnographic accounts by detailing the evolution of settlement structures with increasingly rigid distinctions between public and private space. In the Near East, for example, the advent of more permanent, segmented buildings during the PPNB were accompanied by increasingly restricted social networks and the development of more formalized mechanisms for social organization (Banning 1996; Banning and Byrd 1987; Byrd 1994). Changes in the built environment are strikingly similar to those noted above for LBA Cyprus: restricted access to courtyards, compartmentalization of interior space, elaboration and increased frequency of storage facilities within buildings, increasing focus of domestic activities in discrete locations, and the introduction of special-purpose buildings of a nondomestic nature (e.g., political decision making, ritual and ceremonial activities, and redistributive storage facilities). With the exception of the nondomestic structures, these changes attest to the increasing privatization of domestic production, including such basic daily activities as food storage, preparation, cooking, and dining (Wright 2000).

Halstead has observed similar patterns of development for domestic architecture of the Neolithic period of northern Greece (in particular Thessaly) by tracing the progressive isolation of the household over the course of three–four millennia (Halstead 1989). During the Early/Middle Neolithic, the segregation of the household from the larger community, achieved by the construction of buildings with rectangular plans, was overcome to some degree by the placement of cooking installations in between buildings. In later phases of the Neolithic, the sharing of domestic cooking facilities among households was restricted to immediate neighbors, while during the Final Neolithic they were completely enclosed within courtyards, effectively limiting interactions between neighboring households (Halstead 1989:90). Other studies of the domestication of space in early societies have emphasized the impact on social relations of the adoption of intensive agriculture and sedentary village life (e.g., Hodder 1990). With the growth of sedentism and the domestication of plant and animal resources, economic production became channeled increasingly through the medium of the household, and this, in turn, had an important impact on the ways in which individuals and groups interacted with one another and negotiated access to social space.

One of the aspects of gender that would have been most affected by these developments is the allocation of time and division of labor. Ethnographic research on present-day agricultural societies (Boserup 1970; Ember 1983; Sanday 1973) shows a decline in women's contribution to primary economic production in societies where intensive agriculture is practiced. Ember (1983), citing time-allocation data gathered by Minge-Klevana (1980) on simple and intensive agricultural societies around the world, has shown that, on the one hand, adult women in intensive agricultural societies average 10.8 working hours per day, as opposed to 6.7 working hours per day in simple agricultural societies. Women in intensive agricultural societies, on the other hand, spend more time working indoors than women in simple agricultural societies (5.9 vs. 2.9 hours a day). In both types of society, women spend an average 4.5 hours daily working outdoors, so outdoor work doesn't decrease under conditions of intensive agriculture—but indoor work markedly increases. Convinced that the adoption of the plow per se cannot adequately account for these differences, Ember suggests the following four reasons for the changing work patterns associated with agricultural intensification:

1. Increasing reliance on domesticated animal stocks and lesser reliance on hunting draws men away from hunting and into plowing as a major economic activity
2. Greater reliance on cereal crops requires that a proportionately greater time be spent processing process crops and preparing food, tasks that are allocated primarily to women
3. As the result of agricultural intensification, other domestic work increases (e.g., tending/feeding draft animals, butchering, food processing, spinning, weaving, and other activities that prehistoric archaeologists, following Sherratt 1983, have ascribed to a Secondary Products Revolution)
4. Increasing levels of sedentism appear to be linked to a decrease in birth spacing and hence an increase in number of offspring. Intensified production requires a

greater labor force, and higher levels of fertility demand that more time be spent in child rearing, a task that is allocated primarily to women

Ember's conclusions contradict the notion that "biological" reasons are causal factors in the male/female division of labor among intensive agriculturalists. Men do not take to the plow and women to the home because of men's greater physical strength or women's "natural" role as mothers. Rather, the division of labor along male/female lines is a *cultural* solution to the problem of increased workloads and accelerated birthrates that accompanied the adoption of more sophisticated agricultural techniques.

In Cyprus, evidence for the changing relationships between men, women, and children can perhaps to be inferred from the well-known scenic compositions in clay found in tombs of the EC–MC, which, in the absence of extensive settlement evidence, have furnished particularly important details for activities of daily life (for details, see ch. 4, as well as Swiny 1989:23–24, Morris 1985:264–90, and Karageorghis 1991:ch. 3). A central pictorial theme running through some of these scenes is the division of male and female labor. While men are depicted tending or guarding animals, women perform domestic tasks that have been variously interpreted as grinding grain, kneading dough, or washing clothes. Regardless of the particular interpretations of the activities portrayed, it is clear that by the end of the third millennium B.C. economic production had become more clearly segregated along lines of gender and that a new system of task allocation, not noted previously in the archaeological record of the Neolithic and Chalcolithic periods, had been adopted. Since the changes in domestic architecture documented earlier in this chapter evolved in part to cope with changes in socioeconomic structures, it is worthwhile exploring a bit further the ways in which social relations were renegotiated during the early phases of the Bronze Age.

The cultural solution that emerged toward the end of the third millennium B.C. to cope with the impact of agricultural intensification must be judged as nothing short of revolutionary, for it is likely to have involved a departure from earlier kinship networks and communally based modes of production and the emergence of a household consisting of a husband, wife, and their children. Moreover, a new emphasis was placed on the mutually dependent roles of husband and wife in order to ensure the economic survival of the household. By the same token, the weakening of family ties outside of the household, together with the increasing gendered division of labor, the exclusion of women from primary roles in economic production, and the predominance of males in public life, would have encapsulated the egalitarian relationships between males and females that characterized the earlier prehistoric periods on the island (see ch. 3). Social stability now rested on a much more precarious foundation than it did within older kinship-based system.

The tensions surrounding these developments are effectively illustrated by one of the chief works of coroplastic art of the ECIII–MCI, the Vounous bowl (fig. 2.7), which Peltenburg has interpreted as a symbolic depiction in clay of the existing social order (Peltenburg 1994). Due to its discovery in a burial context, this scene has traditionally been interpreted as a sanctuary, a sacred enclosure, or a funerary ritual (Dikaios 1940; Frankel and Tamkavi 1973; Karageorghis 1991:140; Mogelonsky 1988:216–22; Morris 1985:281–83).

Peltenburg, however, focuses on the vessel's content rather than its context by analyzing the formal arrangement of the figures positioned within the bowl. Only one female is present in the composition, a woman holding an infant. All but two of the other human figures are clearly indicated as males, including the four figures seated against the wall, the six standing in a circle, and the large figure seated on the chair in the center of the scene. On the basis of the clear separation of the sexes in this scene, as well as the size and arrangement of all the figures, he argues that the constellation of figures in the Vounous bowl thus portrays a particular view of a fitting EC social and religious order. Hierarchy is depicted spatially by the separation of groups into different graded levels, with female, infant, and animals in the lowest order, and a seated male, perhaps a deity, in the highest order. The emphasis here is on a social order in which men rather than women are the active agents and in which the parameters of "proper" male and female behavior are clearly defined and segregated. Finally, the "bowl" should be identi-

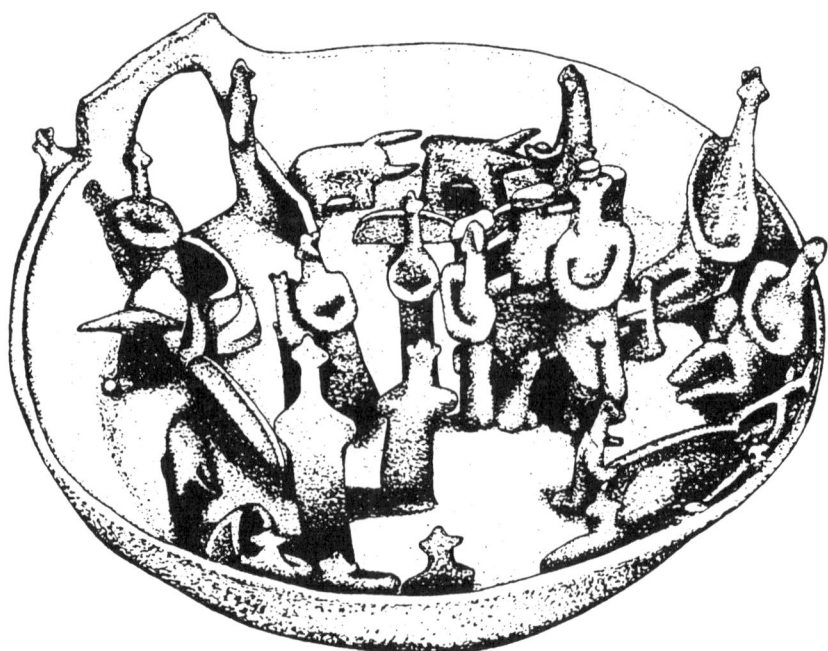

Figure 2.7. Scenic composition inside a Red Polished pottery bowl from *Vounous* (after Morris 1985:fig. 6).

fied not as a sacred enclosure or tomb but as a building; the Kissonerga building model provides a precedent, and this interpretation conforms well to Hodder's definition of the *domus* as "the locus of production and reproduction which constitute society and social relations" (Hodder 1990:41).

In attempting to chart the dynamics of gender relations in prehistoric Cyprus through the mechanism of the household, we have seen some of the ways in which domestic structures were transformed over the course of several millennia, and I have argued that these changes can be correlated to growing levels of sedentism and social complexity. We have also linked the marked separation of male and female roles in economic production during the Cypriot Bronze Age to the increasing use of domestic structures as focal points of economic and social activity.

But more than simply reflecting social and economic changes of emerging complex social groups, the shifting boundaries of domestic space actively contributed to those development. Within the medium of the household, potentially threatening social and economic tensions appeared to be harmoniously resolved since households were portrayed as joint economic enterprises, or mutually dependent teams, rather than as antagonistic actors in an ever-widening social hierarchy. In this sense, the emergent Cypriot household masked underlying social realities and helped create new gender ideologies in which male authority was presented as natural and preordained. In a fundamental way, then, the transformations of the built environment during the Chalcolithic and earlier phases of the Bronze Age helped to produce and reproduce the distinctions on which newly emerging cultural constructions of gender were based. In order to view the continuing ramifications of these developments into the later phases of the Bronze Age, in the final section of this chapter I will turn to evidence for settlement hierarchy and architectural innovation during the LCII–III.

Settlement Hierarchy in the Late Bronze Age

Our present understanding of settlement structure in LBA Cyprus is based on a model first proposed by Catling in the early 1960s, which classified all known sites into three distinct groups: urban centers along the coast, inland villages, and rural towns associated with copper mining (Catling 1963). Although he did not explore the nature of the interactions between these groups in depth, Catling was the first to observe explicitly that this newly emerging settlement pattern constituted a social hierarchy based on differential access to the island's copper resources and that it was generated by the increasing importance of metallurgy and foreign trade to economic expansion.

In recent years, Catling's basic model has been developed more extensively by several other scholars and has been confirmed by excavations at sites such as Hala Sultan Tekke, Kalavasos-*Ayios Dhimitrios*, and Maroni-*Vournes*, all of which would fall into Catling's group of urban coastal centers. In this regard, it is significant that the island's earliest urban polities (Enkomi, Toumba tou Skourou, Hala Sultan Tekke, and Kourion-

Bamboula) are positioned on or near the coast. Coastal locations were also favored by polities of later date such as Kalavasos-*Ayios Dhimitrios* and Kition (both with initial dates of LCII). These urban centers are differentiated from rural villages by their quantities of imported pottery, prestige goods, ashlar masonry, metal objects, Cypro-Minoan inscriptions, and seals, as well as by their considerably larger areal extents. In addition, it is possible that each polity possessed its own political, economic, and cultural status (Knapp 1996:65).

Keswani (1993) has taken Catling's model a step farther by investigating the nature of the economic relations of LBA settlement sites, focusing in particular on the ways in which various settlement types may have been integrated into a coherent economic system. According to her analysis, this system most probably lacked a central, island-wide authority (Keswani 1996b). Instead, power was regionally based, with each major center or polity holding sway over a distinct geographical sphere. The principles of staple finance and wealth finance are used to explain how subsistence goods, raw materials, and luxury items were produced, distributed, transported, and administered by individual polities (cf. Brumfiel and Earle 1987: Earle 1991). In this way, smaller rural outposts and larger urban centers are linked into a hierarchical arrangement in which urban polities exercised political and economic authority over smaller inland sites. As a corollary to those developments, the breakdown of the LBA economic system was a central factor contributing to the instability and ultimate collapse of most urban centers by the end of LCIIIB (Keswani 1989:210–11).

In another important contribution to this discussion, Peltenburg (1996) has explored the political and military aspects of this emerging hierarchy by suggesting that the many fortresses on the island dating to MCIII may have been built to protect and maintain the transport of raw materials from the hinterland to the coast. This, as well as other kinds of evidence from the fifteenth century B.C. [MCIII/LCI], suggest a period of "instability and disruption" that can very likely be attributed to the dynamic processes associated with the emergence of polities in the fourteenth century B.C., particularly the rise to power of the key site of Enkomi on the island's east coast. As Peltenburg observes, the settlement at Enkomi demonstrates "impressive levels of organization" and evidence of copper working already at an early date (LCI), both of which would have required a "highly developed regional infrastructure" (Peltenburg 1996:29).

The social, economic, cultural, and political changes that characterize the LBA of Cyprus must have had a tremendous impact on the construction of gender roles, whether in the domestic sphere or the workplace. This aspect of settlement hierarchy has received little or no scholarly treatment and it is one of the primary objectives of this book. Before doing this, however, we need to look briefly at the architectural remains of some of the key settlement sites of the LBA. Because settlement evidence for the later phases of the Bronze Age is more substantial and widespread than in earlier periods, I will only discuss a selected group of sites here: Kourion-*Bamboula*, Kalavasos-*Ayios Dhi-*

mitrios, Enkomi, and Kition. All of these sites fall into Catling's group of urban coastal centers and collectively provide evidence for the development of an increasingly hierarchical social system on the island during the sixteenth through thirteenth centuries B.C.

Kourion-Bamboula

Weinberg undertook excavations at Kourion-*Bamboula* from 1937–1939 and again in 1948 (Weinberg 1983). His most important achievement was the excavation of sixteen houses surrounded by a circuit wall; these were grouped into four structural phases that jointly range from LCIA–LCIIIB, a period of about four hundred years (c. 1600–1200 B.C.) and still constitute some of the best evidence for domestic architecture in LBA Cyprus. While the domestic structures at Kourion are certainly departures from earlier architectural traditions, it is important to note that they were not freestanding, as is indicated by many of the illustrations in Weinberg 1983 (and fig. 2.7), but existed as parts of large agglomerative complexes like those we have seen at Marki, Kaminoudhia, and Episkopi. In this respect, the settlement plan of Kourion represents a continuation into the LBA of longstanding architectural traditions. It is also important to note that buildings at Kourion, regardless of their plan, are all about the same size, underscoring once again the increasing levels of uniformity in domestic structures and suggesting the persistence of relatively egalitarian social structures, at least at some sites, well into the LBA.

One of the most significant architectural innovations at Kourion was the standardization of domestic building types to a degree not previously known on the island. The most common type was rectangular in plan, with six rooms arranged in three rows around a central courtyard (fig. 2.8); this building type occurs at a number of other LBA sites on the island, including Pyla-*Kokkinokremos*, Toumba tou Skourou, Idalion, Enkomi, Hala Sultan Tekke, and Alassa-*Pano Mandilares*. A second type, which also occurs at other sites (albeit less frequently), is what Weinberg termed the "L-type" plan; it first appears at Kourion in LCIIC.

Another important aspect of domestic structures at Kourion is the evidence they furnish for the increasing privatization of domestic activities; this can be observed both in the inaccessibility of certain rooms, the functional differentiation of workspace, and the construction of permanent installations for household activities. In House A.VI, for example, the main entry was from the street into Room 2 (fig. 2.8). Although some rooms in this structure (e.g., rooms 4, 5, 6) were connected by doorways, there was no way for persons entering Room 2 from the street to gain direct access to adjacent Rooms 1 and 3. This was probably due to the desire to effectively separate "indoor" and "outdoor" space by furnishing greater privacy for household members.

As was usually the case in Bronze Age houses, finds from floor deposits were limited, but there is some evidence for functional divisions within the buildings, with different rooms likely to have served as kitchens, storage areas, and workspaces for

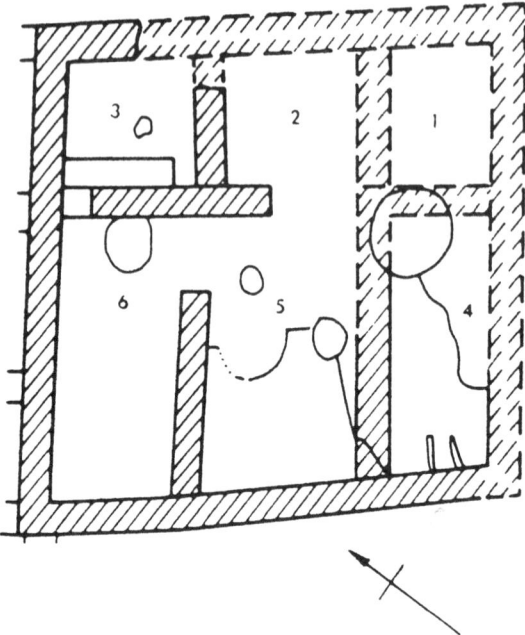

Figure 2.8.   Reconstructed plan of structure A. VI at Kourion-*Bamboula* (after Weinberg 1983:fig. 6).

subsistence activities such as grinding grain. In addition, the regular occurrence of permanent installations for work activities, storage facilities, and water supply (e.g., grinding installations, storage vessels in pits, plaster bins and platforms, cisterns) meant that functional divisions were conceived of as fixed and long-term arrangements of space. The location of cisterns inside buildings is a particularly good example of this since it signifies the "privatization" of water supply and illustrates once again the importance of the interior space (rather than extramural areas) as the primary locus for day-to-day economic pursuits.

House A.VI was constructed initially in Stratum D and reconstructed in Stratum E on precisely the same plan. This pattern, which Weinberg observed for many of the buildings at Kourion, is important for its implications concerning the kinship structures and domestic arrangements of LBA society, such as the emergence of nuclear family groups, the private ownership of domestic structures, and the transfer of property from one generation to the next. I will say more below about the possible correlations between changes in domestic architecture and kinship structures during the LBA.

Kalavasos-Ayios Dhimitrios

Alison K. South directed excavations of a major LBA site at Kalavasos from 1980 to 1999. Although one volume of the final report has already appeared (South et al.

1989), most of what we know of the site's architecture must still be gleaned from preliminary reports (most recently, South 1997).

While a number of wealthy tombs at this site suggest initial settlement in LCIIB (see ch. 6), the architectural remains date initially to LCIIC, by which time the site had become an extremely wealthy, hierarchically organized urban entity. Unlike Kourion, where domestic units shared party walls and comprised joint functions of residential and industrial activities, the structures at *Ayios Dhimitros* were largely independent of one another. Domestic buildings stood side by side with buildings of a nondomestic nature, and variations in size, construction materials, and techniques appear to have distinguished "public" (i.e., economic, administrative) and "private" (i.e., domestic, residential) structures. In addition, some of the buildings seem to have been reserved for special functions. Streets between the buildings, which allowed for the efficient transport of goods to the industrial and administrative areas, may have further promoted the separation of buildings and the segregation of social space (South 1997:156–58).

In her preliminary reports on the site, South reports evidence for functional variation between rooms of individual buildings (e.g., B III); there is also evidence for the existence of special purpose buildings for purposes of administration and large-scale storage (B X), olive pressing (B XI), and metalworking (B IX). The largest and arguably the most important building at the site is B X (fig. 2.9), which has been interpreted as a residence for elites as well as an administrative center (South 1989, 1992, 1997). Its large size, massive construction, and use of ashlar masonry set it apart from all other buildings at the site. The largest single room within the buildings (19.5 × 7.25 m) was a storage area containing a minimum of 47 *pithoi*; together, it is estimated that they would have provided approximately 33,500 l of storage capacity (South 1989:321).

Although there were no metal artifacts within the building, the importance and wealth of its residents can be measured by the overwhelming number of imported ceramic vessels (60 percent Mycenaean) and by the discovery of five cylinder seals inscribed with multiple rows of Cypro Minoan symbols (South 1989:321–22). Whether or not B X can be regarded as an architectural and social product of an emerging state, it is clear that its residents must have constituted the upper echelon of an increasingly bureaucratic and hierarchical society. In any case, *Ayios Dhimitrios* was not unique in this regard; the selective use of ashlar masonry for imposing public structures was increasingly typical in the later Bronze Age of a new type of settlement seen at many other contemporary urban centers such as Enkomi and Kition.

Enkomi

Located immediately beside the modern city of Famagusta, Enkomi is the largest and arguably the most important urban center of the Cypriot Bronze Age (fig. 2.10). Successive teams of French, Swedish, British, and Cypriot archaeologists worked at the site beginning with the British Museum expedition in 1896 and continuing intermittently

Figure 2.9.   Plan of Building X complex at Kalavasos-*Ayios Dhimitrios* (after South 1997:fig. 1).

until the 1960s. The differing goals, excavation methods, and recording techniques of the numerous archaeological missions at Enkomi, together with the political events of 1974, which rendered the site off-limits to archaeologists, make the interpretation of this important settlement an extremely difficult task. The most reliable results were obtained by the Cypriot archaeologist Porphyrios Dikaios during his 1948–1958 campaigns at the site; the following overview is based largely on his final publication (Dikaios 1969).

Dikiaos's excavations established, among other things, that Enkomi was founded in MCIII (or at the latest, LCI). Little remains of this earliest phase of occupation, but what scant architectural evidence there is in Area III clearly predates the initial construction in LCIA of a substantial building that Dikaios called "the Fortress," due to its heavily built walls and similarity to other structures on the island termed "fortresses" by Gjerstad earlier in the century. It is important to keep in mind, however, that the excavated remains of this imposing structure represent only what was probably its basement; its massive walls undoubtedly carried upper stories, and the building is more likely to have functioned as an economic and administrative center ("palace").

The Fortress (with maximum dimensions of 45 m × 13.3 m) is among the earliest large-scale freestanding structures (other than the MCIII forts) known on the island and

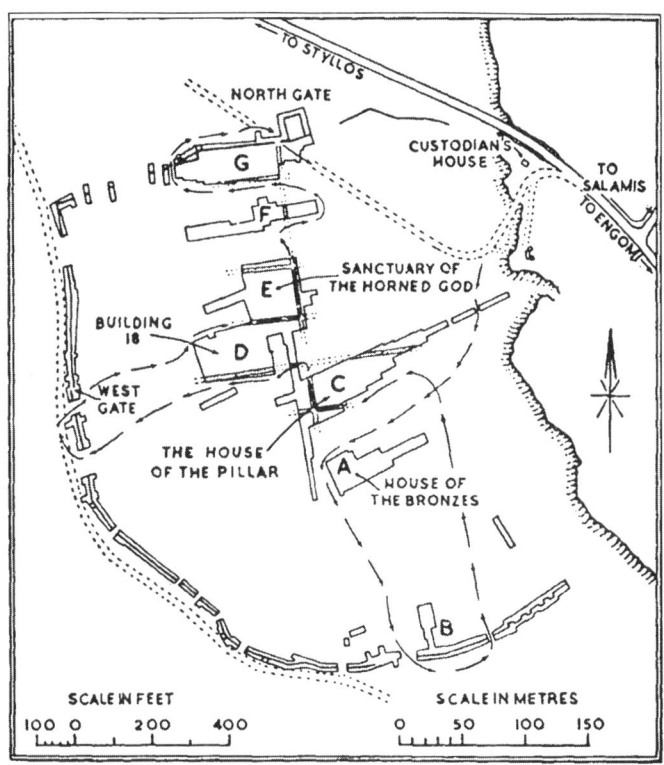

Figure 2.10.   Reconstructed town plan of Enkomi (after Dikaios 1969:pl. 241).

links the rise of state-level society to the construction of monumental edifices. It had two entrances (both in its south facade) flanked respectively by a tower and buttresses. Within several of its eighteen rooms, Dikaios uncovered evidence for industrial activity, in particular copper working. In a later phase (Level IIA), the Fortress was replaced by an even larger structure that appears to have functioned as a complex of residential and industrial units with a domestic wing to the east and copper workshops to the west. In a further rebuilding of the site (LCIIC=thirteenth century), the first ashlar buildings were constructed and the Fortress was furnished with 2–4-m-thick walls and an imposing "gate house." Not surprisingly, evidence for metalworking at the site increases at this time.

Area I, which yielded substantial architectural remains, was also occupied as early as MCIII, although the first remains of buildings were found in LCIA. The structures of Area I, Level IA consisted of two courtyards with attached rooms (Dikaios 1969:pls. 268–69). In contrast with the structures in Area III, they appear to have been exclusively domestic in nature and were destroyed and abandoned at the end of Level IB (=LCIB).

In the next phase of occupation (Level II), construction took place in a new locale; although the latter was only partially excavated, the plan clearly consists of a complex of rooms around three courtyards. The domestic architecture in this area was considerably more complex than at other contemporary sites (e.g. Kourion-*Bamboula*), and Dikaios drew parallels between structures at Enkomi and those of Mycenaean Greece. The increasing proportions of imported Mycenaean pottery wares in the successive phases of Area III also reinforce the view that Cypriot society from LCIIB onwards began to undergo significant levels of acculturation from the Greek mainland.

Kition

Karageorghis excavated this important Bronze–Iron Age urban center in the modern town of Larnaca between 1959 and 1974 (see Karageorghis 1976b for a general account). Strictly speaking, the site lies outside of the chronological parameters of this book, but I mention it briefly here since it illustrates the further development of architectural trends seen at earlier sites. The two main sectors of the excavations, Areas I and II, were correlated by a series of occupation levels, Floors I–IV (but see Kling 1989:68–73). The earliest remains in Area I (Floor IV, dating to LCIIC) comprised a series of rooms of both residential and industrial character. Demas, who published the domestic architecture from the site, concluded that the complex was "a private residential area, perhaps the residence of a local craftsman" (Karageorghis and Demas 1985:10). The remains stratified above Floor IV (i.e., Floors IIIA, III, II, and I) represent a series of destructions, abandonments, and reconstruction phases dating from LCIII to the Cypro-Geometric I period (CGI); following the abandonment of Floor I, Area I remained unoccupied until the Phoenician settlement of the ninth century B.C.

Like Area I, Area II was initially occupied in LCIIC and continued through to CGI, with abandonment thereafter until the Phoenician reoccupation. Rather than functioning as a residential/industrial complex, however, Area II was a sanctuary complex furnished with industrial workshops of metalworking and textile manufacture. The concentration of religious and administrative power in this area has been the basis for much of the current discussion concerning the role of religion in the construction and legitimization of elite power in the Bronze Age (see especially Knapp 1986).

Both areas at Kition incorporate ashlar masonry in the construction of important public buildings and show increasing proportions of imported Mycenaean pottery, wealthy tombs bearing the bodies of elite family groups, and substantial remains of metalworking and textile manufacture. Industrial activities were carried out in special purpose workshops dedicated to metallurgy and textile production (see ch. 3). Before LCIIC (i.e., the thirteenth century B.C.), weaving took place exclusively in the home (see ch. 3 and Smith 2002). This tradition apparently continued into the thirteenth century B.C. in some centers. In Area II at Kition, on the other hand, textiles were manufactured in an area known as the Western Workshops (Karageorghis and Demas 1985). Here, textile manufacture was undertaken indoors in permanent structures, implying that weaving been raised to the level of a full-fledged, full-time industry (Smith 2002). These and other change in the organization of the workplace are likely to have had an important impact on gendered divisions of labor, as we shall see in chapter 3.

Gender and Spatial Innovation during the Late Bronze Age

The settlement evidence from Kourion, Kalavasos, Enkomi, and Kition, as well as other sites of the LBA in Cyprus not discussed here, enables us to outline the following changes in the structure of domestic space during the sixteenth–thirteenth centuries B.C.:

1. The replacement of traditional, agglomerative settlement plans with independent, freestanding structures
2. A greater degree of standardization in construction methods and architectural plans, both within and between sites
3. The positioning of doorways to limit public access and afford greater privacy
4. The functional segregation of work activities, including the construction of special purpose buildings
5. An increasing privatization of domestic activities (i.e., interior courtyards), including the privatization of water supply (i.e., digging of cisterns inside buildings)
6. The construction of streets between buildings
7. The rebuilding of destroyed or abandoned structures on same spot, with identical plans
8. The use of special materials and techniques for the construction of special structures (i.e., ashlar masonry)

Of course, not all of these innovations took place at every site, nor did they occur simultaneously throughout the island. While more traditional settlement plans persisted at some centers (e.g., Kourion), others abandoned those traditions by replacing them with clusters of buildings arranged into discrete sectors (Enkomi, Kition) or with independent, freestanding structures separated by streets (Kalavasos). And, while some sites show greater degrees of standardization of buildings and privatization of space than others, the changes observed in the domestic arrangement of space during the LBA generally demonstrate a more restricted social network for subsistence activities. They also indicate a shift in some categories of industrial production from domestic to extra-domestic contexts and the emergence of more bureaucratic, institutionalized mechanisms for integrating and administering economic pursuits. Finally, they signify important changes in the domestic social sphere, particularly the emergence of a prominent "ruling class" and increases in the gendered divisions of task allocation and working space in both domestic and nondomestic environments.

The emergence of state-level society in the ancient Near East is generally considered to have had a severely negative impact on women's roles and statuses (see, for example, Lerner 1986 and Wright 1996). In Cyprus, however, the situation may have been different, and it appears unlikely that Cypriot society of the LBA ever reached the level of a fully centralized, bureaucratic state. Alternative models based on the concept of heterarchy rather than centralized hierarchical modes of political organization based on regional polities may, in fact, be more in accordance with the archaeological evidence (Keswani 1996b). The evidence of the built environment of LBA Cyprus portrays this distinction particularly well, for although we can trace the emergence of increasingly standardized, symmetrical, structures over time, many of the latter were nondomestic in character, and the island never produced the sort of massive administrative complexes that emerged in ancient Mesopotamia, for example, as early as the fourth millennium B.C.

These important distinctions in the use of space and the construction of the domestic environment point to important distinctions in social organization as well and suggest that patterns of gendered behavior in Cyprus did not conform to the more rigid structures observed in the larger polities further to the east (or, for that matter, to the west). The controversy surrounding the nature and scale of political organization in LBA Cyprus is thus fundamental to an understanding of the dynamics of gender during the second millennium B.C. We will return to it in chapter 7, after we have explored other bodies of evidence for gender in the material culture of the island (tools, technology, figurines, and mortuary evidence), which allow us to view socioeconomic developments in ancient Cyprus from a variety of gendered perspectives.

Working Actors: Gender, Technology, and Labor

> The division of labor by gender is rarely absolute. . . . Which person performs which tasks may be a matter of talent, training and convenience as often as constructed by gender considerations. Furthermore, cautions should be heeded about assigning specific tools to men or women without evidence.
>
> —NELSON, *GENDER IN ARCHAEOLOGY: ANALYZING POWER AND PRESTIGE*

THE EVALUATION OF MALE AND FEMALE ROLES in the past, as in the present, is never more prone to essentialist thinking than in the spheres of economic production, exchange, technology, and the division of labor. The stereotypical model of hunter-gatherer societies, in which men are linked to hunting activities and women are associated with gathering and processing vegetable resources, for example, has served as a powerful paradigm for the universal division of male and female labor into segregated spheres stretching far back into the early phases of human prehistory (Lee and DeVore 1968). In these androcentric narratives of human behavior, the activities of males, which are presumed to have involved the manufacture and use of stone tools, are more highly valued than that of females who, on account of their supposed exclusion from hunting and tool-making activities, are thought to have played less active and integral roles in subsistence (Gero 1991; Watson and Kennedy 1991).

To this have been added unmediated assumptions about women's capacity to undertake physically demanding tasks, due to their lesser physical strength and their biological roles as child-bearers and mothers, all of which are presumed to have restricted female participation in both hunter-gatherer and agricultural subsistence activities. In a similar vein, Ortner's male/female:culture/nature analogy (Ortner 1974) and Rosaldo's domestic/public dichotomy (Rosaldo 1974), which have been adopted by many anthropologists and archaeologists as particularly cogent and compelling explanations for differences in the sexual division of labor, link sexual inequalities to essential biological traits, a linkage that was subsequently given apparent scientific backing by sociobiological research on primate behavior that regarded physiological differences between males and females as prime determinants of adaptive strategies for survival, particularly among early human groups (e.g., Isaac 1978).

Challenges to these and other essentialist narratives of the past have been issued during the last twenty years by a number of anthropologists and archaeologists who have exposed many of the biases inherent in the "man the hunter" model (Browne 1998; Dahlberg 1981; Fedigan 1997; Zihlman 1998). Moreover, recent contextual analyses of division of labor, technological innovation, and material culture, as well as the concept of social agency, have succeeded in defining more extensively women's roles in economic production and have begun to reinterpret various aspects of economic production and exchange from gendered perspectives. While early attempts to revise traditional narratives aimed at "finding women" in the archaeological record, more recent studies have gone beyond the documentation of women's participation in past economies to an analysis of gendered relations of production and exchange, and in particular the gendered division of labor.

Little or no attempt has been made to date to apply these new ways of thinking to the societies of ancient Cyprus, however. In contrast with other exegetical models (most notably, paradigms of socioeconomic complexity), which have gradually encountered a more positive reception by prehistorians working on the island and have now become part of mainstream interpretations of the island's (prehistoric) archaeological record, gender has been neglected as an objective of scholarly research. Social agency, which is currently a central conceptual theme in many theoretically based studies of the past, has yet to be applied to an analysis of the roles and statuses of women in prehistoric Cyprus, of hierarchical divisions within various gender groups, or of the gendered division of labor. Instead, its use has been restricted to the phenomenon of social aggrandizement among elites of unspecified or "neutral" gender (see ch. 1 and Knapp 1986, 1990, 1993, 1996; Manning 1993, 1998b; Rupp 1993). As Gero has observed, this avenue of thought embodies ethnocentric and often androcentric assumptions regarding the identity of social agents (Gero 2000). At the heart of the problem lies a confusion of agency with individual (often implicitly male) achievement, a modern, Western ethnocentric viewpoint that reveals more about the world of the archaeologist than that of the period under study (Johnson 2000:212).

Models of social complexity in Cyprus have focused primarily on the societies of the Bronze Age, but there has been an increasing tendency to extend these models backwards in time (e.g., Knapp 1993; Rupp 1993). Recent excavations of Cypro-PPNB sites, which have begun to furnish important evidence for the island's earliest-known sedentary populations, now make it possible to search for the origins of non-egalitarian political and economic structures as far back as the ninth millennium B.C., although it may be some time before there are sufficient published data with which to do so. In this chapter, I will examine some of the points of intersection between gender, technology, and the division of labor by looking at five particular examples of economic production and exchange that collectively span the entire time frame of this book. These are: (1) the division of labor among epipaleolithic hunter-gatherer populations; (2) gender and the adoption of agricultural subsistence strategies during the Neolithic; (3) gender and craft specialization in ceramic production during the LNeo-MBA; (4) gender and the organization of labor in the Cypriot LBA textile industry; and (5) gender, metallurgy, trade, and social complexity during the LBA. Discussion will focus on themes of gender and agency, the gendered division of labor, and changing patterns of gender relations in the workplace, particularly during the LBA, when the growth of metallurgy and foreign trade drew the island into a wider economic sphere. We begin, however, with the earliest-known archaeological site on the island, the Akrotiri rock shelter.

Man the Pygmy Hippo Hunter?

Until about a decade ago, there was not a shred of evidence in Cyprus for a hunter-gatherer phase of human subsistence. In fact, many archaeologists assumed that the earliest phase of human occupation on the island occurred quite late (i.e., during the seventh millennium B.C. when colonists from the mainland arrived on the island, bringing with them a stock of domesticated plants and animals and establishing permanent farming communities at large, sedentary sites like Khirokitia). However, the recent excavation of a collapsed rock shelter on the southern edge of the Akrotiri peninsula by a team under the direction of Alan Simmons has altered that picture entirely, and it now appears that Cyprus was the first island in the Mediterranean for which mainlanders showed more than just a passing interest (fig. 3.1). As the only known site of its kind in Cyprus, Akrotiri furnishes us with the best, albeit unique, evidence for possible interfaces between gender and the social organization of labor prior to the Neolithic period.

Radiocarbon dates indicate that Akrotiri-*Aetokremnos* was occupied early in the tenth millennium B.C.; its duration is uncertain, but the excavator has proposed that it may have existed for no more than a few centuries or even a few generations (Simmons 2001:5). While the geographical origins of these first known inhabitants are obscure, and their reasons for choosing to leave their homeland and risk a journey by sea to a remote, uninhabited island are not clear, their activities on reaching Cyprus have been the subject of intensive investigation by Simmons and his team (Simmons et al. 1999).

Whatever their origins, the people arriving at *Aetokremnos* c. 9800 B.C. found themselves on a large island with a fairly limited variety of food resources. Wild plant remains, it seems, were scarce (Simmons et al. 1999:329), a situation that at least in part accounts for the failure of hunter-gatherer populations to secure a more permanent

Figure 3.1   Excavations at the Akrotiri rock shelter (Simmons et al. 1999: fig. 2.9).

foothold on the island (Peltenburg et al. 2000, 2001a, 2001b). Excavations revealed no evidence of plant foods at the site, despite the extraction of phytoliths and the flotation of soil samples at the site (Simmons et al. 1999:229).

Faunal remains were also limited, but one species of animal appears to have been available in considerable abundance: the pygmy hippopotamus. Excavation over the course of several seasons yielded nearly 300,000 faunal remains, and more than two-thirds were identified as *Phanourios minutus*, a species of pygmy hippo that has never been recorded outside of Cyprus (Simmons et al. 1999:ch. 7). Other edible food remains found in the excavations included small numbers of pygmy elephant, birds, mice, genet, and snails, and a large variety of marine molluscs (70,000 fragments), of which the primary types were topshell and limpet. As only a single fish bone was discovered, it seems that only invertebrate marine resources were exploited at the site (Simmons et al. 1999:187–90).

In addition to plant and animal remains, a variety of cultural remains were discovered in the excavations. These included a number of rudimentary ashy features known as "casual hearths," about a thousand chipped stone fragments from tools identified as blades, flakes, scrapers, and burins, several ground stone artifacts, and a few stone ornaments and pieces of worked bone (Simmons et al. 1999:ch. 6). While the various features and artifacts from Akrotiri furnish solid evidence that humans were active here sometime after the start of the tenth millennium B.C., there has been a fierce controversy surrounding the relationship between the cultural material and the vast numbers of hippo bones excavated at the site. The bones belong to a lower level (stratum 4) than that of the artifacts (stratum 2), with an intervening stratum (stratum 3) separating the faunal remains from the cultural material. Because of this dissociation, some critics continue to maintain that there is no connection between the faunal remains and the cultural material (e.g., Bunimowitz and Barkai 1996).

In his final report, Simmons discusses stratigraphy and taphonomy in detail in order to defend his belief that the pygmy hippo remains arrived at the Akrotiri rock shelter through the deliberate efforts of humans (Simmons et al. 1999:ch. 12). The lack of cut-marks on the excavated bones, as well as the frequent remains of entire hippo skeletons, he argues, need not necessarily mean that the animals died of natural causes. There would appear to be more than one way to skin a hippo, but since there is no ethnographic literature available on methods of butchering pygmy hippos, it is not easy to imagine how butchering could have been accomplished. Meat could have been obtained without the use of a knife, perhaps by boiling or roasting, but the fragmented nature of most of the bones due to the collapse of the rock shelter makes these hypotheses extremely difficult to test.

After carefully weighing all the evidence, Simmons concluded that Akrotiri was not a kill site, but a place to which hippo carcasses were transported for cooking and processing (Simmons et al. 1999:ch. 13). This view is supported by the near total disarticulation of all faunal remains from the site. As all parts of the animal are represented, Simmons argues, processing of the hippo carcass must have entailed more than simply butchering and cooking and may have involved the manufacture of secondary products. Moreover, the fact that more than a quarter of the bones had clear traces of burning suggests that a large proportion of unused bones were cached and used as fuel after processing.

For purposes of this discussion, let us assume that humans *were* responsible for the butchering and processing of pygmy hippo and other small fauna at Akrotiri. What can we glean from this evidence that might contribute to an understanding of gender and the division of labor at the earliest known archaeological site on the island? Should we imagine groups of male hunters bravely traversing the hinterland of the Akrotiri peninsula, clubs in hand, in search of small errant hippos, while women worked closer to home base, collecting topshells and limpets and boiling up leftover hippo bones into a tasty stew? Since there is no discussion of gender or the division of labor in this otherwise detailed report, we are left to speculate independently on the possible scenarios of social organization and the division of labor among the island's only known hunter-gatherer population.

We can begin by assuming that women as well as men occupied the rock shelter at Akrotiri and that both were actively engaged in subsistence activities. Excavations yielded no traces of human remains since the site appears to have been abandoned as hippo sup-plies started to decline. However, we can safely imagine that any colonizing attempt on Cyprus from a mainland source would have required the participation of males and fe-males to ensure the survival of the group, even if they did not intend to stay forever. But once they were there, what did they do, and who did what? Although there is no direct evidence linking specific subsistence activities with particular individuals or gender groups, the behavior and morphology of *Phanourios*, as well as the excavator's proposals concerning the processing of pygmy hippo remains at Akrotiri, offer several valuable clues.

The particular strategies involved in pygmy hippo hunting are not known, but the large numbers of bones found at the site suggest that they were killed in groups (Sim-mons et al. 1999:314). Archaeological evidence from Madagascar, consisting of the re-mains of a group of five adult and three immature pygmy hippo, suggests it was a herd animal, and this is a likely scenario for *Phanourios* as well (Simmons et al. 1999:304). Groups of pygmy hippo could have been tracked easily since related species are known to defecate liberally, leaving behind ample quantities of spoor. Given the lack of pro-jectile points from Akrotiri, Simmons proposes that the animals may have been clubbed to death or driven off cliffs and retrieved from the sea, strategies known among mod-ern hunter-gatherer groups in various parts of the world. While modern pygmy hippos vary from 150–170 cm in length with a shoulder height of 50–100 cm (Simmons et al. 1999:306), Mediterranean island pygmy hippo are much smaller than their mainland counterparts, akin to the size of a large pig (Simmons et al. 1999:28). Since the latter are not known to travel quickly, chasing and clubbing them would not have presented great problems to any adult hunter intent on pursuit.

The morphology and behavior of *Phanourios* thus offer no obstacles to the hypothe-sis that women as well as men were engaged in pygmy hippo hunting. The herding be-havior of known species of pygmy hippo makes it likely that several were killed in a sin-gle foray. As multiple kills require multiple killers, it seems plausible that hunting would have been undertaken as a group endeavor. The large number of hippo bones, repre-senting more than 500 individual hippos, supports the notion of group-based hunting. Moreover, as clubbing or stampeding the wild pygmy hippo would not have entailed great physical strength, there seems to be no reason to exclude women from this activ-ity. On the other hand, as an average adult pygmy hippo weighs in at 180–270 k (Sim-mons et al. 1999:306), transporting whole carcasses from kill sites may have required considerable stamina; it is therefore likely that men rather than women were obliged to carry *Phanourios* back to camp.

According to the excavator, hunting constituted the initial stage in a long chain of activities involving the processing of *Phanourios* remains. Ethnographic data indicate a va-riety of exploitable resources from pygmy hippo carcasses, including hide, hair, sinew, bone, horn, marrow, grease, blood, viscera, fat, meat, juice, brains, and hooves (Simmons et al. 1999:308–309). Bones left over after processing could have been used as fuel, as suggested by the high percentages of burnt bones from the site. If, as Simmons believes, the inhabitants of Akrotiri exploited some or all of these resources (as they may well have done given the limited food resources in the environment), daily activities at the site would have entailed repeated processes of evisceration, disarticulation, bone and marrow extraction, bone grease extraction, skinning and hide removal, defleshing and meat extraction, brain and blood extraction, bone juice production, and sinew or tendon removal (Simmons et al. 1999:tab. 13.1). Most of these tasks are fairly labor intensive and are therefore unlikely to have been performed by a single gender group. Moreover, since there were apparently few edible plant resources in the environment, the collection of nonvertebrate marine resources would have constituted the only real "gathering" activity suggested by the excavated remains, and that cannot have been the only work engaged in by women.

An integrated model of labor in which men and women worked together to hunt and process animal remains, gather marine resources, and manufacture and utilize chipped stone tools seems the most reasonable scenario for the organization of labor at this time. Indeed, it was a remarkably successful subsistence strategy until resource depletion through over-kill led to diminishing returns and the limited resources of the environment were no longer able to sustain the population. According to Simmons, the abandonment of Akrotiri rock shelter can probably be linked directly to the extinction of *Phanourios* (Simmons et al. 1999:323–36). While other groups of people may have survived elsewhere on the island, *Aetokremnos* was abandoned forever. There is no evidence connecting the erstwhile hunter-gatherers of the Akrotiri rock shelter with the more successful colonizing efforts that followed about a millennium later and involved the transport of domesticated plants and animals to Cyprus from the mainland and the transfer of new subsistence strategies by those destined to become the island's first farmers.

Gender, Agriculture, and the Division of Labor

In economic terms, the invention of agriculture and the widespread development of food- producing economies and sedentary farming villages are among the most significant achievements of prehistory. The material remains associated with these new techniques, including the manufacture of specialized stone tools for clearing and farming land in the Neolithic and Chalcolithic periods and introduction of the plow during the EBA, are thus accorded a great deal of attention by archaeologists concerned with processes of domestication, sedentarization, and socioeconomic growth. However, little attention has been given, particularly in Cyprus, to the impact on gender relations of these important developments or to the gendered division of labor in early farming communities (see Petersen 2002 and Watson and Kennedy 1991 for valuable exceptions).

It is perhaps significant that none of the intensive research on colonizing episodes on the island during the early Aceramic Neolithic period that established the island's first farming communities has addressed issues of gender. One could argue here, though, that this evidence is still too fresh to have taken on board all but basic archaeological reporting. The same thing cannot be said, however, for sites of the later Aceramic period, such as Khirokitia, where excavations have been carried out for many years (Dikaios 1953; Le Brun 1981, 1984, 1989, 1994). Le Brun has touched on several aspects of gender at Khirokitia in a recent article, but he has not discussed these in great detail nor has he addressed economic issues such as the gendered division of labor (Le Brun 2002). While evidence for stone tool manufacture at Khirokitia and contemporary sites is considerable, there has been no attempt to engender either the lithics industries of early communities in Cyprus or the subsistence strategies in which they were used. This is due in part to conservatism in archaeological interpretation but also to the fact that most lithic specialists continue to engage in typological analyses and thus overlook technical aspects of tool production and tool use that might provide better evidence for socioeconomic practices (McCartney 2002).

A notable exception to the rather barren landscape of gender and economy in the Cypriot Neolithic exists in the form of an appendix by Stekelis to Dikaios's final report of Sotira-*Teppes*, one of the principal sedentary agricultural sites of the LNeo (see Stekelis in Dikaios 1961:231–32). In this brief analysis of the chipped stone assemblage from the site, Stekelis distinguishes between "pointed" and "squarish" blades (fig. 3.2), the former of which he attributes to females and the latter to males on the basis of ethnographic evidence from aboriginal groups in Australia where a similar typological division exists and where there is evidence for a sharp sexual division in the organization of labor.

Stekelis's proposals have recently been reexamined by McCartney, who is highly critical of their exclusive focus on formal attributes of the tools, their simplistic parallels to ethnographic groups far removed from Cyprus both spatially and temporally, and their failure to contextualize the relevant artifacts (McCartney 2002). She argues instead that "it is more likely that stylistic preferences varied from one society to the next and, equally if not more probably, that the various pointed and squarish blades found within the Sotira assemblage were selected on the basis of situational performance-related characteristics" (McCartney 2002:239–40).

If, indeed, the two types of knives identified by Stekelis were attributable to a gendered division of labor, we would expect them to show discrete spatial distributions. As McCartney demonstrates, however, there is little or no contextual differentiation between pointed and squarish blades, either at Sotira or any other Neolithic site (McCartney 2002:fig. 3). In contrast, distributions of similar blades among Australian Aboriginal groups are spatially segregated and reflect a strict division of male and female spheres of activity linked to strongly dimorphic gender ideologies. Much more in keep-

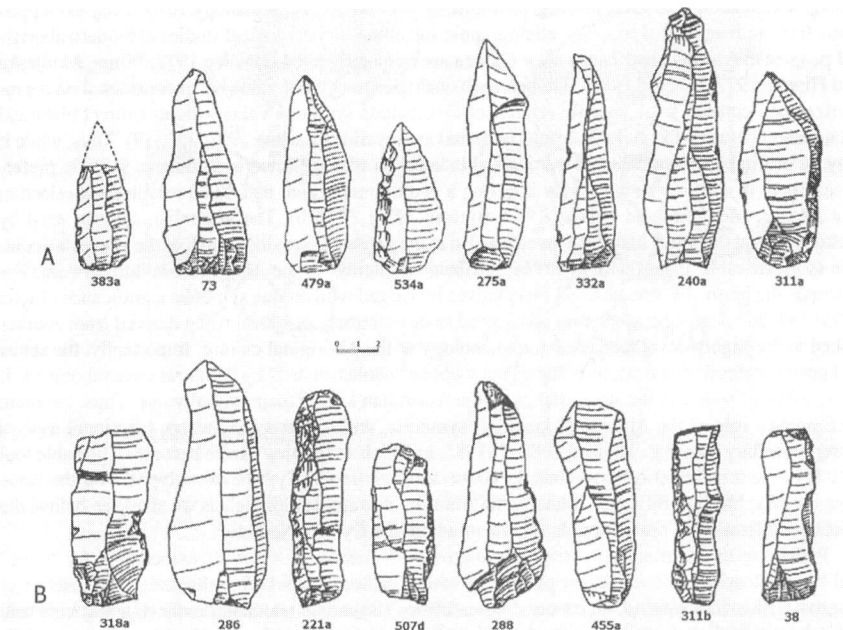

Figure 3.2.   "Square" and "pointed" blades from Sotira-*Teppes* (after McCartney 2002:fig. 2).

ing with the evidence for Neolithic Cyprus is the model of an integrated labor force proposed by McCartney in which females and males were involved in all aspects of production. Variations in form and function of tool assemblages, such as those identified by Stekelis, do not necessarily reflect differential patterns of social organization, but are more likely to have been the result of variations in site function (i.e., settlements vs. non-settlement sites) as well as other factors such as the availability and selection of raw materials (McCartney 2002:245–46). As this case illustrates, archaeologists arguing in favor of gendered divisions of labor in prehistoric societies must base their arguments on careful analysis of archaeological remains rather than on a priori assumptions based on extraneous ethnographic parallels.

McCartney's conclusions for the Neolithic Cyprus accord well with results of a more intensive, wide-ranging study by Peterson on the effects of agriculture on gender relations in the Neolithic of the southern Levant (Peterson 2002). Peterson is highly critical of broad, unilineal models of social change (whether by traditional or feminist scholars) that attempt to link the adoption of agriculture to more sharply defined programs of task differentiation between males and females, a reduction in levels of participation by women in subsistence activities, and a corresponding diminution in female status. Her analysis of human skeletal remains of the Natufian to EBI periods for signs of musculo-skeletal stress offers little support to proponents of these generalized models. Female skeletons, in fact, show virtually no significant changes in levels of musculo-skeletal stress over time, implying that female activity levels remained relatively stable with the introduction of agriculture. Evidence from male skeletons, on the other hand, suggests that male activity levels gradually decreased over time, perhaps, as Peterson has suggested, as the result of a decreased reliance on hunting and engagement by males in a greater range of activities (such as herding) that by the EBA had become physically less demanding (Peterson 2002:118–25). Thus, from the point of view of physical anthropology, the adoption of farming techniques in the southern Levant may have resulted in greater equality, rather than an increasing dichotomy, in the sexual division of labor.

If there is little evidence for a division of labor during the Neolithic period, either in Cyprus or the Levant, when, if ever, *did* it occur? During the Cypriot Chalcolithic, there is firm evidence for low levels of economic and social divisions in various aspects of material culture, some of which coincide with changes in gender relations (Bolger 1993, 1994a; Peltenburg 2002). The increasing importance of pottery vessels, for example, is bound to have had an impact on the organization of labor and allocation of time (Bolger 1998; Shiels 2003), and the intensification of agriculture may have fostered the growth of task differentiation along lines of gender to accommodate more intensive work schedules (fig. 3.3). Certainly by the Bronze Age, it appears from evidence of scenic compositions depicting humans performing activities of daily life that male and female roles had begun to diverge (see chs. 2 and 4 for further details). How and why did this happen? Although the arrival of new people on the island at the end of the Chalcolithic period may have contributed to the transformation of previous cultural norms, changes in technology, social organization, and the division of labor are likely to have been linked to processes of culture change involving indigenous developments as well (Frankel 2000; Peltenburg 1991).

Changing means and strategies of attaining of wealth, status, and prestige, as well as a reconfiguration of the overall structure of economic exchange, may have contributed

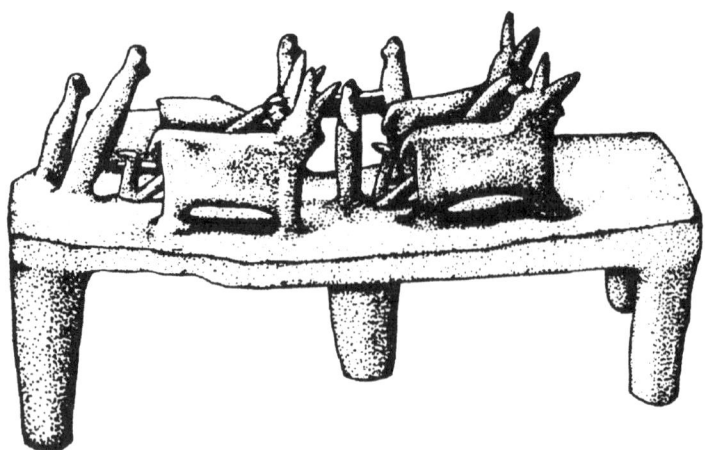

Figure 3.3.   Red Polished pottery scene of plowing (after Morris 1985: fig. 499).

to a reorientation of social and economic roles for women during the Bronze Age (Bolger 1993, 1994a, 1996). This is suggested by the end of reciprocal exchange networks such as the picrolite exchange system of Neolithic–MChal, in which women are likely to have participated (Peltenburg 1992). As the relations of production began to be reorganized in terms of membership in corporate kinship groups, personal exchange networks were replaced by corporate control of resources, with the family, rather than individuals, as chief producers and beneficiaries. Moreover, as inheritance within lineages is transmitted vertically, through paternal or maternal lines, it restricts access to material wealth and circumscribes other forms of economic and social privilege. If, on the basis of cross-cultural data, we may infer that patrilineages were operative in prehistoric Cyprus, and, following Frankel (1978), that residency was virilocal, men would have enjoyed greater access to social and economic prerogatives, and women would have been increasingly restricted in their ability to own or inherit property and other forms of wealth. It should be noted, however, that the emergence of a more highly stratified society during the later phases of the Bronze Age is associated with the rise of powerful and wealthy elites that included women as well as men (see ch. 7); one of the outcomes of increasing social complexity is our inability to treat "women" and "men" as universal, monolithic categories (Gilchrist 1999:52–53).

Ethnographic research shows that changes in modes of kinship and production can be correlated to changes in the relations of reproduction (Peletz 1995:353–54). These approaches emphasize the social context of reproduction by distinguishing its biological and cultural aspects (Holy 1996:56). While only the mother-child relationship is necessary for the successful biological reproduction of the species after fertilization, the reproduction of individuals capable of full social life involves acknowledgment by society at large. Cross-cultural analysis of modern pre-state societies has shown that in many cases, individuals are not eligible to become a full-fledged member of the community if they lack a socially recognized mother and father. In this way, the family becomes the only acceptable means by which the necessity for the replacement of deceased members of a social group is met.

The importance attached to the social context of reproduction can often be discerned in the archaeological record through iconographic portrayals of women and children. Olsen, for example, has recently proposed a sharp distinction in gender constructs between Minoan and Myceanean society on the grounds that Minoan iconography fails to associate women with children, while Mycenaean iconography stresses mother-child relations (Olsen 1998). In her view, "this represents, if not a fundamental difference in gender construction between Minoan and Mycenaean societies, at the very least a fundamentally different approach to a gendered social role" (Olsen 1998:390).

During the third millennium B.C. in Cyprus, women's reproductive roles appear to have been redefined within the context of emerging family structures (Bolger 1996). The control of female sexual behavior, which often accompanies new social demands involving the restriction of kin and legitimization of heirs, probably became more stringent as society attained higher levels of sedentarization. These and other changing definitions of "appropriate" social behavior are linked to the intensification of agriculture and the corporate ownership of land, both of which require a means of passing on inheritance to socially recognized heirs. In Cyprus, the best evidence for the change to corporate kinship structures exists in the form of large communal cemeteries dating to the EBA and MBA, replacing the individual pit graves and small chamber tombs of the Neolithic and Chalcolithic periods; I will discuss this evidence in greater detail in chapter 6.

The need to establish paternity and to socially recognize offspring would have had an important bearing on the role of children as well. With the emergence of lineages and the intensification of agriculture, reproductive strategies are likely to have evolved in accordance with newly emerging forces of economic production. In agricultural societies, children are valued as laborers and as future partners in marriage with members of other corporate groups. At the same time, though, there is a tendency to regard children as commodities, reducing their status in much the same way as that of women. Unwanted children may have been neglected or disposed of, and while infanticide in traditional societies lacking adequate methods of birth control usually occurs during conditions of economic exigency, it can also result from unwanted pregnancies due to illegitimacy (Mays 1993).

Infant burials, including neonates, form a substantial proportion of the Chalcolithic mortuary record, but we have no way of knowing what proportions of these deaths occurred naturally or deliberately; nor do we have evidence on the sexes of the deceased infants that figure so largely in graves of Chalcolithic date. Outside Cyprus, several cases of infanticide have been identified in the archaeological record (Mays 1993, 1995; Smith and Kahila 1992), but it is not known whether the infants in question were males or females, owing largely to the difficulty of sexing skeletons of infants and young children. Ethnographic evidence indicates that infanticide is more likely to be practiced on females in cultures where women's economic input is undervalued and female status is low (Smith and Smith 1994).

The reconstruction of gender during the Cypriot Bronze Age can be linked to the indigenous social transformations that first began to manifest themselves during the MChal as well as to the migration of new ethnic groups from the Anatolian mainland during the second half of the third millennium B.C. (Frankel 2002). The arrival and successful establishment of new cultural groups may have contributed to the transformation of the island over the course of the second millennium B.C. from a relatively small-scale, egalitarian, subsistence-based society to a larger, more dynamic complex of communities in which some groups secured increasingly greater access to wealth. These developments fostered the growth of population, the production of economic surpluses, and the corporate control or ownership of land (Manning 1993). It seems likely, however, that changes in gender relations within the economic sphere initially emerged during the third millennium B.C. within a structural milieu that could still be considered egalitarian, and that they anticipated the emergence of state-level society on the island by a millennium or more. However, we must be careful not to equate division of labor with prestige hierarchy (Gilchrist 1999:52). While the evidence points to a gendered division of labor at an early stage of the Bronze Age, it does not attest to a hierarchy of values for the various tasks allocated to women and men.

Were They All Women? Gender and Pottery Production

In contrast to the androcentric narratives discussed earlier in this chapter that credit men rather than women with the technological know-how that enabled our ancestors to master the environment and develop more effective strategies for subsistence and survival, narratives of prehistoric pottery production generally tend to attribute the manufacture of the earliest ceramic vessels (i.e., household production) to females. Although ethnographic evidence generally appears to support this view, we cannot rely on modern cultural parallels to argue the case. We must also question the assumption, widespread in the anthropological literature on ceramic production, that with increased levels of specialization linked to the evolution of more complex societies, the manufacture of pottery became an exclusively male prerogative and women's roles proportionally diminished (e.g., Leacock 1983; London 2002). Such simplistic models of the division of labor may hold true for many modern pre-state and state level societies, but they cannot be applied uncritically to the societies of the prehistoric past.

In a seminal article on gender and pottery production in prehistory, Wright questioned the anthropological evidence used in support of a gender-based division of labor in the manufacture of pottery, citing gender bias in the recording and analysis of ethnographic reports (Wright 1991). Archaeologists wishing to cite ethnographic evidence in support of arguments about gendered divisions of labor in past cultures must closely scrutinize ethnographic records for probable bias or omission of female participation. In addition, as Wright has suggested (1991:198), we must begin to revise the standard definition of "potter" from "the person who forms or fires vessels" to "all individuals participating in the various phases of ceramic production." Pottery making is a multiphase process and one that in the small-scale societies of prehistoric Cyprus undoubtedly involved large segments of the community, including men, women, and children.

While the various stages of pottery production are likely to have been divided up among several individuals, it is not clear whether men and women were assigned different tasks. Indeed, there may even be something fundamentally misguided in the attempt to differentiate male and female labor in ancient societies since assumptions about the division of labor in the past are likely to incorporate modern Western concepts, such as the gendered division of labor (Gero and Conkey 1991:20–22). Yet, since so many biased accounts of female participation in economic production have been written in the past, it is equally important to expose and critique the theoretical and methodological weaknesses of earlier research and to furnish plausible alternative explanations for the relationships between gender, technology, and economic production. In the pages that follow, I call traditional models of pottery production in Cyprus into question by examining the results of several recent studies of prehistoric hand-made wares. These demonstrate the limits of traditional approaches and offer alternative narratives of pottery production based on close study of ceramic evidence from the Neolithic to MBA periods and on the experimental replication of pottery types during the Chalcolithic.

Challenging Traditional Narratives of Pottery Production

In a recent article on gender, economy, and ceramic production of the LNeo of Cyprus, Clarke challenges hypotheses formulated in the 1960s and 1970s by Deetz, Longacre, Whallon and others concerning the gendered division of labor (Clarke 2002). These theories, which were intended to account for inter- and intra-site variation in early agro-pastoral societies of North America, rested on a priori assumptions concerning descent and postmarital residence patterns. Ceramic designs were used as evidence for establishing those patterns, and, since it was assumed that women made pots, it followed that exogamic practices involving the movement of women should foster greater levels of intra-site variation and lesser degrees of inter-site variation as new ideas and techniques were transmitted between villages. By the same token, endogamy would have had the opposite effect by fostering greater homogeneity within a given village and limiting opportunities for interaction between villages.

The assumption that women made pots has been widely criticized in recent years, as have similar attempts to impose universal prescriptions on subsistence tasks and the organization of labor in general. Clarke reveals the weaknesses of the Deetz/Longacre hypothesis by attempting to apply it to ceramic evidence from LNeo Cyprus. Comparisons of motifs of RW ceramics from three LNeo sites show that closely spaced sites exhibit weaker stylistic links than those more distant from one another. This contradicts the Deetz/Longacre model, since exogamic practices would be expected to foster closer ties between spatially proximate sites rather than more remote ones. Hence, exogamic marital practices are not likely to have been responsible for the diffusion of stylistic elements in ceramic production on the island during its early phases. As Clarke has observed, "the models of Deetz, Longacre, Whallon, and Hill . . . highlight the theoretical inconsistencies of archaeological interpretation with regard to both gender based divisions of labor in prehistoric subsistence strategies, and socio-cultural interactive patterning" (2002:253).

Following the lines of argument presented by the Deetz/Longacre model criticized above, Frankel has argued for many years that pottery production in prehistoric Cyprus was a nonspecialized household industry for most of the prehistoric period in which women made pots within the household and, by marrying out of their villages, spread ceramic knowledge and practices from one locality to another, a practice thought to account for regional divisions in pottery styles (Frankel 1974:11, 51; 1978; 1993a).

In a forthcoming article, however, Frankel and Webb have reversed this position as the result of close statistical analysis of pottery production at Marki; according to their calculations, the estimated minimum vessel count at the site is approximately 15,000 vessels from a total of 300,000 sherds (Frankel and Webb in press). This number, which takes into account the probable patterns of use, consumption, and discard of pottery vessels, and is based on an estimate of between five and thirteen households per year over approximately 500 years of settlement history, yields an average annual discard rate of only thirty-nine–forty-nine vessels. Such a small annual output has led Frankel and Webb to question the model of household production during the earlier phases of the Bronze Age whereby each household manufactured and used its own pottery vessels, on the grounds that it would have been extremely inefficient. Instead, they propose a model of local small-scale specialization or elementary specialization as characterized by Rice (1987).

With regard to the division of labor within this more specialized model of production, however, Frankel and Webb have said very little other than to assert that small-scale specialization involving part-time specialists is likely to be linked to kin-related or other residence groups. While the social correlates of models of incipient specialization need to be explored more thoroughly, both at Marki and elsewhere, it seems likely that Frankel's earlier notions involving exogamy and the movement of women from place to place will have to be revised, as will his earlier assumption that only women made pots.

If marriage practices are not responsible for stylistic patterning, and if we are willing to abandon the exclusive association of women with small-scale pottery production, what alternative explanation can account for the ceramic variation between sites? On the basis of environmental evidence and agricultural practices associated with the island's early farming communities, Clarke (2002) insists that other factors should be taken into consideration, in particular the fissioning of communities as has been suggested by Sherratt (1980) for agricultural exploitation elsewhere in the ancient Near East. According to this model, primary sites are expected to have greater degrees of cultural heterogeneity, while smaller secondary sites, after "budding off" from a primary community, exhibit a more homogeneous range of designs since they would have represented a small subset of the original repertoire. These results need to be tested against a greater body of evidence from a larger number of sites, but they clearly demonstrate the need to approach issues of gender and pottery production from a critical, gendered viewpoint. In particular, we are compelled to doubt the most fundamental basis of the Deetz/Longacres model—that women were the sole pottery producers in early sedentary societies. Evidence suggesting that this may have been impossible has recently emerged in replication studies of Chalcolithic ceramics at the Lemba Experimental Village in the Paphos district, to which we now turn.

Gender and Craft Specialization during the Chalcolithic Period

During the Chalcolithic period, ceramic production developed into a vibrant industry that increasingly required the skill of specialized craftspersons. Experiments at the Lemba Archaeological Research Center involving the replication of Chalcolithic pottery have been conducted intermittently since 1992, when two undergraduates of the University of Edinburgh launched experimental projects as part of their master's dissertations in archaeology. In recent years, experiments were undertaken to replicate a particular type of EChal pottery known as Glossy Burnished Ware (GBW), as a complimentary study to the typological analysis of the EChal assemblages of Kissonerga-*Mylouthkia* (Bolger 2003; Shiels 2003). GBW was chosen on account of its prevalence during the EChal and on account of the attractive sheen of its highly burnished surfaces that, when well preserved, appear to be glazed. It was also decided to begin experiments on EChal vessels as an initial stage, to be followed up in future seasons with the replication of MChal and LChal wares.

For the earliest stages of pottery production in Cyprus, it is impossible to talk about pottery "wares" in the standard canonical sense (i.e., where a distinct surface treatment is applied to a distinct fabric in a particular range of shapes). Multivariate analysis of vessels and sherdage from Mylouthkia effectively demonstrates a high degree of variability in ceramic production, with GBW surface treatment, for example, found in association with at least five different fabric types. One of Shiels's most recent experiments involved the manufacture of a GBW tray in coarse fabric; she was particularly interested in measuring the labor time required to manufacture a single, relatively simple vessel and was surprised to observe the considerable amount of time required to bring the vessel from assortment of unprocessed raw materials to a fired and finished pot (Shiels, personal communication).

That EChal pottery production was labor intensive is shown indirectly by the discovery of high proportions of sherds with mendholes, indicating the repair and reuse of pots after breakage. The use of mendholes all but disappears during the MChal and LChal (fig. 3.4). With the MChal, the technique of "layering" with multiple coats of slurry and slip is likewise abandoned, and less time is spent burnishing vessels. In addition, clays were not as coarse and may not have demanded as much time to prepare; as a result, more time could be invested in the creation of painted designs, and, in fact, the repertoire of design motifs expands dramatically at this time (Bolger 1991). As only some of the buildings at MChal Kissonerga have yielded high quality painted vessels, it is possible that pottery vessels began to be used and displayed as status symbols in part of an increasingly complex social structure.

During the LChal, marked technological changes, including the mass production of vessels with more consistent diameters and thinner walls, became the norm. It is likely that higher firing temperatures were attained as pottery is harder and more durable and mendholes no longer appear in sherdage. Also, greater durability can be attributed to the deliberate addition of angular chert temper and to the selective and regular use of non-

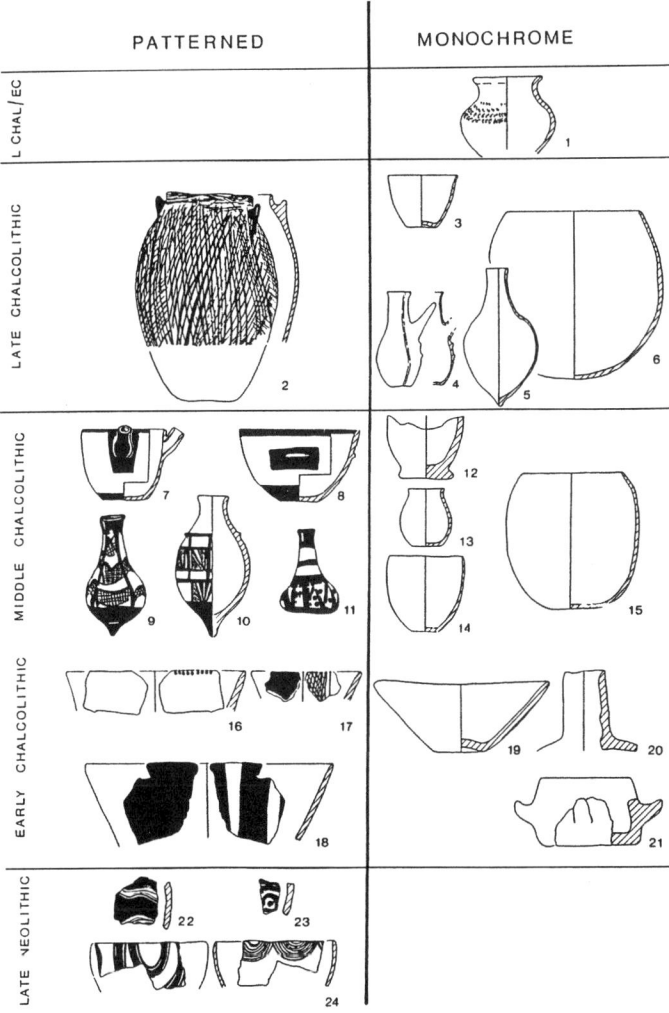

Figure 3.4.   Major pottery types of the Middle and Late Chalcolithic periods (after Peltenburg 1978: fig. 1).

calcareous clays collected from more remote sources. More successful control of firing temperatures is suggested by the manufacture of vessels with considerably higher tensile strength and the rare occurrence of fire shadowing. From these and other innovations in ceramic production, we can infer that new technologies and manufacturing techniques were being adopted during the LChal at a time when new clay sources were being exploited. In addition, pottery was being produced on a more massive scale and clay recipes were more standardized, replacing earlier fabric types that were largely unadulterated and extremely variable in their composition (Wallace 1995).

According to Arnold (1985), Rice (1987), van der Leeuw (1977), and other experts on ceramics, technical innovations such as these are normally associated with the advent of specialized production, which itself is often linked to higher degrees of social complexity. In egalitarian societies, it is argued, access to resources is largely unlimited, and division of labor on the basis of age or sex may be the sole determinants by which individuals come in to contact with given resources. In ranked societies with larger populations and greater population densities, differential access to resources begins to develop, and, while divisions of labor may still be based on age and sex, the emergence of low level or incipient specialization becomes evident.

Perhaps the most salient proof that these developments were indeed taking place during the middle of the third millennium B.C. in Cyprus was the excavation of the Pithos House at Kissonerga (fig. 3.5), where the well-preserved remains of over sixty pottery vessels were found *in situ* on the floor (Peltenburg et al. 1998:37–43). In terms of storage capacity, the Pithos House is without parallel in pre–Bronze Age Cyprus, both in terms of the range of vessel types present and their sheer quantity.

Thirty large-scale storage vessels were isolated in three seasons of conservation from the sea of sherdage found on the floor of the building. While several of these may represent fragments lying on the floor that were not in use at the time of the building's destruction, the building and its contents still convey an impressive capacity for large-scale, long-term storage, larger even than that of other destroyed buildings at Kissonerga. Whatever their precise functions, these vessels furnish compelling proof that pottery production by the LChal had exceeded the level of production for personal use, and strongly suggests the existence of craft specialists capable of producing a more standardized and durable product more efficiently.

On the social scale, of course, this would imply the emergence of a more complex division of labor, and perhaps the first incipient "specialist" class. The technological developments outlined above span nearly two millennia and point to long-term changes in the social forces that engendered them. In particular, the selective use of clays and tempering materials, as well as the attainment of thinner vessel walls, higher firing temperatures, and elaborate design configurations collectively demonstrate the progressively specialized nature of pottery making during the third millennium B.C.. Standardization in various stages of the pottery-making process, including paste preparation, vessel size, and wall thickness, cannot have been fortuitous and may even suggest changes in the organization of ceramic production during the LChal. Although we cannot go so far as to suggest that pot making had become a full-time occupation at this time, it is clear that greater time and effort were expended in the development of the craft during the third millennium B.C. and that higher levels of specialization must have reflected real social needs.

To what degree are we able to link advances in technology and scale of production to gendered divisions of labor? We have seen that simple assumptions equating pottery

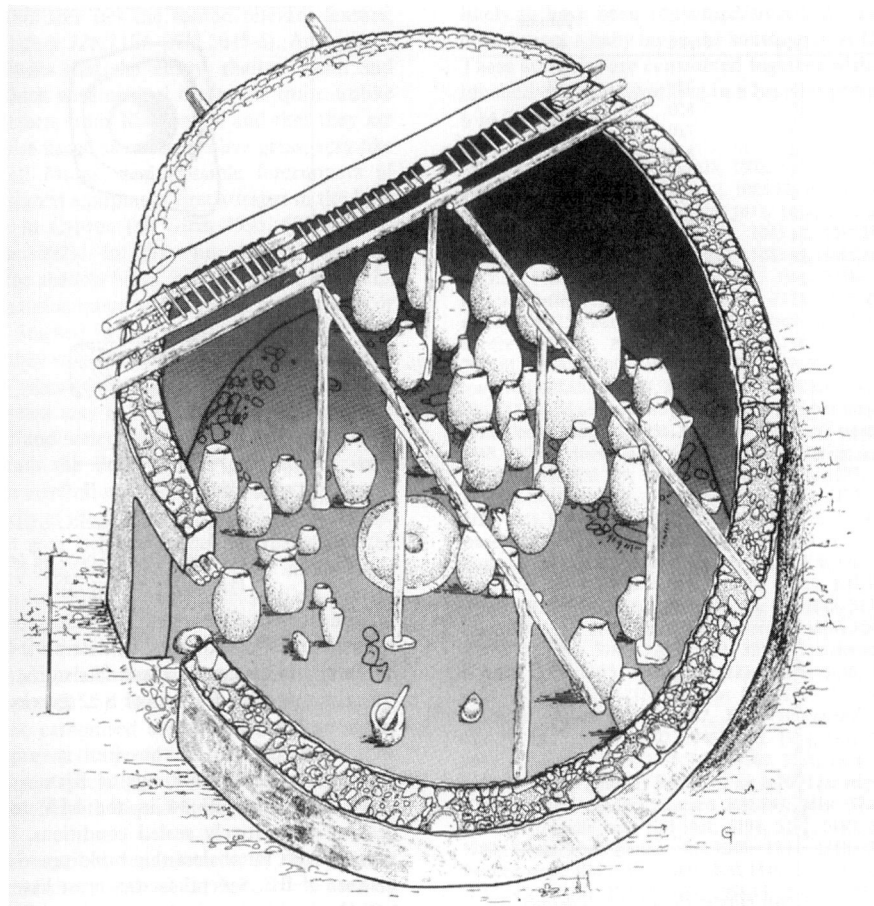

Figure 3.5.   Kissonerga "Pithos House" building 3 (after Peltenburg et al. 1998:fig. 3).

making with females are no longer convincing, despite considerable ethnographic evidence that supports such a view. If, indeed, women contributed to the development of the potter's craft from a simple to a more specialized and complex industry, then they can be regarded as active agents in an area of economic production for which there was increasing demand and whose labor was highly valued. But can we succeed in making such a link between women and pottery production, not by way of ethnographic parallels, but on the basis of archaeological inference?

The results of the experimental work at Lemba convey, at the very least, the considerable amount of time required to make even a single pot. Collection of clay and temper, preparation of paste, vessel formation, decoration, and firing all demanded considerable input of time and energy, and all of these tasks had to be integrated into an already full schedule of activities that had nothing to do with pottery. If we follow Wright (1991) in defining a potter not simply as a person who forms a vessel, but as anyone involved in the technical aspects of the industry, then production at the household level would have demanded involvement of many if not all household members. From this perspective, then, the archaeological evidence accords best with an integrated model of pottery production akin to that proposed by McCartney (2002) for the manufacture and use of chipped stone tools (see above). While it is possible that members of a particular gender group more frequently performed certain aspects of pottery production, it is unlikely that either males or females monopolized the entire range of tasks and skills required to produce a single vessel.

A second line of argument in favor of women's participation in pottery production during the MChal is suggested by the close symbolic and technical similarities between Red-on-White pottery (RW) and figurines. Anthropomorphic vessels, which occur in similar fabrics, shapes, and designs as the figurines, indicate that they were closely connected to ideologies and ceremonial rituals centered on fertility and childbirth. Goring's careful study of many of the pottery figurines points to their use for didactic purposes in ritual or ceremonial performances (Goring 1991a; see also ch. 4 for further details). Since most of these figurines appear to be part of women's birthing rituals, and since in technical terms the figurines are so closely related to the pots, it seems reasonable to imagine that women were involved in their manufacture as well as their use. This is not to argue, of course, that women and only women made pottery during the Chalcolithic period.

Many other types of pottery at this time have no apparent connection with pottery figurines or ritual symbolism, and, as has just been argued above, scheduling demands make it unlikely that women *or* men supervised or engaged in every stage of the pottery-making process. By the same token, one cannot argue that the absence of RW vessels and pottery figurines during the succeeding LChal signified the end of female participation in the ceramics industry. As we have seen, the innovation in pottery technology and the increased scale of production during the LChal cuts across every stage of manufacture, from clay and temper sourcing to vessel manufacture and firing. Thus, the concept of the pottery "specialist" may need to be clarified; rather than being linked to particular individuals or gender groups, the specialization process may have occurred as part of a collective effort of a variety of individuals chosen not for their gender attributes but for their practical knowledge and technical skill.

Gender, Social Complexity, and the Workplace: Evidence of Textiles

Technological studies in prehistoric archaeology have tended to focus on "high tech" industries such as metallurgy, stone tool production, or, to a lesser degree, ceramics, but there has been an increasing interest in recent years in previously neglected topics such as cooking, weaving, spinning, and basketry. Archaeologists interested in the relationships between gender, technology, and society, most of whom are women, have conducted the overwhelming majority of this research. (e.g., Barber 1991; Brumfiel 1991; Costin 1996; Hastorf 1991; Wright 1996, to name but a few). As Wright has observed, the "high tech" industries such as metallurgy have consistently been privileged over other types of labor, and the widespread assumption that men controlled them has led to an undervaluation of women's participation in economic production (Wright 1996:83–84). As a result, there is a pressing need for archaeologists to redefine and reevaluate the meaning of technology and to begin to analyze gendered divisions in the workforce within a larger sociopolitical framework. As Wright (1996), Nelson (1997:ch. 5), Gilchrist (1999:ch. 3), and others have argued, the engendering of technology and material culture enables us to reconstruct previously biased narratives of the division of labor and to restore the human element to processes of economic production.

Several recent studies of women's roles and status with relation to technology have focused on the manufacture of textiles in pre-state and state level societies (Barber 1991; Brumfiel 1991; Costin 1996; Wright 1996). In all of these cases, it can be demonstrated that women were centrally involved in textile production. Before turning to recent evidence in Cyprus, therefore, it will be useful to have a closer look at these related studies in order to provide a framework for interpretation.

In an important article on women's roles in textile manufacture during the Inka empire, Costin (1996) has shown that changes in the gendered relations of production over time are important for understanding social change in general. Prior to the Inka conquest, men as well as women were involved in textile production, although spinning and weaving were tasks associated almost exclusively with females. With the rise of the Inka state, sharper distinctions emerged between male and female labor. Through the implementation of a cloth tax in which the state required local leaders to make tribute payments of cloth, women and girls, who were the traditional spinners and weavers in traditional society, were forced to increase their workloads. In addition, the state increased cloth production by recruiting female weavers and excluding them from other household duties (such as cooking and child rearing) so that they could engage in full-time work (Costin 1996:131). This led to a class of women weavers whose personal lives and reproductive capacity were strictly controlled. Males were also employed as weavers in state-sponsored production, but their status was higher and their personal lives far less restricted. Task differentiation among males and females, which earlier had been regarded as complementary, became segregated and hierarchical. Male and female labor was strictly divided according to the nature of the work they performed, the value attached to their respective work, and the location and conditions of their working environments.

In a similar vein, Brumfiel has considered evidence of textile production from three communities in Aztec Mexico (1991). She bases her conclusions on archaeological evidence since she regards textual and pictorial evidence as too narrowly focused and simplistic to be of much value for shedding light on gender issues (Brumfiel 1991:224–28). After examining the context for women's work and amount of labor expended, she estimates that women's workloads are likely to have increased substantially under Aztec rule due to large tribute assessments to which conquered people were subject (Brumfiel 1991:230); this is corroborated by increased frequency of spindle whorls in Late Aztec contexts (Brumfiel 1991:233, table 8.1). In contrast to Inka weavers, female spinners and weavers under Aztec rule do not always appear to have accepted their fate. By devising various strategies to cope with changing circumstances of production, such as the creation of images linking women's work with pregnancy and birth, women may have managed to resist some of the pressures of an increasingly bureaucratic and repressive state apparatus (Brumfiel 1991:246).

A third case study documenting the relationships between women, textiles, and the emerging state considers textual evidence from Ur III Mesopotamia, where written documents associate weaving exclusively with females; work was performed in workshops from which men and male children were excluded. This gendered division of labor was reinforced in ideological terms by the fact that Uttu, the Mesopotamian weaving deity, was female and had no male counterpart. Within the secular context of the emerging state, however, female labor was not only separate but decisively unequal, and women were paid much less than men, even when they held the same jobs (Wright 1996:tab. 3.2). According to Wright's estimates, women weavers were ranked at the lowest economic status and would have had difficulty surviving if, for any reason, they could not work full time all year round. Working conditions for women weavers were also extremely poor, as illustrated by a case of a workshop where nearly a third of the women and (female) children died in a single year (Wright 1996:93). Wright's close reading of some of the texts suggests, moreover, that women weavers were not attached to families, so there would have been no other claims on their time other than work.

In general, textual evidence for the textile industry in Ur III Mesopotamia points to a highly controlled industry, both in terms of production (especially sexual segregation of the workplace and strictly divided male/female task allocation) and distribution (high-quality cloth available only to elites in society; cloth and dress were markers of prestige and identity). The fact that women made valued items had no positive effect on their status. On the contrary, they were severely exploited either as slaves or at best as semi-free laborers (unlike men, who had the opportunity to work independently for part of the year) and were compelled to work full time all year round. The use of female slaves as textile workers during the LBA was apparently not an uncommon occurrence; for example, Linear B texts from Pylos indicate that this was a standard practice among the Mycenaean city-states, where female slaves imported from Anatolia were indented into the workshops of the palaces (Killen 2003). While conditions outlined for women weavers in Ur III Mesopotamia may have been appreciably worse than those of other early states, they only reinforced the widespread exploitation of female labor in complex, hierarchical societies. Here, as in the Inka and Aztec empires, the state worked deliberately to preserve a division of labor in which male and female roles were strictly differentiated by powerful gender ideologies and male and female labor were sharply segregated, both spatially and economically.

With these results in mind, let us turn now to evidence for textile production in prehistoric Cyprus. In a recent paper on this subject, Joanna Smith has argued that significant changes took place in the workplace of textile production during the course of the LBA (Smith 2002). As there are no known textual or representational sources for LBA Cyprus that might furnish evidence for methods of textile manufacture, the organization of labor, levels of compensation, or status of different task groups within the industry, Smith has been compelled to argue for changes in the gendered division of labor by relying on evidence of the types and distributions of spindle whorls, loom weights, and other artifacts of the industry itself (figs. 3.6 and 3.7). While her conclusions to some degree conform to those of the cases discussed above, they also indicate that women's productive roles in Cyprus were not as deeply affected by the growth of complex society, that male and female labor was not as sharply segregated, and that women's status as textile workers may have been significantly higher than that of their American and Mesopotamian counterparts.

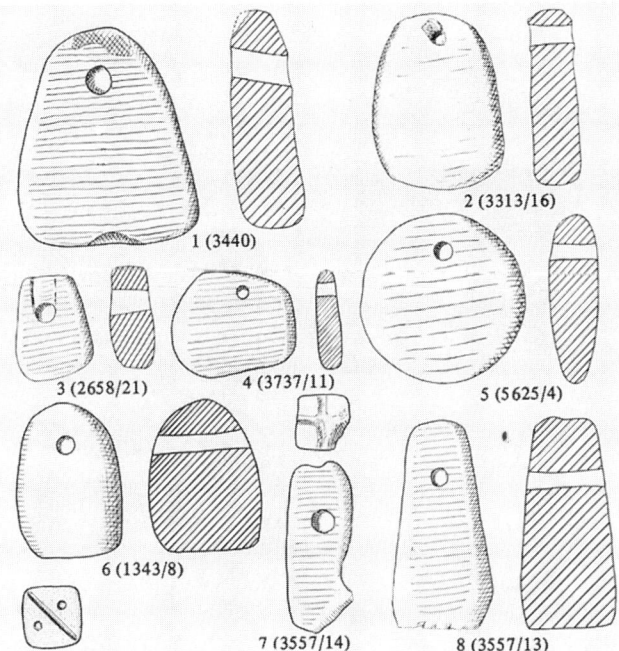

Figure 3.6.   Loom weights from Enkomi (after Dikaios 1969: pl. 165).

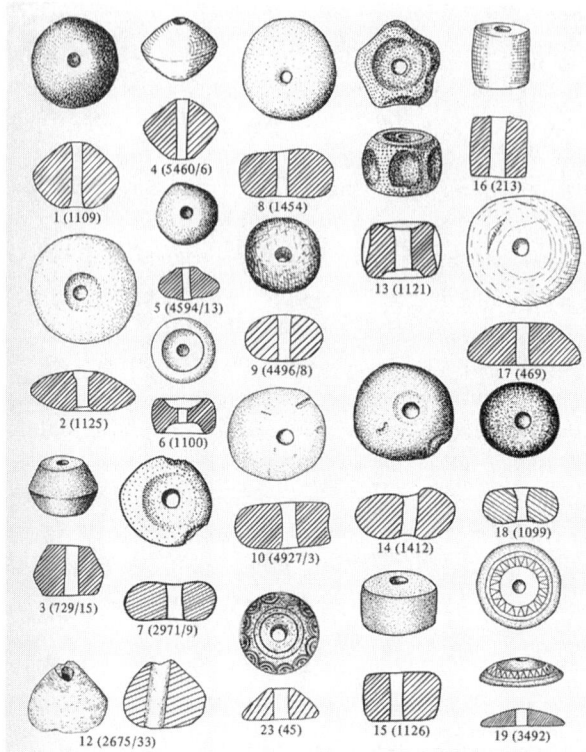

Figure 3.7.   Spindle whorls from Enkomi (after Dikaios 1969:pl. 167).

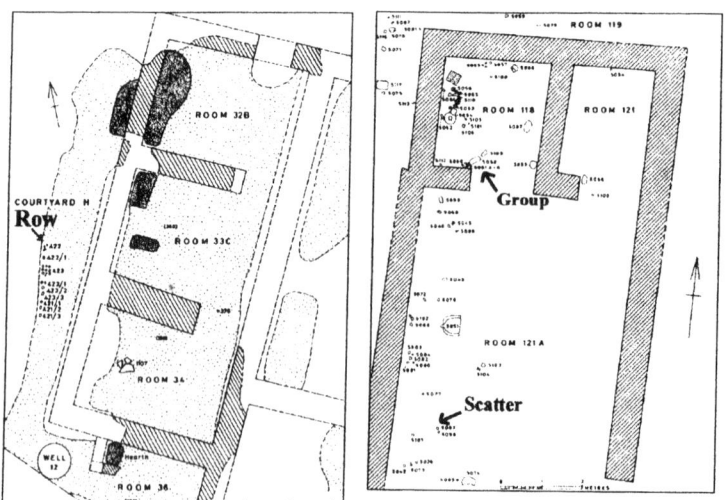

Figure 3.8.   Plan of Kition Areas I and II, showing location of loom weights (after Smith 2002:figs. 12 and 13).

The earliest evidence for textile manufacture in Cyprus dates to the beginning of the Bronze Age, when spindle whorls are first found in archaeological contexts (Crewe 1998:14–15). Prior to LCIIC (i.e., before c. 1300 B.C.), textile production in Cyprus appears to have been undertaken at the household level, although production levels may have increased over time for exchange outside the household (Smith 2002:304–305). The association of spindle whorls with females in burials during this period, and their absence in male burials, also suggests that textile manufacture, or at least certain aspects of production (such as spinning or weaving), may have been exclusively female endeavors. In succeeding centuries (thirteenth through eleventh centuries B.C.), men as well as women became involved, with women very likely continuing to work as weavers in domestic contexts, and both men and women men employed in permanent indoor workshops, such as those at Kition (fig. 3.8). Workshops were located within the structure of large public administrative complexes sometimes referred to as "palaces." The greater amount of space devoted to textile production in these contexts, and evidence for a greater range of industrial tasks (including dyeing and fulling) point to large-scale, centralized manufacture in highly organized workshops that far exceeded the output of domestic production.

In contrast to the conditions faced by women in other areas of the ancient world, there seems to have been little sexual segregation of the labor force in LBA Cyprus, and it is likely that female labor was not as tightly regulated. The higher status of females cannot be readily explained, but it may be due in part to the fact that the island probably never achieved the degree of political centralization and control characteristic of many early states (see Keswani 1996b; Manning 1998). Indeed, a heterarchical social structure may have fostered a diversity of economic and political strategies that in turn would have had varying impacts upon the labor force. Unfortunately, there is no textual or representational evidence with which to test this view, and our ability to generalize about male and female roles in the workplace is hampered by the fact that the site with the best evidence for textile production at this time (Kition) was probably a Phoenician colony and may not be entirely representative of labor practices at other contemporary industrial centers where archaeological evidence for textile production is far more elusive.

Although it is certainly regrettable that there are no documentary sources that might help characterize more extensively the socioeconomic organization of the textile industry during the LC Bronze Age, Smith has been able to draw provisional conclusions about changes in the workplace on the basis of archaeological remains alone. Indeed, as Wright, Costin, and Brumfiel emphasize, texts are often biased, especially when they have been composed as official documents of a repressive state; future studies of gender and status in textile manufacture would benefit considerably from careful analysis of the material remains of the various components of the industry itself and their spatial distribution in both burial and settlement contexts.

With regard to trade in textiles and other valuable commodities, we also need to consider the evidence of ancient shipwrecks. In a recent report on Uluburun, Pulak has characterized the ship's final journey in c. 1400 B.C. as an "official dispatch of precious cargo of raw materials and manufactured goods" originating in the Levant and destined for a port somewhere in the northern Aegean or western Black Sea (Pulak 2001:48). While much of the scholarly interest in this "precious cargo" has centered on its ten tons of copper ingots (probably of Cypriot origin), luxury items, and vast quantities of Cypriot pottery in its hull, a number of storage jars contained fibers dyed purple and red, representing the remnants of colored textiles (Pulak 2001:44). The transport of bolts of material across the sea in the company of a variety of other luxury items leaves no doubt about the value attached to high-quality textiles by emergent elite groups throughout the Mediterranean region. The lack of substantive inquiry into the importance of textiles in the complex societies of the Cypriot Bronze Age cannot, therefore, be ascribed to a lack of evidence for their demand and use as prestige items in systems of large-scale manufacture and wide-ranging trade. As we shall see in the following section, scholarly preoccupation with the mining, manufacture, and trade of metals has precluded investigation of other important sectors of the economy, such as the textile industry, in which women are likely to have made significant contributions.

Gender and Metallurgy: Untapped Mines of Evidence

In contrast to textiles, which have not generally been given substantial scholarly treatment, the study of metallurgy can be regarded as something of an obsession, especially among male archaeologists. Introductory reports on the archaeology of Cyprus are always quick to point out the association between the island's name ("Kypros") and the copper resources of the Troodos Range, which are known to have been exploited as early as the fourth millennium B.C. Moreover, evolutionary models of socioeconomic change, now widely adopted by prehistorians working in Cyprus and the Levant, rest to a large degree on the development of mining and metallurgy during the Bronze Age since the latter are regarded as the primary source of wealth that allowed elite groups to enter the profit-oriented world of the international market. Such monumental changes in technological and economic structures are likely to have had a tremendous impact on men's and women's lives, yet there has been little or no interest in the various discussions on the growth of metallurgy, trade, and socioeconomic complexity of changes in the gendered division of labor. This is probably due to the tacit assumption that women were not involved in metallurgical activities in antiquity, a "presentist" view based to a large extent on the almost exclusive participation of men in modern industrial production of metals, as well as images of itinerant (male) blacksmiths in earlier times (Sorensen 1996:46).

Men and Metal in Ancient Cyprus

Studies of the development of metallurgy in ancient Cyprus can generally be classified into one of three basic approaches: (1) scientific analyses, which examine the composition of ingots and artifacts, the sources of raw materials, the techniques of smelting of ores and manufacturing finished products, and the like (see, e.g., most contributions in Muhly, Maddin, and Karageorghis 1982); (2) typological treatments of metal artifacts, which are devised to identify parallel types in outlying regions for purposes of establishing patterns of trade and chronological frameworks (e.g., Balthazar 1990; Matthäus 1982; Swiny 1982); and (3) socially based approaches linking increased levels of socioeconomic complexity to the development of metallurgy and international trade (e.g., Knapp 1986, 1988; Knapp and Cherry 1994; Manning 1993; Muhly 1982, 1996; Sherratt 1994; Sherratt and Sherratt 1991). While the first two categories are "faceless" narratives that simply report on technological aspects of metalworking or the distribution of metal artifacts within spatial and/or chronological frameworks, the third is of potential interest for understanding the dynamic interactions between technology and society during the LBA and thus merits closer attention for the purposes of the present discussion. We will return to it later.

A somewhat different line of evidence relevant to the gendered division of labor in metallurgical production has been provided by the results of a series of copper-smelting experiments conducted by Walter Fasnacht's team at the Iron Age copper-smelting site of Ayia Varvara-*Almyras* over the course of several seasons (for the most recent report, see Fasnacht, Peege, and Hedley 2000). *Almyras* falls well outside of the chronological range of the present volume, but I have included it in the present discussion since no other extensive experiments have been made for earlier periods. In the following excerpt, Fasnacht reports that women participated in most of these experiments and proved to be particularly skilled at operating bellows:

> Two excellent bellows operators, both women, were taking turns of about one hour each. This job requires not so much physical strength as coordination, stamina and a good feeling for what is happening inside the furnace. During the last ten years of copper working experiments, the best bellows operators have always been women. Historical records of women involved in mining and metalworking are numerous and small-scale operations like Almyras may well have depended on the work of women and even children. (Fasnacht, Peege, and Hedley 2000:104)

Like textiles and ceramics, copper smelting is a labor-intensive activity involving a series of tedious operations, and it is therefore likely to have required the labor of more than a single sex. This view is supported by ethnographic evidence in Cyprus and Europe documenting the participation of women in the mining industry well into the twentieth century (Fasnacht, Peege, and Hedley 2000). Whereas women's roles in modern Cypriot mining operations appear to have been heavily circumscribed (see Maradi 1996 for ethnographic accounts), this need not have been the case for the considerably simpler mining and smelting operations of the prehistoric period. On the other hand, Fasnacht's use of the term "master of the furnace" to characterize the proposed coordinator and director of the operation seems to indicate that his definition of female participation in antiquity did not extend to a supervisory role, a view that is reinforced by the visual reconstruction of copper-smelting activities discussed in chapter 1 (fig. 1.1).

Regardless of whether we agree with Fasnacht's interpretations of the gendered division of labor in metallurgical production in Cypriot prehistory, the results of the copper-smelting experiments, as well as the information obtained from Maradi's interviews with Cypriot mine workers, are potentially valuable resources with which to investigate the interfaces between gender, social complexity, and metallurgical production in the Cypriot past. It is ironic, therefore, that, apart from the illustration referred to above, these results have not been integrated into Fasnacht's own metallurgical research at *Almyras*, nor into any other discussion of early metallurgical production in Cyprus. As we shall see, current research on early metallurgy in Cyprus situates copper extraction, smelting, artifact production, and trade within a broad socioeconomic framework and has addressed large-scale issues of economy and trade rather than issues of gender, agency, and the division of labor.

Gender, Metallurgy, and Society in the Cypriot Bronze Age

The importance of private entrepreneurship and commercial trade to the economy of LBA Cyprus was first articulated by Merrillees (1968:195-97) and was formulated as an alternative to simple and unsubstantiated "thalassocracy models" of earlier decades. More recently, Knapp and Cherry have examined the mechanisms and dynamics of international trade in the ancient Mediterranean by differentiating it into a variety of types, including state-level trade, freelance commerce, and ceremonial gift exchange (Knapp and Cherry 1994:142–51). The impetus in LBA Cyprus to participate in international trade networks has been widely attributed to the increasing demand by elites for exotic luxury goods; these prestigious objects had symbolic as well as economic value, as they could be displayed and manipulated to enhance personal or group status and to legitimize their positions within an increasingly hierarchical social structure (Keswani 1989; Knapp 1986). Elites seeking to import precious foreign goods needed to exploit indigenous sources of wealth in order to trade with their neighbors, and, according to most interpretations, the export of smelted copper was the best means of doing so. The rise of large, coastal towns ("gateway communities") such as Enkomi and are thus linked to the expansion of international markets and copper production in the economy of LBA Cyprus (Peltenburg 1996).

Within a generalized scenario of increasing socioeconomic complexity during the Cypriot Bronze Age, there are a variety of ways in which the identities of social actors have been characterized. As discussed in chapter 1, most adopt a relatively faceless, impersonal terminology (e.g., the use of the term "elites") linked to the aggrandizing behavior of groups rather than to individuals (Knapp 1986, 1993; Manning 1993; Peltenburg 1996; Rupp 1993). Recently, Manning has developed these ideas further by attempting to reconstruct the "biographies" of aggrandizing individuals at the LBA site of Maroni-*Vournes*. While the gender of these groups is not explicitly discussed, one can infer from a close reading of the text that the "central authority" referred to was thought of as a male:

> The autobiographies and biographies of individual human lives center on, and at the same time are invented and reinvented by, key events and signs which signify. . . . The most basic and pervasive usually involve nature, reproduction, and life: death, and the attempts of each human culture to rationalize, manipulate, control, or otherwise transcend those fundamentals. *The basic axioms of human culture, for example the differing roles of men and women, clearly stem from these structural realities.* (Manning 1998:39–40; emphasis mine)
>
> A key individual in Cypriot prehistory may have been based in the lower Maroni Valley at Vournes. If the Alashiya of Near Eastern texts is Cyprus (or part thereof), then this pattern of political structures on LBA Cyprus raises an interesting issue when one comes to consider the identity and especially the location of the 'king' of Alashiya referred to in texts of the 14th and 13th centuries B.C. (Manning 1998:53–54)

The link by Manning between the proposed (male) king or chief of Maroni and the evidence for copper working at the site is explicitly stated in the following passage:

> From LCIIB, if not earlier, there is also evidence of copper working at *Vournes*, and so evidence of specialist craft production, presumably of the materials and types of crafted goods that would be necessary in order to engage in exchange with the foreign traders who were the source of the desired prestige imports buried in the contemporary tombs. The head of the *Vournes* group/lineage is now asserting big man, great man, and chiefly claims and station. This is clearly at the expense of others. (Manning 1998)

Although these passage constitute a rather obvious case of essentialist thinking that "naturalizes" perceived sexual dichotomies (i.e., the association of female roles with "natural" biological phenomena such as reproduction and the tacit assumption that chiefs and kings are likely to be men), most models of socioeconomic complexity for LBA Cyprus rest on similarly shaky theoretical grounds when it comes to the gender of the individual(s) purported to have been involved. We will return to this topic in chapter 7.

Neo-evolutionary models of complexity that trace the rise to power of prominent individuals and social groups often fail to consider the full gamut of archaeological evidence from Cyprus that led to dramatic changes in political and economic structures during the LBA. The development of the metal industry, particularly the introduction of iron smelting and its associations with changes in political organization in the LBA, has been the subject of a recent article by Pickles and Peltenburg (1998). Here the focal point is the gateway community of Enkomi, whose rise to power as a major economic center may have occurred as early as MCIII and is clearly linked to developments in metallurgy (Peltenburg 1996). Dikaios's excavations of an imposing structure he referred to as the Fortress indicate that copper was produced there as early as LCI. The Fortress would have dominated the town then, suggesting the existence of an over-arching authority of unspecified gender who probably lived in the upper stories (Pickles and Peltenburg 1998:87).

Copper production at Enkomi appears to have peaked during the thirteenth century B.C., during which time it is likely to have controlled the mining of copper in Troodos and the transport of raw material from mountains to production center. Later in the century, however, production declined dramatically and the previously aggregated Fortress structure was disassembled into a group of smaller independent structures (Pickles and Peltenburg 1998:88 and fig. 2). These changes in architectural layout signify the breakup of a centralized metalworking center into a group of "autonomous family businesses specializing in copper production"; according to Pickles and Peltenburg, they are also associated with the advent of new techniques of metal extraction involving the exploitation of iron.

While events at Enkomi during the thirteenth century B.C. lie beyond the boundaries of this book, they are important for understanding the vacillations of political, social, and economic power in Cyprus during the later phases of the Bronze Age. The apparent fluctuation and instability of central political organization in Cyprus are not typical of developments at urban polities further to the east and must be due, in part, to strong regional tendencies on an island that has almost always been politically and geographically divided. The decentralization of politicoeconomic control in the late fourteenth–thirteen centuries B.C. is likely to have had an impact on the division of labor, and women's economic roles are likely to have been affected as well, but these issues remain virtually untouched in the growing literature on social complexity of the island's LBA polities. Were extraction, production, manufacture, and trade of Cypriot copper controlled and supervised exclusively by men? If metallurgy during the LBA in Cyprus was indeed a male-dominated industry, how would this have affected gender relations of social elites? Furthermore, how did trade and contact between Cyprus and its neighbors to the east and west alter and redefine gender relations? If, as Knapp has forcefully argued, "elite formation . . . may have been predicated in part on the translation into local terms of foreign cultural and ideological values" (Knapp and Cherry 1994:155), is it not reasonable to imagine that these new ideological values helped reformulate gender constructs by the end of the LBA?

Conclusions

In this chapter, I have looked very selectively at several aspects of gender, technology, and the division of labor in prehistoric Cyprus. There is clearly much more work to be done, but more important still is the need for archaeologists to recognize gender as a salient issue in study of the development of the ancient Cypriot economy. A recent conference on this theme, *"The Development of the Cypriot Economy,"* published in Karageorghis and Michaelides 1996), failed to produce a single paper or even a single paragraph on gender-related issues, thereby missing the opportunity to investigate the effects of changing economic structures on gender relations, and vice-versa. Particularly absent in these discussions is the concept of human agency, which has become a topic of great interest in recent approaches to the past (e.g., Dobres and Robb 2000). In moving beyond broadly based systemic and environmental models of culture change to consider the intentional actions and deliberate choices made by individuals and social groups, agency theory enables archaeologists to place individuals and social groups at the center of the kind of economic and social changes we have been considering in this chapter. Gender is certainly one of the most critical of these issues, and in chapter 7 I shall consider more fully the importance of the concept of agency for generating gender-based theories of social change in prehistoric Cyprus.

Performing Gender: Figurines, Ritual, and Social Identity

4

> Group lifecycle rites are public performances in the theatrical sense, with actors and audience participating in the creation of gender difference and identity.
>
> —GILCHRIST, *GENDER AND ARCHAEOLOGY: CONTESTING THE PAST*

ANTHROPOMORPHIC REPRESENTATIONS, perhaps more than any other category of artifact, furnish powerful and seductive images of the Cypriot past—so striking, in fact, that they have prompted archaeologists who would not otherwise have engaged in social interpretations of material culture to address a diversity of themes such as religion, ritual behavior, political power, kinship structures, and even gender roles. Given the richness and abundance of the figurative material from ancient Cyprus, it is not surprising that so much has been written about them.

By the same token, however, there are a number of serious obstacles inherent in the attempt to interpret much of this evidence. In the first place, the provenances of many of the figurines are not known, owing to their illicit excavation and illegal sale on the antiquities market and to the generally poor standard of recording by archaeologists during the nineteenth and first half of the twentieth century. The recognition that figurines and other artifacts have a particular archaeological importance that transcends their aesthetic value and that can only be appreciated in the light of contextual details is a relatively new phenomenon in archaeology, and it is unfortunate that much of the figurative art from Cyprus was recovered prior to that understanding. Nevertheless, excavations during the last few decades are beginning to provide contextual evidence that allows us to interpret this important body of material within more appropriate spatial and temporal frameworks.

A second obstacle to the interpretation of figurines is that even when *in situ* material does exist, it is rarely found in contexts of primary usage. The ritual deposit from

Kissonerga, discussed later in this chapter, is a good example. The figurines and other objects from this deposit were found in an undisturbed state but were not in contexts of primary usage: clearly these objects had not initially been made for purposes of burial or hoarding. Pre-depositional wear marks, including the deliberate destruction of many of the figurines, attest to their "social life" before burial. Similarly, although most plank figurines of EC–MC dates have been recovered from tombs, their recent discovery in settlement contexts suggests that they too were not manufactured exclusively for funerary purposes.

While scholars in the past have tended to interpret figurines as accoutrements of mortuary ritual, their discovery in settlement contexts at the sites of Alambra and Marki demands that we think more broadly about their functions and meanings. Yet, since abundant contextual evidence is still lacking, figurine studies continue to rely heavily on the intrinsic evidence of the objects themselves. And, although they are being studied increasingly against a general backdrop of socioeconomic complexity or, more controversially, through recourse to ethnographic analogy, typology still forms the basis for analysis and recording. Traditional methods of archaeological classification can certainly be useful for organizing and streamlining evidence of large bodies of material; however, as we shall see later, they also pose problems for interpreting gender constructs.

The lack of contextual evidence for figurines in Cyprus, as well as the general neglect of contextual considerations in their analysis, has generated a wide range of conflicting views on the meaning, function, and significance of figurines and other anthropomorphic images. Many interpretations are highly subjective, relying on essentialist beliefs that mirror modern Western gender categories. In this chapter, I want to explore some of those assumptions. Evidence for anthropomorphic representations on the island from the Neolithic to the LC is therefore followed by a critical look at some of the traditional "mainstream" approaches to figurine studies. Afterward, several recent interpretations of figurative material from explicitly gendered perspectives are presented, among which is the use of figurines as agents in the ritual performance of important life-cycle events during the Chalcolithic period and in the transformation of gender identities during the Cypriot Bronze Age.

Early Anthropomorphic Images in Cyprus

Neolithic and Chalcolithic Periods

On the basis of present evidence, it appears that the manufacture of anthropomorphic images in Cyprus began early in the Neolithic period, during the Cypro-PPNB (Peltenburg et al. 2000, 2001a, 2001b). The only evidence thus far comes from the site of *Shillourokambos* near Limassol, and consists of a two objects from the Early Phase (mid-ninth millennium B.C.), a small lime-plastered figurine with cylindrical neck and backward tilting head and the head of a cat-like creature with pointed ears, made of serpentinite, which appears to incorporate anthropomorphic features (Guilaine et al. 1999; Guilaine and Briois 2001). As only a single cat bone has been dated from the Early Phase, the excavators have suggested that the figurine may have symbolic significance, perhaps connected with ritual or cult practices originating from the mainland (Guilaine and Briois 2001:51–52). Representations of cats are known from mainland sites such as Jerf el Ahmar in Syria (Stordeur 1999); thus the origins of figurative representation on the island would appear to stem from mainland traditions of PPNA, which began about a millennium earlier than the first-known figurines in Cyprus. Unfortunately, these early representations are highly schematic and reveal very little useful evidence for the interpretation of gender constructs.

The next known representations do not appear until the seventh millennium B.C., and, despite excavations at a number of Aceramic Neolithic sites around the island, only a single example occurs in clay; this is an unfired terracotta head from Khirokitia (Dikaios 1953:pl. 98). Stone figurines are more common but still relatively rare and highly schematic in form. Nevertheless, three examples are of particular importance for characterizing the earliest phases of anthropomorphic imagery in Cyprus: (1) an andesite figurine from Khirokitia (fig. 4.1, top); (2) a limestone figurine from Sotira-*Teppes* (fig. 4.1, bottom); and (3) a limestone figurine of uncertain provenance and date, probably also from Sotira and dated on stylistic grounds to the earlier phases of the Chalcolithic (Swiny and Swiny 1983:fig. 1).

The Khirokitia figurine displays biologically male attributes, namely a phallic-shaped head and neck, while the two Sotira figurines are dimorphic, combining schematic representations of penis and vulva; together they mark the beginning of a long-lived tradition of "dualism" in figurative art that persisted in this particular form until the end of the fourth millennium B.C. (see Peltenburg 1982b:fig. 1). Despite the dualistic aspect of the figurines, however, many scholars have regarded them simply as "mother figures" or "goddesses" on account of their presumed associations with fertility (e.g., J. Karageorghis 1977; V. Karageorghis 1991). I will discuss these and other assumptions regarding interpretation of early figurine repertoires in Cyprus at greater length below.

Roughly contemporary with the Khirokitia figurine is an even more striking image that remains unparalleled in Cypriot prehistory—a painting in red ochre depicting two human figures with upraised arms on a plastered pier inside a building at the site of Kalavasos-*Tenta* (fig. 4.2; see also Todd 1981; Todd et al. 1987:47). The poor preservation of the painted figures, their lack of discernible sexual attributes, and the absence of any clear parallels on the island or adjacent mainland make them difficult to interpret from the point of view of gender. (The fact that the better-preserved figure is commonly referred to by archaeologists as the "Tenta man" tells us more about our own implicit assumptions than about past gender constructs.) But the representation of human figures in a prominent location within a building strongly suggests that prehistoric

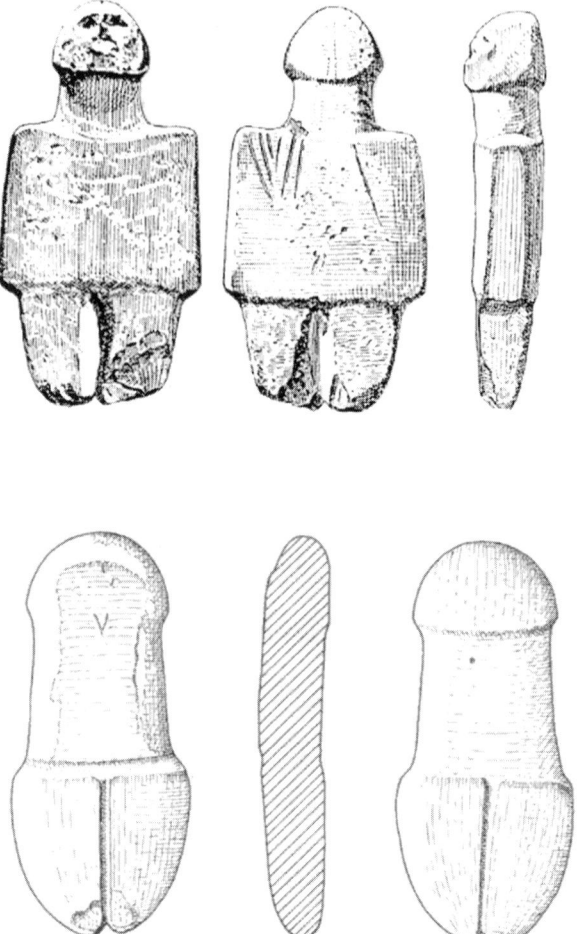

Figure 4.1.   Stone figurines of the Neolithic period: Khirokitia, above (after Dikaios 1953:pl. 98.967); Sotira-*Teppes,* below (after Dikaios 1961:pls. 102 and 106).

communities in Cyprus were endowing certain individuals with special status and recognition at least as early as the sixth millennium B.C.

During the Chalcolithic period, the repertoire of figurines increased dramatically to include schematic and naturalistic forms as well as typical "cruciforms" with stubby outstretched arms (fig. 4.3). In addition, a wider range of materials was used in their manufacture (including limestone, chalk, calcarenite, diabase, picrolite, and several pottery fabrics), and greater stylistic elaboration was achieved through the addition of clothing, facial features, and other anatomical details such as digits on hand and feet (Goring 1991a, 1991b). Pottery figurines exhibit the greatest diversity of form and are decorated in a range of painted designs that have been interpreted as hair, jewelry, clothing, make-up, and tatoos (Bolger 1988; Goring 1991a, 1991b, 1998, 2003).

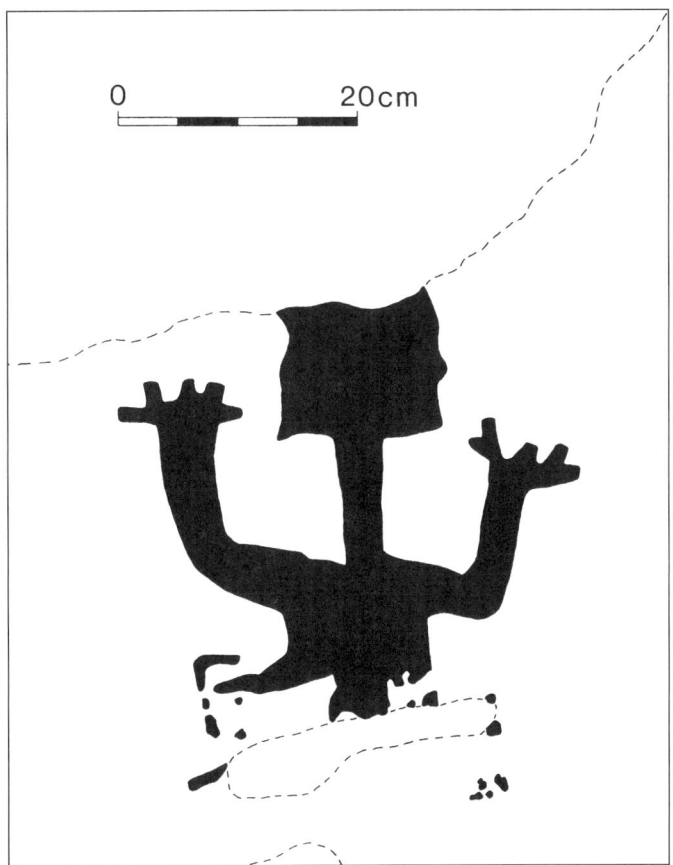

Figure 4.2.   Section of a wall painting of human figure(s) from structure 82 at Kalavasos-*Tenta* (after Todd et al. 1987:fig. 39).

Although the majority of figurines from Chalcolithic contexts are fragmentary and many have unknown provenances, a substantial body of *in situ* material has emerged in recent years as the result of excavations at Lemba-*Lakkous*, Kissonerga-*Mosphilia*, Kissonerga-*Mylouthkia*, Kalavasos-*Ayious*, and Souskiou-*Vathyrkakas*. Much of this is well preserved and includes, in addition to stone and pottery figurines, small anthropomorphic pendants worn around the neck during an individual's lifetime and deposited in graves after death (fig. 4.3, top row). These are made of picrolite, a bluish-green soft stone found in abundance in the Kouris riverbed near Limassol, and their associations in graves of women and children, as well as their squatting posture that mimics the more elaborate seated figurines in clay, argue for their use as birthing pendants (Peltenburg 1992). Other finds include anthropomorphic pottery vessels, hollow receptacles in human form capable of containing and releasing liquids, limestone statuettes representing pregnant females (fig. 4.4), and fragmentary remains of larger ceramic figures that may have measured as much as a meter in height (Bolger 1988; Peltenburg et al. 1991).

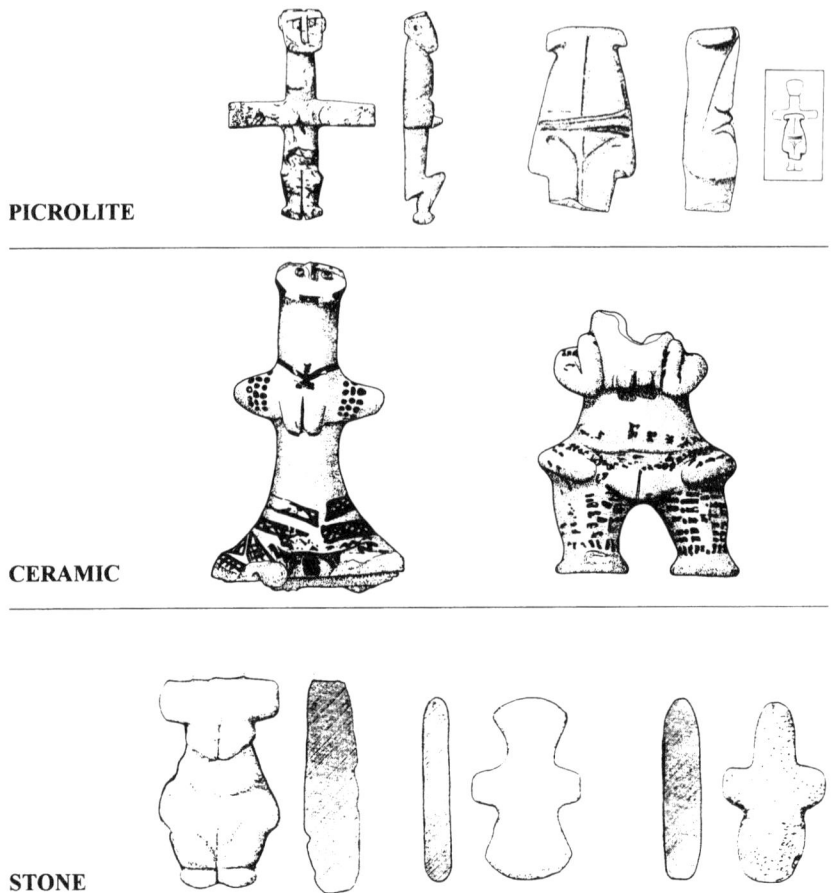

PICROLITE

CERAMIC

STONE

Figure 4.3.   Stone and pottery figurines of the Chalcolithic period: Lemba, top row; Kissonerga, bottomg two rows (after Peltenburg et al. 1985:figs 80.1 and 80.5; Peltenburg et al. 1991:figs. 22, 24–25).

The most significant group of figurines to emerge in recent years is a set of twenty pottery and stone figurines found at Kissonerga-*Mosphilia* in a ceremonial pit with fire-cracked stones, ashy fill, and a building model (figure 4.3, bottom two rows; see also Peltenburg et al. 1991). This deposit is important not only for the sheer number of figurines present but also for the contextual evidence it has furnished, which I will say more about later. The unprecedented output of figurative art during the late fourth millennium B.C., evidenced so spectacularly in the Kissonerga deposit, ended abruptly, however, toward the end of MChal (c. 3000 B.C.). After that time, figurine production ceased and did not resume at any significant scale until late in the EC. The recent discovery at Marki-*Alonia* of a human figurine in White Painted I A ware, however, raises the possi-

Figure 4.4.   Female figurine of limestone from Lemba (after Peltenburg et al. 1985:pl. 45.1).

bility that a limited number of figurines were being manufactured during the Philia facies (Frankel and Webb 2000). Reasons for the decline of figurative art during the
LChal and EB are not clear, but when production of figurines resumed late in the third
millennium B.C., they were of a radically different design and their contextual associations point to significant changes in social organization and gendered meaning.

Plank Figurines and Genre Scenes

Among the most widely studied figurines from Bronze Age Cyprus are the so-called plank figures, dating from the end of the EC (c. 2000 B.C.) and continuing through to MCI, about two hundred years later (fig. 4.5, top row). These clay representations have been named for their peculiar plank-like shape and are decorated with elaborate incised lime-filled designs; most are manufactured in RP ware, the characteristic pottery ware of the period, although a small number are known to occur in other fabrics as well. The overwhelming majority of plank figures were recovered during excavations early in the twentieth century at the large cemetery sites of Lapithos and Vounous in the north of the island and have been widely interpreted as funerary objects. However, recent excavations at two important settlement sites, Marki-*Alonia* and Alambra-*Mouttes*, both in central Cyprus, have yielded fragments of plank figurines in stratified domestic contexts (Coleman et al. 1996; Frankel and Webb 2001:fig. 8), prompting some scholars to reconsider their functions and meanings in broader terms (a Campo 1994; Knapp and Meskell 1997; Talalay and Cullen 2002).

Contemporary with the plank figures is another important group of human representations, the so-called scenic compositions of the EC–MC. Like the plank figures, most are made of RP ware, but instead of representing individual figures they depict an array of human figures attached to the bases, rims, and walls of vessels, performing activities of daily life (see figs. 2.7, 4.10, and 5.4). While many lack secure find contexts, those whose provenances are known have been found in funerary contexts. Given the limited number of settlements excavated from EC–MC, however, we should not assume that they lacked a function within the living communities of the Bronze Age prior to their burial. Although not as numerous as the plank figures (only about twenty are known), these intriguing scenes have attracted scholarly interest for the evidence they provide of day-to-day life in the earlier phases of the Bronze Age (Karageorghis 1991; Morris 1985). Interpreting the content and significance of these scenes, however, has been difficult due to their often damaged, fragmentary states and the absence of contextual information. I will say more below concerning the interpretation of these unique compositions, particularly with regard to the emergence of gendered divisions of labor.

Before turning to material from the later phases of the Bronze Age, it is important to note that the funerary contexts from which the plank figures and the genre scenes are derived differ radically from those of earlier periods. Although almost all Neolithic and Chalcolithic burials were single interments in small pit-graves, those of the EB–MBA were group burials in large built chamber tombs that were reused, sometimes over a period of several generations or more. Changes in burial patterns signify other important changes in the structure of society that must be considered when interpreting the figurines associated with them. It is unfortunate, therefore, that scholarly investigation of this important body of material has tended to focus almost exclusively on their intrinsic formal and stylistic attributes, often at the expense of contextual information.

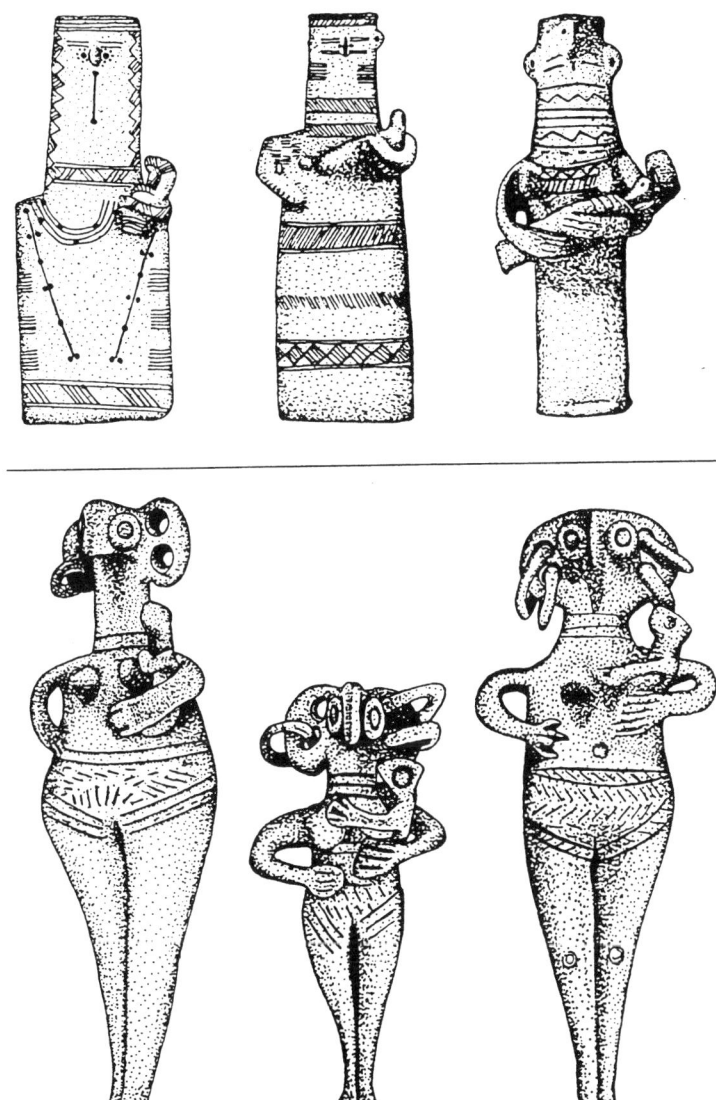

Figure 4.5.   Figurines of the Cypriot Bronze Age; plank figures, above (after Morris 1985:figs. 229–230); "Astarte" figures, below (after Morris 1985:figs. 281–283).

Images of Women during the Late Bronze Age

The LC witnessed the continued production of anthropomorphic figurines in clay; their uniform, large-scale manufacture points to increased levels of standardization and special-ized production beginning as early as LCII (Karageorghis 1993:1). While some of these fig-ures carry infants and thus bear a formal resemblance to the earlier plank figures, their overall iconography is quite different. The most common type occurs in a new pottery type known as Base Ring ware and has a bird-like face identified with the Near Eastern goddess Astarte (figure 4.5, botom row). Most of these examples are standing, but some are seated and many are shown holding infants. Regardless of its particular pedigree, this new class of half-human half-animal figurine has no earlier tradition on the island and is likely to have arrived in Cyprus as the result of expanding trade networks to the east. The latter were matched in importance by intensified links to the west, as indicated by the introduction of new figurine types during LCIII with features similar to figurines from the Aegean, especially Crete (Karageorghis 1993:1). Traditional interpretations of this LC material see them as a continuation of the worship of the "great goddess" in Cyprus (e.g., J. Karageorghis 1977; V. Karageorghis 1993) and have downplayed their overt sexual characteristics (Budin 2002). A recent contextual study of LC terracotta figurines, however, shows that most of the "Astarte" types derive from funerary contexts of wealthy elites, while the Aegean types occur almost exclusively in domestic contexts, perhaps as foundation deposits (Begg 1991).

Additional evidence for Aegean contacts has been provided by the discovery in tombs of a number of impressive Mycenaean pictorial kraters, some of which depict prominent females: the Kourion "window krater," the Aradhippou "homage krater," and a chariot krater with a female figure inside what appears to be a mortuary structure at Kalavasos-*Ayios Dhimitrios* (fig. 4.6; see also South 1997; Steel 1994). In addition, females occur in other media, such as cylinder seals (e.g., Vermeule 1974:pl. 126.343; Webb 1999); these attest to the introduction of new, exotic, and expensive materials to portray the female human form.

The export of various products from Cyprus during the LBA, particularly copper, introduced unprecedented levels of wealth into the economy and accelerated class divi-

Figure 4.6.   Mycenaean chariot krater from Kalavasos-*Ayios Dhimitrios* depicting a woman standing inside a tomb (after South 1997:fig. 6).

sions. The growth of hierarchical social structures in turn fostered new ideologies that may have encouraged elite groups to devise strategies by which to secure more effectively their broadening bases of power, and it is likely that women played important roles in these developments (Steel 2002). Two figurines are of special importance in this context as they are both made of bronze and stand on copper ingots: a male warrior figure from Enkomi traditionally referred to as the "Ingot God" (fig. 4.7) and an unprovenanced female figurine formerly in the Bomford collection and now in the Ashmolean Museum, which has commonly been interpreted as the "consort" of the Enkomi figure (fig. 4.8). Their close iconographic similarities suggest similar functions and meanings that have potential bearing on relationships between gender, figurative art, and social complexity during the LBA, and I will discuss them in greater detail below.

Traditional Narratives of Cypriot Figurines

Goddesses, Wives, and Concubines

The Island of Aphrodite conjures up romantic images to archaeologists as well as to tourists, and this, in turn, has led to a number of myths concerning gender in the prehistoric Cypriot past. The most popular of these has been the myth of the Great Goddess, which has found favor in both popular and scholarly circles. The "goddess" narrative extends back to the nineteenth century with the ideas of Bachofen and others, who believed in the existence of a maternal deity (the so-called Great Goddess or Mother Goddess) in early religion (Russell 1998). Its current popularity, however, can be largely attributed to the work and writings of Marija Gimbutas, whose gynecentric theories on matriarchy and female deities in prehistory have been central concepts in her analysis of the rich anthropomorphic repertoire of "Old Europe" and have had a significant impact on the interpretation of figurative material in many regions of the Mediterranean, including Cyprus (Meskell 1995).

For archaeologists working in Cyprus, the temptation to project Aphrodite, goddess of fertility and sexuality, back into the Stone Age has often led to the interpretation of Neolithic, Chalcolithic, and Bronze Age figurines as "proto" Aphrodites (J. Karageorghis 1977; V. Karageorghis 1991). This suggests that Gimbutas's influence is still felt in some circles, although feminist and nonfeminist scholars alike have discredited her ideas in recent years (Goodison and Morris 1998; Meskell 1995). In his brief discussion of the meanings of the earliest Cypriot figurines, Karageorghis states that "her [Gimbutas's] basic tenet that a common religious ideology did exist among the various regions of the 'old world' in the Neolithic and Chalcolithic periods is correct" (Karageorghis 1991:2). Later in the same chapter, he suggests that more than simple diffusion may have been involved in the transmission of religious beliefs from Old Europe to Cyprus and that the resemblances between figurines of those regions may have resulted from direct contact between those cultures (Karageorghis 1991:43).

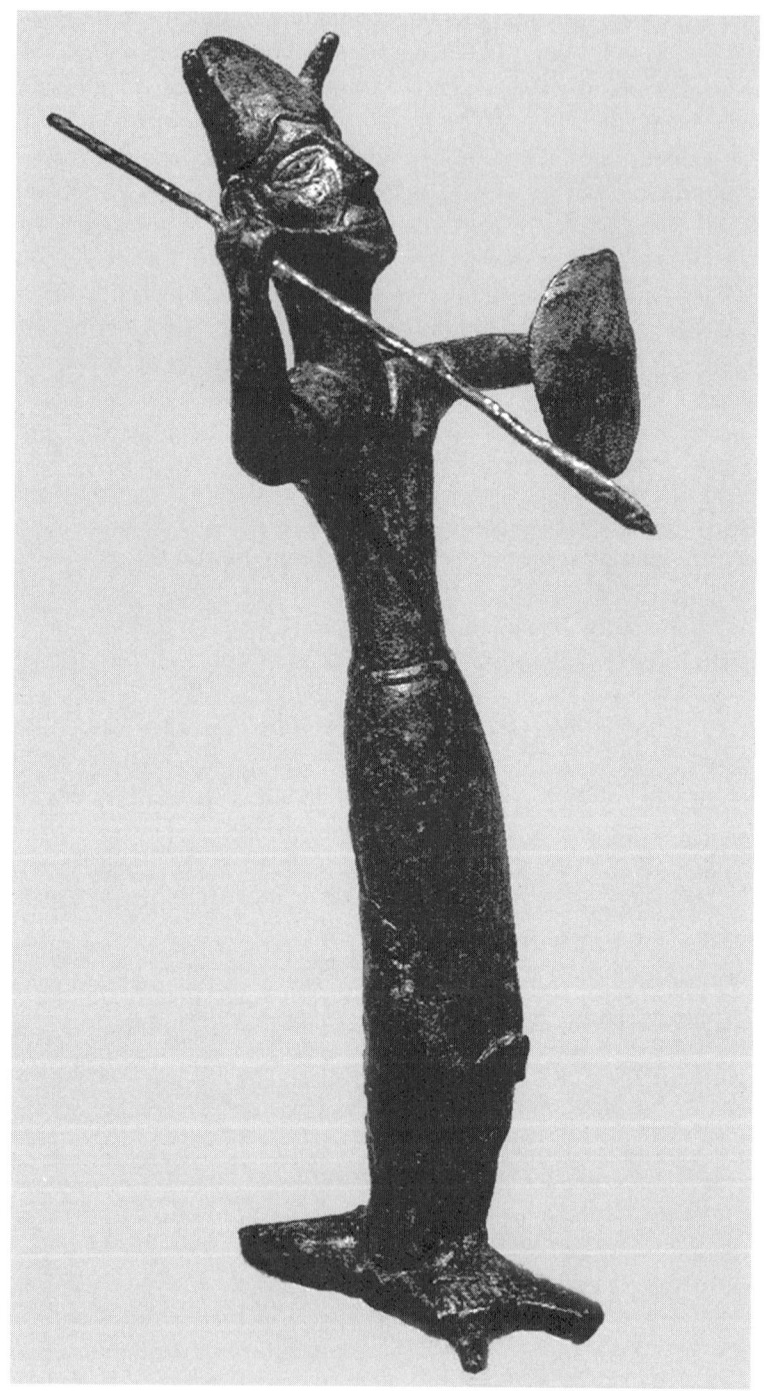

Figure 4.7. The "Ingot God" from Enkomi (after Tatton-Brown 1979:fig. 102).

Figure 4.8.   The Bomford figurine (courtesy of the Ashmolean Museum, Oxford).

In the absence of any material link between Cyprus and the mainland prior to the later third millennium B.C., however, these ideas seem doubtful.

In academic circles, the concept of the Great Goddess has fallen from grace during the last two decades, and scholars engaged in research on figurines no longer regard them as vestiges of early religion (Conkey 1997; Meskell 1995; Rice 1981; Russell 1998). Merrillees was one of first to challenge the idea of figurines as deities within a Cypriot context; he interpreted the plank figurines as human rather than divine representations made for "funerary and fertility purposes" and symbolizing the "continuity of human existence through procreation and life after death" (Merrillees 1980). Several years later, Desmond Morris proposed an even more radical departure from the Goddess theory by proposing a purely secular interpretation of the figurines. His book, *The Art of Ancient Cyprus* (1985), was the first attempt to gather together a significant body of figurative evidence from the Neolithic through the Bronze Age periods. Influenced by Ucko's earlier study of figurines in Greece and Egypt (Ucko 1968), Morris argued for a purely practical, functional interpretation of the Cypriot figurines and forcefully rejected all religious interpretations, including the Mother Goddess theory and religious ideologies relating to death. Figurines were interpreted seen to function as practical aids in the birthing process, "personal good luck charms worn to increase the chances of giving birth" (Morris 1985:116). This view is widely shared by archaeologists today, who, like Morris, have rejected the notion of deities and organized religion in early Cypriot society.

In an article on "the meaning and function" of Bronze Age figurines in Cyprus, Orphanides echoes Morris's skepticism about the divinity of Cypriot figurines and believes that the presence of males and children in the figurative repertoire requires a greater breadth of interpretation (Orphanides 1990). He also criticizes traditional interpretations that fail to draw upon contextual evidence. As he rightly observes, by treating the figurines as a homogeneous group, archaeologists have endowed them with a monolithic meaning that fails to take into account their particular spatial and temporal contexts (Orphanides 1990:46). Unfortunately, Orphanides's own interpretation of the material falls into a similar trap since it rests on unmediated assumptions concerning male and female roles that are not supported by the iconographic or contextual evidence. Despite his observation that both male and female figures hold infants, for example, he concludes that women performed the main roles of childrearing. Other roles assigned to women are unreflectively equated with women's presumed functions in the "real" world: servants, wives, and concubines (Orphanides 1990:46).

Although Orphanides admits that males may sometimes act as fathers, husbands, and sons, they also have more active, public roles, "performing activities of daily life, such as ploughing fields" (Orphanides 1990:47). He provides no evidence to support these ideas, however, and since the figures he refers to are either damaged or lack sexual attributes, they cannot be assumed to represent males. Moreover, as they are not viewed within particular socioeconomic parameters, their "meanings," as well as the roles of the "real" women and men they are thought to represent, are defined by "natural" biologi-cal attributes rather than flexible social constructs: women in terms of their sexual and reproductive capacities and men by their superior physical strength.

While Orphanides claims that the meanings of figurines are inextricably bound to the social structures that produced them, he never investigates or defines the dynamics of social relationships, and he doesn't follow up the statement that "symbols and ideol-ogy can be understood through the way people organize, interpret and categorize their world" with by an exploration of the social dynamics of gender (Orphanides 1990:46). Context is brought into this discussion only in a very general way, by reference to the figurines as "components of funerary ritual" (Orphanides 1990:47). This is a contex-tual link that suggests to Orphanides the continuation of women's biologically deter-mined roles even beyond the grave: through the burial of figurines in tombs, he observes, "women were able to continue contributing towards the maintenance and reproduction of the society they were members of in the Afterlife" (Orphanides 1990:50). In the end, such unmediated and unsubstantiated assumptions about women's roles in the past con-tribute little to our understanding of gender in the Cypriot Bronze Age.

Figurines and Social Elites: The "Ingot God" and the Bomford Figurine

While the so-called Ingot God from Enkomi and the Bomford figurine fall beyond the stated parameters of this book, I have included them in this chapter for the important evidence they provide for gender and social complexity in the later phases of the Bronze Age. The Bomford figurine, a bronze statuette of a female standing on top of a copper ingot (figure 4.8), was first discussed in detail by Catling (1971:15–32) and later by Masson (1973), Karageorghis (1977), and others (see Hulin 1989, with references). Catling considered the figurine to be a local goddess of Near Eastern ancestry and a "consort" to the well-known statue of the Ingot God from Enkomi, who likewise stands on an ingot (fig. 4.7). Although this account is primarily descriptive, providing stylistic details of the figurine and arguing on the basis of parallels in bronze and terracotta for a Cypriot pedigree, Catling ends with the following conclusions regarding its identity:

> The identity of the woman is a matter of dispute—arguments are divided between those who think it is a goddess and those to whom she is no more than a woman, a *hierodoule* [sacred prostitute] perhaps . . . on balance I believe we should identify the Bomford stat-uette as the 12th century B.C. version of a long-established Cypriot female deity whose origins are ultimately to be found in the Near East. In all likelihood she is the same god-dess who was later to become the Paphian Aphrodite.
>
> In her Bronze Age manifestation, at least, she was doubtless a goddess of fecundity. (Catling 1971:29)

Here we see the traditional mother goddess model applied to a bronze figurine. She is regarded as a deity rather than a woman, a goddess of fertility, and a probable precursor of Aphrodite. Catling goes on to compare what must be the closely related roles of the Bomford figurine and the Enkomi Ingot God:

> He is invoked as the protector of the copper and, no doubt, of the city in which the copper is produced. His female counterpart, seen in the Bomford statuette, has quite another role to play. The copper workers looked to her, we may suppose, to ensure the fruitfulness of the mines and even more of the smelting furnaces and the processes by which the raw copper is produced. . . . The naked goddess represents traditional Cyprus . . . and traditional religious beliefs, invoked to play her ancient role in assuring fertility and increase. (Catling 1971:30–31)

On stylistic grounds, the Bomford figurine is very similar to the Ingot God; however, only the latter is considered by Catling to be the controller-protector of the copper industry. By virtue of his management of this important economic resource, the Ingot God is also regarded as having control over the city of Enkomi itself. In contrast, the female counterpart of the Ingot God is apparently not in control of anything: her role is limited to fecundity, interpreted in this case the as "fruitfulness of the mines," and there is no association here between women and political or economic power. Her role as a "symbol of traditional religious beliefs" (i.e., fertility) is once again grounded in the presumed links between females and the life-giving forces of nature.

Until recently, Catling's interpretations of the Bomford figurine and Ingot God have met with wide acceptance. V. Karageorghis, for example, has offered the view that "the statuette may represent Astarte, symbolizing the fertility of the copper mines of Cyprus" (1976a:204), while J. Karageorghis, after expressing the opinion that the Bomford figurine is the same as the Ingot God (she even calls her a "protective divinity"), reverts to a traditional interpretation of the figurine that is very close to Catling's:

> Il est évident que cette "déesse" est apparentée au dieu au lingot d'Enkomi. Le statuette devait représenter une divinité protectrice du cuivre, tout comme le dieu d'Enkomi. Mais le dieu d'Enkomi est d'aspect oriental et sans doute d'origine étrangère. Au contraire, la déesse au l'ingot est dans la lignée des déesses chypriotes de la fécondité. Elle a éntendu ses pouvoirs fécondants à la fertilité de la terre en minerai. On l'a nommée "Astarté au l'ingot." (Karageorghis 1977:104–105)

> It is evident that this "goddess" is related to the Ingot God of Enkomi. The statuette represents a protective divinity of copper just like the god of Enkomi. But the god of Enkomi is oriental in aspect and without a doubt of foreign origin. In contrast, the goddess of the ingot belongs to the tradition of Cypriot fertility goddesses. She devotes these powers of fecundity to the fertility of the earth in the form of ore. One could call her "Astarte of the ingot."

As indicated recently by Hulin, the Bomford figurine has been endowed with a number of other identities as well, and by association with the Ingot God (identified as the

Babylonian god Nergal, the Levantine god Resheph, and even the Greek god Hephaistos), could form the subject of even wider fields of interpretation (Hulin 1989:127). However, the continual insistence by scholars that these figurines represent deities has until recently prevented the consideration of alternative interpretations.

Knapp was the first to radically reinterpret these figurines by shifting the analysis from the religious to the political and economic spheres (1986). Drawing on Marxist models used by Drennan and Rappoport in ethnographic studies of cultures Melanesia and Mesoamerica, he outlined the workings of religious ideology on the island, in which the sacred is seen as a vehicle or instrument of authority by which elites establish and maintain control:

> Special interest groups, whether led by chiefs, kings or emperors, justify their acquisitive enterprises or expansionistic goals through a process of sanctification. The ability to educe and apply sanctity may have facilitated control over resources or manipulation of primary producers, both factors in the formation of elite power, and in the emergence of elite authority. (Knapp 1986:67)

Some individuals were therefore able to organize and control key aspects of resource acquisition and production, transportation, and distribution, and, in doing so, were able to establish and maintain social status and economic advantage in the midst of the organizational changes needed to stabilize their authority (Knapp 1986:72). Elsewhere, Knapp has concluded that "the need to formalise, legitimise, and integrate the copper industry became a critical factor in the urban expansion and sociopolitical development of the ProBA" (Protohistoric Bronze Age) (Knapp 1994:282). While he has managed to shift the discussion of LBA figurines to entirely new ground by placing them within a social context that reveals the links between religious ideology and economic structures, Knapp fails to consider the ways in which personal relations could have been affected by such fundamental social changes. Who precisely were those powerful elites? Did they include women, as might be implied by the Bomford figurine? If so, how were they empowered and to what degree were they regarded as valuable economic and social agents? What effects, if any, did the emergence of elites have on gender relations? From the point of view of gender, Knapp's ideological landscape remains vague and impersonal.

Several scholars have commented on the physical attributes of the figurines. Catling (1971), for example, refers to the Bomford figurine as "the naked woman." Knapp (1986) adds the following details: "the facial and body features are prominent, almost bulging, and the sexual attributes are pronounced." He also comments on her puny size: "the male ingot figurine (35 cm) dwarfs this female statuette (9.9 cm); the main link between the two is the oxhide ingot base" (Knapp 1986:11). How are we to construe the greater emphasis given in these reports to the sexual characteristics of the Bomford figurine, or to her smaller size? What are the ideological links between the two figurines, and what can they tell us about gender constructs in the LBA? If we wish to answer these questions, we need to incorporate issues of gender into the fundamental questions posed by Knapp (1986) at the end of the work: How did elites in the LBA exercise control in what must have been an island divided culturally if not politically? How did they legitimize that control? Furthermore, what is the relationship of the bronze statuettes, miniature ingots, ingot representations, and monumental architecture associated with metallurgical activity (dating mainly to the thirteenth and twelfth centuries B.C.) to the socioeconomic developments that led to the rise of social complexity during the seventeenth through fifteenth centuries B.C.?

Limitations of Classification and Typology

Given the absence of detailed contextual evidence and a widespread unwillingness by archaeologists to draw on ethnographic evidence, most studies of Cypriot figurines rest on typological classification. A variety of typological approaches have been adopted over the last decades by a variety of scholars (Karageorghis 1991; Mogelonsky 1988, 1991, 1996; Morris 1985; Vagnetti 1974). In each of these studies, taxonomic classes are based on perceived similarities and differences of formal attributes; as this is an artificial process arrived at through subjective mental exercises, typologies can never accurately reflect the cognitive meanings of past social groups. Indeed, typologically based modes of interpretation tend to provide greater insight into the mind of the cataloguer than into the cognitive workings of prehistoric cultures who produced the artifacts. Mogelonsky, for example, has selected five anatomical features (head, ears, arms, legs, neck) as the basis for her classification of RP figurines. While her typology is straightforward and manages to avoid the usual proliferation of types and subtypes, it effectively minimizes the importance of other features, such as breasts, hairstyle, and elaborately incised designs, which may have been of considerable significance to the EC–MC cultures that made and used them (see Mogelonsky 1991).

In a recent book on Cypriot figurines of the Chalcolithic to MC, a Campo (1994) has attempted to reduce the subjective element in the taxonomic process by using the computer-based technique of multidimensional scaling (MDS) to establish salient attributes of form. MDS reduces multivariate attributes to basic "normative" patterns that she believes can be used to establish principal and secondary functions and meanings of the figurines. According to a Campo's model, the Chalcolithic "norm" is a female form with bent knees; for the EC–MC it is a flat rectangular form with recognizable facial features. These norms form the basis for further interpretation: attributes that occur most frequently are deemed to have overriding importance with regard to interpretation, an assumption that glosses over other less frequently occurring but potentially significant attributes and can lead to distorted, unfounded assumptions. For example, since breasts do not occur regularly on the figurines treated in a Campo's study, they do not fall into the "normative pattern" and are considered minor or "redundant" features. Figurines without breasts are presumed to be females by analogy with those that have breasts; accordingly, the portrayal of breasts would not have been necessary since anyone viewing the figurine would have assumed their existence. But, as other scholars have begun to demonstrate (Hamilton 2000; Ribeiro 2002; Talalay and Cullen 2002), the absence of sexual characteristics such as breasts may have been a deliberate choice on the part of the artist and may have social meanings that transcend binary gender categories. The concept of "normative form" seems, therefore, to contribute little to our understanding of gender and once again demonstrates the degree of subjective bias inherent in the taxonomic process as well as a methodological bias to minimize or ignore differences.

A second major drawback in a Campo's study, and one that applies to many studies of figurines in Cyprus, is the failure to examine the material first-hand. Line drawings are only as good as the eyes of their illustrators and often omit or overlook important details of form, style, or preservation, while photographs are often of poor quality and may present only a partial view. Few illustrations depict figurines from all angles, and the representation of a three-dimensional artifact in two dimensions distorts the image. For a variety of reasons, then, drawings and photographs are not adequate substitutes for close personal observation and scrutiny with a microscope or high-powered hand lens. An important exception to this rule is the recent work by Goring on Chalcolithic figurines from Kissonerga-*Mosphilia* and -*Mylouthkia* (Goring 1991a, 1998, 2003). These studies have deliberately avoided taxonomic approaches, focusing instead on details of form and decoration as well as on evidence of manufacturing techniques and use. Fragmentary examples are given equal consideration to whole ones, and all have been examined with hand-lens and under a microscope. Goring's methodology can be a useful and effective model for other researchers wishing to investigate larger questions of function and interpretation. It is one of the few to draw conclusions from personal close-range observation of the figurines rather than just illustrations and, as we shall see later, one of the few to interpret figurines within the parameters of their specific find-contexts.

As Kissonerga has yielded figurines that span the range of the fourth millennium B.C., Goring has been in a position to outline some of the important long-term developments in the portrayal of the human form over the course of a thousand years (Goring 1991b). The EChal evidence, she notes, shows increased anatomical details such as more recognizably anthropomorphic outlines, cruciform shapes, and details like divisions for toes and fingers, incised pudenda, and modeled hips; painted decoration is already elaborate. During the MChal, the repertoire expanded to include a greater variety of types and the manufacture of more sizable figurines; in addition, the figurines were decorated more elaborately to indicate hair, clothing, jewelry, and possibly tattoos.

Wear marks, which can only be observed through microscopic examination, furnish important evidence concerning the function of the figurines. Goring has noted that the stone examples from Kissonerga-*Mosphilia* exhibit very different wear patterns from those of the ceramic examples (Goring 1991a:49–52). While the former show a light overall polish, the latter are worn only in small, isolated patches. This may have resulted from their being used in different ways—the stone figurines held or clutched in the hand, and the pottery figurines touched in selected spots. As the stone figurines are not self-supporting, they may have been held or gripped during childbirth; on the other hand, the pottery figures, which are self-supporting, may have functioned as teaching aids to adolescents being instructed about crucial life-cycle events, such as pregnancy and birth. Goring has not attempted to engender her analysis of early figurative art in Cyprus, but she has made a significant contribution to the analysis of anthropomorphic representations in Cyprus that illustrates the fundamental importance of examining the figurines first-hand and reveals the limitations of standard, typological approaches.

Engendering Cypriot Figurines: Mother, Other, and Beyond

Alterity and Complexity

Anthropomorphic figurines constitute an important body of evidence with which to explore the changing gender constructs that shaped, and were shaped by, the dynamics of increasingly social complexity during the Cypriot Bronze Age. Context plays a vital role in this discussion, for without it we are unable to relate finds to their immediate and more remote surroundings. Two types of context are relevant here: the specific archaeological find-spots of the artifacts themselves, which connect them to their immediate surroundings; and the broader economic, political, and ideological contexts that allow us to interpret the material within a broader social framework. None of the studies of anthropomorphic images discussed thus far have provided a contextual treatment of the material in connection to issues of gender. In this section, therefore, I will discuss two recent studies that have attempted to do this. These are a contextual analysis of female figurines of the Chalcolithic, EC, and MC (Bolger 1996) and an interpretation of an important genre vessel, the Vounous bowl (Peltenburg et al. 1991). As both of these studies rely to some degree on the evidence of birthing figurines from a ritual deposit at Kissonerga (Peltenburg et al. 1991), it will be useful to review some of the important contextual evidence provided by ceremonial pit 1015 and its contents (see fig. 4.9).

The Kissonerga deposit dates to c. 3000 B.C. and comprises an interrelated network of pits and ovens in an open, public area adjacent to B 206, the largest excavated building of the MChal (Peltenburg et al. 1991:88). Pit 1015 was the largest of those pits and the only one to yield stone and pottery figurines and a building model; but adjacent pit 1225 contained pottery vessels. Both pits were filled with ash, animal bone, and fire-cracked stones, which had been removed from other pits and ovens and have been interpreted by the excavators as the remains of cooking and feasting activities. Examination of the objects in pit 1015 showed that they were worn and damaged, indicating their use and (in some cases) deliberate destruction before they were placed into the pit. After being deposited in the bottom of the pit, in and around the building model, the objects

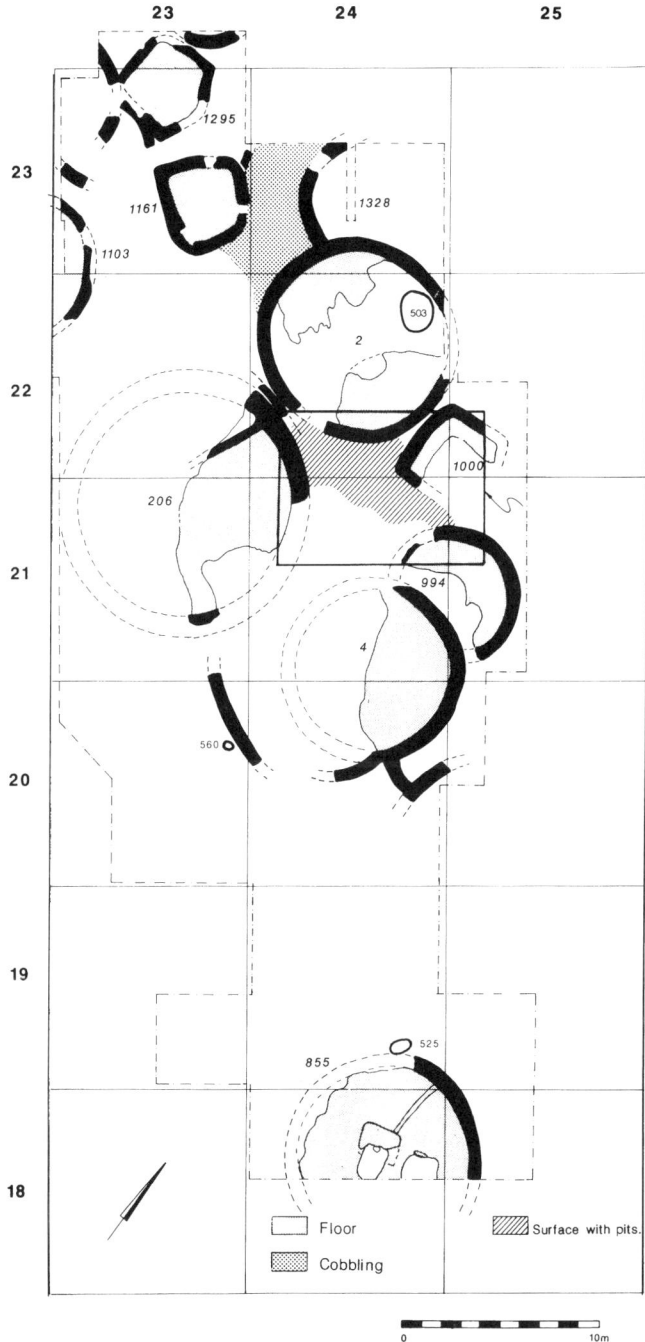

Figure 4.9.   Plan of Middle Chalcolithic Kissonerga showing the area of ceremonial pit 1015 (after Peltenburg et al. 1991:fig. 10).

were covered with two large RW vessel fragments that served as "lids" for the deposit. A third vessel, complete rather than fragmentary, was placed upright over the whole deposit before the pit was filled in with the ashy debris described above. The rim of this vessel (a bowl) would have been visible to residents of a building (B 1000) that was erected sometime after the pit was filled, perhaps, as the excavators have suggested, for the receipt of further offerings.

What is striking with regard to the condition and context of the figurines is the evidence they furnish for reconstructing the sequence of rituals and events that comprised their use, destruction, burial, and abandonment. It allows us to hypothesize a multistaged ceremony involving feasting, the deliberate destruction and burial of figurines in and around a building model, and further ritual activity that may have involved offerings or libations. In these respects, it closely resembles intentional "closure" deposits that sometimes accompany the abandonment of buildings at other prehistoric sites on the island (Peltenburg et al. 1991:99). The domestic nature of the deposit is beyond doubt, as indicated in particular by the building model (which replicates actual, excavated buildings at Kissonerga) and by the presence of stone tools, needles, and spindle whorls. In addition, the absence of typical Chalcolithic grave goods such as pendants and necklaces further attests to the non-mortuary character of the deposit (Peltenburg et al. 1991:100). The contextual information from pit 1015 thus furnishes important evidence against the interpretation of the figurines as deities and should put to rest the many unfounded, anachronistic notions of an ancient "mother goddess" in Cyprus.

The "closure ceremony" at Kissonerga takes on a different meaning and significance when we recognize that it represents the end of ideological beliefs and ritual practices linked to fertility and birth, customs attested on the island for several millennia. Why did this happen? And what do these developments tell us about the construction of gender during the third millennium B.C.? In a recent article, I have explored these questions by considering the evidence of anthropomorphic representations as they relate to the broader contextual issues mentioned above, namely the advances in socioeconomic complexity now known to characterize the Chalcolithic and EC (Bolger 1996). I have considered not only the Kissonerga ceremonial set, but also pendants and other figurines that are related iconographically and occur not just in pottery or limestone but also in picrolite, a soft greenish igneous stone that was popular during the Chalcolithic period for the manufacture of figurines and personal ornaments. The most common picrolite form has arms outstretched a right angles to the body and hence the have been termed "cruciforms." The latter occur as figurines, but also as pendants worn individually or with shell necklaces. One of the birthing figurines from Kissonerga (fig. 4.3, middle row, left) depicts a woman wearing the same type of necklace, suggesting that individuals wore the pendants during their lives. Moreover, the depiction of this figurine in the act of giving birth (parturition is illustrated as the newborn child emerges between her parted legs) furnishes an important link between the cruciforms and childbirth (Peltenburg 1992).

In considering all the figurative evidence from the Chalcolithic period, attention must be drawn to the wide range of symbolic images represented. While anthropomorphic figurines and pendants are manufactured in a variety of materials and shapes, all seem related to birthing rituals. The fact that they appear in both domestic and funerary contexts demonstrates the degree to which the birthing icon permeated social life at this time. The public nature of the use, display, and disposal of figurines at Kissonerga and their association with a typical Chalcolithic domestic structures, as well as the absence of special religious structures or precincts, are in keeping with practices in traditional prestate societies known from ethnographic research where there is little separation between public and private spheres. Consequently, the system of symbols represented by the birthing figurines must have had an important impact on the beliefs and practices of all social members. Where sex is clearly indicated on Chalcolithic figurines, it is invariably female (although as I shall discuss in the next section, some of these females have phallic-shaped necks and heads). So females were central to the rituals of fourth millennium B.C. Cyprus. The symbolic messages transmitted by the figurines emphasize women's roles in fertility, pregnancy, and birth and suggest that women were regarded in high esteem as fundamental contributors to social reproduction and survival.

The deliberate destruction and burial of these symbols in ceremonial pits at Kissonerga as part of a communal feast signaled an end to Chalcolithic birthing ideologies and associated gender constructs. During the LChal, pottery and ground stone figurines are no longer in evidence, and although a few picrolite cruciforms have been found in LChal contexts at Lemba and Kissonerga, birthing ideology had all but died out. The figurines of the later third millennium B.C. look radically different. Few can be considered birthing figures, and sexual ambiguity is much more pronounced. However, one common type, and the only one to depict women in relation to reproduction, shows them cradling infants in their arms on or their laps. In contrast to the Chalcolithic examples, they emphasize the social role of mother rather than the more generalized role of birthgiver.

As we saw in chapter 2 in reference to the figure scene on a bowl from Vounous (fig. 2.7), the mother figure appears beside penned animals, thus associating her with the control of nature, while the remainder of the bowl is occupied by males (Peltenburg 1994). This scene is thus the visual expression of a new world order in which men and women played different roles than they had in the past. The symbolic presentation of these messages as part of the "natural" world order may have helped to mediate, pacify, or override many of the social contradictions inherent in the transition from pre-state to state level society, in particular the relations between women and men (Yanagisako and Delaney 1995).

Anthropological and archaeological studies in recent years have demonstrated the importance of religious artifacts and rituals in the legitimation of social hierarchy (including Brumfiel and Earle 1987; Knapp 1986; Paige and Paige 1981; Shanks and Tilley

1982). In addition to reflecting ideology, ritual symbols promote political agendas when individuals or groups intent on gaining or maintaining power manipulate them for their own ends. By interpreting the Cypriot figurines as instruments of power rather than as dolls, charms, works of art, or static symbols of fertility, we are able to gain insights into the way changes in gender roles were constructed, performed, and reiterated.

The impact of the growth of social complexity on gender constructs during the Bronze Age must have been considerable and can be observed in the changing conventions of new forms of figurative art, in particular the genre scenes, that emerged at the end of the third millennium B.C. Morris (1985) and others have commented on what appears to be a gendered division of labor in several of the scenes. The most obvious examples show females on one side of the vessel engaged in domestic activities around a trough, while on the opposite side males control animals, tend ovens, and supervise pottery or copper production. From this and other related evidence, it appears that transformations in gender ideology began to emerge at the end of the EBA that began to differentiate the economic and social roles of women and men. Hodder has demonstrated a similar development for southeastern Europe, where, during the fourth and third millennia B.C., gender roles become more sharply segregated and there is increasing social emphasis on burial, men, cattle, and weaponry (Hodder 1990). As in Cyprus, the Secondary Products Revolution appears to have contributed significantly to these developments. The gradual transformation documented by Hodder for Europe, however, was compressed in Cyprus into a few centuries, where it is likely that the emergence of social complexity during the EC–MC transition was accompanied by a loss of female status in several key areas, such as the diminution of prerogatives that, as we have seen above, attended women's previously valued roles in social reproduction and intercommunal exchange.

With the cessation of birthing figurines and the presumed demise of its attendant social constructs, and with the overcoming of previous barriers to social complexity, circumstances were ripe at the end of the EC for new social definitions of appropriate "male" and "female" behavior. The results of recent work on early figurative art in Cyprus have an important bearing on our understanding of the mechanisms of social change, in particular changes in gender constructs, during the third millennium B.C. (Bolger 1996; Peltenburg 1994; Talalay and Cullen 2002). Whereas classic structural models of gender relations argue that the decline of women's roles coincides with the rise of the state, the archaeological evidence from Cyprus shows that gender polarization, or alterity, occurred at an early stage within in the trajectory of developments leading to the emergence of complex society in the LBA. In other words, changes in gender constructs do not occur as passive reflexes to changing economic conditions, but form the basis for the development of socioeconomic complexity. Thus, while female status did not immediately decline as a result of advances in social complexity, the greater degree of differentiation of social and economic roles according to sex may have served as an initial stage in the emergence of the male-dominated hierarchies that characterize the later phases of the Bronze Age in Cyprus. As de Beauvoir has observed, alterity is a powerful social ideology that lies at the root of female oppression in society (1974).

Gender Ambiguity and Individuality

The limitations of binary gender constructs and the failure to consider the possibility of multiple genders have been subjects of critique by "third wave" feminist critiques over the last decade (see Butler 1990). Butler in particular has argued that sex as well as gender is socially constructed and that linking gender constructs to binary male/female sex divisions excludes the possibility of multiple genders and fails to fully disengage sex from gender:

> If gender is the cultural meanings that the sexed body assumes, then a gender cannot be said to follow from a sex in any one way. Taken to its logical limit, the sex/gender distinction suggests a radical discontinuity between sexed bodies and culturally constructed genders. . . . When the constructed status of gender is theorized as radically independent of sex, gender itself becomes a free-floating artifice, with the consequence that *man* and *masculine* might just as easily signify a female body as a male one, and *woman* and *feminine* a male body as easily as a female one. (Butler 1990:6)

In Cyprus, a number of recent studies have adopted this approach by addressing issues of multiple genders and gender ambiguity. In a critical assessment of prehistoric figurines from the Mediterranean region, for example, Hamilton (1994) examines the ways in which figurines have traditionally been classified and assigned to binary (male/female) categories that reflect modern Western categories of gender division. Many interpretations concerning the meaning and function of figurines are likewise questionable due to their unmediated assumptions about gender roles that have little to do with the conditions of the prehistoric past. Male/female dichotomies restrict our understanding of gender to a single pattern, thereby failing to consider the fluidity and multiplicity of gender constructs common in non-Western preindustrial societies.

Hamilton proposes that we approach the figurines not within a framework of dimorphism but from the perspective of sexual ambiguity. Figurines lacking any indications of sex should not be assumed to be female; the absence of breasts, for example, may have been deliberate rather than accidental and may tell us something about attitudes to sex and gender. Dual sexed figurines, like some of the Chalcolithic birthing figurines with phallic necks, although limited in number, furnish evidence of gender constructs that transcend simple binary divisions. Moreover, traditional interpretations of figurines based on binary male/female categories reflect "conservative attitudes to sex and gender roles" that are not shared by many traditional societies (Hamilton 1994:13).

Several recent articles have taken up the issues raised by Hamilton by applying the concept of ambiguity and multiplicity of genders to specific bodies of Cypriot archaeological material. Ribeiro, for example, examines human figures in the genre scenes and explores the possibility that those that lack indications of sex may have been intended to represent children or adolescents (Ribeiro 2002); I will discuss her ideas in chapter 5.

In a recent study of the plank figurines of the EC–MC, Talalay and Cullen (2002) argue that binary categories restrict our understanding of gender constructs and have adopted a new approach centered on gender ambiguity. Citing evidence from ethnographic sources, they observe that the functions and meanings of anthropomorphic figurines are complex and dynamic and that their meanings may have changed according to the requirements of an increasingly hierarchical, complex society. Context is important in this discussion, and, as the authors note, the mortuary context of the figurines must be treated cautiously due to the fact that few settlements have been excavated from EB–MB sites. Recent excavations at Marki and Alambra, however, have yielded a number of figurine fragments, indicating that they were not intended exclusively for mortuary purposes and may have served as emblems of status or identity in life as well as death (Coleman et al. 1996; Frankel and Webb 1996a).

Still, the overriding association of most Bronze Age figurines with mortuary contexts cannot be overlooked. It is unfortunate that so little is known of the specific find contexts of the figurines. Associations of figurines with particular burials are obscured both by the Bronze Age custom of multiple internment and failure of excavators to record details of context. What evidence there is suggests that the plank figurines were placed in only a small percentage of EC–MC burials and then only in wealthy tombs containing bronze objects as well (Talalay and Cullen 2002). This indicates that not all members of society had access to their use.

Were the plank figurines meant to portray individuals? This question is taken up in a recent article by Knapp and Meskell (1997) in which the authors propose to demonstrate the emergence of the individual in Bronze Age society by relating details of style, anatomy, and decoration to advances in social complexity. Unfortunately, the evidence does not convincingly support this proposition since, stylistically speaking, the plank idols are no more "individual" than their Chalcolithic predecessors. Recent work by Goring (2003) shows elaboration of detail on RW figurines as early as the start of the fourth millennium B.C. In contrast, the two-dimensional forms of the plank figurines, the absence of limbs on most examples, and the stylized character of their decorative motifs convey a high degree of uniformity among them (a Campo 1994).

In many respects the earlier Chalcolithic figurines display more "individualized" traits, and, on the basis of the archaeological evidence, one could well argue that individuality began to decline rather than increase during the Bronze Age. Closer attention and study needs to be made of the entire range of figurative evidence during the prehistoric period, and close scrutiny of the objects is essential to determine how we might define "individuality" in the prehistoric past. Most importantly, theoretical considerations need to be balanced by an equally rigorous examination of the actual "bodies of evidence" amassed from decades of fieldwork and research.

A decline in individuality would accord well with the trajectory of social changes that characterize the emergence of the state, in particular the declining role of kinship in economic production and exchange and its gradual replacement by impersonal bureaucratic institutions. By the same token, it is unlikely that the move away from collective social structures had begun by the early second millennium B.C. As Talalay and Cullen conclude, "an emphasis on collective or group identity is more aligned with the ethos of the earlier Cypriot Bronze Age, particularly since many of these images were recovered from collective or multiple burials" (2002:187). In their view, the figurines may have served as powerful symbols that "subsumed male and female and stressed instead the collectivity and ancestral ties of the community, a message of particular power for an emerging elite" (Talalay and Cullen 2002:191).

The conclusions Talalay and Cullen reached demonstrate, among other things, the ways in which archaeological context can help illuminate changes in the social construction of gender over time and through space. While these types of investigations allow us to define general, long-term trends in trajectories of social relations, they tend to preclude consideration of shorter temporal spans, such as that of the human life cycle. In the final section of the chapter, therefore, I will attempt to interpret the figurative material of ancient Cyprus from a life-history perspective so that we can better appreciate the role they played in the performance of gendered identities through their use in important life-cycle events.

Figurines and the Life Cycle

One of the criticisms of gender studies of the previous decades has been its focus on women as a monolithic category that fails to acknowledge the real and palpable differences between them. More recent approaches have attempted to address difference by assessing the effects of factors such as age, class, status, and ethnicity on gender constructs (Meskell 1998). A consideration of gender difference, however, should not be restricted to intra- or intercultural disparities of social groups over long stretches of time and space: it needs also to reckon with the biological and social changes that characterize the life histories of individuals (see Foxhall 2000; Gilchrist 2000; Joyce 2000; Morbeck, Galloway, and Zihlman 1997).

Anthropomorphic images from prehistoric contexts in Cyprus provide substantial evidence with which to investigate these changes. The multiplicity of forms and styles, as well as their varied contextual associations, signify a multiplicity of meanings linked to major biological stages in the female life cycle. Figurines, however, do not just reflect the bio-behavioral changes that took place in past lives; they are also focal points in the performance of rituals that allowed individuals to negotiate gender identities within their respective communities. As key instruments in the performance of life-cycle rituals, figurines were the media through which the experience of the body was communicated and enacted within a larger social sphere.

Gender, Ritual, and Life Experience

While biological developments form the basis of life-cycle events, it is important to view them within a cultural framework. Biology is not destiny, and although the developing body provides occasions for life-cycle rituals, it does not determine their meaning and significance since the very definition of what constitutes important biological developments is culturally prescribed and variable (Vitzhum 1997).

Traditional approaches to life-cycle rituals within the social sciences (e.g., Durkheim 1912; Turner 1969; and van Gennep 1960) begin with the etic observation that most societies display "intense emotional beliefs" and "almost obsessional interest" concerning major events of the human lifecycle (Paige and Paige 1981:1). In many cases, beliefs and emotions surrounding these events are so strong that the latter are heavily couched in myth and ritual or even become taboo. According to ethnographic accounts, the most commonly occurring life-cycle processes ritualized in this fashion are menarche, male reproductive capacity (often ritualized by circumcision), pregnancy, childbirth, and death, and the rituals surrounding these events express particularly intense emotions.

According to van Gennep (1960), fears, risks, contradictions, and social stress emerge at these important transitional junctures and threaten to destabilize social groups; rituals thus function to reduce stress and instability and reinforce social structures by dramatizing the transition from one life stage to the next and educating the community about the rights and obligation of new social roles (Paige and Paige 1981:3). Individuals and groups demonstrate allegiance to established social norms through the performance of rituals and thereby help to promote group solidarity by "reinforcing society's collective view of itself." This view was most forcefully expressed by Durkheim (1912), who believed in the unifying power of ritual as a kind of "social cement" to promote and maintain group solidarity.

More recent approaches to ritual interpret it not as a means to solidify group identity but as a means by which sub-groups (such as "elites") can acquire and maintain social control (Paige and Paige 1981). According to this model, ritual is not reflective but strategic and dynamic, and processes of bargaining or negotiation are implicit in its use. Douglas (1966), for example, has demonstrated an inverse correlation between male dominance and pollution beliefs (i.e., where male dominance is undisputed, there is normally an absence of pollution beliefs, and women are not kept apart from men during pregnancy and menstruation). Segregation occurs in societies where male dominance is not clearly defined, and thus serves as a means by which female sexuality and reproduction can be regulated. Similarly, Brown has observed that menarchal rituals are found in matrilineal societies that practice matrilocal or bilocal residence patterns: when women marry outside the group (i.e., patrilocal exogamy), there is no need for ritual since the move to a new locality itself serves as the marker of new social status (Brown 1963). Menarchal and other related rituals can thus be regarded as cultural markers for societies in which women enjoy a relatively high status. Paige and Paige (1981) have drawn on these findings as support for their view of reproductive ritual as a "political event" with implications that (while perhaps unknown to participants in ritual) go well beyond the purely biological developments they purport to deal with; in this way, the subjective body is appropriated by those seeking to acquire and maintain power for purposes of social regulation and control.

Although it is crucial to acknowledge the deliberately political dimensions of reproductive ritual in many human societies, the approach advocated by Paige and Paige (1981) and others is limited in its adoption of a purely etic approach that denies ritual subjects a role in political interactions. Implicit in their view is the belief that reproductive rituals are political operations orchestrated by a small partisan (probably male) group to establish and maintain control over female reproduction and to safeguard paternity. This rather mechanical, one-dimensional view of communal ritual obscures its flexible and complex role throughout the human life course; moreover, it minimizes the importance of the female life experience and fails to consider the possibility that women were more than passive participants in male-dominated ritual agendas.

On the contrary, in pre-state societies that were relatively egalitarian, it is highly likely that women actively engaged in rituals in order to maintain or elevate their own social status. Through ritual performances, women dramatized the tensions involved in the acquisition of gender roles and were a means of negotiating and altering those roles over the course of their own lifetimes. Reproductive rituals thus provided occasions for women to "enact" new gender roles. Since involvement in reproductive rituals required repeated actions by women at various stages throughout the life cycle, the continual process of enactment confirmed the *appearance* of social norms and thereby helped promote the social stability deemed so crucial by Durkheim and van Gennep. This subtle distinction is a key point in arguments by Judith Butler, who views gender as a dialectic between actors and audience and performance as the means by which gender roles are constructed and reconstructed over the course of one's life (Butler 1990).

More radical approaches to gender over the last decade take the view that sex as well as gender is culturally constructed. Earlier theories of gender processes drew a sharp division between sex, which was regarded as being biologically determined, and gender, which was interpreted as a social construct. According to Butler and others, this should be regarded as a false dichotomy, on several grounds (Butler 1990).

Recent studies in primatology focus on "sex" as a mosaic of similarities and differences among males and females (McLeod 1997). Sex, like gender, is socially constructed in that it operates within particular political and cultural parameters. And, as Butler has argued on theoretical grounds, sex (biology) cannot be dissociated from gender (culture) since this implies a false dichotomy between mind and body that fails to recognize the centrality of life experience to the cultural construction of social norms (Butler 1990). In other words, sex and gender are not merely constructed extrinsically, outside of the body within "society" at large. In part, they are constructed from within, in accordance with bio-behavioral changes experienced subjectively throughout the life cycle. Butler's theories represent an entirely new understanding of gender that can be used to interpret ritual behavior by focusing on ritual subjects and by incorporating emic perspectives into our understanding of societies of the remote past. Life history approaches promote such an understanding by emphasizing the importance of personal experience as an analytical category and by charting the parallel courses of biological and social developments throughout an individual's lifetime.

Figurines, Context, and Community

It has been argued earlier in this chapter that we cannot fully appreciate the meanings and functions of figurines unless they are studied contextually. Context helps establish the life histories of artifacts and links them to the people who used them. Since anthropomorphic figurines from prehistoric Cyprus derive from domestic as well as funerary contexts, their function and meaning must have been significant throughout the life course, although that significance may have altered considerably from one stage to another.

At Kissonerga, the site that has yielded the most extensive and detailed contextual information for figurines of pre–Bronze Age date, anthropomorphic figurines have been found in a communal deposit that closely resembles a closure ceremony, as well as in isolated domestic contexts; picrolite figurines and pendants in birthing postures have also been found in tombs where they are associated with women and children. In addition, several sites, including Kissonerga, have yielded figurines wearing birthing pendants around their necks, indicating once again their function in life as well as death as symbols of personal identity. Contemporary with these finds are an important group of figurines from Souskiou that are found in group burials and in some cases can be associated with particular individuals.

While figurines and pendants are thus likely to have been highly valued objects and associated with individual identity, especially before the Bronze Age, we must be careful not to sharply demarcate "personal" and "public" spheres within the pre-state cultures of the island. As ethnographic evidence demonstrates, personal identity in small-scale agricultural societies is normally defined in terms of larger social constructs. Along these lines, Goring (1991a) has suggested that figurines are best understood in a communal context and that they may even have belonged to the community rather than to individuals. Similarly, Talalay (1987) has argued that figurines in Neolithic Greece were exchanged as tokens in marriage agreements, a phenomenon that illustrates particularly well the role of these objects as vehicles of social interaction.

The communal significance of figurines apparently became even more pronounced in the succeeding millennium when the vast majority of figurines known from the

EC–MC were deposited in large communal tombs such as Vounous and Lapithos. The fact that figurines cannot be clearly associated with particular burials within those tombs further supports this notion, as we saw earlier (Talalay and Cullen 2002). Although it could be argued that the lack of clear associations is due at least in part to poor recording practices of the excavators (the tombs were uncovered early in the twentieth century), it may also reflect their increased use during the Bronze Age as symbols of corporate or group identity. As Talalay and Cullen suggest, the ambiguous nature of the RP figurines may have allowed individuals to negotiate and reconstruct gender with greater facility at a time when increased levels of complexity, including the emergence of elite groups, were beginning to create new social tensions.

Anthropomorphic Figurines and Stages of the Life Course

In what ways did social identities change during an individual's lifetime and what role(s) did figurines play in the process of adopting and transforming gender? To try to answer these questions, we must first try to classify their multiplicity of forms and stylistic variations within a within a life-history framework. Table 4.1 outlines the stages of the life cycle as represented by various classes of figurines from the Chalolithic to the MC periods (Neolithic figurines have not been included due to their abstract forms, small numbers, and often fragmentary states). Figurines from the Chalcolithic, EC, and MC have been combined in this table, but there are important differences in their repertoires.

During the Chalcolithic period, figurines reiterate a limited set of themes (i.e., sexuality, fertility, and reproduction). Formal and decorative attributes vary widely, especially in the case of the pottery figurines, making formal typological

Table 4.1.   Cypriot Figurine Types as Stages of the Human Life Cycle

Life-cycle Stages	Corresponding Figurine Types
Pre-pubescence (infancy, childhood, adolescence)	cradled infants (EC-MC) "sexless" figurines (Chal, EC-MC) "sexless" figures in genre scenes (EC-MC)
Puberty (adulthood, reproductive capacity)	sexual emblems (Chal) figurines emphasizing breasts and other secondary sex characteristics (Chal) "dual" figurines (Chal, EC-MC)
Partnering (marriage)	twin plank figures? (EC-MC) couples in scenic compositions (EC-MC)
Childbirth (pregnancy, parturition, couvades)	birthing figurines (Chal) birthing pendants (Chal) anthropomorphic vessels (Chal) building model—seclusion? (Chal) "lactation" models (Chal)
Parenting (nursing, cradling)	planks with infants (EC-MC) figure scenes with infants (EC-MC) "Astarte" figurines with infants (LBA)

classification difficult if not impossible (Goring 1991a). Moreover, it is clear that although the ritual function of Chalcolithic figurines centers on childbirth, the latter is understood as a multi-stage process encompassing sexuality, fertility, pregnancy, parturition, nursing, and childrearing. The identification of figurines corresponding to each of these developmental stages suggests that they were used at different times during the life cycle. Moreover, evidence of wear points to different functions for stone figurines, which are formally abstract and lacking in detail and cannot stand on their own; and pottery figurines, which are morphologically complex, highly detailed, and self-supporting (Goring 1991a). The multiplicity of materials, forms, styles, themes, and contexts present during the Chalcolithic period has often been overlooked in the attempt to come to general, overarching conclusions concerning their function and meaning. The evidence demands, however, that we move beyond the search for monolithic meaning and begin to link the diversity of figurative types with an equivalent diversity and complexity of human life experience. It also demands that we move beyond male/female dichotomies and begin to view human sexuality, fertility, and procreation as an overlapping mosaic of biological and social characteristics. The repeated performance of ritual enactments throughout the life course would have enabled individuals to display and confirm publicly their engagement in the ritual system of human sexuality and reproduction with which the communities of Chalcolithic Cyprus appear to have been particularly concerned and to which they attached considerable social value. As Butler's theory of performativity suggests, these actions need not have reflected subjective reality or personal identity; rather, they served as a means by which women could actively demonstrate their engagement in, and manipulation of, the political and social structures of their constituent communities.

Like the figurines of the Chalcolithic period, those of the EC–MC display a considerable degree of stylistic variation, particularly with regard to the elaborate incised lime-filled motifs that may represent alteration of the body with cosmetics, tattoos, scarification, clothing, jewelry, and other accessories. Their anthropomorphic forms, on the other hand, are highly stylized and conform to a standardized "plank" shape that is less individualized than in the previous period. Talalay and Cullen have suggested that this unity of form may have been a deliberate feature that enabled their owners to adopt and transform identities throughout their lives (2002).

As table 4.1 indicates, figurines were still being used during the Bronze Age in association with life-cycle events, but pregnancy, sexuality, and birth do not appear to figure among the themes that were of concern to those who used them. The broad hips, swollen bellies, enlarged breasts, and parturient poses that characterized anthropomorphic figurines of the previous period have been replaced by two-dimensional planks whose sexual and reproductive attributes are ill defined and, in most cases, absent. Only a small proportion of the plank figures show individuals with infants, and these focus not on pregnancy or parturition but on post-partum parenting roles in which the plank figure supports a cradled infant in the arms or on the lap (Bolger 1996). The arrangement of partnerships, such as marriage alliances, may be depicted by the so-called twin plank figurines and by the placement of couples on the bodies of some RP genre vessels. Clearly, the emphasis has switched from fertility and reproduction to mating and parenting, and this may be correlated with changing kinship structures. An important example of this shift is the figurative scene on a RP bowl from Marki, of ECIII–MCI date.

THE MARKI BOWL: A FEMALE BIOGRAPHY?

In addition to figurines and vessels, an important group of ceramics, the "scenic compositions," give evidence of women's changing roles within the life course. These depict groups of individuals (some clearly male, some clearly female, others apparently "sexless" according to Ribeiro 2002) engaged in activities of daily life, either in groups as free-standing scenes or as figurative attachments to the exterior or interior of a variety of RP bowls and jars. Although about a dozen well-preserved examples of these genre scenes exist, the best preserved and most relevant for the present discussion is a bowl from Marki-*Alonia* with loop handle and twin spouts, with a series of human figures attached to its outer wall immediately below the rim (fig. 4.10). The arrangement of the

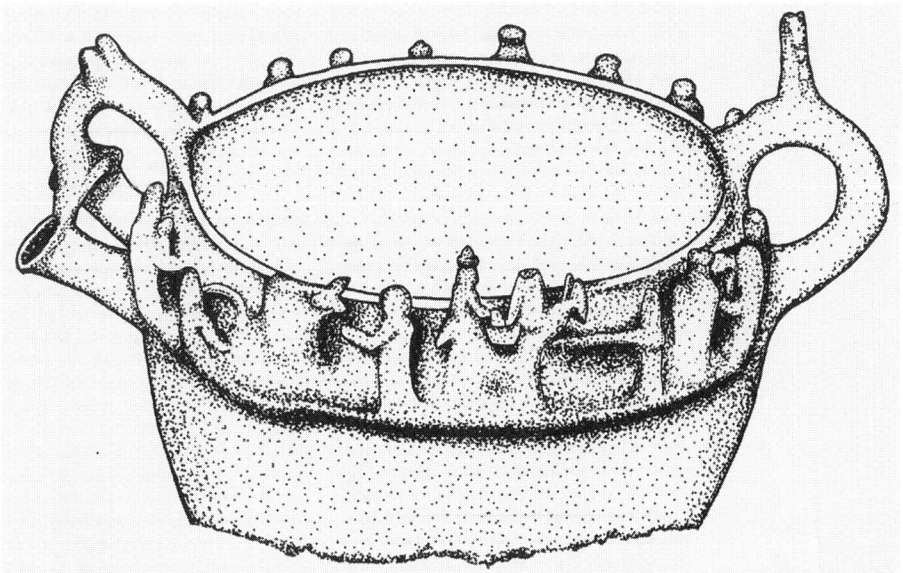

Figure 4.10.   Scenic composition on a Red Polished bowl from Marki (after Morris 1985:fig. 488).

figures is significant for a discussion of the female life cycle and so a detailed description is provided here:

Side A:
1. Damaged figure at a trough (sex unknown, only feet remain)
2. Male and female couple; arm of male wrapped around female; female wears turban and has four rows of puncture marks on her body; male wears a headband
3. Pregnant female with prominent breasts and genital groove; she wears a turban
4. Fragmentary human figure with a pounder working at a trough (sex unknown)
5. Damaged figure (sex unknown) next to an oblong trough
6. Pregnant female with prominent breasts; clay pellet in genital groove may indicate the emergence of a child from the womb; female wears a wide band across her upper body and a horizontal band across her head

Side B:
1. Male/female couple with sexes clearly indicated; female wears headband and has two rows of incised dots; she is positioned next to a ledge with a pounder; male wears a headband
2. Cradled infant positioned next to female described immediately above
3. Six figures (two badly damaged) standing on low platform with arms stretched towards a ledge (sex unknown)
4. Two human figures (sex unknown) on either side of a large structure, usually interpreted as an "oven"

The figures on this vessel appear to form a coherent composition that depicts a particular female life cycle. Although the sex of the first figure (A1) is unknown as the result of heavy damage, it is portrayed as standing alone. It probably represents an individual (adolescent female?) prior to partnering or marriage, as the succeeding element in the scene comprises a male and female next to one another as a couple (A2). The next element (A3) consists of a pregnant woman next to a woman who appears to be giving birth (A6). On the opposite side of the vessel, a male/female couple face outward (B1); next to them, at the side of the female, is a cradled infant (B2). Procreation is portrayed here not as abstract "fertility ritual" but within a context of a male-female partnership that presumably formed the smallest unit of extended kinship groups.

Clear indications of sex are indicated only on figures associated directly with life-cycle stages (partnering, pregnancy, childbirth, parenting). In contrast, figures intermediary between those just mentioned are depicted as "sexless" and are engaged exclusively in tasks of daily life (pounding or grinding, working in groups on a platform) rather than life-cycle roles; these "intermediary" figures may serve as narrative devices that epitomize the passage of time between major life-cycle events. Finally, the transition from one stage to the next is marked in several instances by changes in headdress and body decoration (indicated by puncture marks and perhaps representing tattoos, jewelry, or scarification). The female initially wears a turban (A2, A3), but her headdress changes from a turban to a headband in the childbirth scene (A6) and in the parenting scene on the other side of the vessel (B1). The male in (B1) and cradled infant in (B2) also wear identical headbands, thus symbolically linking mother-father-child and perhaps signifying their status as a nuclear family group. The final scene on side B (B4) signifies the end of the female life cycle, and logic dictates that the feature traditionally interpreted as an "oven" must in fact represent a tomb. While there is no way to be certain that this is the case, it makes sense both in terms of technological constraints (i.e., the tomb is depicted above ground since it must be modeled in relief) and overall thematic conformity to the rest of the figures on the vase.

RECONSTRUCTING MALE LIFE CYCLES

Female bodies visibly display many of the processes of human reproduction, and life-cycle events are therefore embodied on many of the figurines that have been considered in this chapter. In contrast, there are few figurines from prehistoric contexts that can be securely identified as males, perhaps because the male body does not undergo similar demonstrable changes during the life cycle. Until recently, the only unambiguously "male" example known before the Bronze Age was the seated figure allegedly from Souskiou, and one of the Souskiou shaft graves has also yielded a phallic figurine modeled in stone (Christou 1989:fig. 12.9).

Stone phalli have been recorded at other Chalcolithic sites such as Lemba and Kissonerga, suggesting that male participation in reproductive rituals may have been more common than is usually acknowledged (fig. 4.11; for additional illustrations, see Peltenburg et al. 1985, 1998). At Kissonerga, for example, twelve artifacts of phallic form were found, and all are made of stone (Goring 1998:158–59): one was from the EChal, four each were associated with MChal and LChal deposits and the rest were not from datable contexts. Only two were found in primary *in situ* deposits, and both of these derived from a MChal building, incorporated respectively into its hearth and wall. Another phallus (Peltenburg 2003:fig. 61.4) has arm-like projections that liken it to an anthropomorphic figurine. Goring has observed that none of the phalli from Kissonerga was self-supporting and that they were probably intended to be held in the hand (Peltenburg et al. 1998:159). As the most visible element of the male reproductive process, the phallus was an appropriate symbol of male sexual maturity and reproductive capacity, and phallic representations may have been modeled for use in male initiation ceremonies or other puberty rites.

The seated male figure from Souskiou mentioned above still remains the only example of a complete male figure prior to the Bronze Age (fig. 4.12). While its large size (36 cm high), intense facial expression, and erect penis have drawn considerable attention in the archaeological literature, its meaning remains enigmatic (Karageorghis 1991;

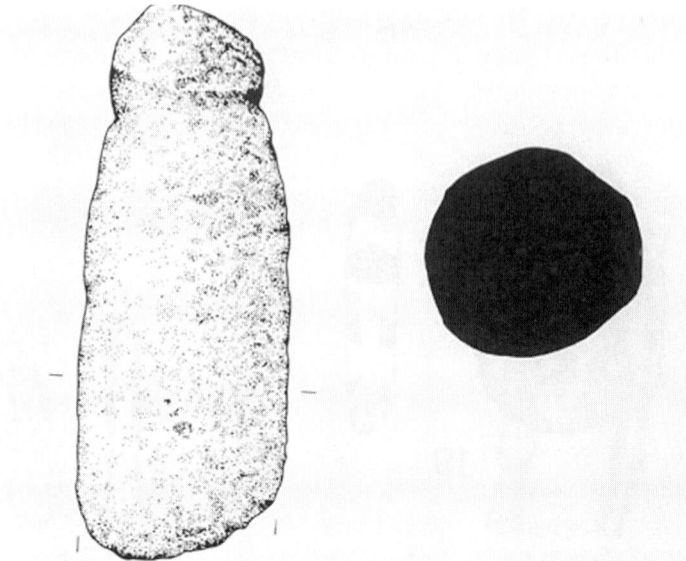

Figure. 4.11.   Limestone phallus from Lemba (after Peltenburg et al. 1985:fig. 82.8).

Karageorghis and Vagnetti 1981; Morris 1985). A detailed reconsideration of this figure by Hamilton, however, has led her to suggest that the figure may have been intended
as a representation of couvade (Hamilton 1994). As evidence for this interpretation she
has cited the iconography of the figure itself (seated on a stool, intense facial features
with a grimacing expression, perhaps representing the pain of labor), as well as parallels
to an anthropomorphic vessel in the Kissonerga deposit (Peltenburg et al. 1991:fig. 20)
that is probably male and displays a similar grimacing expression. Hamilton suggests
that the Souskiou male figure may be interpreted as an example of gender ambiguity
since he is shown "crossing" boundaries of sex and gender as defined by modern binary
constructs (Hamilton 1994). In Butler's terms, this figure might be regarded as a "parody." Parody, according to Butler, involves more than imitating an original prototype—
it undermines the whole idea of an "original" gender and thus "constitutes a fluidity of
identities . . . and deprives hegemonic culture and its critics of its claim to naturalized
or essentialist gender identities" (1990:38).

Within the traditional societies of ancient Cyprus, life-cycle events such as birth provided females with occasions to perform and reiterate important social roles. While the
particular rituals enacted by men and women may have differed according to gender,
the mechanisms of their performances were similar, involving the display and manipulation of anthropomorphic figurines. The widespread distribution of birthing figurines, as
well as their varied repertoires, indicates the great degree to which ritual behavior formed
the *habitus* of Chalcolithic society and illustrates the importance of the human body as an

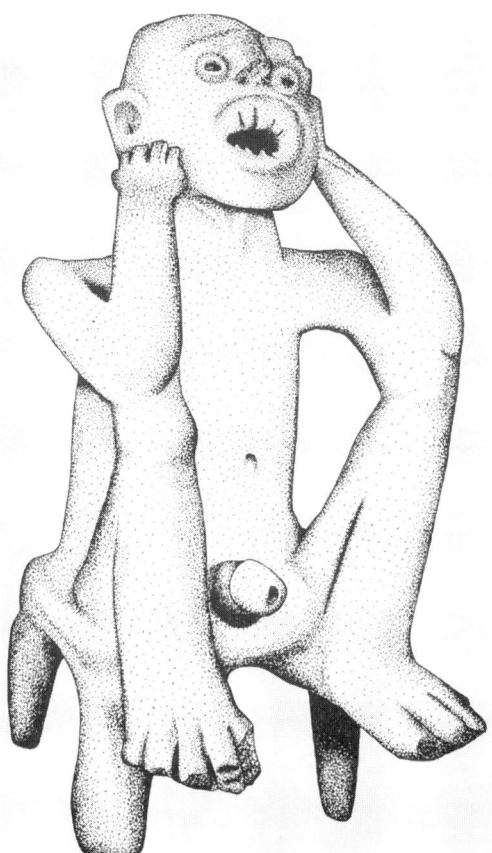

Figure 4.12.   Seated male pottery figure, allegedly from Souskiou-*Vathyrkakas* (after Morris 1985:fig. 175).

important site for the negotiation of gendered identities. This is likely to have been the case for the other classes of figurative material considered in this chapter as well. As material constructions of the body at various stages of development, the anthropomorphic figurines and vessels, as well as many of the genre scenes, served as important metaphors for the dialectical interplay between subjective and objective experience, between individual and community (Butler 1990:133).

The End of Communal Ritual

As socially significant acts, life-cycle rituals in traditional Cypriot society were important mechanisms through which gender was continually constructed and reconstructed, and figurines, which were centerpieces in those rituals, played important roles in that process. Ritual enactment enabled performers to create, display, and transform social meanings in accordance with evolving experience and circumstance; to a large degree, then, ritual enactment can be regarded as a deliberate "adaptive" strategy whose meaning and mechanisms changed in accordance with evolving social structures. Changes in ritual practice and performance can be seen at several crucial junctures during the third–second millennia B.C.: at the end of MChal (c. 3000 B.C.); during the EC III–MCI transition (c. 2000 B.C.), and at the start of LCII (c. 1400 B.C.). By focusing on these three "transitional points" we can witness the development of ritual process from individualistic enactments of life-cycle events to communal rituals whose meanings were more ambiguous and which were more closely linked to large corporate kinship groups (for ECIII–MCI), and finally to rituals using standardized, repetitive symbols whose manipulation was the prerogative of smaller groups of elites (LC II–III).

Peltenburg has discussed some of the changes occurring at the first of those junctures when the system of birthing rituals, which had been a hallmark of MChal culture, began to dissolve (Peltenburg 1992, 1993). The destruction of ritual paraphernalia in a ceremonial area at Kissonerga, discussed in detail earlier in this chapter, constitutes a closure ceremony enacted in a public precinct adjacent to a large MChal structure (fig. 4.9, B206), and the actions in the ceremonial area must be associated with inhabitants of that building (Peltenburg et al. 1991). By taking figurines out of circulation, the inhabitants of B206 "demonstrated their authority in exercising control of such an exclusive system." In this way, the deposit of ritual paraphernalia in pit 1015 can be interpreted as an attempt to curb the power of those elites by appropriating their ritual objects.

While this argument is to some degree plausible, it also poses certain problems regarding gender constructs during the fourth millennium B.C. In the first place, B 206 is a prestigious building, the largest in diameter of any known building of the period, containing red painted plaster walls and quantities of elaborately painted vessels. Although elites associated with the building may have been attempting to regulate, control, or suppress birthing rituals, there is no real evidence to suggest that figurines of the MChal were being manipulated by elites prior to their destruction and burial in pit 1015. Although it is likely that there was competition among emerging elite groups toward the end of the MChal, it is more likely that the struggle to control figurines and perform the rituals associated with them represents an attempt by incipient elites to establish and solidify power bases on a different ideological footing. The rituals they sought to control need not have been under previous control of other groups; given the great degree of variation and pronounced "individuality" of Chalcolithic birthing figurines, it is more likely that reproductive rituals were appropriated from individuals in order to be subsumed within the rubric of newly emerging kinship structures.

Finally, we need to interpret the evidence of MChal birthing ritual, not just within the vague political framework of emerging "elites" but from a gendered perspective that considers the effects of social complexity on relationships among men, women, and children, and between individuals and communities. Reproductive rituals tend to occur in relatively egalitarian, matrifocal societies where women have relatively high status; here, where other forms of social or political control are absent, rituals often function to regulate sexuality and control reproduction (Brown 1963). As has already been suggested above, however, this is not a clear case of ritual performers being controlled by outside groups or individuals; rather, participants in life-cycle rituals play active roles in the construction and reconstruction of gender and elevate or enhance their status by publicly corroborating social norms. The existence of reproductive rituals during the EChal and MChal and probably also earlier (see Le Brun 2002) implies a certain degree of tension within communities as a whole, and the Kissonerga deposit can serve as a case study in which emerging elite groups attempted to dominate the power of individual performers by appropriating, destroying, and concealing their ritual symbols. The fact that a small number of birthing figures are found in LChal contexts suggests that their efforts at transforming reproductive ritual were considerably, though not entirely, successful.

The encapsulation and ultimate disappearance of fertility and birthing rituals during the first half of the third millennium B.C. marked the final stage of a long tradition on the island extending back at least as far as the LNeo, a period of nearly two millennia. The Kissonerga deposit signifies the beginning of the end of that tradition as society became more sedentary and complex and as interest groups began to transform existing egalitarian structures according to their own needs. Peltenburg (in Peltenburg et al. 1998, ch. 4.2) has suggested greater visibility of family identities at this time in the mortuary record, as evidenced by the first inhumations of adults and children together within large purpose-built chamber tombs.

Around the middle of the third millennium B.C., the ritual traditions of the fourth and earlier third millennia B.C. were apparently replaced by new ideologies accompanying the introduction of new technologies and ideologies from abroad (Frankel and Webb 1999). Although the material attributes of the Philia culture do not generally include anthropomorphic figurines, the recent discovery of a White Painted (Philia) figurine at Marki suggests that they in fact have been part of the new technological and ideological package introduced to the island from abroad during the second half of the third millennium B.C. (Frankel and Webb 2000). Further evidence is needed, however, to determine the extent to which they might have been accompanied by new gender constructs. Figurines appear in Cyprus again in large numbers only at the end of the third millennium B.C. As I indicated earlier, these are clearly of a different form and purpose than those of the late fourth millennium B.C., and those who participated in the new rituals apparently operated within a different socioeconomic sphere that valued membership in corporate kinship groups. This restructuring of ritual performance represents a first major stage in the transformation of communal ritual among the prehistoric communities of Cyprus.

Unfortunately, there is limited contextual evidence that might furnish clues to the rituals associated with the figurines and genre scenes of the EC–MC. As I have suggested elsewhere (Bolger 1996), the development of socioeconomic complexity may have had an important impact on social structure and hierarchy, which, in turn, may have caused a decline in status for women. Along the same lines, Peltenburg (in Peltenburg et al. 1991 and Peltenburg 1994) and others (Knapp and Meskell 1997; Manning 1993) have used the genre scenes of EC–MC date as evidence of the presence on the island of aggrandizing male elites. But if we understand ritual behavior within a relatively egalitarian social context as the strategic performances of active social agents, then the opposite may have been the case: women may have deliberately chosen to adopt and perform new gender roles during the Bronze Age in order to consolidate their positions within emerging corporate groups and thereby maintain a relatively high social status. The ambiguous, abstract forms of the plank figurines appear to furnish an appropriate, flexible medium through which political strategies could be tried and tested and by which gender roles could be negotiated and transformed (see Talalay and Cullen 2002).

This relatively "open" system of gender negotiation was abandoned during the LBA as economic institutions began to replace the older kinship-based structures. The wealthy contexts in which many LC figurines are found suggests that reproductive ritual came to be the prerogative of a small, elite sector of society (Begg 1991), and as the LBA progressed, Cypriot elites increasingly gained status from association with foreign groups whose gender constructs were less flexible and whose impact in Cyprus was so far reaching. The rapid transformation of political and economic spheres during the LBA in Cyprus appears to have brought to an end the ritual practices linked to life-cycle events; the latter were replaced by standardized emblems used to transmit new political messages, and the control of those messages came to rest in the hands of increasingly smaller groups of (elite) individuals.

The observation by Karageorghis (1993:1) that by the LC figurines had "lost their individuality" is true in a certain sense: they were no longer linked to the life histories of individuals but had begun to adopt more generalized, uniform iconographies whose meanings could easily be identified by larger social groups. Mass production and standardization of form on the "Astarte" figurines of LCII–III, for example, endowed them with a "generic" quality that rendered their meaning more easily "translatable" but at the same time less fluid and flexible. Consequently, the search for "individuals" among the bodies of figurative evidence on ancient Cyprus should focus on earlier periods of Cypriot prehistory; with the emergence of social complexity, the ability of individuals to negotiate gendered meanings and influence social norms was significantly reduced and subsumed into the collective identities of groups whose power and prestige were increasingly based on wealth and rank rather than on traditional structures of family and kinship groups.

Invisible Characters: Children and Adolescents   5

> The unresearched is predominantly that which is defined feminine.

> —BAKER, "INVISIBILITY AS A SYMPTOM OF GENDER
> CATEGORIES IN ARCHAEOLOGY"

M Y DECISION TO INCLUDE CHILDREN in a book on gender has been based on the connection between their absence in archaeological reconstructions and the absence of women. Both have remained invisible as the result of widespread, often implicit, assumptions among archaeologists that important activities in the past were performed exclusively by adult males and that women and children did not engage in "real work," at least to the extent that it merits discussion in published reports. Consequently, women and children have not been recognized as agents in their own prehistory (Bolger n.d.; Hastorf 1998; Moore and Scott 1997).

By the same token, the failure to "write children into the archaeological record" can be attributed to the relatively marginal roles granted to children in the industrialized West, a phenomenon that emerged during the nineteenth century as part of a larger pattern of social and economic change associated with the shift from agricultural to industrial production (James, Jenks, and Prout 1998:115). Cross-cultural studies of non-state societies, as well as states in underdeveloped countries of Africa and Asia, have shown that children are often crucial constituents of economic production since they regularly contribute to the labor force both within and outside of the family. Even in the developed world child labor continues to exist, although it tends to be low paid, part time, and often illegal (Boyden and Myres 1994; James, Jenks, and Prout 1998:112–13). Changes in economic and social structures, whether occurring gradually or rapidly, are likely to have a direct impact on relationships within the family, and children, like everyone else, are inevitably caught up in the process. The social construction of childhood, therefore, parallels the social construction of gender, and, in considering the roles of children in cultures of the remote past, we are helping not only to establish and define the identity of its non-adult members but also articulating more clearly the dynamics of gender relations among adults.

In addition to playing important roles in economic production, children serve as recipients and transmitters of socially constructed ideologies, morals, values, and norms. As repositories of spoken and unspoken beliefs about the world, children are ideological as well as material heirs, and, while they may criticize and reject some of the cultural knowledge passed down from their elders, they nonetheless play crucial roles in the reproduction of social relations through enculturation. The assimilation by children of cultural norms can be observed in their imitation of the gendered behavior of adults, a process that is culturally induced rather than biologically determined. Learning and performing gender roles involves more than simply absorbing and imitating culturally defined patterns of behavior, however; it is a complex cognitive process that begins at a very early age. By negotiating gender roles, children function as active agents in the acquisition, transmission, and even subversion of cultural norms. An important dimension of the study of gender in prehistory, therefore, should consider the means by which social constructions of gender are adopted and transmitted by a community's youngest members and the extent to which children play a role in structuring, maintaining, and transforming them.

Childhood, Past and Present

The historical processes by which children in Western society came to be regarded as discrete social categories were first examined in depth by the social historian Philippe Ariès in his classic work, *Centuries of Childhood* (1962). Drawing on evidence of literature, painting, and historical documents dating from the tenth to the nineteenth centuries, Ariès was able to trace in considerable detail some of the changing perspectives on children and childhood from the medieval to the early modern period. One of his most important conclusions is that the conception of "child" as a distinct social category, something we take for granted today, does not appear to have existed during the Middle Ages. It only began to emerge in the sixteenth century with the widespread practice of Christianity, with its emphasis on the immortality of all human souls, including those of children.

Children received further social definition during the eighteenth century as the result of changes in the secular sphere associated with the gradual decline of child employment as apprentices and domestic servants and a renewed interest by adults in children's education. In addition, Ariès ascribes the construction of childhood in modern terms with the general demise of extended family groups later in the nineteenth century and their replacement by the nuclear family. Childhood, in its fully developed modern form, was thus a nineteenth-century invention. Family and school together, he argues, had the effect of removing children from adult society, at least among the middle classes;

as a result, children's roles as contributors to the economic and social well being of extended kinship networks were reduced and marginalized to a state of economic and emotional dependency on a nuclear family group.

While many scholars dispute some of the particular details of Ariès's work, or criticize its failure to consider earlier, classical models of childhood in Western thought, *Centuries of Childhood* is widely recognized as a seminal example of a new perspective on childhood that began to be adopted by social scientists toward the middle of the twentieth century. The treatment of children as a distinct constituent of the social fabric can be seen particularly well in many of the sociological, psychological, and anthropological studies of childhood and personality development, some of which have been incorporated into models of enculturation and of socialization (Lindsey 1997:ch. 3).

An important example within the field of cultural anthropology is the groundbreaking research undertaken by Margaret Mead on several island cultures of the western Pacific, which focused on the ways in which cultures shape and define personality. In one of her best-known works, *Sex and Temperament in Three Primitive Societies* (1935), Mead investigated the variations in social behavior among members of three New Guinea tribes, themes addressed earlier in her classic study *Coming of Age in Samoa* (1928). In these works, behavioral differences were attributed to variations in cultural norms, and nurture (learned processes of socialization) rather than nature (essential biological traits) was regarded as the key component shaping individual personality. In terms of gender, cultural variability of male and female behavior was the central theme in one of her later works, *Male and Female* (1949), which focused on the construction of gender and personality traits in the twentieth-century United States.

Childhood as a culturally determined phase of human development is the subject of another avenue of anthropological research best illustrated by van Gennep's *The Rites of Passage*, published in the same year as Aries's book (van Gennep 1960). According to van Gennep, childhood was bounded by cultural constraints associated with important life-cycle events such as birth, puberty, and marriage. Although influenced by psychoanalytic theory, notably in its emphasis on the function of rituals and taboos to resolve potential conflicts between individuals and society, van Gennep adopted a more social perspective by stressing the role of the community in the difficult and even dangerous passage of its members through critical episodes in the life cycle. By extensive recourse to ethnographic examples, van Gennep demonstrated the diversity of practices by which cultures mark the different stages of childhood and acknowledge them publicly by ritual celebrations. Particular attention was paid to initiation rites celebrating the passage of children to adulthood (so-called puberty rites), a process regarded as crucial to the successful integration of individuals into the wider social sphere (van Gennep 1960:ch. 6).

A similar emphasis on the behavioral and cognitive processes by which children are integrated into society can be seen in twentieth-century perspectives in developmental psychology, which rejected many psychoanalytic theories of early childhood development (including the Freudian preoccupation with primal behavior) by study-ing children within a social context. The work of Jean Piaget best exemplifies this trend (e.g., Piaget 1929, 1955). Piaget was the one of the first psychologists to view children as active agents in the acquisition of cognitive skills relating to the discov-ery and assimilation of cultural norms (Bem 1993). This developmental process was believed to occur in progressive stages and lead ideally to the emergence of fully fledged, mature adults. With the growing dominance of Piaget's thought over the fol-lowing several decades, the processes involved in the acquisition of gendered behav-ior were placed firmly within the social sphere, and children's adoption of polarized gender categories was ascribed to their conscious assimilation of normative gender constructs through processes of socialization.

Piaget's idealist views on children and childhood were seriously challenged in the 1960s and to a large degree have been replaced by new approaches (e.g., Merleau-Ponty 1962), whose emphasis on embodied rather than cognitive knowledge stresses the pri-mary importance of physical experience in the child's negotiation of the world. While the concern with the physical aspects of children's development (body, brain, nerve cells, etc.) still figures largely in the current literature (Christensen 1993; Shilling 1993; Toren 1993), work in developmental psychology attempting to attribute the causes of gender polarization exclusively to biological rather than cultural factors has met with consider-able opposition (Kohlberg 1966). Empirical evidence calls into question these and other sociobiological explanations of social identity (Bem 1993:115), as does the recent map-ping of the human genome, which has failed to ascribe differences in male and female behavior to specific genetic locations. To a certain extent, then, models first proposed by Piaget and others arguing for the situation of childhood within a broader social context still carry considerable weight today.

Archaeology, with its long-term perspective, is the only discipline capable of tracing changes in social constructs over long stretches of time, but, like its neglect of gender issues, it has not generally been inclined to investigate the roles of children. Although we cannot underestimate the difficulties of identifying children in the archaeological record, archaeological evidence can be a useful tool for examining long-term changes in the social definitions of children and childhood and thereby enable us to extend Aries's analyses back beyond the Middle Ages and the Classical world, into the remote past. Yet children have been marginalized in discussions of ancient societies, and only recently has research begun to be undertaken by a small handful of scholars in European prehistory (see especially Lillehammer 1989 and Moore and Scott 1997), while in Cyprus children have been almost totally neglected in archaeological investigations (see Bolger 1996, 1998; Le Mort 2000; and Lorentz 1998 for previous work).

This chapter aims to remedy the situation to some degree by considering several strands of evidence that shed light on the identities of infants and children in Cypriot prehistory. Rather than trace a broad range of social developments over the course of sev-eral millennia, however, I have chosen to consider four particular aspects of the archaeological record that demonstrate some of the ways in which an archaeology of children and childhood can shed light on our understanding of gender and social complexity during the Neolithic, Chalcolithic, and Bronze Ages. The first concerns the high incidence of infant mortality recorded at sites of the Neolithic and Chalcolithic periods. Recent work by the French at Khirokitia suggests physical rather than cultural factors as the principal causes, but this interpretation is open to question. The second theme is based on mortuary evidence from the Chalcolithic period, a topic treated also in chapter 6, where I will focus on other gendered aspects of the prehistoric burial record. Here, mortuary evidence is examined from the point of view of children's roles in changing kinship networks. A third body of evidence consists of the scenic compositions of the EC–MC, a topic addressed in some detail in chapter 4, which provide important evidence for the relationships between gender and age among sub-adult social groups, focusing on the premise that they may have constituted a "third gender" category (Ribeiro 2002). The fourth and final theme looks at the practice of cranial deformation, a phenomenon observed on human skeletal remains from all phases of Cypriot prehistory; various methods of head shaping are used to evaluate the participation of children in the formation of collective identities of emerging elite groups during the LBA.

Infant Mortality and Infanticide

High incidences of mortality among infants and children characterize most of the ancient populations of Cyprus, but explanations for this phenomenon have not been investigated in any depth until quite recently (Le Mort 2000; Lorentz 1998). Western ethnocentric assumptions regarding attitudes to children in developing countries (e.g., that children's lives are somehow valued less, that infanticide is widely practiced on newborn females, or that primitive cultures are somehow inured to the loss of children owing to its frequency) have been reflected in the archaeological literature by a near complete absence of scientific research in this area (but see Mays 1993, 1995 and Scott 2002).

Investigating the potential causes of infant mortality in past societies, therefore, confronts us with our own values and assumptions about the status and importance of children in traditional, non-Western cultures. As we shall see in more detail in chapter 6, human skeletal remains from archaeological excavations in Cyprus have not often been given the scientific treatment they deserve, with much of the material poorly excavated, inadequately recorded, and hastily analyzed, if studied at all. There are exceptions to this general rule, however, especially for the periods prior to the Bronze Age where more substantial collections of carefully excavated, scientifically studied skeletal material exist. We turn first to the evidence of the largest body of prehistoric skeletal material, the Aceramic Neolithic site of Khirokitia.

Excavations at Khirokitia between 1936 and 1943 by Dikaios and from 1975 to the present by Le Brun have yielded a total mortuary population of approximately 250 individuals. Nearly 60 percent of the deceased (n=141) were infants and children (Le Mort 2000:tab. 1). Le Mort's recent study of skeletal material of sub-adults from the site has determined that nearly 50 percent of the dead at Khirokitia were infants under one year old, with almost all of those (98 percent) falling within the perinatal period (including fetuses older than six lunar months and infants of less than one month old). In contrast, children and juveniles between five and fourteen years of age were markedly underrepresented in the mortuary record of the site (Le Mort 2000:tab. 2).

Moyer's study of mortuary remains at Kalavasos-*Tenta*, a site near Khirokitia and partly contemporary with it, has yielded similar results with regard to child and infant mortality (10 percent children, 45 percent infants), although the minimum number of individuals from burials at *Tenta* was less than twenty (*Todd 1998*). The general picture emerging from these recent studies of the Aceramic Neolithic skeletal material suggests higher ratios of perinatal mortality than is normally the case in ancient populations (Le Mort 2000:67). In attempting to explain the high incidence of perinatal infant mortality at Khirokitia, Le Mort has considered cultural attitudes and practices such as infanticide but feels that infanticide was unlikely on account of homogeneity in the mortuary rituals associated with perinatal infants at the site (Le Mort 2000:68). Instead, she cites pathological conditions as the likely cause of the high perinatal infant death rate. Medical examination of sub-adult skeletons revealed that most children and some infants at the site suffered from porotic hyperostosis, a bone condition frequently caused by severe anemia; while this condition is most often linked to iron deficiency anemia, it can also result from genetic varieties such as thalassemia and sickle cell anemia. It is interesting to note that infants at nearby *Tenta* appear to have suffered from some form of anemia as well (Todd 1998:46).

Although preliminary analytical results on the Khirokitia and *Tenta* material suggest that the causes of high infant mortality during the Aceramic Neolithic were biological in nature, we should be careful not to polarize biological and cultural factors into discrete, non-negotiating spheres of influence. Ethnographic evidence of traditional societies has found that in many cultures infanticide is a benign rather than a deliberate practice, with weaker offspring or offspring of one or both sexes becoming increasingly ill and eventually dying from parental neglect (Keesing and Strathern 1998:123). In these contexts, infanticide can be viewed as a mechanism for regulating reproductive processes, restricting population growth, and maintaining ecological balance. It is possible, therefore, that cultural beliefs and practices played some sort of role in the high incidence of infant deaths at Khirokitia and other early sites on the island, particularly if it can be proved that the anemia was due to iron deficiency rather than genetic dysfunction.

Arguments for the construction of infancy as a discrete social category at Khirokitia can be inferred from evidence of mortuary rituals associated with various age-grades of sub-adults. The concentration of infant burials in certain structures (e.g., tholos XLVII had twenty-five infants and four adults), the burial of five infant skulls without post-cranial remains, and the fact that 75 percent of burials from Dikaios's excavations were found without pit association are indications that infants, particularly very young infants, were regarded as a distinct social group and were thus accorded separate mortuary rites (see Niklasson 1991:ch. 2, esp. pp. 58–60 for further details).

Unfortunately, mortuary evidence from other contemporary Neolithic sites is not sufficient to provide comparisons with patterns observed at Khirokitia. Excavations at several Chalcolithic sites in the Paphos district, however, have yielded human skeletal material in sufficient quantities for comparison with Khirokitia. In general, the evidence suggests equally high rates of infant mortality during the fourth and third millennia B.C., but fewer perinatal deaths. At Lemba, for example, over 60 percent of all burials were of infants and children, but only one of the thirty-one total child burials (c. 3 percent) was possibly a perinatal infant (Grave 31, burial of an infant 0–3 months of age; see Peltenburg et al. 1985:tab. 148). At Kissonerga, children represent about 63 percent of the mortuary population, but published data are not sensitive enough to indicate how many deceased infants were of perinatal age (see Peltenburg et al. 1998:tabs. 4.3–4.4). Age data provided in the final report group together infants and young children from birth to 2.9 years, but the fact that this group accounts for only 28.6 percent of the total means that proportions of deceased infants of perinatal age must have been relatively low.

The evidence from Kissonerga also points to significant changes in attitudes toward infants and children during the Chalcolithic period itself. Despite the small number of specimens in the Period 3 (MChal) sample at Kissonerga, statistical tests showed significant differences between the Period 3 and 4 groups (Peltenburg et al. 1998:75). Statistics on age distribution according to period show that the proportion of infants/young children (i.e., between 0 and 2.9 years) decreased from 66.7 percent in Period 3 (MChal) to 17.9 percent during Period 4 (LChal) (Peltenburg et al. 1998:tab. 4.3).

Age distributions for Period 4 suggest the introduction of a complete age structure at the site. Peltenburg has attributed these changes to an under-representation of adults in the Period 3 mortuary record and has proposed the existence of separate adult cemeteries during the MChal, either in extra-mural cemeteries that have not yet been located, or in remote regional cemeteries such as Souskiou-*Vathyrkakas*, 20 km east of Kissonerga, where the ratio of adults to children found in burial contexts was 4:1 (Peltenburg et al. 1998:ch. 4). Either way, the evidence of mortuary ritual during the Chalcolithic period signifies profound changes in social attitudes toward infants and children during the first half of the third millennium B.C., as well as toward changes in the reproduction of social relations between adults and children.

While more evidence is clearly needed to explain changing patterns of infant mortality in prehistoric Cyprus, the fact that these patterns change rather dramatically between various periods and phases of prehistory, and vary even within the confines of a single site, makes it likely that cultural factors played an important role, even in cases where biological factors may be judged to have been the immediate cause of death. Social attitudes toward infants and children may have been more sharply differentiated in the past than today, and studies attempting to "write children into the archaeological record" of Cyprus should therefore be sensitive to cultural divisions within the monolithic categories of "child" and "infant."

Identifying Children in Chalcolithic Mortuary Rituals

Substantial evidence for mortuary ritual during the Chalcolithic period occurs at several sites in the west of the island, largely as a result of the work by the Lemba Archaeological Project. Excavations at other Chalcolithic sites, such as Erimi-*Pamboula* (Bolger 1988; Dikaios 1936) and Kalavasos-*Ayious* (Todd 1991), have yielded little in the way of funerary remains, so our knowledge of mortuary ritual during the mid-fourth and mid-third millennium B.C. is restricted almost entirely to the Paphos district. Although excavation and study of material from the Souskiou sites are still in progress, evidence from Lemba and Kissonerga was extensive enough to assume that the burials are representative of a presumed population (Niklasson 1991:237).

At Lemba, fifty-nine graves were excavated within the boundaries of an important Chalcolithic settlement (Peltenburg et al. 1985). Graves were simple pit-type inhumations, the vast majority (c. 65 percent) comprising burials of infants and children (see figs. 5.1 and 6.2); multiple inhumations were rare, accounting for only three (5 percent) of the total graves at the site. Interesting patterns emerge when we look at differences in the treatment of children in burials of MChal and LChal dates. These involve differences in structural features of the burials as well as in the nature and number of grave goods accompanying the dead.

In an extensive review of the mortuary material from Lemba, Niklasson isolated what she termed "special features" in a number of the graves (Niklasson 1991:130–33). These included the construction of ridges in havara and pisé around the rims of several pits (Graves 31, 32, 34); rings of stones around pit rims (Graves 29, 50); double pits (Graves 4, 5); a circular extension for a skull (Grave 45); tubular apertures within graves interpreted as libation holes (Graves 12, 13, 15); linked networks of pit graves (Graves 12–15, 20); and capstones (graves 48, 50). Although it was not possible to assign relative dates to all of the Lemba graves due to limited stratigraphical evidence and lack of sufficient pottery, some graves could be attributed to Period 1 (MChal) and others to Period 3 (LChal). The important pattern that emerges with these special features is their exclusive association with infants and children during the MChal and their exclusive association with adults during the LChal.

Grave goods show similar patterns. Infants and children were frequently accompanied by querns, pottery, necklaces, and pendants during the MChal, but not in LChal contexts. Examples include querns discovered in burials of an adolescent (Grave 18) and

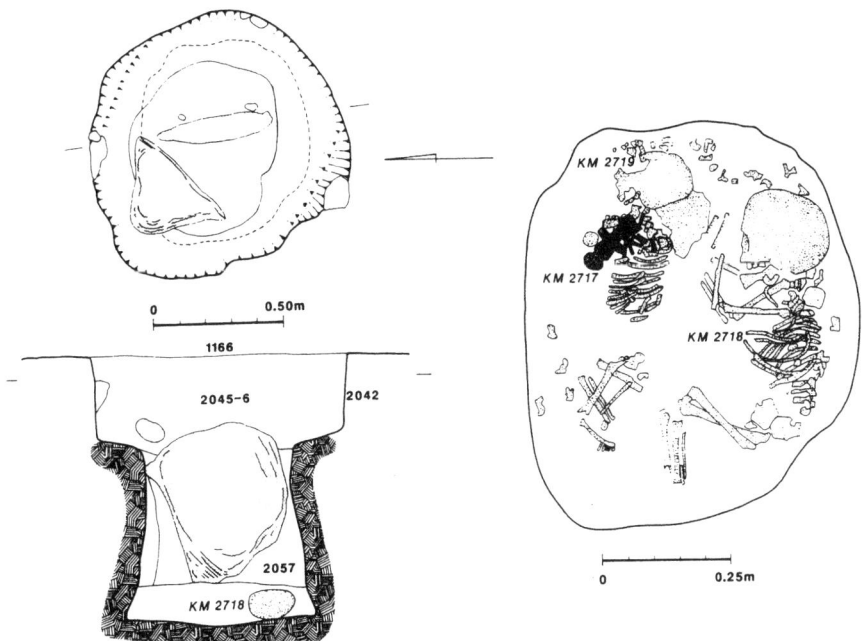

Figure 5.1.   Plan of child burial in grave 563 at Kissonerga (after Peltenburg et al. 1998:fig. 57).

a child (Grave 38); the ceramics associated with this grave indicated that the latter belonged to the MChal. In addition, a dentalium shell necklace was recovered from infant burial Grave 47, and picrolite pendants were found in several child burials (Graves 21, 44, 46). The only grave at Lemba to contain a cruciform figure (Grave 20) formed part of the children's burial complex under Building 2. Stratigraphic evidence places this burial complex within the MChal, or, at the very latest, the earliest LChal. Grave goods in child burials disappear during the LChal at Lemba (Lemba Period 3), and adult burials do not appear to have been furnished with grave goods during either period. Differential treatment of adults and children in MChal–LChal contexts occurs at Kissonerga as well, although in a somewhat different manner (see Peltenburg et al. 1998:ch. 4 for a full report on the mortuary evidence). One of the most remarkable features of the Kissonerga mortuary population is the low proportion of adult burials at the site during the MChal (tab. 5.1). Burials are almost exclusively of infants, children, and adolescents; adults, who occur rarely in Kissonerga burials, may have been inhumed in remote cemeteries such as Souskiou where greater proportions of adults are attested. This trend reverses itself during the LChal with a return to a complete age structure in the burial population, a development regarded by Peltenburg as a "major ideological shift" between MChal and LChal Kissonerga (Peltenburg et al. 1998:84).

Table 5.1.   Burial Evidence from Lemba and Kissonerga

Burial Record	Lemba	Kissonerga
Total Graves & Tombs	59	73
Total with Human Bone Analyzed	48	60
Total Graves with Single Inhumations	55	51
Total with Human Bone Analyzed	45	51
A) Single Adult	19	19
B) Single Child	26	32
Total Graves with Multiple Inhumations	3	9
Total with Human Bone Analyzed	3	9
A) Adult Males		1
B) Adult Females		2
C) Multiple Children	1	2
D) Adult Male + Adult Female		
E) Adult Male + Infant/Child	1	
F) Adult Female + Infant/Child	1	2
G) Adult Male/Female + Infant/Children		2
Total Chamber Tombs	0	13
Chamber Tombs with Multiple Inhumations	0	7

Another innovation at LChal Kissonerga is the appearance of chamber tombs, which may have been introduced to accommodate adult and family burials (see fig. 6.4). With regard to grave goods, child burials during MChal are rich in picrolites and other grave goods, but in LChal children's grave architecture declines, as do the frequency and quality of grave goods; the only exceptions are instances where children are buried together with adults in chamber tombs. These and other related phenomena signify a fundamental shift in attitudes toward adults and children within society as a whole and suggest closer ties within kinship groups during the first half of the third millennium B.C. Strong bonds of kinship during the LChal are further attested by the introduction of unprecedented mortuary features such as the tube-like apertures in the children's burial complex below Building 2 at Lemba, which were apparently used to facilitate contact between the living and the dead (Peltenburg et al. 1985:116–18). These tubular shafts may have been used as libation holes as part of recurring funerary rituals. The demonstration and reinforcement of social bonds between family members is paralleled at Kissonerga, where the deceased were sometimes buried inside ruined buildings or at the edges of their walls and may have had prior residential connections with them (Peltenburg et al. 1998:ch. 4). One of the buildings (B375), in fact, has been termed a "mortuary enclosure" by the excavator as it contained no less than six interment facilities within an area of about eight square meters (Peltenburg et al. 1998:88–89). These and other similar burial patterns furnish us with explicit "maps" of social relations in which the association of graves with houses may symbolize hereditary rights to land and other resources.

Perhaps the most significant development suggested by the changes in funerary practices during the LChal at Lemba and Kissonerga is the transformation of kinship structures. In ethnographic accounts of preindustrial societies, a major distinction is drawn between kindreds and lineages; while kindreds are associated with nomadic or semi-nomadic hunter-gatherers and horticultural groups, the emergence of lineages ascribed to infrastructural changes are associated with increasing levels of sedentism, agricultural intensification, and social complexity. The principal structural feature of kindreds is the unrestricted span and depth of bilateral reckoning due to the lack of a uniform principle for limiting the extension of the kinship circle (fig. 5.2). Similarly, there is no possibility for large-scale social segmentation, as only ego's siblings have same relationship to kindred as ego. This kinship structure is normally found in societies that are not agriculturally based and where corporate ownership of or rights to land are not central to economic production. Egalitarian societies, in which there is little social hierarchy and minimal ownership of property or wealth, most frequently fall into this category. Divisions within the social structure of egalitarian groups normally occur along lines of age and or gender, such as age sets and the sexual division of labor. Equally characteristic of kindreds are communal rites of passage, such as those in celebration of birth, marriage, or death, which help promote and maintain group identity and cohesion.

Lineages, in contrast, are groups related vertically by descent from a common ancestor (fig. 5.3). In patrilineages and matrilineages, membership in a kinship group is reckoned along a single line of descent, either paternal or maternal. Here, the cultural restrictions used to define "kin" lead to group segmentation (lineages and sub-lineages),

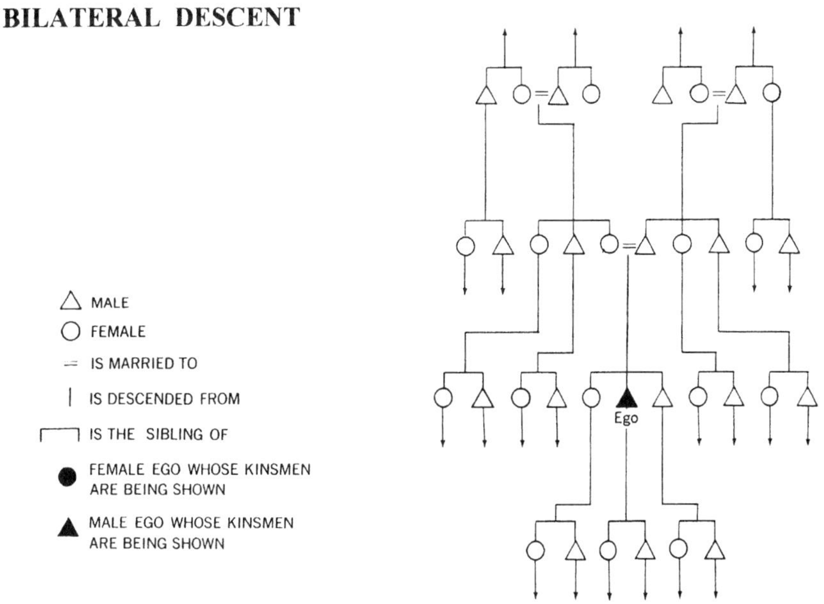

BILATERAL DESCENT

Figure 5.2.   Diagram of bilateral descent (after Harris 1971).

potentially posing threats to group integrity. Incipient divisions within society are to some degree resolved by affinities, or marriage links, which are important for creating economic and social bonds and for maintaining group cohesion. Marriage thus takes on new functional importance as the far-ranging networks of social relations characteristic of kindreds is replaced as an organizing principle by smaller, domestically differentiated groups or "nuclear families" consisting of husbands, wives, and children.

The emergence of lineages in Cyprus is strongly suggested by major developments in mortuary ritual during the third millennium B.C.: the gradual phasing out of single inhumations and burials according to age sets (represented by multiple child burials), the appearance of chamber tombs; the advent of communal burials of mixed ages and sexes, a decline in attention paid to children in mortuary rituals, and the transformations of birthing symbolism within life-cycle rituals. The most dramatic example of the latter is the disappearance during the LChal of birthing figurines in clay and stone, objects widely attested during the MChal. Not until the EBA, over half a millennium later, did the *koutrophouros* ("child bearer") reappear as a theme in representational art. In the following sections, we shall consider the impact these changes may have had on children's social roles during the Bronze Age.

Gender Identity in the Early–Middle Bronze Ages

We return now to the scenic compositions, discussed in chapter 4, which form the subject of a recent article by Ribeiro on gender ambiguity in Cyprus during the EBA and MBA (Ribeiro 2002). Ribeiro cautions against adopting simple binary oppositions in interpreting these scenes and regards the absence of sexual characteristics on many of the figures as deliberate rather than fortuitous acts that may be correlated to non-binary

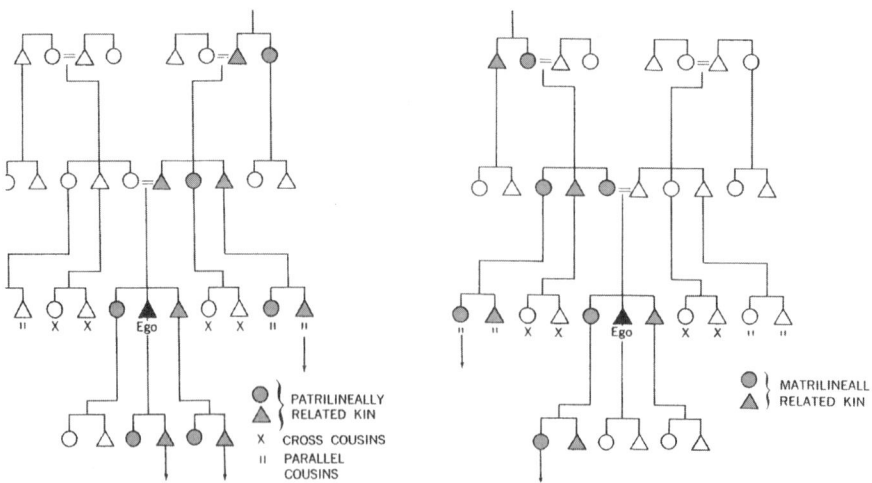

Figure 5.3.   Diagram of unilineal descent (after Harris 1971).

gender constructs. Human figures lacking sexual traits, she argues, should not be attributed to the binary sex categories "male" or "female" but were possibly intended to portray physically immature, prepubescent children who thus constitute a third sex and separate gender grouping.

This proposal merits further consideration. Let us first consider the evidence of the vessel compositions used to interpret sexless figures as prepubescent children. The fragility of the forms on these scenes, projecting as they do away from the vessel surface, makes them particularly prone to damage and wear (e.g., fig. 5.4). Even in cases where the vessel appears to be relatively well preserved, it is impossible to be certain that no damage has occurred. Small bits of clay, for example, representing anatomical features like breasts or penises, may easily have broken off or eroded from the figures, either as post-depositional wear or as the result of excavation. This may account for the high proportions of "sexless" figures in these scenes. To determine actual numbers with greater accuracy, the objects would have to be examined at close range with the aid of a high-powered lens, and, as we saw in chapter 4, few studies of Cypriot figurines have done so. Reliance on photographs, descriptions by others, and even personal observation through a museum case are limited in the kind of evidence they can provide.

Secondly, and perhaps more fundamentally, we must question whether it is sufficient to distinguish and define a sub-adult age set or "third gender" on the basis of missing secondary sex characteristics. Evidence other than anatomy (i.e. jewelry, headbands, costume, tattoos, etc.) could be taken into consideration as possible signifiers of gender.

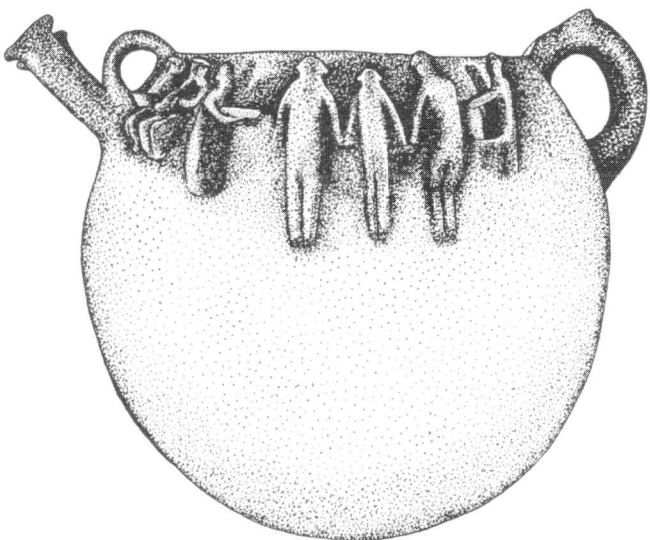

Figure 5.4.   Scenic composition with "sexless" figures from the Hadjiprodromou collection in Cyprus (after Morris 1985:fig. 491).

Moreover, if sexless figures are deliberately meant to be children or adolescents, why were they made at adult size? And why was Bronze Age society apparently so concerned with their portrayal? Ribeiro's suggestion (2002:207) that prepubescent individuals represent "the next generation of the ruling elite" offers one possible explanation, but we need to question the degree to which economic hierarchy and social rank characterized social organization in Cyprus before the LBA. Further examination of the evidence in lights of advances in social complexity during the EBA and MBA might offer additional clues concerning the role of children and adolescents in the definition of hierarchical social systems. Some of the ethnographic parallels cited in Ribeiro's article are interesting and compelling, especially the concept of prepubescent childhood as a gender-neutral period among traditional pre-state cultures, which she cites as a possible explanation for the lack of anatomical features on many of the figures in the scenes. Still, her model remains highly speculative and might gain more credence if it could be based more firmly on archaeological evidence rather than primarily on ethnographic parallels. A more detailed investigation along these lines would certainly be worthwhile.

Let us assume for the sake of the present discussion, however, that Ribeiro is correct in thinking that some of the figures on these vessels represent adolescents. What would their presence in these scenes tell us about the role of sub-adults in the daily life of the EBA and MBA? For example, what role(s) might they have played in economic production? What other kinds of work might they have pursued, and would they have carried out those activities independently or in a more ancillary fashion as members of kinship groups, household groups, or age sets? In what contexts, in other words, is child labor likely to have been situated, and to what extent would patterns of sub-adult labor have corresponded to the gendered division of labor suggested by some of the scenes on these vessels? As Ribeiro herself has not explored these aspects of the evidence, it is useful to look more closely at the details on some of the better-preserved scenes. The state of preservation of the compositions is crucial to this discussion, since the sex of abraded or damaged figures may not be clear.

Table 5.2 shows distributions according to sex of figures on six scenic compositions (biological males have been determined by the presence of a penis and females by the presence of prominent breasts). For purposes of this discussion, the sexless figures included in this table are assumed to represent prepubescent children. Columns indicate males working alone, females working alone, females in groups, sexless figures alone and in groups, male/female couples, sexless couples, and figures with infants. Several interesting patterns emerge when work activities are correlated with age sets and gender groups. Adult males, for example, appear always to work independently. Only in one instance, the Marki bowl, does a male appear jointly with another figure: this is a male seated next to a female. Apart from that single instance, male activities are not group oriented. While adult females may work independently, they also engage in joint activities with other women in tasks such as washing laundry, making bread, or shaping pottery vessels.

Table 5.2. Indications of Age and Sex on Figures in Red Polished Scenic Compositions (grp=group; cpl=couple; inf=infant)

	Male	Female	Fem Grp	Sexless	Sexless Grp	M/F Cpl	Sexless Cpl	Fem/Inf	Sexless/Inf
Kalavasos Bowl	1	1	1	2			1		
Oxford Bowl	3			6	1				1
Marki Bowl				3	2		1		
Pierides Bowl		2		2	1	2			
Hadjiprodromou Bowl				3	1		2		
Sevres Jar	2	2	1					1	
Washing Scene		2		4				1	

Figures with clear indications of sex (the presence of penis, breasts, etc.) comprise only a minority of the elements in these compositions. By far the majority of figures lack indications of sex and, according to Ribeiro, can be regarded as prepubescent children. If her hypothesis is correct and these figures are meant to represent adolescents, the latter would appear to contribute more than adults to the economic activities being depicted. On the six scenes include in this analysis, figures without sexual demarcation appear twenty-one times: sixteen times as individuals and five times in "peer" groups. By comparison, males appear only six times and females only seven times.

Activities of the "sexless figures" follow the female work pattern: sometimes they work alone, and other times they work in groups. From the full repertoire of scenic compositions, only one clear example exists of a sexless figure associated with a group of adults. This is the so-called Washing Scene (Morris 1985:fig. 502) in which two women and three sexless figures stand in front of a washbasin. They are accompanied by a third woman, who is holding an infant, and a small figure standing on the rim of the basin, also unsexed and probably a child. The headgear and necklaces on the three unsexed figures are identical to those of the women, so only the lack of explicit sexual features (i.e., breasts) sets them apart. The close association in this scene between women and children suggests that they worked together in groups to perform certain domestic tasks. It may be significant, moreover, that there are no known examples of children associated with males on any of the compositions.

Within the entire known repertoire of scenic compositions, sexless figures appear in the following constellations: associated with a bowl or basin (the Kalavasos bowl); seated next to a spout, standing next to conical lumps, an oven, and a pestle and mortar (the Oxford bowl); seated on a bench and wearing turbans, facing a bowl, seated on a pack animal, facing an oven, and stretching toward a bull (the Marki bowl). While some of the activities are difficult to interpret, the wide range of contexts in which sexless figures appear suggests that adolescents were engaged in many aspects of domestic production and thus should not be regarded as ancillary laborers. This view would accord well with ethnographic accounts of preindustrial societies in which the labor of children, especially adolescents, contributes significantly to economic production. As stated earlier, however, more careful scrutiny is needed in the study of the evidence, and the latter must be examined first hand rather than through drawings and photographs before we can argue confidently that anthropomorphic figures that appear superficially to be sexless do not, in fact, exhibit any sexual traits. Such rigorous, detailed analysis has been seldom undertaken for the Cypriot anthropomorhic material.

Research by Goring provides additional criteria for investigating the possible representation of sexless figures and hence a "third gender" category for the MChal (Goring 1991a). Nineteen figurines were found in the Kissonerga deposit, nine made of pottery and ten of several types of stone. Secondary sexual attributes are indicated on all of pottery figurines but on only one clear example of the stone figurines. On the one hand, Goring attributes this to the material differences of stone and clay (i.e., the greater difficulty of depicting physical features in stone). But she also argues that the use of the pottery figurines as demonstration pieces in puberty rituals, as indicated by wear marks, would demand that they exhibit a greater degree of realism in the portrayal of the human form. While the pottery figurines are "anatomically correct" and detailed, the stone figurines are more abstract and schematic. The latter may have been rubbed or clutched as fetishes, perhaps during childbirth itself to ensure a successful birth and thus required no great degree of anatomical detail.

Given the fact that one of the stone figurines in the Kissonerga deposit was rendered in greater detail and that several stone figurines from other sites contain clear renditions of adult anatomy, we must also consider the possibility that the schematic stone examples were not intended to represent adults, but children. While none of the stone figurines in the Kissonerga deposit is self-supporting, Goring describes the single stone example rendered in anatomical detail, KM 1471 (Peltenburg et al. 1991:fig. 21) as "the only stone figurine unambiguously shown standing," and that "it makes better visual sense upright than recumbent" (Goring 1991a:41). She then compares this figurine to the well-known "Lemba lady," a large limestone figurine of an adult female (fig. 4.4). As adults are normally depicted upright and standing and children recumbent, the stone figurines, which are highly schematic and not self-supporting, may represent children, while more detailed examples, such as KM 1471, may represent adults. As on the scenic compositions of the Bronze Age, children of the Chalcolithic period may not have been attributed to one or another class within a binary system of gender categories but to a third gender group. This hypothesis remains highly speculative, however, and needs to be supported by further evidence.

If we move from the limited evidence of the Kissonerga deposit to a more general consideration of the entire repertoire of Chalcolithic anthropomorphic representations, there is very little unambiguous evidence for the portrayal of sub-adults prior to the Bronze Age. Some of the picrolite pendants, which as we saw in chapter 4 are closely associated with children in many Chalcolithic burials, may represent children, but apart from their seated posture, which replicates that of the birthing figures from the Kissonerga deposit, they provide very little relevant information; they are simply too small and schematic to provide sufficient detail. In fact, there is only a single unambiguous portrayal of a sub-adult prior to the Bronze Age: the painted image of an infant emerging from legs of a RW birthing figure (KM 1451), and we know that it is an infant from its orientation and position on the female figure, not from the schematic form of the image itself. Overall, there appears to be very little intrinsic interest in children per se during the Chalcolithic period. Apart from their frequent occurrence in mortuary contexts, children remain archaeologically invisible. This situation is likely to have changed, however, as children took on more clearly defined roles within emerging kinship groups.

Consequently, we should expect to see more evidence of children in pictorial represen-tation during the Bronze Age, and indeed we do.

Shaping Identity in the Late Bronze Age

In this section, I will consider skeletal evidence from a number of prehistoric sites in Cyprus in order to investigate the practice of cranial deformation. While artificial cra-nial deformation (ACD), or head shaping as it is sometimes called, is well attested to in the Neolithic and Bronze Age periods, its use in the Chalcolithic is uncertain. Evidence for the practice comes from scientific study of prehistoric Cypriot crania, mostly of adults as those of infants and children tend to be poorly preserved. However, it can be assumed that the practice was carried out during infancy when the skull was soft and malleable, and it is thus relevant to a discussion of children. The earliest known instance of ACD has been identified on the skull of an adult male from a Cypro-PPNB well at *Mylouthkia* (Peltenburg et al. 2000), but it was observed on many crania studied by An-gel from Khirokitia (Angel 1953, 1961), by Hjortsjö at LNeo Karavas and EB *Vounous* (1947), and by Domurad (1986), Fischer (1983), Fürst (1933), Schulte-Campbell (1983)), Schwartz (1974), and others at LBA sites of Akhera, Pendayia, Lapithos, Ayios Iakovos, Chrysopolitissa, Enkomi, Kition, Hala Sultan Tekke, Kalavasos, and Kourion.

Three basic types of ACD have been observed in these studies: (1) occipital flat-tening; (2) plagiocephaly; and (3) postbregmatic flattening. The first type, occipital flattening, shortens and widens the cranium through pressure applied to the rear of the skull. It is very likely to have been the result of cradle boarding or consistently laying swaddled children on their backs to sleep. Cradle boarding is widely attested to in the ethnographic literature and appears as a frequent theme in the coroplastic art of the EC–MC (fig. 4.5). The infants cradled in these figures are often described as having "bands" on their heads, as if cranial deformation had been achieved delib-erately, but if we look closely they look more like "caps" than "bands"; many have no such caps, and, in any case, bandages applied by wrapping around the skull would have produced a very different effect.

As stated earlier, occipital flattening has been recorded at many prehistoric sites, in-cluding nineteen skulls at Khirokitia, and at least one instance each at Cape Andreas, *Tenta, Mylouthkia*, Karavas, and *Vounous.*; in addition, clear evidence of head shaping has re-cently been observed by Kirsi Lorentz on a skull from Marki (Frankel and Webb, per-sonal communication). The actual numbers were no doubt higher, but crania must be well preserved in order to assess deformity.

Other than the single example from Karavas, occipital flattening does not appar-ently occur during the LNeo (e.g., Sotira skulls are normal), nor has it been reported from sites of Chalcolithic date (Lemba, Kissonerga, Erimi). It does occur during the Bronze Age, at EC sites such as *Vounous* (Angel determined this from photos), and during the LBA along with other types of ACD, suggesting that the practice of cradle boarding was a long-lived tradition on the island. As we shall see in chapter 6, however, there is no clear evidence to suggest that occipital flattening was either applied deliberately as a marker of social status or that it was differentially applied to males and females.

The second type of ACD, plagiocephaly (from *plagios* = oblique, asymmetrical), involves the flattening of one side of the skull, resulting in a slight to pronounced bulging of the opposite side (fig. 5.5). This type of ACD has been reported on the Karavas skull (Hjortsjö 1947), where it apparently occurs in tandem with occipital flattening. Plagiocephaly becomes much more common during the LBA, however, being represented for example on all skulls (twenty-two total) studied by Schwartz from Kition and Hala Sultan Tekke (Schwartz 1974). Hjortsjö (1947) reported plagiocephaly on eight of ten skulls studied from Enkomi; of these, six are what he called "crossed-plagiocephaly," in which infants were bound differentially on both sides rather than consistently on one side. Like occipital flattening, plagiocephaly is likely to have resulted from cradle boarding if the child rested more frequently on one side, or, as suggested by Schwartz, on the stomach with the head to one side. Plagiocephaly in modern infants is commonly attributed to positional preference during sleep and is thus unintentional; in many cases, when a child begins to walk, the effects of plagiocephaly are reversed due to the ability of bones to remodel themselves (Lorentz 1998:app. 12).

The third type of ACD, post-bregmatic flattening, results from pressure applied to the vertex posterior to bregma (*bregma* = craniometric point on top of skull where the coronal and sagittal sutures intersect). This type of deformation can only be brought about intentionally, and was probably achieved by means of a padded board held in place with a bandage (fig. 5.5). Pressure applied in this way affects the obelion arch of the parietals and slightly widens and lengthens the head. With one possible exception (a male skull from Erimi), post-bregmatic deformation has been reported only from sites of the LBA, and there among varying proportions of the population. For example, it has been reported on eleven of forty-four skulls (just over 30 percent) at Kourion-Bamboula; nineteen of forty-four skulls (roughly 43 percent) at Enkomi; five of eleven skulls (roughly 45 percent) from Hala Sultan Tekke; and in even greater proportions at other LBA sites such as Pendayia (three of five = 60 percent), Kition (nine of eleven = 82 percent) Akhera (six of six =100 percent). At other sites, it does not appear at all (e.g., Ayios Iakovos near Enkomi, where not a single example was found among the thirty-seven skulls studied).

In sum, post-bregmatic deformation appears to span all phases of the LBA, occurring most frequently in LCII. The only possible exception is a skull from Erimi, first described by Rix in Dikaios' final report on Erimi (Dikaios 1936: 80). Angel, who apparently remeasured the skull sometime later, claimed that the Erimi skull exhibited "extensive obelion flattening," possibly the result of post-bregmatic deformation (Angel

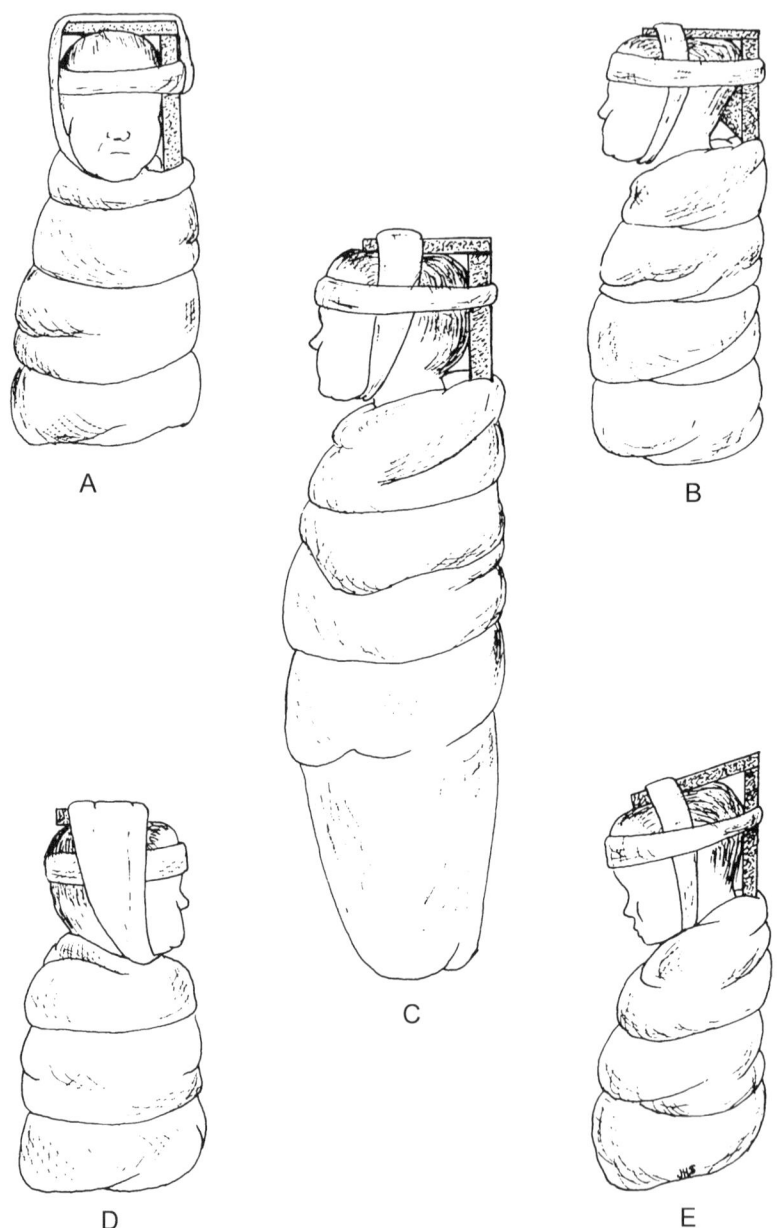

Figure 5.5. Diagram illustrating treatment of infant's skull to produce plagiocephaly, A–B; and post-bregmatic flattening, C–E (after Schwartz 1974:fig. 1).

1972:149). However, the entry for Erimi in Angel's craniometric table published in the final report of Sotira (Angel 1961:tab. 1) specifically states "no deformation" for this skull. Perhaps Angel changed his mind between 1961 and 1972 after considering the Bamboula material with its widespread post-bregmatic deformation.

In any case, the Erimi skull had been badly damaged and required extensive restoration before it could be examined. The most severe damage occurred on the vertex, precisely the area of interest here, and a place where even slight misalignments in reconstruction can throw off actual measurements by substantial proportions. The Erimi skull ought actually to be reexamined, for if it truly provides evidence of post-bregmatic flattening, we might be forced to agree with Angel's original conclusion, based on this evidence alone, that this type of ACD originated in the fourth millennium B.C. For the time being, however, this argument is far from certain, and it seems more likely that post-bregmatic deformation was initiated at a much later date, during the LBA.

Post-bregmatic head shaping occurs differentially not only between sites but also among populations at a single site. In Fürst's collection from Enkomi, for example, the practice was almost universal in some tombs—nine out of ten in Grave 6, for example; it appears sporadically in others and is entirely absent elsewhere (Graves 3, 17). Angel, too, observed what he termed "striking differences" in local practices, with skulls at Enkomi more severely deformed than those at Kourion. Moreover, at both of these sites deformation is absent from some tombs and almost universal in others, suggesting that family customs played an important role.

It seems, then, that different cultural factors were involved in the practice of ACD during the LBA. While occipital flattening and plagiocephaly were probably functional in origin, post-bregmatic deformation appears to have been purely cosmetic: no "natural" position can produce it, for it requires binding of the skull, and there is no practical reason to bind a child's head to the top of a cradleboard. It thus seems that sometime during the LBA, ACD became a *deliberate* practice. Why was this the case and what does it tell us about the role of children during the Bronze Age?

One possible explanation is that certain social groups adopted the technique for purposes of marking identity and enhancing social status. Ethnographic evidence indicates that deliberate cranial deformation is often related to status, as are other practices involving alterations of the body (such as foot binding in Japan or neck elongation in Burma). The deliberate practice of ACD during this time might be considered what Shilling has termed "physical capital" in which the body itself becomes an endowed entity and integral to the process by which class relations are reproduced (Shilling 1993) and thus may have served as a means by which emergent elites attempted to distinguish themselves as discrete corporate entities by physically dissociating themselves from other social groups.

Viewed within a context of advancing social hierarchy, the deliberate practice of cranial deformation at this time becomes significant, not only because it provides yet another means by which elite status may have been attained but because of the implications it has for children within those elite groups. By deliberately shaping the skulls of young infants, elite groups marked their newest constituents with a particular identity, one that made manifest their membership in the group and one they would carry with them into adulthood as a permanent emblem of their elite status. Although children presumably had no choice in the matter, and thus played rather passive roles in shaping their own identities in this regard, from the perspective of changing social constructions of childhood, it is significant that infants and children were now recognized by adults as valuable members of their constituent groups, worthy of bearing physical insignia of collective identity. Investigation of other aspects of mortuary ritual during the LBA might reveal the degree to which ACD was correlated with other aspects of mortuary ritual, including the number and richness of associated grave goods.

The mortuary record of LBA Cyprus shows sharp status distinctions, especially in the size and wealth of grave good assemblages; this was particularly the case from LCII onward (see ch. 6). This phenomenon has been strikingly illustrated at recent excavations at Kalavasos-*Ayios Dhimitrios*, where a number of high-status burials of adults and children of LCII date have been found in close proximity to burials of lesser status (South 1997).

Another example is Tomb 9 at Kition, a chamber tomb that yielded quantities of imported Mycenaean pottery and in which eleven adult females were found with post-bregmatic deformation (Karageorghis 1974). These developments can be seen to coincide with the special treatment of children in mortuary contexts and the adoption of differential burial programs for non-adults. In some instances, children were interred separately from adults, either in discrete chamber tombs, in pots, or, in the case of small children and infants, in niches specially cut into the walls of *dromoi* (Keswani 1989; Lorentz 1998). To judge from the accompanying grave goods, the children in these burials were members of elite groups; Tomb 12 at Kalavasos, which contained the remains of three infants and a five–six-year-old child along with pottery, gold jewelry, and a Hittite silver figurine, is an important case in point (South 1997:pl. XV:I). Non-elite children, like non-elite women, are archaeologically invisible at this time. This and other evidence points to important ideological links between the social construction of the child and the emergence of powerful economic groups during the LBA; further study along these lines be of fundamental importance for understanding and acknowledging the contribution made by children, both in life and in death, to the legitimizing strategies of incipient ruling classes.

Visions of Childhood in Ancient Cyprus

Most archaeological reconstructions of the past are faceless landscapes, detailed images of houses without households, tools without toolmakers, pots without potters. In chapter 1, however, I discussed an exception to this rule: a brochure advertising the excavations at Almyras, a copper manufacturing site of the Archaic, Classical, and Hellenistic periods in Cyprus, which provides a unique glimpse of one archaeologist's view of the past (fig. I.I). As we saw in that chapter, the cover illustration depicts men, women, and children busy at work in the production of copper. The following is an excerpt from the accompanying text:

> In order to remove the sulphur from the pyrites, it was necessary to roast the ore before it could be smelted. . . . The ores were placed on a bed of wood or charcoal, the fire was kept alive by the natural prevailing winds. . . . The roasted ore was then transferred to the smelting furnaces. . . . In order to obtain the necessary temperature of around 1200 degrees centigrade to reduce the ores and form liquid metal and slag, air had to be forced into the furnace by means of a bellow and blow pipes. . . . The site of Ayia Varvara may therefore provide us with information on the copper production and trade within the political and social structure of the Kingdoms in the first millennium B.C. of Cyprus.

Without the reconstructed drawing that appears on the cover, this brochure would present yet another depersonalized account of the activities involved in the production of copper without explicit reference to age or gender. The addition of the illustration, however, offers an insight into the excavator's view of the division of labor in metallurgical production during the Iron Age. Women and children are depicted as assistants in this activity, which is presumably managed by the males working at the furnaces. In the foreground, a woman and four children are shown collecting and preparing fuel to roast the ore. They are drawn in stationary positions, seated near the fuel in all but one instance where a child stands holding a basket of fuel. In contrast, the two men in the hinterground are shown actively engaged smelting and roasting the copper ore. Both men are standing; while one tends the flames of the roasting fires, the other dumps roasted ore into a cylindrical smelting furnace. The assumptions regarding the roles of men, women, and children are obvious in this picture. Men's activities involve primary production of copper, while women and children are relegated to the status of helpers. Men are active, in motion; women and children are inactive, still. Only men engage in pyrotechnics and thus, given the widely acknowledged contribution of copper production to the ancient Cypriot economy, are given primary credit in this important enterprise. According to this image, the roles of women and children were considerably less crucial. Although this may very well have been the case, it needs to be demonstrated rather than simply assumed.

Similar portrayals of women's and children's roles have been observed in the archaeological literature of northern Europe (Hurcombe 1997). In an article investigating the role of children in the flint-knapping industry, Finlay describes reconstruction drawings of flint knapping at the Late Glacial site of Trollesgave in Denmark that interpret flint production as the product of a skilled master and child apprentice (Finlay 1997:207–208). The apprentice is described by the excavator as a "small boy training under the guidance of a skilled knapper," and the reconstruction drawing accompanying the text shows the adult male flint knapper in the company of his wife (shown scraping hides) and children (playing with spears). In a similar vein, although as a text-only reconstruction, excavators at Pincevent give flint knappers imaginary names, all of them male (Finlay 1997:208). Such imaginative scenarios make manifest the underlying male-centered agendas of many archaeological interpretations and offer little solid evidence for the actual division of labor among men, women, and children in cultures of the remote past.

Just as androcentric narratives of the past have tended to underplay the role of women in the workplace, they have also undervalued the economic roles of children, who remain truly invisible in archaeological accounts of the past. Gero (1991) explored the androcentric bias inherent in the characterization and interpretation of prehistoric stone tool industries and considered several potential constraints on tool production and their implications for gender that could be equally applied to older children. The constraints include (1) scheduling—children have amply free time and could have learned from adults; tool production could have taken place in domestic environments; (2) access to raw materials—in Cyprus, most materials are locally available, so they could have been obtained by children who were taught to recognize the necessary types of stone; (3) physical strength—along with coordination, a lack of sufficient physical strength would have excluded young children from chipping or grinding stone tools, but older children would not have had a problem.

In conclusion, there are no theoretical grounds for excluding children from lithic activities in prehistoric Cyprus. While it is fairly easy to dismiss arguments against the participation of sub-adults in stone tool production, however, finding positive proof of their involvement is a much more difficult task. Finlay's discussion of Mesolithic flint-knapping assemblages from Islay in the Hebrides demonstrates the potential of analyzing tool assemblages in terms of skill levels acquired at different stages of the life cycle (Finlay 1997). By examining definitions of childhood, theories of apprenticeship, and ethnographic evidence against the material record of flint assemblages, she has been able to construct a plausible model of flint knapping based on the cumulative acquisition of skills by child apprentices. Application of similar models, which move away from technological and typological analyses per se to more cultural investigations of stone tool production, could help us evaluate the potential roles of children in the economy of ancient Cyprus as well. Such innovative approaches to material culture would also help us to visualize more clearly the people behind the tools, pots, houses, and other artifacts of conventional, and often biased, archaeological reconstructions.

Endings: Gender and Mortuary Ritual   6

> [Funerary custom] is not so much about the dead themselves as the living who buried them.

—PARKER PEARSON, *THE ARCHAEOLOGY OF DEATH AND BURIAL*

MORTUARY EVIDENCE HAS TRADITIONALLY BEEN USED by archaeologists to evaluate the status, identity, and wealth of the deceased, establish differential patterns of grave goods and burial customs among contemporary communities, and trace long-term changes in funerary practices through successive cultural phases. Recent models, however, have begun to shift the emphasis from the identity and status of the dead to an examination of ways in which rituals of death and burial reveal the motives and identities of the living (e.g., Campbell and Green 1995; Downs and Pollard 1999; Parker Pearson 1999; Tarlow 1999). This new way of interpreting mortuary evidence has developed out of the recognition that in many traditional societies, unlike those of the industrial West, death is commonly regarded as a process rather than event. In examining funerary remains from the past, therefore, we not only gain a better understanding of the physical traits and social statuses of individuals but of the cognitive processes, ideological constructs, and political motives of social groups.

Since the study of mortuary evidence can shed light on the beliefs and customs of entire living societies, it must also be capable of exploring the ways in which cultures of the past defined and negotiated gender. In other words, the engendering of funerary evidence not only helps us distinguish and define gendered identities, it allows us to discover underlying patterns of social and political relations between and within various gender groups. An essential ingredient in the attempt to distill gendered meanings from mortuary remains is contextual analysis of mortuary structures, skeletal remains, and associated burial goods, as well as the broader analytical framework of socioeconomic structures. By correlating changes in mortuary practices to advances in socioeconomic complexity in ancient Cyprus, we can begin to appreciate some of the means by which gender identities were redefined and transformed, particularly during the third and second millennia B.C.

Before turning to the evidence for these developments, however, we must acknowledge the difficulty of the task at hand. First, the poorly preserved state of much of the human skeletal material from excavations often makes it difficult to determine the sex of the individuals being studied. The sexing of children's skeletons is particularly problematical in this regard. Second, the process of sexing skeletons is apparently prone to gender bias. Parker Pearson, citing Weiss (1972), has observed that the assignment of biological sex in favor of males may distort relative percentages of males and females in a funerary population by as much as 12 percent (Parker Pearson 1999:96). Third, the poor excavation and recording techniques adopted by most excavators prior to the mid-1900s limit our ability to investigate questions of gender in anything more than the most general fashion. Unfortunately, this applies to excavations of many of the large cemetery sites of the Cypriot Bronze Age where very little skeletal material was analyzed at the time of excavation and much or all was discarded, resulting in the absence of such basic data as the age and sex of the deceased. In addition, many ancient tombs have been subject to intensive looting over the years, so that a great deal of information concerning the island's ancient populations has been irretrievably lost. Finally, we must be critically aware of the many androcentric assumptions that have influenced the interpretation of burial evidence in archaeological reports. The recent challenge to the sexing of the individual in the well-known Iron Age burial at Vix in Burgundy is a case in point (Arnold 1991, 2002). While the presence of elaborate ornaments and lack of sword led initially to the conclusion that the individual must have been female (hence the title "princess of Vix"), the decision was later reversed by several scholars who challenged it on the basis of a second unfounded assumption—that it was highly unlikely that a female of the period could have held such a powerful position in society. Although recent studies of the skeleton seem to have confirmed that the Vix "princess" was, in fact, a female, the thorny process of claim and counterclaim reveals the all-too-prevalent role of essentialist thinking in interpretation of funerary remains.

These difficulties notwithstanding, mortuary evidence provides some of the best data for gender studies since it occurs as the result of deliberate human acts that reveal communal attitudes toward particular members of society. In certain cases, it can also furnish insights into the socioeconomic structures of society as a whole, shedding important light on such phenomena as economic stratification, political hierarchies, and patterns of kinship. For these reasons, then, it furnishes ample scope for the examination of gender constructs, not only with regard to the differential treatment accorded to women and men but also for identifying multiple genders. Numerous cases of nonbinary gender categories in ethnographic accounts of traditional societies serve to emphasize the mutability of gender cross-culturally and demonstrate the limitations of applying binary models to pre-state cultures of the past. Moreover, by tracing diachronic developments in mortuary ritual, we can monitor changes in social attitudes toward death and dying and long-term changes in gender constructs.

I want to begin this chapter, therefore, by discussing some of the principal developments in mortuary ritual in prehistoric Cyprus during the third–second millennia B.C. that shed light on the processes by which gender was negotiated. Emphasis will be placed on sites that have yielded the most substantial, well-documented evidence of funerary remains, but other sites will also be included when they are relevant to particular aspects of the discussion. As the Epipaleolithic remains at the Akrotiri rock shelter left no traces of human burials (see chapter 3), I will begin by looking at evidence of the earliest-known burials on the island dating to the Aceramic Neolithic period.

Gender and Death before the Bronze Age

The earliest-known evidence of human burial in Cyprus has emerged quite recently through the excavation of sites of the Cypro-PPNB (c. 8500–7000 B.C.). While certain burial practices, such as multiple interments, disarticulated skeletons, and secondary depositions, clearly differ from those of the late Aceramic Neolithic, it is hard to gauge their social significance or significance for gender as little skeletal material has been sexed. Unfortunately, since it is still quite new and skeletal material has not yet been sexed, it furnishes little evidence for gender analysis. Mortuary remains from the mainland, at sites such as Jerf el Ahmar (Stordeur 1999), Göbekli Tepe (Schmidt 1999), and Kfar Hahoresh (Goring-Morris et al. 1998) offer intriguing evidence for Near Eastern burial customs at this time, but it is unlikely that they parallel precisely the burial practices on Cyprus, which are likely to have evolved along their own trajectories. For more substantial evidence, we must move to the late Aceramic period, dating from the seventh to mid-sixth millennium B.C.

Gender and Mortuary Remains at Khirokitia

The late phase of the Aceramic Neolithic is best represented at Khirokitia, where its discoverer and first excavator, Porphyrios Dikaios, uncovered over one hundred intramural burials below the floors of the round houses (Dikaios 1953:fig. 6.1). These yielded skeletal remains from sixty-two infants, twelve children, and seventy-four adults (Le Mort 2000:tab. 1); males and females were equally represented among the adult population (Angel 1953). The recent excavations by Le Brun have unearthed more than ninety additional remains and have greatly increased our knowledge of the mortuary population, particularly with regard to the high incidence of infant mortality (Le Mort 2000). The skeletal material is still being analyzed, but preliminary data have been published in several lengthy reports that provide important insights into the mortuary practices at the site (Le Brun 1984, 1989; Le Mort 1994, 2000).

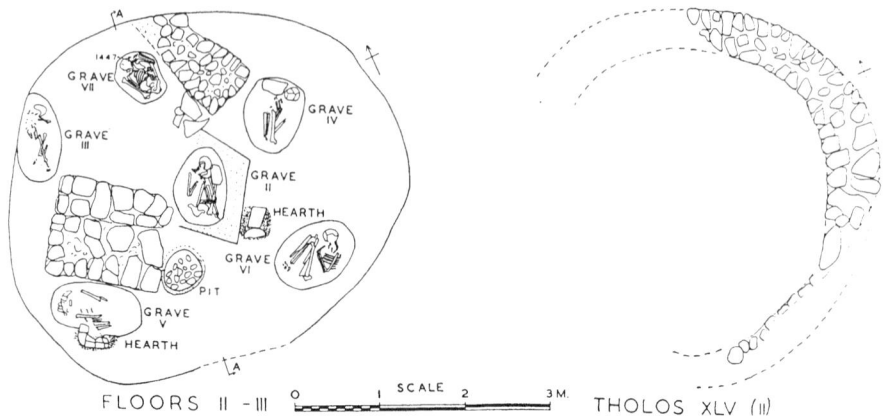

Figure 6.1.   Intramural burials at Khirokitia (after Dikaios 1953:169).

According to a recent publication on the mortuary data from the site, the total burial population at Khirokitia currently numbers 107 adults, 23 children, and 118 infants (Le Mort 2000:tab. 1). All burials are individual primary inhumations; most of these are simple, unmodified pits, but among the more elaborate burials, men and women were equally represented (Le Brun 2002). Le Brun has stressed the relatively egalitarian nature of burial customs at the site with regard to the gender of the deceased but has observed differences with regard to burial position and grave goods associated with males and females. For example, male skeletons were oriented exclusively toward the northeast, while women's were oriented in different directions. Women were buried with items of personal adornment (such as picrolite and carnelian beads on dentalium shell necklaces), and female burials had higher percentages of raw materials and diabase vessels than those of males. Males, in contrast, were more likely to be buried with quernstones.

While some differences exist, however, these are relatively minor in comparison to differences observed in later periods on the island and seem to be outweighed by overall similarities in the construction methods and distribution of the graves, as well as in the numbers and types of associated grave goods. Generally speaking, the evidence points to very low levels of gender differentiation during the Aceramic Neolithic period, but two aspects of the mortuary record provide insights that carry the analysis of gender beyond questions of equality or inequality of individual burials and beyond the differential identities, roles, and statuses of male and female deceased to an understanding of some of the ways in which gender was constructed during the Aceramic Neolithic period. These are the practice of ACD observed on some of the skulls and the occurrence of gender-aligned sequences of burials within discrete groups of superimposed buildings.

Artificial Cranial Deformation: A Gendered Trait?

Cranial deformation, or the deliberating shaping of the human skull in infancy, was widely practiced in all period of Cypriot prehistory (see chapter 5). Its occurrence was noted as early as 1931, with Buxton's study of crania LBA and Iron Age Lapithos (Buxton 1931) and soon thereafter in studies by Fürst (1933) and Hjortsjö (1947). At about the same time, Lawrence Angel, a noted American anatomist, conducted a thorough examination of the skeletal material from Dikaios's excavations at Khirokitia (Angel 1953). One of the most important results of this work was the identification of a particular type of cranial deformation known as occipital deformation, an artificial flattening of the rear of the skull thought to have resulted from contact with cradle boards during infancy, as indicated on many clay images of infants dating to the EBA and MBA (see Morris 1985:148–52).

Angel believed that ACD was more frequently associated with females than males (Angel 1953:416). Of the thirty-eight measurable skulls of known sex (of which twenty-two were adult males and thirteen adult females), only four males (29 percent) exhibited the trait, while seven of the female skulls (54 percent) were artificially deformed. Some scholars have attached great significance to the seemingly higher frequency of occipital flattening on females at this time (Domurad 1986:161; Le Brun 2002), and the issue merits further discussion since it has now come to be regarded as an important mark of gender differentiation.

In the first place, we must acknowledge that we are dealing with only a fraction of the total mortuary population of the site. Angel was able to measure less than a third of skulls from Dikaios's excavations (38 of a total of 123 skulls), owing to the poorly preserved state of much of the skeletal material. Moreover, the task of determining whether or not a skull exhibited traces of ACD rather than deformity due to other circumstances such as post-deposition stress cannot always have been straightforward. This is suggested by Angel's attribution of skulls to various "levels" of deformity (1961:tab. 2) and by his changing statistics on the frequency of ACD occurring at the site, from "a minority" in the original report to "over 50%" in a later study (Angel 1961:229). There is also a discrepancy between the original numbers of males and females with ACD listed in his 1953 report and the information provided in the table accompanying his 1961 report, which shows five adult males and six adult females (i.e., roughly equivalent numbers) with ACD (Niklasson 1991:60–61). Furthermore, if skulls recorded with "trace" levels of ACD are incorporated into these statistics, then the proportion of male skulls exhibiting the trait far outnumbers that of female skulls.

Unfortunately, it is not possible to resolve these discrepancies on the basis of present evidence. Additional study, including a reexamination of skeletal material from Dikaios's excavations and a full report on the sexing and examination of skulls from Le Brun's excavations, is required to determine more accurately the frequency of ACD at the site and to test the hypothesis that it was applied differentially to males and females. If it can be confirmed that women and men exhibited different degrees or frequencies of ACD during the

Neolithic period, we must then try to explain why this was the case and whether it applied in all burial sequences. Differential patterns of cranial deformation might have been associated with different kinship groups, for example, rather than with an across-the-board selection according to gender. Contextual information on the occurrence of ACD could help us to pinpoint the areas (i.e., clusters of buildings or vertical sequences of buildings) in which the highest incidences of ACD occurred and to determine whether the custom was applied with the same degree of frequency during all phases of occupation at the site.

Clearly, there is a need to explore in more detail the physical and cultural causes of ACD during the Neolithic period. Angel suggests that the occipital location of the cranial flattening could indicate the practice of cradle boarding, rather than a deliberate attempt to shape infants' heads for purposes of social distinction. Angel himself posited, somewhat enigmatically, that the differences might be due to differential physical (biological) factors: that male skulls somehow "resisted" deformation more successfully than females, or "recovered" more completely from deformations imposed in infancy, leaving fewer discernible traces on their skulls later in life (Angel 1953:416). However, it is equally likely that cultural factors, such as the cradle boarding of infant girls for longer periods of time than boys, might better account for differential patterns of ACD, if the latter indeed exist. In sum, the practice of ACD at Khirokitia as a gender-related phenomenon is highly questionable on the basis of present evidence, and further analysis is required to comprehend its social significance in Cypriot prehistory.

Burial Sequences as Lineages?

Intriguing evidence for age and gender sets at Khirokitia has emerged from recent studies by the French team working there (Le Brun 2002). Examination of burial sequences within superimposed dwelling units has led to the proposition that burials were made selectively according to sex. In some sequences (such as Dikaios's tholoi V, VIII and in structures 125 and 126), burials were exclusively of adult males; other sequences (such as tholos XV(II) or structures 117 and 122–124) contained only female burials. Does this suggest sexual segregation of living populations as well, or even polygamy, as Le Brun has recently suggested (Le Brun 2002:115)? While no firm answers can be reached on the basis of current published evidence, it seems clear that the mortuary record at Khirokitia, occurring as it does within the context of domestic structures, argues against the existence of nuclear residential groups at the site.

The arrangement of buildings at Khirokitia around common courtyards appears to support this view (see figure 2.1), but it furnishes little evidence for the particular types of kinship structures adopted by local inhabitants. Moreover, although vertical sequences of burials exhibiting distinct gender differentiation may constitute lineages, it is not certain that they signify the existence of "achieved" rather than "ascribed" status for individuals, as Le Brun has recently proposed (2002:27). However, the patterns of behavior implied by the placement of graves in vertical sequences of gender and age sets

contrast sharply with burial practices in later periods where the deceased were buried extramurally in large communal tombs used and reused for generations and comprising individuals of all ages and sexes. The fundamental nature of those changes, as well as their
significance for an understanding of gender in prehistoric Cyprus, will be explored further below in the discussion of burial evidence from the Chalcolithic period, when the
first real evidence of the shift from individual to group burials appears.

Gender and Mortuary Ritual in the Chalcolithic Period

While a certain degree of continuity can be observed between the funerary practices of
the early phases of the Chalcolithic period and those of the Neolithic, significant differences began to emerge during the third millennium B.C. that may be linked to changing
gender constructs. Many of the artifacts typical of the MChal, such as dentalium shell
necklaces, cruciform pendants, figurines, and painted pottery vessels, disappeared during
the LChal and were replaced by monochrome vessels of new morphological types, annular shell earrings, and beaded necklaces of faience and stone (Peltenburg 1991). Along-
side the traditional Neolithic-Chalcolithic pit graves, moreover, there appeared new types
of mortuary facilities, most notably the rock-cut chamber tomb, a long-lived design that
persisted on a larger, more elaborate scale throughout the Cypriot Bronze Age. These were
accompanied by new sets of social relationships during the third millennium B.C., as can
be seen from evidence at several key sites of the Chalcolithic period.

Three sites are particularly relevant here: Lemba, a fairly small settlement four km
north of Paphos, which was occupied during the middle and late phases of the period,
from roughly the mid-fourth to the mid-third millennium B.C.; Kissonerga, a site that
was only two km away from Lemba but was wealthier, larger, and longer lived, with a
chronological range of nearly two millennia; and Souskiou-*Vathrykakas* near Palaepaphos
(Kouklia), which falls entirely within the MChal (c. 3500–3000 B.C.) and constitutes
the only exclusive cemetery site of Chalcolithic Cyprus.

With the exception of Souskiou, burial facilities at Chalcolithic sites in Cyprus occur within the built environment and have not been found in separate cemeteries. Unlike burials of the Aceramic Neoltihic period, which occurred intramurally under the
floors of domestic structures, few Chalcolithic burials are located inside buildings; however, the association between interments and buildings remains strong since interments
are often placed adjacent to exterior walls. At Lemba, for example, all fifty-nine graves
of MChal–LChal date were pit graves, and the overwhelming majority comprised single
inhumations of infants and children (see fig. 6.2 and tab. 5.1). Multiple inhumations
were rare, accounting for only three of the total excavated graves (roughly 5 percent),
and they occur only in certain combinations: either a single adult (male or female) is
buried with a child or infant, or children are buried with other children. Adults, it seems,
were never buried together; and men, women, and children do not appear to have been
interred in what might be interpreted as "nuclear family" groups.

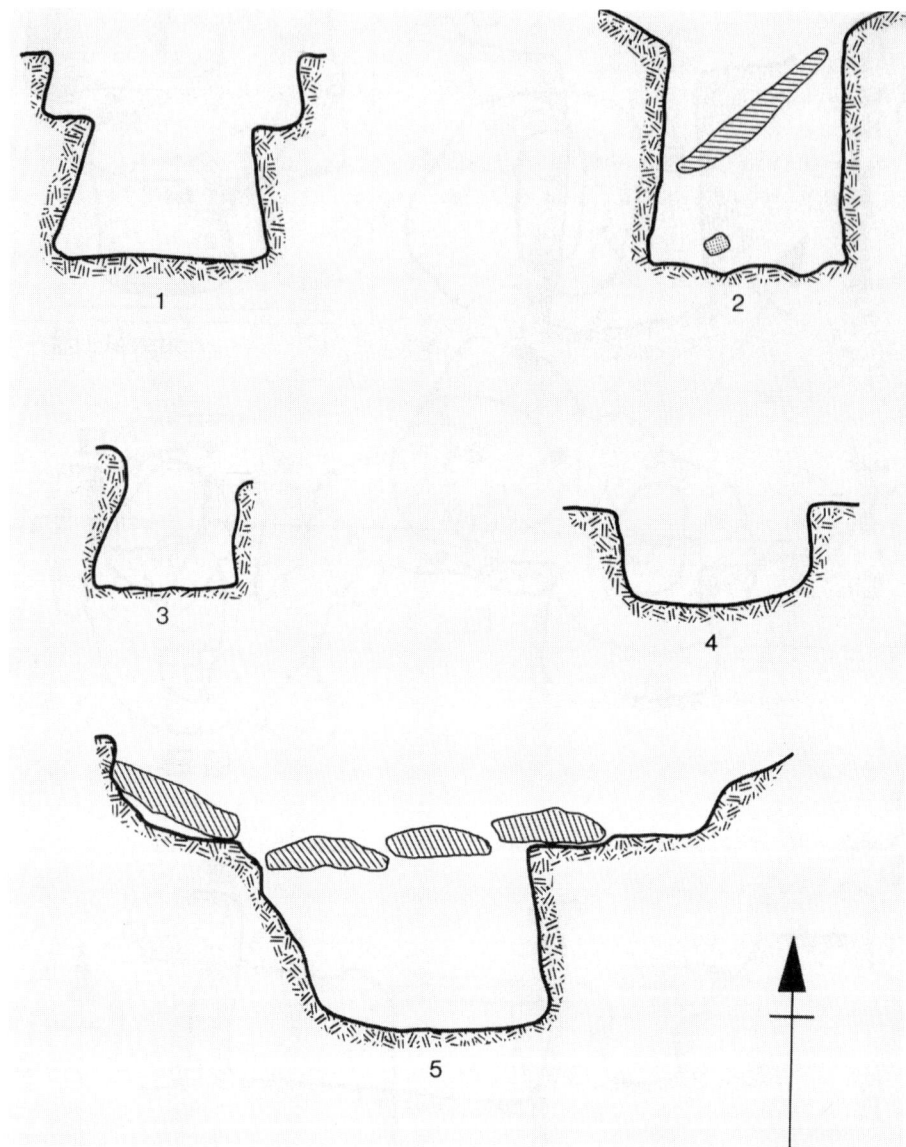

Figure 6.2.   Pit burials at Lemba (after Peltenburg et al. 1985:fig. 43).

Differential treatment of adults and children, a phenomenon observed at Lemba, occurs at Kissonerga as well, although it manifests itself in a somewhat different manner.
The low proportion of adult burials at the site constitutes one of the most remarkable
features of the Kissonerga mortuary population (Peltenburg et al. 1998:fig. 4.5). Adults
may have been buried extramurally in remote cemeteries such as Souskiou-*Vathyrkakas*. By
the LChal, however, this trend had reversed itself, and mortuary data indicate a return

to a complete age structure in the burial population, a development regarded by the excavator as a "major ideological shift" between MChal and LChal Kissonerga (Peltenburg et al. 1998:84). The inclusion of adult burials within the built environment at Kissonerga is in keeping with the evidence at Lemba Period 3 (also LChal), where special structural features previously reserved for children were transferred to adults. These and other related phenomena signify a fundamental shift in attitude toward adults and children within society as a whole and suggest closer associations within family groups during the middle of the second millennium. The cemetery of Souskiou-*Vathyrkakas* near Kouklia village is situated on the edge of a plateau overlooking the Dhiarrizos River and is composed of deep bell-shaped shafts cut into the bedrock (see fig. 6.3). Due to the richness of their associated burial goods, the Souskiou tombs have been targets of repeated illicit digging, but excavations by Iliffe and Mitford in 1951, Maier in 1972, and the Department of Antiquities in 1972 and 1991–1997 have yielded a great deal of information on this important cemetery site of the MChal (for a preliminary report, see Christou 1989).

Multiple burials of adults in deep shaft-like tombs represent a significant departure from funerary traditions elsewhere on the island. Moreover, the unusually rich and unorthodox character of grave goods sets this site apart as something extraordinary. A

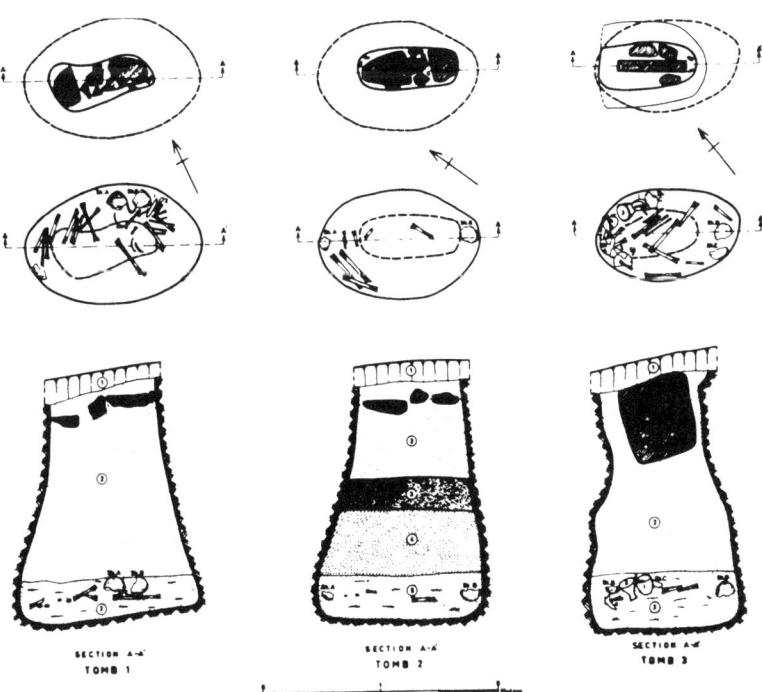

Figure 6.3.   Shaft graves at Souskiou-*Vathyrkakas* (after Christou 1989:fig. 12.3).

particularly spectacular example from a recent campaign at the site was the discovery of an anthropomorphic pottery vessel in the form of a pregnant female, now on display in the Cyprus Museum in Nicosia. It was found in a multiple burial of an adult together with three small children and a possible adolescent; unfortunately, the sex of the adult could not be determined due to its poorly preserved state.

The final report of the Souskiou cemetery is currently in preparation, and, although not all of the human skeletal material has been fully analyzed, a thorough examination of the human dentitions suggests much higher proportions of adult inhumations than were recorded at Lemba and Kissonerga (Dorothy Lunt, personal communication). Many of these appear to be adult females, with or without accompanying children. Figurines with characteristics similar to those of the Souskiou vessel are known from other contemporary sites in Cyprus, but these have usually been recovered in disturbed contexts or as the unprovenanced spoils of illicit digging. An important exception to this rule was evidence for birthing ritual at Kissonerga, where a group of nineteen figurines of stone and pottery were found in a ceremonial pit together with pottery vessels, stone tools, a triton shell, and a ceramic building model (Peltenburg et al. 1991). One of the most important finds, a RW female figurine shown in the act of childbirth, clearly demonstrates that these objects were connected to birthing rituals (figure 4.3, KM 1451); the child, painted in red, emerges between her legs. A second figurine in RW ware was hollow and may actually have been an anthropomorphic vessel like the one from Souskiou (figure 4.3, KM 1475). As we saw in chapter 4, variations in attributes of form and wear suggest that the stone figurines were held or clutched in the hand, while the ceramic examples were free standing and had restricted areas of wear, indicating their possible use as didactic models in puberty rituals (Goring 1991a).

Birthing symbols may also exist in the form of picrolite anthropomorphic pendants incorporated into dentalium shell necklaces in MChal graves (Peltenburg 1992). These necklaces are associated with women, as depicted in paint on the Kissonerga birthing figurine (KM1451), and children, as in Grave 563 at Kissonerga (figure 5.1). From the relative scarcity of these ornaments in graves, we can infer that they were regarded as luxury items. Only a handful of the seventy-three graves excavated at Kissonerga, for example, and five of fifty-nine graves at Lemba contained picrolites. Similarly at Souskiou, only one of the five tombs excavated by the Department of Antiquities in the 1970s contained picrolites, and that ratio has not increased significantly as the result of the recent excavations. The single tomb in question, Tomb 3 (figure 6.3), contained twenty picrolite pendants, sixteen of which were the anthropomorphic cruciform variety; the pendants were found in association with the burials of three adult females and an eight-year-old child (Lunt, personal communication). Similar patterns recur at Kissonerga and Lemba. To date, no picrolite cruciform pendant has been found in the burial of an adult male, and the repeated association of picrolites with certain women and children suggests restricted, differential access to the procurement of raw picrolite and the possession of picrolite ornaments during the MChal. It thus seems likely that women were centrally involved in the production and exchange of this highly valued material.

The deliberate breakage of several of the Kissonerga figurines and the careful placement of all the objects into a ceremonial pit together with burnt debris are ritual acts that signify the end of a long tradition of birthing ritual (see chapter 4). Anthropomorphic figurines are not found in LChal contexts at Lemba or Kissonerga, nor are the birth pendants and cruciform picrolite figurines with bent knees that Peltenburg (1992) has argued constituted a continuation of the same symbolic set. The adoption of mortuary facilities designed for multiple burials appears to have taken place at Souskiou during the MChal, and during the LChal at Kissonerga, where multiple burials occur in multichambered facilities (fig. 6.4).

In attempting to sum up what we have seen so far regarding the development of mortuary ritual during the EChal–MChal, the following patterns emerge: high proportions of children and infants in intra-settlement burials; segregation of children from adults in

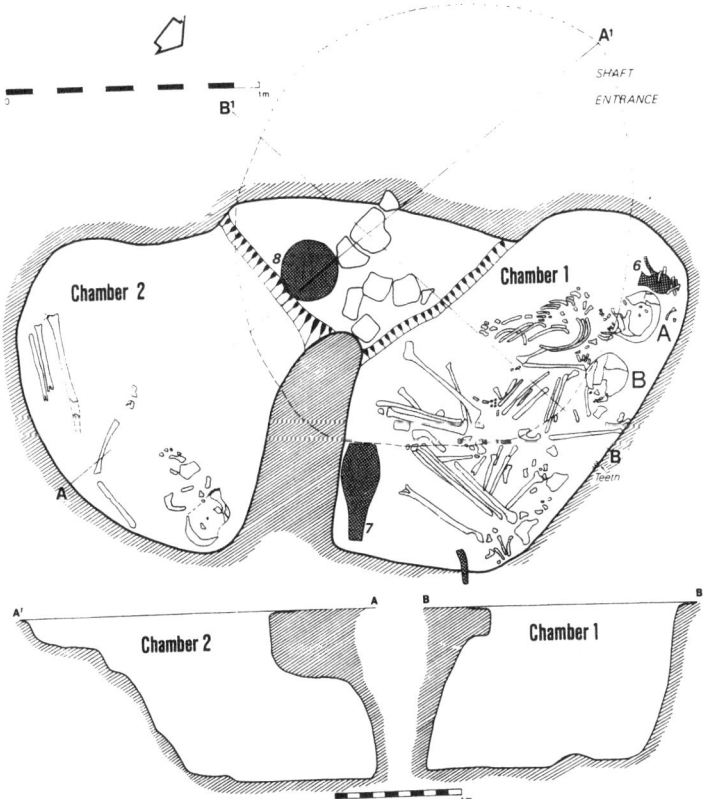

Figure 6.4.   Chamber Tomb 505 at Kissonerga (after Peltenburg et al. 1998:fig. 53).

intra-site burials; the predominance of single inhumations in pit graves; and the possibility of separate, remote cemeteries for adults; the segregation of male and female adults; the linking of "special" architectural features and grave goods with children; and the association of women and children with fertility and birthing symbolism, in general, and picrolite figurines and pendants, in particular. These practices changed dramatically during the LChal with the introduction of chamber tombs; an increase in multiple inhumations, the decline of birthing symbols; and the first recorded instances of group burials comprising women, men, and children. As we have seen in chapter 5, the joint burial of adults and children during the LChal marks a dramatic ideological shift that can be understood only within the larger perspective of changing socioeconomic conditions. The reinforcement of social bonds between adults and children implied by these acts, as well as by the joint burial of adults and children elsewhere during the LChal, indicate that children as well as adults were affected by advances in social complexity and that changes in treatment and status of children were bound up with changing gender constructs that exercised an equally marked impact on the relationships between women and men.

Gender and Mortuary Ritual during the Bronze Age

Group burials are first attested to in the MChal, but it was only later, during the EBA, that the practice of burying the deceased in large communal cemeteries separate from their associated settlements became standard mortuary practice. This trend continued into the MC and LC, and, as we have seen in chapter 4, may express new ideologies and practices associated with the emergence of descent groups during the course of the later third and second millennia (Keswani 1989:500). Unfortunately, there is very little evidence concerning the human populations buried in these tombs as most were excavated early in this century, prior to the adoption of modern excavation methods. These early campaigns did not, as a rule, record information on sexes or ages of the deceased nor did they focus on health issues such as stress, diet, and disease. On the other hand, there is fairly detailed evidence for construction techniques and architecture of the tombs, as well as for the position and alignment of bodies and the range and quantities of associated grave goods, which has been used to support models of low or incipient socioeconomic differentiation (Davies 1997; Keswani 1989). However, little attention has been paid to the emergence of new kinship structures implied by the number, size, and arrangement of tombs within these large mortuary complexes or to their lengthy temporal spans, all of which have potential links to changing gender constructs. In the following sections, I will try to distill some of the important social developments relevant for issues of gender that are suggested by mortuary evidence at several key sites of the EBA.

The Early Bronze Age and the First "Corporate" Burial Grounds

Cemeteries of the Cypriot Bronze Age consisted of large networks of chamber tombs cut into bedrock and furnished with a long rectangular entry passages known as *dromoi*, limestone slabs used as blocking stones, and single or multiple burial chambers (fig. 6.5). The use of chamber tombs on the island can traced back to the middle of the third millennium B.C. at sites such as Kissonerga, as can certain classes of grave goods, including spiral earrings, annular shell pendants, and biconical spindle whorls (Peltenburg 1991). During the Bronze Age, group identity and ancestral links were reinforced in mortuary rituals by the repeated use and reuse of tombs over many generations. During his excavations at Philia-*Vasiliko*, for example, Dikaios noted that some of the tombs had been reused and that previous occupants had been swept "unceremoniously" to the back of the chamber; the reuse of tombs gradually became a common custom, leading to multiple burials collectively spanning long periods of time (Dikaios 1961:160–65).

More extensive evidence of the EBA mortuary record on the island is to be found at the cemetery of *Vounous* near the north coast (fig. 6.6). Excavations by Dikaios, Schaeffer, and Stewart during the 1930s revealed 164 tombs of EC–MC date (Dikaios 1940; Schaeffer 1936; Stewart and Stewart 1950). These are similar in architectural form to those at Philia but appear to have involved more complex mortuary rituals (Baxevani 1994:177–202). According to Stewart, the dead at *Vounous* were laid out in orderly arrangements, with the first burials placed in the west of chamber, to the right of the entrance, and later burials in back, with respect maintained for previous dead. Grave goods, including bronze spiral earrings, annular shell pendants, and incised, biconical spindle whorls link these tombs to the Philia deposits at Kissonerga and Marki, but the size of this cemetery, the reuse of tombs over many generations, and the degree of reverence

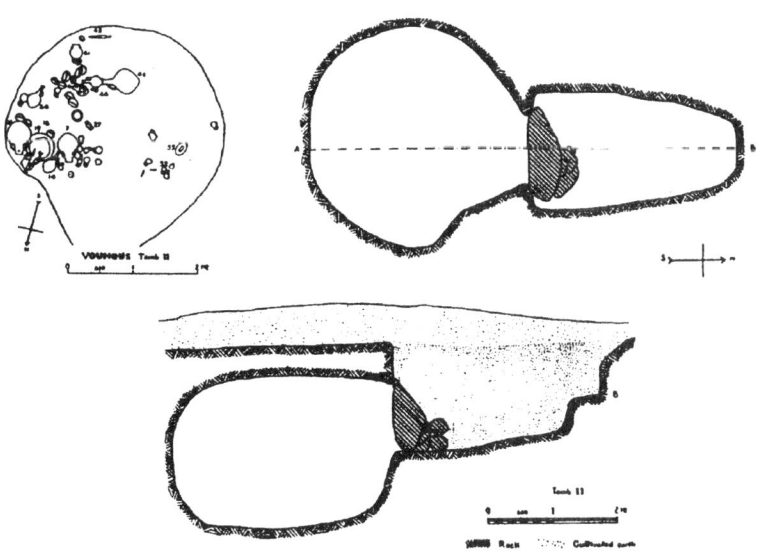

Figure 6.5.   Early Bronze Age chamber tomb with *dromos* from *Vounous* (after Dikaios 1940:fig. 9).

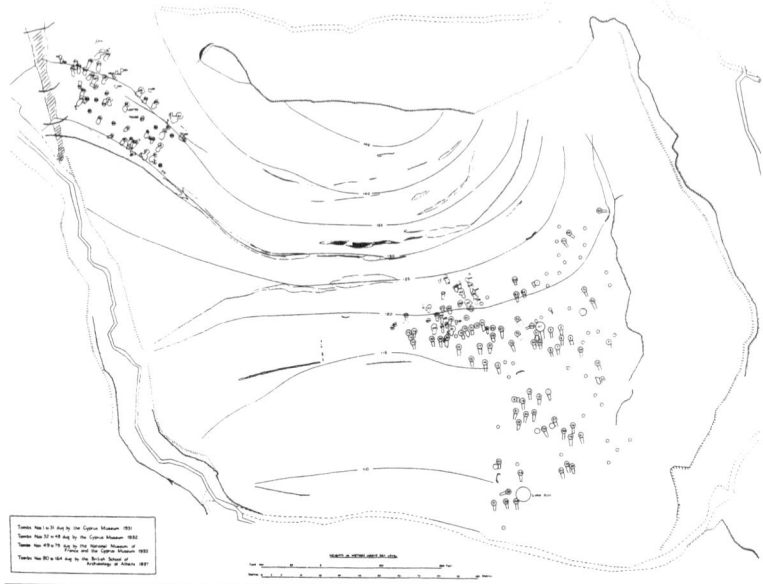

Figure 6.6.   Plan of the Bronze Age cemetery at *Vounous* (after Dikaios 1940:fig. 1).

shown for ancestral dead suggest the emergence of social groups with more sharply de-fined communal interests. In some of the more elaborate tombs, the deceased were ac-companied by figurines and modeled scenes incorporated into pottery vessels, some of which have been discussed in chapters 4–5.

In addition to furnishing evidence for increasing levels of social hierarchy and sex-linked divisions within society, the scenic compositions demonstrate the collective na-ture of productive labor and situate the processes of production and reproduction within the context of family and household groups. As we have seen elsewhere in this book, concepts of complementarity conveyed by much of the sculpture, while perhaps indicative of a relative degree of equality between the sexes, embrace categories of al-terity and difference. Recent discoveries of figurines in settlement contexts at Marki, dated to EC III, broaden the function and meaning of these objects by indicating their use among the living as well as their burial with the dead (Frankel and Webb 1996a:187–88). Nevertheless, they clearly suggest the growing importance of commu-nal enterprise to the economic success of newly emerging kinship groups that may have constituted the island's earliest ranked societies.

Incipient Hierarchies? Mortuary Patterns during the Middle Bronze Age
The transformation of socioeconomic traditions first seen during the EBA manifests it-self more clearly during the succeeding cultures of the MBA and LBA. Detailed work

in this area by Keswani has demonstrated strong correlations between the greater elaboration and diversity of burial customs, greater differentials in mortuary wealth, and fundamental advances in social complexity (Keswani 1989, 1991, 1996a).

During the MBA, burials exhibiting relatively low levels of wealth and structural elaboration existed in proximity to burials containing unprecedented amounts of wealth. According to Keswani, the latter constitute substantial mortuary events that may have involved "months or even years of accumulation of goods and food to be disposed of, consumed, and distributed" (Keswani 1996a:4). While these should be not be confused with the kind of elite system of rank associated with the emergence of the first state societies on the island several centuries later during the LBA, they can be regarded as examples of what she terms "generalized prestige competition," which served to reinforce kinship ties and strengthen the development of corporate identities (Keswani1996a:6). The site that most conclusively attests to these developments is the large cemetery of Lapithos-*Vrysi tou Barba* on the north coast (Baxevani 1994:203–18).

Burial Customs at Lapithos

From 1927 to 1931, the Swedish Cyprus Expedition undertook small-scale excavations at Lapithos-*Vrysi tou Barba*, but in the early 1930s the University of Pennsylvania carried out more extensive work involving the excavation of ninety tombs. The cemetery, which was in use from ECII–MCII, consisted of chamber tombs with an entry corridor (*dromos*) and multiple chambers. Herscher, who studied the Pennsylvania tomb material for her doctoral dissertation, noted that some tombs and individual burials were richer than others, both in terms of the number, variety, and elaborateness of their grave goods (Herscher 1978:790–91). Tomb size also varied, as did the number of chambers per tomb, but there was little variation in tomb architecture (Herscher 1978:791). The overall picture was characterized as one of "religious egalitarianism; rich and poor, young and old were buried in the same cemetery with apparently the same rites" (Herscher 1978:796).

Keswani has since reconsidered this evidence and has come to somewhat different conclusions regarding the social structures of the Lapithos community, particularly with regard to variations in the elaboration of mortuary ritual. At least six tombs, she believes, provide evidence for simultaneous interments, while others such as T 322, one of the richest and largest, contained few bones, a phenomenon that is ascribed to pre- or post-interment ritual (Keswani 1991:17). In addition, a series of shallow rectangular pits reported by Herscher as occurring over the entire surface of the bedrock at Lapithos may, in fact, have functioned as primary mortuary features from which burial remains were later removed for redeposition into tombs (Keswani 1991:17–18).

Kesani's interpretation is strengthened by the fact that some of the pits were cut into by the *dromoi* of tombs, indicating that the pits were dug earlier. The frequently haphazard arrangement of skeletal remains within the tombs, as well as their disarticulated state, ascribed by Herscher to successive interments of the deceased and poor preservation of skeletal remains, could therefore be indicative of multiple stages of mortuary ritual. Ongoing ritual behavior is given further confirmation by the vertical shafts connecting holes in the *dromos* of Tomb 806, enigmatic features that possibly functioned to facilitate periodic communication between the dead and the living (Herscher 1978:790). It therefore seems likely that burial customs during the MBA evolved from simple short-term events into complex, long-term mortuary programs in which some social groups managed to inter (and perhaps re-inter) remains of their deceased kin, and to accumulate, display, and dispose of funerary wealth over longer periods of time than had previously been the case (Keswani 1991). It is thus significant that the largest and richest tombs at Lapithos, and those that entailed the most elaborate funerary rituals, occur only during the final phases at the site, while smaller, more modest tombs first appear during the early phases and continue throughout the sequence. Once again, the evidence suggests a considerable diversity in the mortuary record that can probably be attributed to advances in social complexity and the emergence of limited degrees of social ranking (Keswani 1989:226).

With regard to the role of gender in the developments of MBA funerary ritual, we are hampered by the deficiency of the excavation records. No attempt was made during the excavations or in subsequent study of the skeletal material to determine the sexes of the deceased. Instead, assumptions were made about the sex of skeletons on the basis of associated grave goods, with pins, ornaments, and spindle whorls ascribed to females; razors, knives, and tweezers to males (Herscher 1978:787). Today we realize the biases inherent in such a priori judgments, but unfortunately for Lapithos, that realization has come too late. Most of the remaining cemetery sites of the Cypriot MBA likewise fail to provide evidence of sex and age data, either because skeletal material was never analyzed because of insufficient evidence (e.g., Dhenia, Palealona, Politiko, Ayia Paraskevi, Alambra, Paleoskoutella). Regrettably, very little skeletal material from these sites was saved for future study. A notable exception to this otherwise bleak picture, however, was provided by chance in 1978 when construction works in the village of Kalavasos revealed (and partially destroyed) a series of MBA tombs in the locality of Panayia Church.

Excavation of a portion of a MBA cemetery in Kalavasos village was undertaken as a rescue project by the Vasilikos Valley Project under the direction of Ian Todd in 1978 when construction work threatened a number of tombs. The final report, including plans and sections of the tombs, detailed descriptions of the finds, and a study of the human skeletal remains, was published several years later (Todd 1986). Thirteen tombs were investigated, comprising a total minimum population of eighteen adults and three children; many had been disturbed and damaged prior to excavation, and it is certain that a considerable number of others exist. Nevertheless, Todd's report is still the only substantive study of a MC tomb group excavated by modern scientific methods. For this reason, it is worthwhile taking a closer look at the mortuary remains from the site, in particular for the evidence they can provide on issues of gender.

Although the circular shape of these tombs, their lack of entrance corridors, and their relatively small, uniform sizes (2–3 m in diameter) do not conform to tomb groups at the larger cemetery sites further to the north, other aspects of the mortuary record, especially the variations in funerary ritual, corroborate some of the ideas proposed by Keswani about MC burial customs generally. In the first place, many of the tombs provide evidence of multiple phases of ritual activity. Tomb 36, for example, the largest known tomb from these excavations (fig. 6.7), was cut well before its use as burial chamber, while the stratigraphy of many other tombs clearly indicates successive episodes of ritual activity. In addition, the disarticulated state of many of the skeletal remains may be have been the result of secondary interment.

Tomb 36 contained the largest group of individuals (seven total); others contained far fewer, with nine tombs containing interments of a single adult. Children were represented by only three of the twenty-two individuals identified among the skeletal remains, and there were no infants. One wonders whether infants were given special treatment distinct from that of adults and children, or whether perhaps they were buried elsewhere. Because many tombs had been partially destroyed, and not all tombs

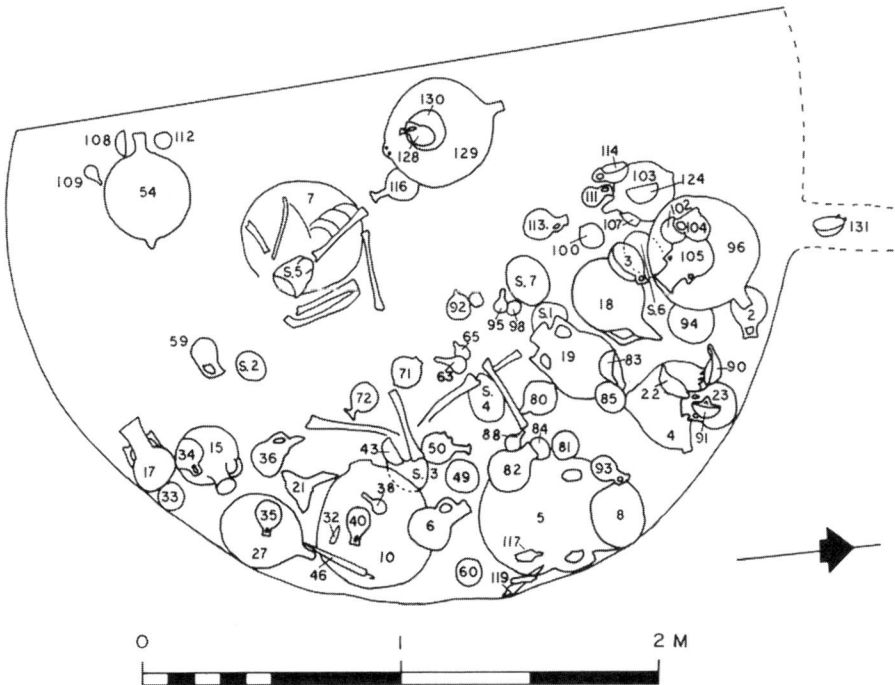

Figure 6.7.   Plan of Kalavasos-Panayia Church Tomb 36 (after Todd 1986: fig. 6).

could be fully excavated, we must also acknowledge the possibility that a greater number of children, as well as some infants, were buried in the tombs although their
remains were not discovered. When considering the totality of evidence from this relatively small group of thirteen tombs, one is struck by the variation in the numbers of
individuals buried within a given tomb as well as the differences in number and richness of their associated artifacts. As mentioned above, Tomb 36 alone contained a fairly
large number of burials. Three individuals were distinguished in Tomb 38, two in Tomb
41, and only a single individual in each of the remaining tombs with skeletal remains
(nine total); a thirteenth tomb, Tomb 44, yielded no diagnostic skeletal remains. In apparent contrast to contemporary sites in the north, then, tombs at Kalavasos consisted
primarily of single inhumations, a pattern that we have seen reflects earlier traditions
on the island, including the earliest burials at Lapithos. Tomb 36 stands out, not only
for its larger size and greater number of interments but also for the quantity and richness of its funerary offerings (fig. 6.8). A total of 132 objects were catalogued from
this tomb, probably fewer than the original total prior to the tomb's partial destruction
by bulldozing. This was by far the greatest number in any single tomb, illustrating the
ability of some kinship groups to amass and dispense with considerable wealth for
the purpose of burying its deceased kin.

While the sum total of wealth in Tomb 36 is considerable, artifact numbers are not as
impressive when one considers the relative large number of individuals interred. Tomb 40,
for example, which contained the remains of a single young adult, yielded seventy-six artifacts; and Tomb 39, again of a single young adult, contained thirty-five grave goods. Tomb
37, containing a minimum of two adults of indeterminate age and sex, yielded fifty-two
artifacts. In contrast, other tombs had relatively few finds: Tomb 42 and Tomb 57, both
single adult burials of indeterminate sex, contained only twelve artifacts and little or no
bronze; Tomb 43, an adult female burial, contained only six objects and no metal objects.

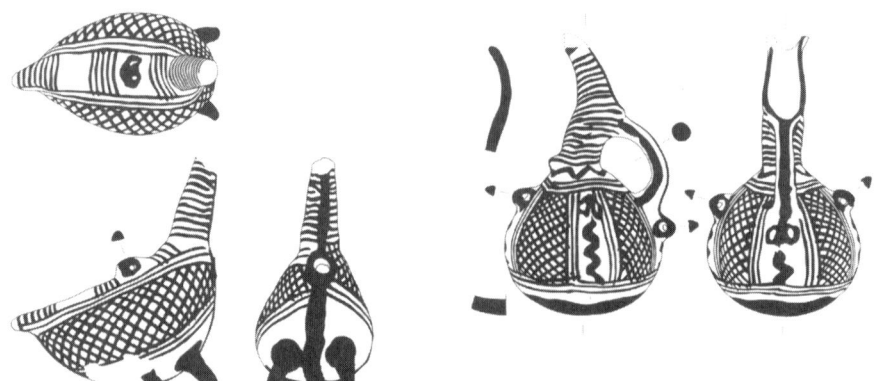

Figure 6.8.   White Painted II Pottery from Kalavasos-Panayia Church Tomb 36: bird vessel no. 22, left;
juglet no. 85, right (after Todd 1986:fig. 37.1).

In general, burials of single adults are furnished with the fewest grave goods, and the young female in Tomb 43 had the smallest number of all. Whether this pattern was applicable to all of the tombs of the Kalavasos cemetery is difficult to judge given the limited nature of the excavations, but it may be worth noting that Tomb 41, which contained the burials of an adult female and a child, yielded a mere eleven artifacts, including only a single fragment of copper or bronze. The contrast with Tomb 36, in which four adult females were buried along with two adult males and a child, is significant. Important for an estimation of social ranking within the Kalavasos tomb complex are the varying numbers of metal objects associated with the different burials. Most were of copper or bronze (metallurgical analysis was not undertaken for these rescue operations), but one tomb (Tomb 37) also yielded an imported silver bracelet. This tomb, which contained the remains of two adults of indeterminate age and sex, also contained the highest per capita number of metal artifacts (8.5:1). Tomb 39, which yielded seven metal artifacts in association with the burial of a single young adult, was a close second, while Tomb 36 contained the greatest overall number of metal finds (eighteen total). In contrast, burials of single adults, and especially adult females, had lower number of metal finds.

The evidence from the MC cemetery at Kalavasos, although limited in scope, appears to indicate a relatively low status for single adult females or females interred only with children, a pattern that may reflect social attitudes to women who, for whatever reason, were interred separately from their respective kinship groups. While one can draw only preliminary conclusions at this juncture concerning the gender-related aspects of the mortuary remains, it seems likely that female status during the MBA was linked to membership in a corporate group. This is a phenomenon not observed in earlier phases of Cypriot prehistory and must be regarded as the result of changes in the relationship between individual status and the increasing power of kin-related groups to accumulate and dispose of surplus wealth. Rather than being "ascribed" at birth, female status was now more flexible since it was linked to the negotiation and attainment of greater privileges within the context of prestige competition. This situation changed during the LBA, however, with the introduction of exotic goods into mortuary contexts and the emergence of social hierarchies based on the growth of metallurgy and the increasing demand for imported luxury goods through long distance trade networks (Peltenburg 1996). The impact of these developments on gender constructs in Cyprus will be explored in the following sections.

Gender and Mortuary Ritual in the Late Bronze Age

To understand the ways in which mortuary evidence can illuminate changes in gender constructs during the second millennium B.C., it is important to keep in mind some of the socioeconomic developments of the LBA, in particular the political, social, and economic transformations associated with the emergence of the first state-level societies on the island in LCII (c. 1400 B.C.). Instabilities and upheavals before 1400 (MCIII–LCI) can very likely be attributed to a gradual demographic shift away from the north and central regions to the southern and eastern coasts (Peltenburg 1996:28) that occurred as part of the expansion of metallurgical production on the island during the LC and the increasing ability of Cypriot elites to exploit international markets for purposes of trade. Unfortunately for our understanding of the processes by which these developments arose on the island, evidence for the transitional period is limited; no substantial group of intact, carefully excavated and recorded tombs exists for the end of the MBA in Cyprus (MCIII) (Keswani 1989:516). I will turn, therefore, to a consideration of mortuary remains for the period of the MC–LC transition and then for the LBA proper, for which there is better evidence, both quantitatively and qualitatively, of differential burial practices.

Although Enkomi is the only settlement site with substantial remains of the MC–LC transition (see chapter 2), tombs groups from several other sites point to changes in mortuary rituals that are linked unambiguously to advances in social hierarchy. Three sites have been chosen for discussion, all of which are situated in the north of the island and positioned inland rather than on the coast: Dhali-*Kafkallia* (in the village of Idalion, between Nicosia and Larnaca), Stephania (several miles from the north coast to the east of Morphou Bay), and Ayios Iakovos (northeast of Nicosia at the start of the island's panhandle). Unfortunately, these sites have been subject to considerable looting and destruction. In addition, recording levels vary, and sexing of skeletal material was not undertaken at Dhali and Stephania and was undertaken on only a portion of the human remains from Ayios Iakovos. Despite these limitations, the mortuary remains from these sites allows us to outline some of the broad changes in mortuary customs that began to occur at the end of the MC and continued into the LBA.

A looted cemetery at Dhali, comprising approximately 110 tombs, was surveyed by Overbeck and Swiny in 1970 (Overbeck and Swiny 1972). One of these tombs was completely cleared and appears to have been in use from MCIII/LCI to the Cypro-Geometric. A survey of tomb morphology revealed the standard chamber tomb type with *dromos*, already known during the EC. While the looted state of the tombs precludes a meaningful study of burial and mortuary population, the evidence evinces an aspect of burial customs not seen before this time, namely the use and reuse of tombs over considerable periods of time. This contrasts with the temporally shallow burial sequences noted for earlier periods of the Bronze Age.

Fourteen tombs of MCIII–LCII date were investigated at Stephania in 1951 by a joint team from the Ashmolean Museum and the University of Sydney under the direction of Joan du Plat Taylor and Veronica Seton Williams. A brief report, comprising largely a catalogue of finds and plans of the tombs, was later published by Hennessy (1963). Although two of the tombs had been completely looted, and an additional two turned out to have non-tomb features, evidence from the remainder can be used to reconstruct some of the developments in mortuary ritual during the early phases of the LBA.

Several important patterns emerge. The first has to do with the long chronological range of most of the tombs (LCIB– LCII for most, LCIA–LCIIIA for tomb 2), a feature observed also at Dhali. The second concerns the relative sizes of the tombs. While the two tombs of the MCIII (Tombs 10, 13) are fairly small and consist exclusively of a single chamber with a *dromos*, some tombs of the LC have significantly larger chambers (Tombs 4, 9), and others have multiple chambers (Tombs 4, 14). The smaller tombs continue in LC as well, so it appears that inequalities in rank and status have become more sharply defined at this time.

A third pattern concerns the differential levels of wealth represented by contemporary tombs, a phenomenon that apparently existed already in MCIII as indicated by the respective groups of finds in Tombs 10 and 13. Whereas the former was relatively rich (the chamber was found to contain twenty-six objects, five of which were copper), the latter was more modestly appointed, containing only seven objects, none of which was metal. Likewise for the LC, Tombs 2, 4, 5, 7, and 14 were rich in finds, while Tomb 9 had only eleven objects and no metal finds; and although Tomb 12 yielded several objects that could be regarded as prestige items (a Mycenaean IIIB stirrup jar, as well as several bronze, copper, and lead rings), it yielded only twenty-two objects. Tombs with double chambers normally contained a disproportionate amount of wealth in one of the two chambers (T 4, Chamber A; T 14, Chamber A). Yet it appears that the majority of tombs of the LBA were furnished quite lavishly; the number of wealthy tombs far outweighs the more poorly provisioned ones, and no tomb lacks grave goods. The overall view provided by the data, therefore, is that burial at Stephania was a prerogative of elite members of society.

The skeletal remains from Stephania were not studied by specialists, but catalog entries include general descriptions of the skeletal material found within each tomb and, when possible, an estimated minimum number of individuals for each chamber. This allows us to consider a final aspect of the burial customs at the site, namely the number of finds in tombs relative to the number of individuals estimated to have been interred. Tomb 12 had a minimum population of fourteen but only twenty-two total finds, whereas Tomb 14, perhaps the richest tomb at the site, had over sixty objects. Other rich tombs contained low numbers of burials (Tomb 4 with five skulls; Tomb 5 with two burials; Tomb 7 with three individuals). Unfortunately, the lack of a proper study of the skeletal material precludes comparison of tomb wealth according to gender, but mortuary patterns at Stephania strongly suggest that the accumulation of disposable wealth during the LBA was no longer the result of the joint effort of large corporate groups, as had been the case during the EC–MC. The growing power and prestige of smaller groups with greater access to nonagricultural wealth were central to the growth of socioeconomic complexity that ultimately resulted in the advent of more centralized, bureaucratic forms

of political organization. Both Dhali and Stephania furnish essential clues to that trajectory of developments. A third site, Ayios Iakovos, takes the analysis a step further by in-
troducing evidence for the human populations that comprised elite groups.

The cemetery at Ayios Iakovos-*Melia* was in use from MCIII–LCII. Fourteen tombs
were excavated at the site by the Swedish Cyprus Expedition in 1934 (Gjerstad et al.
1934:302 ff.), and an additional tomb excavated by the Department of Antiquities in
1959 at locality *Kakotris* was later published by Åström (1966). All are large chamber
tombs (up to 33 sq. m) that apparently served as collective burial facilities averaging
ten–twelve bodies per burial. Evolution in tomb morphology can be gauged by differences between the earliest tombs (MCII), which are variable in form and size, and late
ones (MCIII/LCI onward), which appear to be more standardized and elaborate. Skeletal remains from the site were preserved in this case and studied by Fürst (1933) and
later by Fischer (1986). Both noted the disproportionate number of male and female
skulls in these burials (Füerst identified twenty-eight males and eight females; and Fischer identified twenty-five males, seven females, three possible males, and one possible
female). Fischer attributed this to differential preservation of male and female crania.
Viewed in context, however, it is more likely to have been associated with changes in gender roles during the LBA, which, in turn, can be linked to the demographic and economic changes outlined earlier. This was apparently not an anomalous occurrence, for
similar patterns of male/female ratios are visible at two other key sites of the LBA,
Kourion, and Enkomi.

Invisible Women: Enkomi and Kourion

Studies of human populations of the LBA are hampered, as always, by the exiguous
amount of skeletal material that has been studied by experts. A review of the skeletal
remains of the LBA twenty years ago concluded that "none of the existing collections
can be representative of the populations that occupied these sites . . . from an archaeological standpoint the overall sample does not have sufficient regional or temporal control to provide evidence of universality" (Schulte-Campbell 1983:251).

Regrettably, the situation has not improved substantially in recent years, although it
is hoped that the final report on the human skeletal remains from *Ayios Dhimitrios* will constitute an important step in the right direction. For now, however, we must continue to
rely on studies conducted in the mid-twentieth century of poorly preserved skeletal material from excavations that were not carefully excavated or recorded, many of which were
analyzed by anthropologists working without access to or guidance from archaeological
records long after the excavations were complete. Skeletal remains from Kourion and
Enkomi, considered below, fall into this category, but their fairly sizable mortuary populations, and the fact that the skeletal material from both sites was saved and a portion
examined scientifically at a later date, make them the best available candidates at present
for examining the interfaces between gender and mortuary ritual during the LBA.

Excavations at Kourion were first carried out by the British Museum early in the twentieth century, following the discovery of plundered tombs. The expedition can be characterized as more of an up-market looting operation than a scientific excavation, however, and the results were never published. Some years later, J. F. Daniel excavated forty additional tombs at the site for the University Museum of the University of Pennsylvania, but his premature death in 1948 prevented analysis and publication of his results. This task was later undertaken by J. L. Benson, who published the tomb material with an appendix by Lawrence Angel on the human skeletal remains (Benson 1972). Angel identified eighty-one individuals in the final report (published as Appendix B in Benson 1972). These included sixty-four adults, of whom forty-one were males and twenty-three females, a figure that approximates the 2:1 M-F ratio observed at Ayios Iakovos.

Angel also identified the remains of fourteen children and three infants, but most of these could not be sexed. Twenty-four skulls were sufficiently preserved to determine the frequency of cranial deformation (fifteen males, four possible males, and five females). Deformities of "Cypriote" type (i.e., post-bregmatic deformation) were detected on six males, two possible males, and one female, suggesting that females at Kourion were not frequently subject to induced cranial deformation. If, as argued in chapter 5, the practice of post-bregmatic head shaping was a status-related behavior, the rarity of its application to female skulls may signify a more circumscribed status for females at Kourion. Extensive looting of the site, unfortunately, precludes any meaningful study of the finds to determine whether different types, qualities, or quantities of grave goods were provisioned to males and females in mortuary contexts.

Enkomi's long and important history has been outlined in chapter 2, but here our focus shifts to the mortuary remains from the site, which were so extensive that early excavators didn't realize they were in the middle of a settlement when they uncovered the many rich and elaborate chamber tombs of LBA date. According to Keswani, who has studied these remains in detail (see especially Keswani 1989:ch. 6), there was a fairly clear evolution of burial practices from MCIII onward. For the transitional MCIII–LCIA, only a small number of intact tombs are extant; finds from these tombs are mostly ceramic, although French T 32 had metal, faience, a scarab, and a hematite weight. During the LBA, the chamber tomb with *dromos* is most common type and is found in every area of the site. Each tomb held from one–fifty-five burials, with an average of twelve burials per tomb. Some of the tombs apparently were used for very long periods of time (i.e., as much as 300 years, judging from the pottery). Tombs vary in size from 1 to 10 sq. m, but there appears to be no correlation between tomb size and wealth of grave goods. Overall, tombs of the LBA at Enkomi are extremely rich, with most tombs containing some quantity of gold.

In addition to chamber tombs, five tombs of LCIIA or IIB date were corbelled tombs constructed of ashlar masonry; all were exceptionally rich. As four of the five were situated in the same quadrant of the site (Q4E), and the fifth was immediately adjacent (Q3E), they may have belonged to a highly ranked lineage; at the very least, they attest to the existence of rich and powerful elites (Keswani 1989:55). The wealthiest tombs contain items of symbolic prestige value, such as carved ivories with motifs of sphinxes, hieroglyphs, and exotic animals. These objects do not appear in tombs prior to LCII, and their pronounced symbolism strongly suggests the emulation of Near Eastern customs and the manipulation of Near Eastern ideology for the purpose of legitimizing political power. Moreover, and especially important for understanding the impact of these developments on gender constructs, are the disproportionate numbers of males in the Enkomi tombs, suggesting perhaps that some women had a lower social status and that elite groups at Enkomi may have been preponderantly male (Keswani 1989:503).

Skulls of seventy-five individuals from some of the Swedish tombs at Enkomi were examined and published by Fischer in 1986. Earlier studies of human remains from the site by Fürst (1933) and Hjortsjö (1947) are probably not as reliable and were made on the basis of smaller collections. Fischer identified thirty-one adult males, thirteen possible males, fifteen adult females, four possible females, three adults of uncertain sex, and nine children. These results are strikingly similar to those obtained by Angel at Kourion, who likewise calculated a 2:1 ratio of males to females. Keswani (1989:424–25) is quick to observe, however, that not all tombs yielded a disproportionate representation of males and females (Swedish Tomb 11, for example, contained the remains of four adult females and three adult males); she also notes that two out of three females in Enkomi burials are older women, so perhaps high status females were more often accorded the right of burial than younger women of lower status. Swedish Tomb 18, dating to LCII, would seem to support this hypothesis. It contained the body of a thirty-six-year-old female accompanied with a gold diadem, gold mouthpiece, three pairs of gold earrings, a bronze mirror, a gold necklace, gold toe-rings, bronze ankle-rings, a gold finger ring, and an ivory box.

Fischer did not attempt to examine the Enkomi skulls for evidence of cranial deformation, but Fürst, who studied forty-four of the skulls earlier on, found nineteen (seven males, ten females, and two children) with post-bregmatic flattening (fig. 5.5). If indeed this form of ACD was status related, then it is evident that elite females at Enkomi were designated with this status marker on an equal or greater footing with men, implying higher status than that suggested by their underrepresentation in burial contexts.

We must exercise caution, of course, in interpreting studies that do not consider full assemblages of skeletal material from tombs. Given the small proportion of skeletal material that has actually been studied from LBA sites, we should be mindful of Schulte-Campbell's assertion that it is not possible to draw general conclusions concerning the populations who inhabited the sites of LBA Cyprus on the basis of the present evidence. For now, we can merely conclude provisionally that Schwartz's results from Kition and Hala Sultan Tekke, as well as from the smaller skeletal collections at Akhera and Pendayia, appear to contradict evidence from Enkomi and Kourion concerning the presence of women in LBA graves. They also suggest that certain burial customs, including decisions on which individuals were entitled to be buried within the settlement, as well as their manner and location of burial, may have been regulated heterarchically by local or regional customs rather than emanating from a central authority. Further evidence of elite burials from three sites not yet considered in this discussion (Akhera, Toumba tou Skourou, and Kalavasos) illustrate what may have constituted yet another regional or local burial custom, the spatial segregation of males and females during the LBA.

Segregation and Alterity in Late Bronze Age Tomb Groups

Skeletal remains from two tombs at Akhera, located in the northwest part of the island, were studied by in the 1970s by Schwartz, who identified eight individuals from two different tombs; one of them (Tomb 2) contained three adult females while the second (Tomb 3) contained two adult females (Schwartz 1974). A child is also reported, but Schwartz doesn't report its context. In any event, the two tomb groups appear to be composed exclusively of females, a phenomenon not noted in the mortuary ritual of the earlier Bronze Age. The three chamber tombs from the nearby site of Pendayia, for example, dating to LCIA, had mixed sex burials.

The site of Toumba tou Skourou in Morphou provides a second example of segregation according to sex, although here the nature of the spatial separation is different. In the latest chamber of a multiple chamber tomb in use from LCI (Tomb 2, chamber 4), the single inhumation of an adult female of about twenty-five years of age was uncovered (Vermeule and Wolsky 1990:247 ff.). The burial dates to about 1350 B.C. (LCIIB) and was apparently the last body deposited in the tomb. The intact nature of the burial, as well as the lack of other extraneous skeletal material, indicate that the woman had been buried on her own, although the remains of a baby's skull in a pocket of ash near the entryway may have been interred at the same time in a nearby niche. Moreover, the skull of the adult female exhibited clear signs of post-bregmatic flattening. Grave goods associated with the skeleton included Mycenaean pottery, gold beads, fragments of ivory pyxides, and a cylinder seal in lapis lazuli with gold foil caps. According to the excavator, this was the richest individual burial at the site (Vermeule and Wolsky 1990:248). Although there had been earlier burials in this chamber (dating to LCI), the older skeletal material had been cleared away prior to the interment of the female. The latter, therefore, constitutes one of the few occurrences of an elite female buried on her own in the LBA.

By far the most conclusive evidence for sexual segregation in LBA tomb groups comes from the site of Kalavasos-*Ayios Dhimitrios*, one of the few sites of this period that has been methodically excavated, recorded, and analyzed (see South 1997 and South et al. 1989 for preliminary reports). While some of the skeletal material has yet to be examined, the evidence to date indicates a recurrent pattern of sexual segregation among the richest tombs. Although children are sometimes interred jointly with either adult males or adult females, males and females do not occur together, and there are no known groups of "nuclear family" burials comprising men, women, and children. Tombs 1 and 14, for example, contained adult males, the former with children and the latter without, while Tombs 11, 13, and 16 contained adult females (with or without children). The similar range of luxury goods (most notably Mycenaean kraters) from Tombs 11, 13, and 14, their common orientation (parallel to the large administrative structure, Building X) and successive chronological occurrences (T 11 earlier than 13; T 13 earlier than 14), and the respect for earlier burials with regard to space attest to a common burial program of a distinct and spatially differentiated group of elites in which males and females were interred separately.

Tomb 11 can justifiably be regarded as the most prestigious female mortuary facility known from prehistoric Cyprus (see fig. 6.9). This important tomb of the LBA (LCIIA/B), which is known only from preliminary reports (Goring 1989; Moyer 1989; South 1997:163–65), was the usual chamber and *dromos* type, with a large chamber (c. 2.5 x 4.2 m) to the north of the *dromos* and a much smaller chamber (Tomb 9) to the south; the latter contained only the bones of a newborn infant. Tomb 11, in contrast, contained seven individuals: three young women, a three-year-old child, and three newborn infants. The spatial arrangement of the skeletons was unique in that the adult females had been placed on benches against the wall of the chamber, while the infants and child found lying on the floor. The remains of two adult females, twenty-one–twenty-four years and seventeen years, lay on a bench built against the eastern wall of the chamber (skeletons [Sks.] 2–3 in fig. 6.9). Both skeletons were disarticulated, probably as the result of secondary burial or rearrangement. On the western bench, a nineteen–twenty-year-old female (Sk.1) lay on her back in extended position, adorned with a full set of jewelry. Evidence of wear indicated use of the jewelry before interment, so it is possible that these ornaments were the property of the woman in life as well as in death (Goring 1989). The remains of a young child (Sk. 4) were recovered from the floor of the chamber, while the remains of three infants were found on the floor near the western bench (Sks. 5–7); their bones were disarticulated and had probably been interred in an organic container that has not survived.

The finds from Tomb 11 are quite remarkable, consisting primarily of luxury goods such as gold, ivory, glass, and a number of Mycenaean vessels. Goring, who studied the gold jewelry from this tomb, has calculated that the twelve gold earrings found in the tomb (six on the female on the western bench and an additional six on the eastern bench) were of a standardized weight known at other sites such as Enkomi, where earrings of identical weight were unearthed in Swedish Tomb 18. She has proposed that the women of Tomb 11 may have been buried with their dowries (Goring 1989:104).

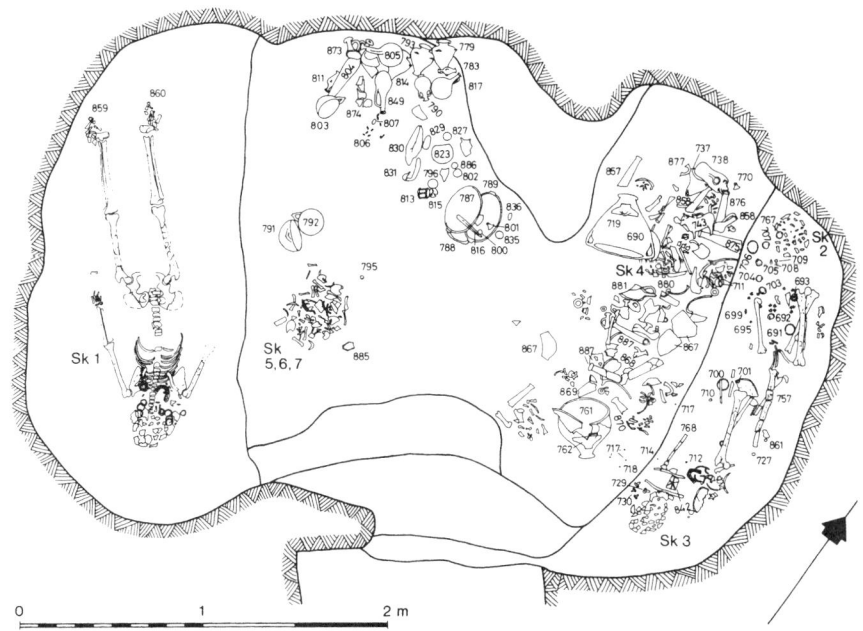

Figure 6.9.   Plan of *Ayios Dhimitrios* Tomb II (after Goring 1989:fig. 13.1).

Ethnographic evidence generally correlates dowry systems with lower female social status; however, dowries can often ensure women's financial security since they represent wealth transferred to her husband's family conditionally, as long as the marriage remains intact. For this reason, cultural rules governing remarriage (known anthropologically as the levirate and sororate) normally function to keep dowry wealth within the family on the death of a husband or a wife. The fact that the luxury goods in Tomb II can be regarded by their association with particular women as items of personal adornment and wealth, that some of these items had been used prior to burial, and that their owners exercised control over them even after they died by taking them to their graves, lends support to Goring's proposal and provides clues concerning the rights and prerogatives of elite women to possess, manipulate, and dispense with wealth. In addition, the standardized weight of the gold earrings, which would have made them a source of convertible currency, may indicate that women were actively engaged in trade or exchange of luxury items during the LBA.

The final excavation report on *Ayios Dhimitrios* is still in progress, so we cannot determine if similar patterns recurred in other areas of the site. It is possible, of course, that some of the tombs containing larger numbers of interments (such as Tombs I and 5) and not as wealthy as those just cited contained adult members of both sexes, but sex could be identified on only several of the adults in these tombs (see Moyer 1989). Present evidence suggests, however, that the sexual segregation of burials at the site was a common practice. As we have seen in chapter 3, patterns of alterity involving binary male/female divisions were noted in some of the coroplastic art of the EBA–MBA, but the binary spatial division between sexes was applied to mortuary contexts for the first time in the LBA.

Ethnographic evidence for ritual segregation of males and females in pre-state societies is widely attested to and is usually found in societies where women's privileges are circumscribed (e.g., Strathern 1972). Yet, in LBA Cyprus, the correlation of male/female segregation with lower female status is contradicted by the luxurious nature and copious numbers of finds associated with elite female burials. The gendered lens, therefore, reflects status differences between women: elite females of considerable wealth and status appear to have been buried lavishly at Kalavasos (such as Tomb 11 or the considerably more modest Tomb 16), while women of lower status remain archaeologically invisible. In contrast, lower-status males appear to have been accorded burial rights, as evidenced by the Enkomi Tomb 10 (French) and Ayios Iakovos Tomb 8 (Sks. 11 and 26), both of which contained skeletons of adult males associated with locally made pottery (White Shaved, Base Ring, and Monochrome wares) but with no metal or imported objects (Fischer 1986:32–33, 35).

Similar practices involving the segregation of male and female elites and invisibility of lower-status women have been identified in the mortuary record of the Early Dynastic IIIA period in Mesopotamia, which dates to c. 2100 B.C. Although there is a lack of analyzed skeletal material from the "Royal Cemetery" at Ur, grave goods within these elite Sumerian tombs occur almost invariably in discrete male and female groupings (Pollock 1991). Where sex can be determined, females are associated with hair rings, earrings, combs, and "dog collars," while males are found together with axes, whetstones, daggers, and brims, a kind of head ornament (Pollock 1991:373–76).

These grave goods appear in nonoverlapping sets in all but two of the Royal Cemetery tombs. The exceptions are two burials found with "male" and "female" objects *in situ* on the same skeleton, an occurrence that perhaps parallels the gendered mix of burial goods in some elite tombs of LBA Cyprus (discussed below). Unfortunately, in the case of the Ur ED III material, the sexes of these two skeletons are unknown, but Pollock notes that lower status individuals at other contemporary sites (such as Kish, where a contemporary cemetery contains greater numbers of non-elite individuals) are not gender differentiated in the same way; this is especially true for lower-status females who, in terms of gender marking with identifiable object sets, are wholly invisible in the burial record (Pollock 1991:377–78).

Similar developments involving a diminution of power for women have generally been linked to the emergence of states, although the extent and particular form of female circumscription varies spatially and temporally (Silverblatt 1988, 1991). The emergence of the state in Cyprus, as elsewhere, can therefore be seen to have had a po-larizing effect on females by bringing about differences between women with regard to identity and status. For the first time, it is possible that differences in economic stature and social rank began to fragment monolithic gender categories of "men" and women" into a multiplicity of disparate and competing sub-groups.

Gender Mutability in the Late Bronze Age

Gender mutability has been widely attested to in ethnographic studies of traditional so-cieties but has seldom been considered in gender studies of mortuary evidence from prehistoric sites. Instead, archaeological attention has tended to focus on the sexing of skeletal remains and the search for patterns of associated finds according to binary male/female categories, the approach undertaken so far in this chapter. Ironically, how-ever, mortuary remains can provide some of the best evidence for nonbinary gender structures since the purposeful nature of the evidence can indicate, with a lesser degree of ambiguity than is normally the case, the social messages transmitted by the deceased individuals themselves and by the living groups who managed and participated in their funerary rites. Although the evidence for third gender categories may often be obscured by the fragmentary state of the evidence, the lack of archaeological inquiry into the ex-istence of nonbinary gender structures is more likely to reflect modern Western as-sumptions than past realities.

As is often the case in studies of mortuary populations from prehistoric sites, one can expect to encounter numerous obstacles when attempting to isolate and identify in-dividuals. We have seen how the collective nature of burials during the Bronze Age of Cyprus, with tombs used and reused over considerable periods of time, as well as loot-ing in the past and in more recent times, pose particular problems in this regard. The looted condition of many tombs makes it unlikely that grave goods excavated from them comprise the original total number of finds or that those finds were found *in situ*. As a result of these and other taphonomic problems, the attempt to associate specific sets of grave goods with individual skeletons can prove to be an exercise in extreme frustration.

These difficulties notwithstanding, burial evidence of the LBA demonstrates the limitations of binary categories for analysis mortuary evidence. At least five burials from different sites of the LCIIB–IIIA and one from MCIII appear to meet the biological, material, and taphonomic requirements for a "third gender" or "transgender" burial. These are described immediately below in chronological order, beginning with the most recent example (Hala Sultan Tekke Tomb 23) and moving backward in time. After pre-senting this evidence, I will discuss some recent, nonbinary approaches to gender and identity and offer possible interpretations of what appear to be incontrovertible in-stances of third gender burials of the Cypriot Bronze Age. Apart from Tomb 23 at Hala Sultan Tekke, which was a shaft grave, all of the tombs considered here are the typical Bronze Age chamber tombs with doorway and *dromos*.

Hala Sultan Tekke Tomb 23 (LCIIIA, c. 1175 B.C., fig. 6.10) contained the single inhumation of a male found *in situ* in an intact shaft grave (Niklasson 1983). The burial was of a single adult male in his late thirties or early forties at the time of his death; the bones were in poor condition, being extremely fragmentary and completely decomposed in places (Schulte-Campbell 1983). The skull shows signs of artificial cranial deformation (i.e., post-bregmatic flattening). Finds from the tomb include twenty-one pieces of jewelry found on the chest and neck of the skeleton itself (fig. 6.11, 1–9); some of these originally formed an elaborate necklace, at the center of which was a gold-mounted faience scarab with cartouche; near the chin rested various pieces of jewelry, including a gold finger ring, a disc-shaped gold pendant, and another gold, crescent-shaped pendant; an additional two earrings and a silver finger ring with engraved bezel were found as a result of careful sieving of the soil from the grave.

The body had apparently been covered with a piece of cloth (garment? shroud?). Three ivory buttons and several bronze pins resting *in situ* near his femur and elbow probably formed part of his dress (see Niklasson 1983:172–87 ff. for detailed catalogue descriptions of the finds from T 23). Several pieces of weaponry accompanied the deceased (fig. 6.11, 10–11), and other burial items (near but not on the skeleton) include two ivory boxes or gaming boards, several faience gaming pieces, three ivory

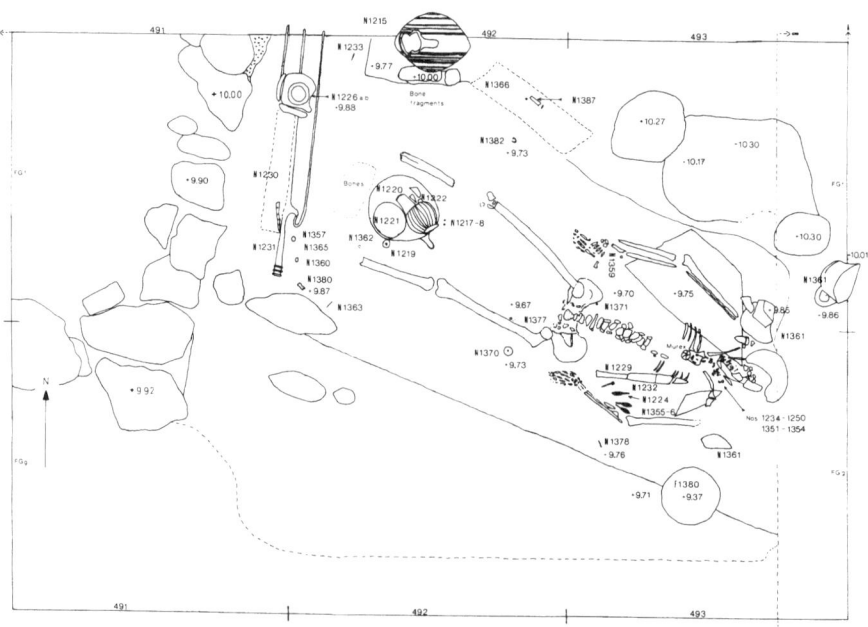

Figure 6.10.   Plan of burial in Tomb 23 at Hala Sultan Tekke Tomb 23 (after Åström et al. 1983:fig. 419).

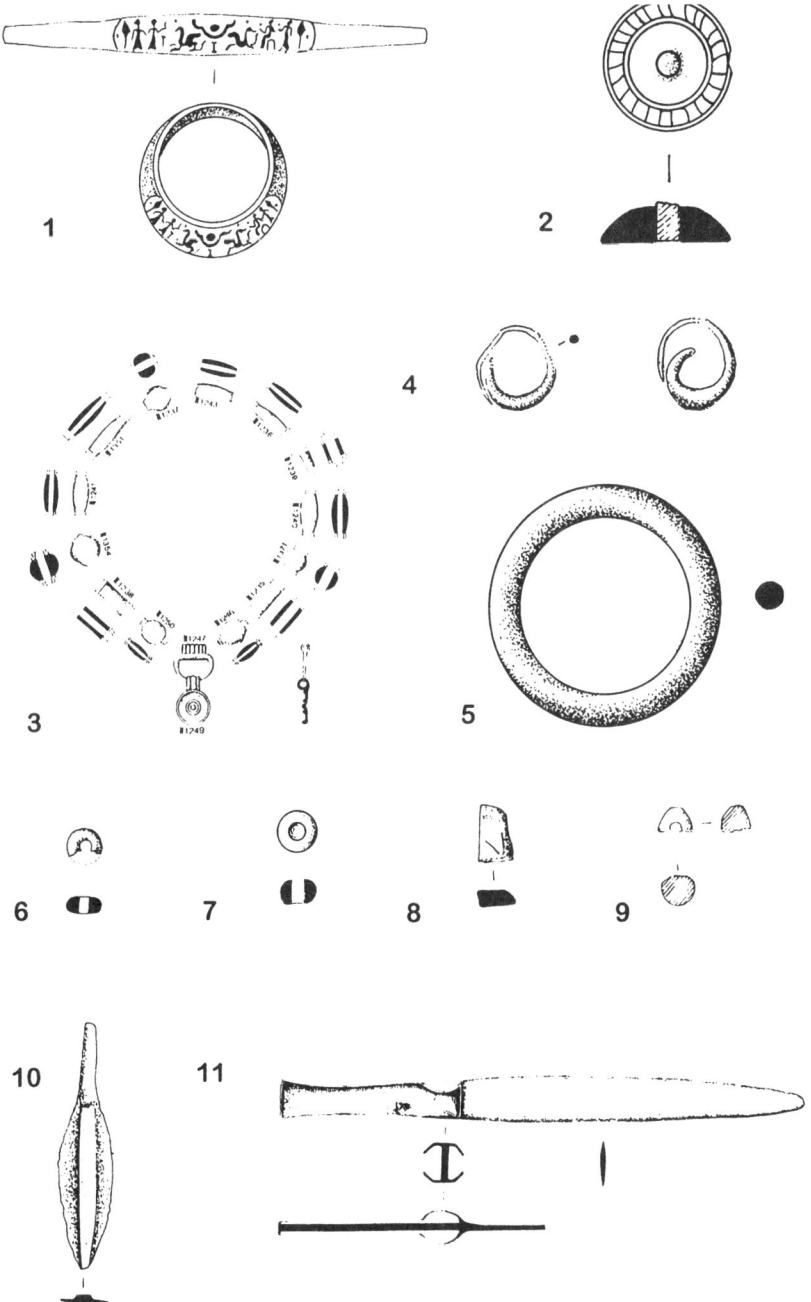

Figure 6.11.   Finds associated with male burial in Hala Sultan Tekke Tomb 23 (after Åström et al. 1983:figs. 492, 497, 510–511, 516).

spindle whorls, a turquoise gold-capped bead near the pelvis, a bronze dagger, and three arrowheads. Parallels for many of the finds in this tomb come from Kition Tomb 9 (LCIIC). Enkomi Tomb 17 (Swedish) Skull No. FCE 38 (LCIIB?) contained the burial of a single individual described in the report as an "old male," who was apparently the last body to be brought into the chamber (reported in Fischer 1986; Fürst 1933; Gjerstad et al. 1934). The skeleton was found *in situ* with feet toward the entrance in outstretched dorsal position. His left hand held a gold bowl (no. 61), and a gold diadem (no. 62) and a mouthpiece of gold leaf (no. 63) were found *in situ* on the skull. His clothing had been fastened by a silver pin (no. 78). Parallels for the gold diadem and mouthpiece come from Swedish Tomb 18 (Skull FCE 43) dated to LCIIC, in association with the burial of a thirty–thirty-six-year-old female.

Ayios Iakovos Tomb 13, level 3, skeleton 2 (LCIIB) contained the burial of a male of indeterminate age (Åström 1972:292; Åström and Åström 1972:801; Fischer 1986: 33; Fürst 1933:27, 52–105; Gjerstad et al. 1934:345–48, 351). The skeleton was found *in situ* to the left of the entrance with its head toward the entrance and was enclosed by a thin stone curbing; finds were found within the curbing, thereby demarcating them from the other burials in this level. Finds associated with the burial include Mycenaean and Base Ring vessels, a faience cylinder (part of a necklace), several gold beads, and one paste bead.

Ayios Iakovos Tomb 13, level 3, Sk. 3 (LCIIB date) was the burial of a forty-eight-year-old male found *in situ* to the right of the door with its head toward the back wall of the chamber (for references, see skeleton 2 above). Finds associated with the skeleton included a White Slip II bowl, a White Shaved bottle, and a set of bronze hair rings.

Kalavasos-*Ayios Dhimitrios* Tomb 14 (LCIIB) contained the remains of two adult males in its large, 3.7 m long chamber (South 1997:165–67). The final report on the skeletal material, including information on the ages of these individuals, has not yet appeared, but information on this tomb has been provided by the excavator (South, personal communication). Like other tombs in the area, Tomb 14 contained a bench, which had been cleared off as if to make room for an additional burial that never took place. Skeleton 1 was a definite male adult, a mature individual with an estimated age of thirty-seven to forty-five years at the time of death. The sex of skeleton 2 is less certain since it was less than 5 percent complete; however, on the basis of dental attrition and size and morphology of the humerus fragments, it appears to be a late middle-age male. Finds from the tomb included a Mycenaean krater and other Mycenaean vessels, a Red Lustrous arm-shaped vessel, Cypriot wares such as base ring cups and White Slip II bowls, three bronze daggers, two gold diadems, finger rings and beads, faience gaming pieces, fragments of gold foil, fragmentary ivory pyxis lids, and a fragment of an ivory duckling from a duck-shaped cosmetic vessel.

Lapithos Swedish Tomb 29 (probably MCIII) contained the remains of an individual described as "a male, not young" (Fischer 1986:30; Myres 1946:78–85, pls. 24–25;

Åström and Åström 1972:184). Finds from the tomb number at least seven bronze objects, including an axe head, a chisel, a pair of tweezers, three eyelet toggle pins, and a needle. The lack of jewelry, however, distinguishes this burial from the other examples above, suggesting perhaps that the practice of interring biological males with objects gendered "male" and "female" was not as pronounced before the LBA.

Dressing for Death: Gender and Social Identity

The notion that people use clothing and other accoutrements of dress to shape individual identity and that identity itself is influenced to varying degrees by the attitudes and customs of society at large, is a growing theme in archaeological investigations of material culture (see Barnes and Eicher 1992; Sorensen 1997; Sorensen 2000:ch. 7). Its history in other social sciences (such as anthropology, sociology, and psychology) is considerably more extensive: catalyzed initially by research on phenomenology and perception in the 1960s (e.g., Merleau-Ponty 1962); developed in writings on semiology (e.g., Barthes 1967); and transmitted from the 1970s onward into sociology, cultural anthropology, and social psychology (e.g., Barnes and Eicher 1992).

Applications of these concepts in archaeology have tended to focus on artistic representations of dress (sculpture, wall painting, etc.) rather than on burial evidence (see Arnold 2002 for an exception). By transmitting social messages, dress serves as a non-verbal means of constructing and communicating identity. It includes clothing, jewelry, hairstyles, cosmetics, body painting, tattooing, scarification, body piercing, and any other kind of ornamentation to the body (Lee 2000). In the case of the "third gender" evidence presented above from tombs of the Cypriot LBA, we are dealing, of course, with three types of material evidence: clothing (the remains of garments on males from Tomb 23 at Hala Sultan Tekke and Enkomi Tomb 17), jewelry (all of the tombs had evidence of various types of jewelry associated with the burials), and cosmetics (Kalavasos Tomb 14). It should also be noted that several other categories of finds conventionally associated with female burials (spindle whorls and needles) were found in several of the tombs.

So, how might we interpret this evidence from a gendered perspective? Or, in semiotic terms, what social messages were being transmitted by the elites of the LBA (whether in reference to the deceased themselves or those who buried them) through their association of male bodies with bodily ornaments frequently associated with biological females? Do these "third gender" burials constitute examples of "cross-dressing" in the LBA, or are there other, more appropriate explanations for these particular sets of mortuary remains? Arguments in support of transgender categories should theoretically demonstrate the existence of two distinct gendered sets of behavior, for which the six burials cited above would constitute "exceptions to the norm."

As always, evidence is scanty, but the most reliable data come from the LCII site of Kalavasos, which has been excavated over the last twenty years in a detailed and scientific manner (see South 1997 and South et al. 1989 for a recent preliminary report). Here, as we have seen earlier in this chapter, several tombs containing burials of adult females (e.g., Tombs 11, 13) have been found with similar repertoires of grave goods as the six male burials cited above; the only difference is that the female burials lack daggers. The other examples of exclusively female burials with similar ranges of luxury goods I was able to identify were Toumba tou Skourou, Tomb 2, chamber 4; Enkomi Swedish Tomb 18, skull no. FCE 43; and Enkomi French Tomb 5 (dating to LCIIIB). What is surprising here, in reference to normative reconstructions of LBA burial customs, is that there aren't more. In other words, a search through the same literature that produced the *six* examples of "third gender" male burials yielded only *five* instances of elite women buried with a similar array of luxury items. As with many other regions of the ancient Near East, it may very well have been the norm rather than the exception for men of high status to be adorned with jewelry, at least for purposes of burial. And, indeed, the inclusion of jewelry and other luxury ornaments in burials may have been more frequently associated with deceased males than with females.

In the attempt to resolve these contradictions, we must first consider what is meant by "identity" in the context of Cypriot mortuary ritual. In the first place, it is highly unlikely that the deceased were projecting merely their own, subjective identities; it is far more likely that the identities of deceased individuals were transmitted, manipulated, inflated, disguised, repressed, or in some other way constructed, by the living members of society in charge of the burial, perhaps by kin or close associates.

The conviction that burials are more about the living than the dead situates mortuary ritual within a social context that enables us to move beyond the concept of individual, subjective identity and to transcend polarized behavioral categories in the effort to distill gendered meanings from customs of funerary dress. By its very definition, then, the concept of "transgendering" rests ultimately on a binary approach, since it involves "crossing the boundary" between dimorphic patterns of male and female identities. In effect, the act of performing gender becomes assimilated to either the male or female pole, once again reflecting the exegetical force of Western thinking. Perhaps, as Arnold has suggested, it would be more helpful to view these polarized categories as part of a continuum rather than as opposite terminals in a system of discrete non-overlapping divisions (Arnold 2002:239).

The Social Context of Mortuary Ritual

An alternative approach to questions of identity, and one that might avoid the theoretical objections just referred to, situates questions of gender, identity, and perception firmly within the dynamic framework of social relations. Such an approach has been adopted in recent work in social psychology, but because of its emphasis on context, it would apply equally well to archaeological analysis. Barrie Thorne, a leading proponent of the "social relations" approach in psychology, has summarized the importance of this perspective:

> Shifting the level of analysis from the individual to social relations and from sex cate-
> gories to the variable social organization and symbolic meanings of gender further
> unravels dichotomous constructions . . . the presence, significance and meanings of [gen-
> der] differences are refocused when one asks about the social relations that construct
> differences—and diminish or undermine them. . . . How is gender made more or less
> salient in different situations? In specific social contexts, how do the organization and
> meanings of gender take shape in relation to other socially constructed divisions like age,
> race and social class? (Thorne 1990:106)

To examine the question of third gender in LBA Cyprus within a more socially oriented framework, we need to keep in mind some of the major socioeconomic developments associated with the period. LBA material culture, and in particular mortuary evidence, presents a picture of greater social-economic division within society than the culture of the earlier phases of the Bronze Age. As we have seen, this is due in large part to the increasing importance of metallurgy, trade, surplus wealth, and demand for foreign products from Near Eastern polities with whom the island increasingly interacted. These behaviors are coupled with the growing presence in the mortuary record of LBA Cyprus of elites buried in tombs with unprecedented wealth and symbolic objects with foreign affiliations used as symbols of empowerment to achieve and maintain prestige and legitimize political control. In the course of these developments, some males and females began to play more prominent roles; but while lesser-status males remain archaeologically visible, lower-status women disappear entirely from the mortuary record.

All six burials cited earlier in this section date to the period between MCIII and LCIIIA, in other words to the period associated with the socioeconomic developments just outlined, and all are instances of biological males adorned with female dress, rather than vice-versa. In earlier periods of the Bronze Age, however, gender fluidity involving females did apparently exist. Lapithos Swedish Tomb 322, chamber B, for example, dating to ECIII, contained a female eighteen–twenty-four years old, with finds including two knives, a sword, and dagger in addition to tweezers and a needle. Fischer dubbed her an "E.C. Amazon" and remarked that "if the finds are personal tomb gifts, the tomb should contain the burial of a female warrior . . . these different tomb gifts should perhaps lead to the conclusion that there are no 'typical male' and 'typical female' tomb gifts, at least during ECIII" (Fischer 1986:29). It thus appears that a significant role reversal may have taken place in mortuary rituals during the MBA and that women and men had begun to negotiate gender in profoundly different ways.

Another interesting pattern present in the six burials under consideration concerns the age of the deceased males, who in every case where age could be determined, were in their late middle ages or older. This suggests that in the LBA, identities of elite males were not always static but changed during the course of the life cycle. With the attainment of a particular age and status, individuals formerly defined as "male" appear to have been transformed to a different gendered state or may even have transcended socially designated gender categories entirely. Similar phenomena are attested to cross-culturally in a number of pre-state societies where specific age sets (i.e., older individuals and prepubescent children) are regarded as gender neutral, and archaeological evidence shows this pattern to have had a wide geographical scope within the Mediterranean region (Treherne 1995).

The burials of these elderly elite males by the surviving members of the group were invariably marked with great ritual and fanfare, and a considerable amount of surplus wealth was disposed of in the process. A proportion of this wealth may have comprised the personal belongings of the deceased, but much of it had no doubt been accumulated over long periods of time by members of his social group, who chose deliberately, whether through social obligation or vested interest, to alter the status of precious commodities by taking them out of economic circulation and placing them in mortuary offerings. Such practices are known, for example, in the eastern Solomon Islands where funerary celebrations and commemorative rites involve the transformation of special objects formerly treated as commodities (which can be bought, sold, or exchanged) to spiritual objects taken out of economic circulation (Davenport 1986). If, indeed, the unprecedented wealth deposited in tombs of LBA Cyprus represents a cultural revaluation of material objects from commodity to noncommodity status, then perhaps the transformation of gender identities among select elite males was intended as a similar passage of the human body from gendered to transgendered state.

On the other hand, if the prime concern of those engaging in the ritual celebrations of the deceased was an ostentatious display of wealth, perhaps it didn't matter what form of wealth was deposited as part of the funerary rites. In this case, wealthy objects would retain their status as precious commodities despite their new ritual context. Goring has shown in her study of jewelry from Tomb 11 at *Ayios Dhimitrios* that earrings probably served as convertible currency at this time, so perhaps the interment of males with "female" jewelry signified not a transformation in gender identity but a blatant display of wealth (Goring 1989). Yet, the absence of traditional "male" artifacts such as knives and daggers is striking, and the fact that elite females do not seem to have been accorded similar "rites of passage" with regard to burial goods may be further proof that men's and women's roles had become more sharply differentiated during the LBA, in death as well as in life, and that for the first time in Cypriot prehistory, men and men alone were privileged to attain the highest ranks within the social, political, and economic structures of society.

Denouement: Themes and Threads   7

> An engendered past addresses many longstanding concerns of
> archaeology: the formation of states, trade and exchange, site
> settlement systems and activity areas, the processes of agriculture,
> lithic production, food production, pottery, architecture, ancient
> art—but throws them into new relief. An engendered past replaces
> the focus on the remains of prehistory with a focus on the people
> of prehistory . . . and concentrates instead on the continuities and
> dialectics of life, the interpersonal and intimate aspects of social
> settings that bind prehistoric lives into social patterns.
>
> —GERO AND CONKEY, "TENSIONS, PLURALITIES, AND ENGENDERING
> ARCHAEOLOGY: AN INTRODUCTION TO WOMEN AND PREHISTORY"

WHILE THE PRECEDING CHAPTERS HAVE CONSIDERED various bodies of evidence for gender in ancient Cyprus—architecture, economy, technology, figurative art, skeletal remains, and mortuary evidence—the cross-cutting themes that link them have been obscured to some degree by their treatment as discrete cultural entities. The aims of this chapter, therefore, are to reconsider some of the salient aspects of gender that cut across the boundaries between the various classes of material evidence and to attempt to distill meaningful patterns from the evidence concerning the ways in which gender identities were realigned and reconstituted over the course of many millennia.

The richness and depth of the archaeological record allow me to present only a partial view of those developments, and the selection of particular themes for discussion has been based both on the contextual connotations of the archaeological data and on central areas of interest and debate in current research on gender archaeology. I am the first to acknowledge the limitations of this endeavor. Post-processual approaches in archaeology have fostered a multiplicity of new perspectives that are wide ranging and complex, and many of them are relevant to analyses of gender (Brumfiel 1992). However, the evidence treated in earlier chapters of the book lends itself particularly well to the following topics: gender and agency; gender and the life cycle; the embodiment of gender; and gender ambiguity and multiplicity. Although these themes intersect and overlap, I will consider them separately for the sake of clarity. Finally, I shall summarize some of the main diachronic patterns of gendered behavior that took place during the *longue durée* of successive Neolithic, Chalcolithic, and Bronze Age cultures on the island and will examine the emergence of gender hierarchies against the backdrop of increasing socioeconomic complexity. Particular attention will be placed in this discussion on the interfaces between the construction of gender and the rise of complex society during the LBA.

Gender, Agency, and Power

The concept of social agency has been central to the shift from processual to postprocessual models in archaeology and to the development of archaeology of gender (Brumfiel 1992; Hekman 1995; Hodder 1982; Johnson 2000; Shanks and Tilley 1987). While the application of agency theory to archaeological interpretation is still in its early stages, and while more work is needed to define what we mean by social agents (Dobres and Robb 2000), it has had a tremendous impact on recent research due to its emphasis on subjectivity, female empowerment, and resistance to instruments of social oppression (for recent discussions of these themes, see Barrett 2001; Dobres and Robb 2000; Gardiner 1995; Johnson 2000; Nelson 1997; and Sweeley 1999).

Agency theory has helped restore human features to the "faceless blobs" of archaeological tradition. During the earlier phases of gender archaeology (more appropriately labeled the "archaeology of women"), the concept of agency played an important role in claiming for women a central place within the enormous tide of economic and technological innovations being explicitly or implicitly credited to males (Gero and Conkey 1991; Gero 1991; Wright 1991; Wylie 1991). More nuanced approaches to gender in recent years have taken on board Gidden's concept of "structuration" that positions subjective actors within their particular social and historical contexts (Giddens 1984). As Shanks and Tilley have stated, "individuals are competent and knowledgeable while at the same time their action is situated within unacknowledged conditions and has unintended consequences" (Shanks and Tilley 1987:116). In this way, feminists have been able to embrace theories of agency while avoiding essentialist pitfalls imbedded in Cartesian notions of subjectivity based on a prediscursive, masculinist self (Hekman 1995).

The concept of social agency has been central to discussions in several of the earlier chapters of this book. In chapter 2, the architectural space of the domestic environment was regarded as a stage for the daily performance of gendered identities (see also below, Dimensions of Gender). Rather than simply reflecting underlying social structures, however, the built environment helped to fashion and reshape gender relations. The privatization of space as a long-term process in Cypriot prehistory was seen as contributing to the emergence of the household and the demarcation of boundaries between social groups. Within this revised social framework, there emerged new roles for men, women, and children, and these became more differentiated and less egalitarian over time (see below, Gender through Time).

In chapter 3, I considered a different body of evidence that is equally relevant to agency theory, namely the evidence of lithic, ceramic, and textile production for the gendered division of labor. Androcentric assumptions concerning the introduction of these important technological innovations, as well as the practice of these industries over the course of several millennia, were shown to be unfounded. The acceptance and promotion by scholars of a sexual division of labor early within the prehistoric sequence (in Cyprus as well as most other areas of the ancient world) rests on sociobiological concepts of "naturalized identities" that are divorced from social agency (Yanagisako and Delaney 1995). By questioning these essentialist notions and placing agency at the center of the analysis, we are able to resituate conventional discourses of the gendered division of labor into more appropriate economic, political, and historical frameworks.

Finally, mention should be made of some of the criticisms of agency theory that have been voiced by feminist archaeologists engaged in gender research. Particularly strong arguments against the adoption of agency theory in feminist discourse have been put forth in a recent article by Gero (2000). Her main objection concerns the masculinist bias inherent in applications of agency theory that implicitly link social action to male subjects (activities such as exercising authority, mastering the environment, initiating alliances and trade, etc.). In privileging "active" subjects and by placing agency at the center of social theory, she argues, we "risk promoting and reiterating the deep divide between active males and passive females" (Gero 2000:34).

In several of the earlier chapters of this book, I have drawn attention to what I see as the problems of the gender-neutral terminology used in models of socioeconomic complexity in Cyprus, particularly during the LBA (e.g., Knapp 1993, 1994; Manning 1993, 1998b). Because the gender of emerging elite groups among the urban polities of LBA Cyprus is never specified, implicit assumptions privileging male participation in the developing copper industry, the emergence of hierarchical political structures, and the involvement of Cypriot polities in international trade and politics are allowed to emerge. Future discussions of such important topics as the development of the Cypriot economy and the shift from egalitarian to hierarchical modes of social organization should make deliberate efforts to avoid this pitfall. Placing gender at the forefront of the discussion of socioeconomic complexity would help to reveal the faces of elite social actors and might begin to resolve some of the critical objections Gero raised about the role of agency theory in current archaeological interpretation.

Gender, Age, and the Life Cycle

Important contributions to the archaeology of gender have been made in recent studies examining the relationships between gender and age (e.g., Fedigan 1997; Gilchrist 1999:ch. 5, 2000; Moore 1994; Morbeck et al. 1997; Thomas 1996). Central to these discussions have been changes in gender identities associated with transitions in the human life cycle, underscoring the fluidity of gender constructs not only over long stretches of time but within the relatively brief time spans of individual lives. The biological and cultural transitions from "cradle to grave" vary considerably both spatially and diachronically, and the most crucial of them are often marked by ritual ceremonies such as initiation rites, marriage ceremonies, and mortuary feasts (van Gennep 1960). In pre-state societies, men and women frequently participate in different sets of rituals that both reflect and reiterate gendered identities and help to define and reconstruct their social roles. It is thus possible to argue that time itself is gendered and that gender alters one's experience of time (Gilchrist 1999:81; Thomas 1996).

In chapter 4, I discussed some of the gendered aspects of the life cycle in prehistoric Cyprus through an examination of various classes of anthropomorphic representations. The unprecedented production during the Chalcolithic period of female figurines and pendants in birthing postures, for example, was interpreted within a system of ritual beliefs and ceremonial acts associated with fertility, pregnancy, and birth that does not appear to have existed in earlier times (Lorentz 1998:33). In displaying, clutching, and manipulating these objects, women engaged in ritual behavior that affirmed their powers and capacities in social reproduction and substantiated their roles as valued members of society. Males, too, are likely to have been involved in rituals of initiation at this time, but, as we have seen, evidence for male imagery is extremely scanty.

An extension of the repertoire of anthropomorphic images during the Cypriot Bronze Age involved the manufacture of vessels with figurative appendages participating in scenes of daily life. One of these vessels, the "Marki bowl," discussed in chapter 4 (fig. 4.10), depicts sequentially the various stages in an individual female's life, including a rare depiction of pregnancy otherwise unknown in the figurative material of the period (Lorentz 1998:46). The diachronic scope of the scenes on the bowl constitutes a kind of visual biography of the various gendered identities experienced during her lifetime; by the same token, the mortuary contexts of many of the scenic compositions attest to their value and importance to the community of the living beyond the lifetime of the deceased.

Considerations of age and life-cycle stages underscore the lack of attention normally given by archaeologists to childhood and senescence and to the ways in which age structures social identities (Gosden 1994; Moore and Scott 1997; Rossi 1983; Thomas 1996; Zihlman 1999). As learners and practitioners of gender, children play important roles in the transmission of gendered identities (Deverenski 1997). Frequently neglected or marginalized in archaeological studies, a consideration of children's roles is integral to our understanding of the constructive processes of gender.

In chapter 5, I looked at selected aspects of the social construction of childhood in ancient Cyprus, focusing in particular on the ways in which definitions of the child varied through time and overlapped with gender constructs. The differential treatment of children in pit graves of the MChal–LChal, for example, was shown to coincide with the segregation of males and females in mortuary contexts and with changing economic and kinship structures. Later in the same chapter, I demonstrated some of the ways in which skeletal evidence of cranial deformation during the Bronze Age constituted an important means by which children's identities were shaped to mark their membership in elite social groups (see below, Gendered Bodies). At the same time, the increased visibility of infants and adolescents in the figurative art of the Bronze Age was seen as underscoring their important roles as social actors at a time when political and economic structures on the island were becoming more complex.

Since the majority of adults in prehistoric societies died by the time they reached modern middle age, it is more difficult to assess the overlaps between gender and age during the later phases of the life cycle. The excavation at many sites in Cyprus of considerable numbers of female skeletons of childbearing age, as well as numerous skeletal remains of neonates and infants, draws our attention to the biological risks of pregnancy and birth, which must have been regarded as dangerous periods of transition in the female lifecycle. Gendered differences in the experience of time are also suggested by mortuary evidence from the LBA in which elderly males of elite status appear to have transcended binary gender constructs (see chapter 6 as well as below, Ambiguity and Multiple Genders). These and other examples (such as Ribeiro's discussion of prepubescent children as a third gender category, discussed in chapter 5) illustrate the reciprocal relationship between age and gender and underscore the fluid nature of gender constructs over time.

Gendered Bodies

Among the most frequently investigated topics in the recent research on gender has been the study of the gendered body. Numerous articles and books on the subject have appeared over the last decade, ranging from theoretical single-authored works by feminists, gay and lesbian authors, social theoreticians, and queer theorists (e.g., Butler 1993; Diprose 1994; Gatens 1996; Grosz 1994; Shilling 1993) to edited works and conference proceedings that apply those theories to various contexts in the past and present (e.g., Barnes and Eicher 1992; Lancaster and di Leonardo 1997; Montserrat 1998; Price and Shildrick 1999; Rautman 2000; Wyke 1998). While much of the recent interest in the gendered body has been influenced by the work of Foucault, in particular his concern with the embodiment of sexuality, power, and social control (e.g., Foucault 1979), Foucault's writings have been criticized by feminists for marginalizing the female subject (e.g., McNay 1992; Sawicki 1991). Current studies on the gendered body in past societies have moved beyond Foucauldian concepts of the body by focusing on the roles of individuals (Bailey 1994; Knapp and Meskell 1997; Meskell 1998, 1999, 2000, 2001). Although there are many challenges to the archaeological interpretation of bodies, owing to the fragmentary nature of the evidence, the possibilities for gendered perspectives afforded by the archaeological record in investigations into the analysis of mortuary evidence, human skeletal material, and representational art are considerable.

It is regrettable, therefore, that excavations during the nineteenth and much of the twentieth century in Cyprus paid little attention to human skeletal remains, many of which were summarily recorded and discarded and are consequently unavailable for study today. An exception to this otherwise dismal picture was the work of Lawrence Angel, a physical anthropologist who served as a specialist with a number of excavation teams in Cyprus during the 1950s and 1960s. His exemplary analyses of skeletal remains from Khirokitia, Sotira, and Kourion have provided the basis for my discussion of practices of head shaping (ACD) among the prehistoric populations of the island in chapters 5 and 6 (see Angel 1953, 1961, 1972). As we saw in those chapters, patterns of occipital flattening on skulls of adults prior to the LBA appear to have resulted accidentally through the practice of cradle boarding, while patterns of post-bregmatic flattening, which first appear during the LBA, cannot have been accidental. The deliberate flattening of skulls in these contexts appears to be connected with the marking of elite identities; moreover, its application to male and female skulls alike indicates its function as a signifier of class affiliation rather than gender ideology.

The treatment of the gendered body in the previous chapters of this book has concerned itself to a great extent with the rich and varied bodies of figurative evidence from Neolithic, Chalcolithic, and Bronze Age contexts (see also below, Gender Ambiguity and Multiple Genders). In chapter 4, I traced the development of anthropomorphic figurines during the Chalcolithic period and Bronze Age and attempted to correlate the changes in the representation of the female body to developments in the social and economic spheres. The cessation of birthing figurines during the LChal and the production of plank figures and scenic compositions during the ECIII–MCI transition was seen as reflecting changes in society accompanying the intensification of agriculture and increasing levels of sedentism over long periods (see below, Gender through Time). At the same time, the use of figurines and genre scenes in ceremonial and ritual performances associated with life-cycle events helped shape and reiterate the gendered identities associated with the aging process and events of the life cycle (see above, Gender, Age, and the Life Cycle).

Chapter 4 also considered the theme of the embodied individual by reviewing recent studies of Cypriot figurines by a Campo (1994) and Knapp and Meskell (1997). While a Campo's reductionist typology was shown to conflict with her suggestion that they may represent individuals, Knapp and Meskell's focus on decorative rather than formal attributes offers greater latitude to this hypothesis by emphasizing the variations between, rather than the similarities among, the different types. Nevertheless, their claim that individuals can first be observed in the archaeological record of the Cypriot Bronze Age is undermined by the richly varied corpus of RW painted figurines of the Chalcolithic period; their decorative elements express a variety of stylistic traits that, according to this line of argumentation, might support their candidacy as individuals. The evidence of figurines would thus appear to situate the initial appearance of recognizable individuals in the archaeological record of Cyprus within MChal rather than the Bronze Age, that is, within a framework of incipient rather than more fully fledged complexity (Knapp 1993). There is clearly plenty of scope for further research on this subject, but, as I have suggested in chapter 4, arguments for individuality could be strengthened by a more careful scrutiny of the figurines and a closer consideration of their contextual associations.

Gender Ambiguity and Multiple Genders

Theories of embodiment have taken critical issue with Cartesian dualities of mind/body, inside/outside, self/other, male/female, and sex/gender (e.g., Butler 1990, 1993; Grosz 1994; Marks and de Courtivron 1980; Price and Shildrick 1999; Rautman 2000). Butler's concept of performativity, as well as Bordieu's *habitus*, have been instrumental in attempting to understand the mechanisms by which conventional social norms, including gendered behavior, are constructed and reiterated (Bordieu 1977, 1990; Butler 1990). The pervasiveness of binary social categories in Western thinking has given them the appearance of "natural" rather than culturally constructed phenomena and consequently has had a strong impact on archaeological interpretation of the past. Polarized categories of sexual classification are evident in most traditional analyses of figurines in Cyprus, which are presumed to represent either male or female forms (Hamilton 2000). In fact, many prehistoric figurines in Cyprus display no clear indications of sex. There are a variety of possible reasons for this: perhaps the sex of these images was not important to those who made them and other messages were being communicated; alternatively, the sex may have been encoded in ways that we cannot fathom or could only be deduced from contextual information that we are currently lacking. It is also possible that that they represent multiple or fluid gender categories that were deliberately intended to be ambiguous.

Several studies cited in previous chapters have raised the issue of gender ambiguity and the possibility of third gender categories. In chapter 4, I summarized recent work by Talalay and Cullen, who interpret the RP plank figurines of the Bronze Age as expressions of communal solidarity rather than individual identity (Talalay and Cullen 2002). The lack of clear sexual markers on most of these figurines, as well as their find contexts (most were found in multiple chamber tombs of large communal cemeteries that were in use for several generations or more), supports this hypothesis and underlines the importance of contextual considerations in the interpretation of figurative material. According to Talalay and Cullen, the sexual ambiguity of these classes of figurines may attest to the relative unimportance of individuality or sexual classification within the framework of social messages they were intended to communicate.

In chapter 5, I considered evidence presented in a recent article by Ribeiro in which sexless figures in scenic compositions of the Bronze Age were interpreted as prepubescent adolescents (Ribeiro 2002). Ribeiro believes that gender ambiguity on the figures in these scenes was deliberate, and that children of sub-adult status may have held a "genderless" or "third gender" status. While there is ample ethnographic evidence to support this view, there are difficulties with the archaeological interpretation of the material; these have been discussed in chapter 5. Nevertheless, Ribeiro's work is a rare attempt to go beyond simple dimorphic gender groupings in the treatment of figurative evidence.

The performativity of gender can be seen not only in the production and use of figurines in life-cycle events but also in the strategic performances and ceremonies associated with mortuary rituals. Since funerary ritual tells us as much about the living community as it does about the deceased, the analysis of funerary evidence can highlight the important role of community and society in the cultural construction of gender (Parker Pearson 1999). Curiously, the engendering of mortuary evidence has only recently become a subject of major investigation in archaeological research (Arnold and Wicker 2001).

In chapter 6, evidence for multiple gender categories was discussed in reference to mortuary remains from elite burials of the LBA (see also above, Gender, Age, and the Life Cycle). There, the skeletal remains of elderly, high-ranking males were adorned with costume and ornament and jewelry that in other contexts could be regarded as gendered female; they were also adorned with personal accoutrements and weapons that were gendered male. The difficulties of interpreting this evidence within a nonbinary framework were addressed in chapter 6, as was the importance of looking beyond Cyprus to relevant bodies of evidence from the Mediterranean region and beyond, where the construction of identities among elite warrior classes was effected through a similar "transgendering" or "ungendering" of male bodies (Treherne 1995). Although it is unlikely that the individuals in the Cypriot burials constituted a warrior class, their age (over fifty years of age), social status (elite), and associated sets of finds are similar and may indicate the adoption of foreign gender constructs on the island through processes of acculturation that helped reshape masculine identity during the later phases of the Bronze Age.

The gender mutability of deceased individuals in mortuary contexts of the LBA demonstrates with particular clarity the ways in which the various categories of gender analysis considered in the preceding pages can overlap and intersect, for it combines factors of age, the life cycle, the gendered body, gender difference, gender fluidity, and social agency within a single body of evidence. Although many additional themes could be singled out for investigation here, I will leave them for another occasion and turn instead to a consideration of some of the fundamental diachronic changes in gender and social complexity in ancient Cyprus that, by reference to some of the evidence presented in the previous chapters, I shall attempt to throw into greater relief.

Challenging Unilineal Modes of Social Change

In considering various aspects of gender in ancient Cyprus from the hunter-gatherer rock shelter site at Akrotiri down to the urban polities of the LBA, I have drawn on evidence for social developments that occurred over the course of more than eight millennia. Here, I wish to distill from the details of the previous chapters what I regard as the central transformations in gender constructs during that *longue durée* of Cypriot prehistory and assess the degree to which changers in gender relations and gender identities can be correlated with other trajectories of social, economic, and political change.

Transformations of Gender in Early Cypriot Society

It is unfortunate that so little is known in Cyprus of what may have been a lengthy if sporadic hunter-gatherer past. It is hard to imagine that the Akrotiri rock shelter, discussed in chapter 3, constitutes the only attempt by early seafarers to colonize the island during the 1,000 or so years between its abandonment and the first appearance of settlement during the Cypro-PPNB. It is therefore highly likely that marine transgressions during the Early Holocene have obscured the visibility of former coastal settlements (Peltenburg et al. 2001a, 2001b). Nevertheless, these early attempts, if they existed, are likely to have been short-lived enterprises, and, as has been reported elsewhere in this book, it was not until about 8500 B.C. that colonizing efforts on Cyprus met with a greater degree of success.

Much has been written in the literature on gender about changes in female roles and statuses with the shift from hunter-gatherer to agricultural life styles (for a recent discussion, see Peterson 2002), so it is important to ask whether the transition to an agriculturally based economy in Cyprus during the Neolithic period can be correlated with changes in gender relations. On the basis of evidence presented in chapters 2–5 on Neolithic and early Chalcolithic societies, we would have to argue that the adoption of agriculture per se does not seem to have made a significant difference. This concurs with recent research by Bender who, in searching for the "roots of inequality" in the past, has likewise maintained that the adoption of agriculture did not dramatically affect gender hierarchies (Bender 2000). As I have shown in chapter 3, various lines of evidence, from the production and use of chipped stone tools and the introduction of ceramic technology to the lack of substantive evidence for a division of labor among early agricultural communities, point harmoniously to the persistence of egalitarian social structures throughout the Neolithic period and EChal.

Visible differences began to emerge during the MChal–LChal, and these may be correlated with increasing degrees of sedentarization toward the end of the fourth millennium B.C. In chapter 4, I traced some of the major developments in the long tradition of figurative art produced during most phases of Cypriot prehistory. Schematic figurines were prominent among the island's Neolithic and Chalcolithic cultures. Many early examples incorporated dual elements of male and female anatomy or were so schematic as to be merely suggestive of a generic human form, but others became more naturalistic and differentiated during the Chalcolithic period, culminating in the remarkable production during the MChal of a set of human figurines that are recognizably sexed as female. The latter formed part of a symbolic system associated with pregnancy, fertility, sexuality, and birth linked closely in mortuary and other ceremonial contexts to women and children.

Many of the figurines are likely to have been displayed and manipulated in female initiation rituals, while the cruciform pendants (whose seated postures mimic birthing figures) may have been worn as personal talismans or jewelry by individual females throughout their life cycle; some clearly accompanied their owners to the grave, as they were included as burial items in some MChal pit graves. At the same time, the evidence of male figurines and emblems of male sexual anatomy suggests the practice of male initiation rites, although contextual evidence for the objects associated with those rituals is extremely limited. The gendered division of ritual performance, therefore, appears to have been central to the construction of gendered identities during the MChal. While many of the more schematic figurines from Kissonerga show no evidence of sex, those that do are clearly female (Goring 1991a). The greater degree of social differentiation presented by figurative art in domestic and mortuary contexts is also visible in other types of material evidence, in particular the segmentation of space within the domestic structures, first observed in the later fourth millennium B.C. at Lemba and particularly Kissonerga, which may be linked to changes in sociopolitical structures and gender relations (Peltenburg 2002).

Similar shifts in gender relations have been observed by Draper in research on the social effects of sedentarization among the !Kung (Draper 1997). Although Draper's research applies to hunter-gatherer rather than horticultural groups, her results enable us to make important correlations between sedentary life styles and degrees of social differentiation. In particular, sedentarization appears to be associated with higher levels of gender segregation among children and adults. These changes, both for the !Kung and for early farming communities in Cyprus, did not immediately result in a hierarchical ranking of gender statuses. However, they may, in fact, be indicative of an early stage in a long-term trajectory of social changes that, under certain circumstances, led to the establishment of social norms involving separate spheres of male and female activity and a nonegalitarian ranking of gender roles.

The deliberate breakage and defacement c. 3000 B.C. of many of the figurines in the Kissonerga ritual deposit marks an end to a set of gender-related rituals that appear to have played an important role in the island's early cultures for more than a millennium. Although still a unique event in Cypriot prehistory, this ritual act may signify the first stage in the restructuring of gender relations, a process that continued during the third and well into the second millennium B.C. Patterns of alterity also continue, as we have seen in evidence of some of the scenic compositions of EC–MC date showing gendered divisions of labor. The new "communal spirit" that emerged during the Bronze Age, as suggested by the construction of larger settlements with agglomerative architectural plans and by the abandonment of individual graves and tombs in favor of large communal cemeteries, was also characterized by new forms of economic activity and social interaction associated with the intensification of agriculture and the Secondary Products Revolution (Sherratt 1983).

The latter did not exclude women from contexts of primary productive labor or public life, but it is likely that they required greater time commitments by females to economic pursuits and child-rearing responsibilities within the domestic environment, as suggested by new figurine types depicting parental figures whose sex, when indicated, can usually be regarded as female (but see Hamilton 2000). A newly emerging division of labor along the lines of gender would have been further reinforced by the shift from larger kin groups to smaller nuclear units of economic production ("households"), a development that is clearly apparent from the architectural record of the later third millennium B.C. and characterized by increasing privatization of the domestic sphere (see chapter 2).

In summarizing the changes in social constructs in Cyprus prior to the LBA, it is important to emphasize that shifts in gender relations occurred in different contexts at different times and that changes in some of the more symbolic aspects of gender and material culture, such as the production and use of anthropomorphic figurines, appear to have anticipated the differentiation of gender roles in the economic sphere. The punctuated nature of socioeconomic change, as well as the apparent discontinuity of settlement between the Aceramic Khirokitian culture and the Sotira culture of the LNeo, may help account for the relative stability of gender constructs over long periods of time (such as the 3,500-year time span from Aceramic–EChal). At any rate, the evidence as it now stands does not permit us to infer significant distinctions between male and female roles. The persistence of long-established egalitarian economic structures well into the Bronze Age may, in turn, help explain why the development of incipient levels of socioeconomic complexity on the island did not immediately lead to a hierarchical realignment of gender roles or to the fragmentation of gender identities into communities of difference.

In other areas of cultural interaction, however, gender constructs appear to have been renegotiated as early as the late fourth millennium B.C. As we have seen in several of the earlier chapters of this book, the rapid pace of social change observable during the MChal–LChal marked the start of an accelerated trajectory of socioeconomic complexity that continued throughout the third and into the second millennium B.C. This was accompanied by fundamental changes in the social construction of gender that created "worlds of difference," not only between women and men but within the monolithic category of "women" as well.

Gender and Complex Society in the Late Bronze Age

Due to economic, social, and political developments stemming from earlier phases of the Bronze Age, Cypriot society during the LBA clearly attained a level of complexity not seen previously on the island. But there is still considerable controversy concerning the nature of regional interaction and political organization of the island's first "urban" settlements. Debate in recent years has focused on whether the various regional polities formed what can be regarded as a state, as implied by the evidence of international correspondence during the fourteenth century (the "Amarna letters") between various rulers of Egypt and the "king of Alashiya" now widely accepted as representing all or part of Cyprus (Knapp 1994; Muhly 1996; Peltenburg 1996; but for a contrasting view see Merrillees 1992).

Peltenburg (1996) has made a strong case for the proposal that Cyprus achieved state-level status during the earlier phases of the LBA. A network of fortresses situated between Enkomi and the copper sources of the Troodos in LCI, he argues, may be linked to Enkomi's role in the copper industry and to its exercise of widespread or possibly island-wide political, military, and economic control. By the fourteenth century, however, Enkomi became just one of several important coastal polities, such as Kition and Hala Sultan Tekke, which were impressive both in size and wealth.

An alternative model has been proposed by Keswani (1996b), who points to significant regional differences during LCII and doubts that the island was administered by a single centralized authority at any time. In her view, the absence of archaeological evidence for a centralized bureaucratic control, such as a unified system of ritual practices or iconographic symbols, attests to modes of heterarchical rather than hierarchical political organization. These arguments have been challenged in a study of ritual architecture and iconography in the LBA by Webb, who believes that the standardized character of artifacts such as ritual terracotta figurines and bull rhyta, as well as the content of glyptic iconography, in fact comprise a common symbolic system manipulated by a central authority (Webb 1999:307). On the other hand, while powerful chiefs may have held sway, either regionally or beyond, for short periods of time (as proposed by Manning 1998b), it is unlikely that a single authority ever managed to exercise control over the entire island any time during the LBA. Political organization suggests, instead, a pattern of devolved authority as well as a periodic tendency toward volatility and social unrest: hardly a steady one-way avenue to statehood.

Recent archaeological research has shown that among the prehistoric cultures of the ancient Near East, there were many paths to social complexity (Yoffee and Cowgill 1995; Yoffee and Sherratt 1993). The recursive, parochial character of the growth of socioeconomic complexity in Cyprus is certainly not unique among the societies of the ancient world, and this is crucial to an understanding of gender constructs of the protohistoric and early historical periods of the island since it would have promoted greater latitude and variation in the social construction of gender than might otherwise have been the case. We should also keep in mind that processes of secondary state formation have different causes and effects from those associated with the rise of pristine states, such as the Mespotamian polities, the Aztec empire, or dynastic Egypt (Price 1978). Among pristine states, bureaucracies were more firmly entrenched and leadership more despotic; in the framework of the patriarchal state, women's roles, whether social, economic, or political, were heavily circumscribed, as I have discussed in chapter 3 with regard to women's roles in textile production.

Universalizing models of social change linking gender (in particular, a decline of female status) to the rise of the state are inappropriate here, not only because they fail to muster the necessary supporting evidence but also because they marginalize the role of social actors (groups and individuals) in the transformation of sociopolitical processes (Crumley 1987; Moore 1994:73–74; Silverblatt 1991). In Cyprus, as elsewhere, the construction of more complex political and economic structures during the LBA stemmed from the dynamic interplay of social agents with existing sociopolitical structures and resulted in the restructuring and realignment of human relationships and the fragmentation of gender identities (Moore 1994). Although changes in gender constructs during the LBA were closely linked to the emergence of stratified economic and social classes, the latter varied from region to region and, in the absence of a centralized political apparatus, may have fluctuated over relatively short periods of time.

Under these circumstances, an individual's place in social hierarchies (gendered or otherwise) is likely to have been more effectively enhanced by association or affiliation with emergent elites. This may help explain the apparently contradictory evidence in the mortuary record of the later Bronze Age (discussed in chapter 6) in which high proportions of female elite burials occur at some localities but not at others (Keswani 1989). It may also account for the differential practice of cranial deformation (post-bregmatic flattening) as a status marker on selected individuals at certain sites (discussed in chapter 5) and the representation in bronze statuary of both male and female figures (deities?) standing on oxhide ingots (i.e., the Ingot God and Bomford figurine); both were important ritual symbols used strategically by increasingly powerful groups to legitimize their social status and to maintain their political authority (see chapters 1 and 4). While chiefly women can be seen to enjoy a high status within their rank and class, it is important to acknowledge that it was probably by virtue of their class and not their gender that they managed to do so.

Ethnographic evidence suggests that as rank and class begin to supplant kinship as major structuring principles of political and economic organization, production and reproduction become separated, resulting in many cases in the diminution of female status (Gailey 1987:17–21). For non-elite women in complex societies, productive labor is devalued and reproductive capacities are constrained and controlled to ensure the subordination of non-elite to elite groups. While the status of non-elite males also declines, male identities are not fragmented to the same degree and males retain a modicum of status by virtue of their more highly visible productive roles. Gendered patterns in burial practices of LBA Cyprus (discussed in chapter 6) are relevant to this discussion since they are characterized by differential treatment of lower-ranking men and women. Although the archaeological record contains considerable numbers of burials of non-elite males, non-elite females are virtually absent.

The changes in social status and gendered identities resulting from the emergence and growth of more stratified societies affected individual lives in profound ways and must have led to tensions and antagonisms within and between social groups. Indeed, the political landscape of LBA Cyprus, in which urban polities emerged in fits and starts and centralized authorities remained geographically and temporally circumscribed, adumbrated the tensions and inequalities that must have ensued as older communal forms of social organization became encapsulated by non-kinship-based institutions. As part of this process, gender, like kinship, became an important "arena of struggle" (Gailey 1987:266). The fragmentation of gender identities and the emergence of gendered "worlds of difference" can be attributed to successful attempts by elite men and women to restructure gender identities along economic lines. However, the non-unilineal trajectories of change associated with the rise of urban polities during the LBA, as well as their regionally divergent characters, attests to the ability of non-elites to successfully resist the emergence of a fully integrated, overarching state. While all women in Cyprus may have lost status as women in the transition to complex society, and while the status of non-elite women appears to have dropped to the bottom of the gender hierarchy, women's roles in social, political, and economic life remained more flexible and less rigidly circumscribed than those of many of their Near Eastern sisters.

Dimensions of Gender: Time, Space, and Relativity

The narratives of Cypriot prehistory I have presented in this book treat gender as a process rather than an abstract entity. Time is a crucial element in this process, acting simultaneously on a number of levels: within the lifetime of individuals, where it is linked to the life cycle and the aging process; from generation to generation through processes of enculturation; and diachronically over considerably longer periods, both immanently and extrinsically as the result of acculturation with nonindigenous ethnic groups. I have also tried to emphasize the multidirectional aspect of social change, a concept that is diametrically opposed to the unilinear models adopted in many studies of the remote past.

Contextual evidence for gender in ancient Cyprus argues very strongly against such straightforward modes of interpretation; on the contrary, it privileges models of culture change that are sensitive to particular temporal and spatial contexts and to the complex dynamics of social interaction.

Space constitutes a second critical dimension of gender, as I discussed in particular in chapter 2 where I examined the dynamic relationships between gender and architectural space and focused on the increasing privatization of space as a metaphor for changes in kinship structures and gender relations. The close interaction between social actors and the built environment in prehistoric settlements is neatly expressed by what Tringham has called the "life histories" of houses (Tringham 1994). By reconstructing the built environment, people continually endow space with social meaning; at the same time, the structures they create shape the narratives of their own biographies. From the relatively small scale of architectural space one can extend the analysis of gendered space to larger places, such as villages, towns, and regions. Regionalism as a central factor in political, social, and economic life persisted throughout all phases of Cypriot prehistory, becoming particularly visible during the LBA with the rise of urban centers that despite their similar structures retained distinctly regional traits. Considerable variation can also be seen in mortuary evidence and settlement remains, and these, as I have observed earlier, are likely to have been connected to regional variations in sociopolitical structures, including variations in gender relations.

Finally, we can consider the larger spatial entity of the island itself as a factor in the social construction of gender (Ardener 1993; Massey 1994; Spain 1992). For much of its prehistory, Cyprus was isolated from neighboring cultures of mainland Anatolia, the Levant, Mesopotamia, and Egypt. Even more remote were the cultures of prehistoric Greece and Italy to the west. Although the early colonizing phases of the island testify to interaction between Cyprus and the mainland as early as the tenth millennium B.C., the tentative nature of that interaction can be seen by the failure of early colonizing efforts to effectively take root, underscoring the difficulty of early settlers to survive in relative isolation and to maintain contact with their mainland roots.

Prior to the Bronze Age, Cypriot society was allowed to progress to a large degree along its own lines of development, without significant involvement or interference from foreigners. As we have seen in earlier chapters, that situation began to change during the LChal, when influxes of new ethnic groups from mainland Anatolia arrived on the island and introduced new technologies and a new economic life style (a new *habitus*) centered on the use of the plow and traction animals (Frankel, Webb, and Eslick 1995). From that point on, the island underwent successive though intermittent periods of acculturation that culminated with the Hellenization of the island at the end of the eleventh century (Webb 1999:6–7). Cyprus's entry into the vast space of the Mediterranean world, and the reciprocal influx of foreigners onto its shores, had a particularly decisive impact on its traditional political, economic, and demographic structures. In time, this led to the establishment of a complex, multicultural society in which gender relations were refashioned along lines of "difference."

Post-processualism's greatest contribution has been its break with generalized views of the past that claim to be "scientific" or "objective." The knowledge that "reality" is subjective and that there is no such thing as an absolute truth can be viewed with either considerable relief or profound disappointment, depending on one's critical view of the world. For better or for worse, however, it has made us aware that in neglecting to undertake deliberate theoretical research agendas in our studies of the past, or by failing to take the time to become aware of our unconscious views about society, we are likely to encounter the pitfalls of essentialist or presentist interpretation (Wylie 1998).

It is hard to imagine an archaeology of gender emerging within a traditional analytical framework or within the theoretical confines of ecosystems theory that, owing to its definition of cultures as well-integrated adaptive systems, is incapable of investigating the effects of human interaction on the dynamics of social change (Brumfiel 1992). A key determinant of the future of gender research in Cyprus, therefore, involves a greater willingness among archaeologists to engage in more critical and theoretically based approaches to the past. This means taking risks, both with ourselves and with our material, but it has to be a more intellectually rewarding process than simply describing, cataloging, and summarizing what we find.

Another crucial key to greater acceptance of gendered narratives of the Cypriot past concerns the gender of the narrators, since the pursuit of archaeological fieldwork on the island has always been a predominantly male prerogative. While this situation has begun to change in recent years, the male-dominated structures within the field for more than a century have profoundly shaped the way Cypriot archaeologists think about the past, including the establishment of chronologies, terminologies, and research agendas that have become so entrenched and inert as to defy revision. And, in spite of the acceptance and application of post-processual models by some archaeologists in recent years, research on gender has been virtually neglected.

With few exceptions, discourses on socioeconomic complexity, for example, which fail to treat gender as an integral component, have been narrated by males enjoying solid bases of power within the academic establishment (almost all are tenured professors) who can be regarded as successful competitors for the "prestige goods" of publishing in top-rung journals, securing financial backing for research, and successfully advancing and implementing new research agendas. The disproportionate allocation of academic prestige, distinction, and power along predominantly male lines will continue to perpetuate androcentric narratives of the past. In order for gender to become firmly established as a legitimate domain of research, therefore, archaeologists working in Cyprus need to become more critically aware of the existing political structures within the field, in particular its male-dominated systems of academic appointment, project management, and financial support. The reasons for the gender inequities imbedded in these institutions, as well as the prospects for significant change over the coming decades, are explored in the final chapter.

Epilogue: Cypriot Archaeology— Who Tells the Story?

8

> The androcentric interpretation and presentation of the past is both structured by, but also fed into, the larger ideological and symbolic domain of our contemporary society, as the past duplicates and legitimates present-day norms and values.
>
> —GERO, "SOCIO-POLITICS OF ARCHAEOLOGY AND THE WOMAN-AT-HOME IDEOLOGY"

ALTHOUGH WRITTEN NEARLY TWENTY YEARS AGO, Gero's article "Sociopolitics of Archaeology and the Woman-at-Home Ideology," of which the passage above is an excerpt, is relevant to the practice of archaeology today, particularly in terms of the close correlations it draws between modern ideologies of gender and the interpretation of gender roles in the remote past. Archaeology has been slow in developing a critical awareness of gender, both in its interpretation of the past and in its professional practice. Although women's participation in archaeological fieldwork and research has increased considerably during the last two decades, particularly among those employed in the United States, men continue to be more successful at obtaining high-ranked teaching positions, funding for research programs, management positions as directors of field projects, publications in top-tier peer-reviewed journals, and recognition in the establishment of research agendas. These and other inequities have persisted in promoting and reinforcing gender divisions within the field and in legitimizing essentialist paradigms in the interpretation of the past. In absolute terms, then, men still run the archaeological show.

While there is much cause for continued pessimism regarding issues of equity for women in the field, there is also positive evidence that conditions are beginning to improve. Women's status and visibility rose considerably during the 1990s, to such an extent that Gero's image of the stereotypical male archaeologist as hunter/conquerer/adventurer and the stereotypical female as the "stay-at-home housewife secluded in the base camp or lab or museum, sorting and organizing materials" can not be applied as readily today (Gero 1985:344). As I have tried to emphasize in earlier chapters of this book, post-processual and feminist approaches in archaeology have exposed many of the androcentric biases inherent in many "objective" and unmediated accounts of the past and have encouraged the pursuit of research that is more critically and theoretically grounded. Among other things, this has helped transform the status of gender-based research from a marginal (and highly suspect "political") pursuit to a legitimate area of archaeological inquiry. Strong pockets of conservatism—particularly the public funding of research projects—continue to ignore or discourage research projects in which gender plays a central role, but there have been considerable advances for women over the last decades that enable us to adopt a more positive prognosis for the future (Nelson, Nelson, and Wylie 1994).

For archaeologists working in Cyprus, where traditional interpretive models still dominate most research agendas, there have been significant, positive changes over the last decade in women's participation in fieldwork, research, and publication. Although these developments are only just beginning to be felt, they may ultimately have a significant impact on "who tells the story" of the Cypriot past. This, in turn, should lead to substantial revision of many of the theories and methods currently used in the interpretation of societies of the remote past, particularly with regard to gender.

In this chapter, I will review some of the statistical evidence available for assessing gender roles in the practice of Cypriot archaeology from 1970 to the present. After a brief look at changes within the larger field of classical archaeology in general, I will consider some aspects of gender equity in fieldwork, research, and publication in Cyprus. I will then speculate on what I see to be the likely role for women in Cypriot archaeology during the years to come.

On account of the strong links between Cyprus, Greece, and Rome in historical periods, Cypriot archaeology arose in the United States as a minor subdiscipline of classical studies. It has traditionally been offered as a course of study at only small number of universities (usually in Classics departments) sponsoring field projects in Cyprus. Although the first American excavations on the island were aimed at investigating sites of the island's prehistoric or proto-historic periods (such as Kourion and Lapithos), the practice of Cypriot archaeology remained firmly rooted within the relatively conservative tradition of classical studies.

A recent book by Dyson paints a vivid picture of the staid and restrictive climate in which this tradition functioned in the early decades of the twentieth century by examining the role of the American School of Classical Studies (ASCS) in Athens (1998). During the early years, women enrolled at the ASCS were encouraged to attend classes and participate in its programs, but they were not permitted to join in on field expeditions since the latter constituted an exclusively male domain (Dyson 1998:88). Only a handful of women, intent on careers involving excavation and fieldwork, refused to acquiesce and managed to achieve their research goals outside of the rigid framework of the school. The best known of these renegades, Harriet Boyd Hawes, surveyed Crete on muleback in full Victorian dress and later became the self-appointed director of excavations at Gournia, a non-palatial Bronze Age site in the east of the island (Bolger 1994b). Her final excavation report on this important Minoan town site is still regarded an exemplary piece of scholarship (Hawes 1908).

Despite the successes of Hawes and other like-minded scholars, however, relatively few women in succeeding generations followed in their footsteps; as a result, the direction of field projects continued to exist as an almost exclusively male prerogative throughout the first half of the twentieth century. In Cyprus, which was regarded in the public imagination as a more "foreign" destination offering a far less acceptable working environment for women than Greece, there was no female director of excavations prior to the late 1930s. The volume *Who's Who in Cypriot Archaeology* (Åström 1971), which contains biographical and bibliographical details on archaeologists who were active in Cypriot archaeology at the time, lists Joan du Plat Taylor as the only woman director of excavations during the 1930s–1960s (du Plat Taylor excavated the Byzantine site of Ayios Philon in 1938–1939 and Apliki, an important metalworking site of the Bronze Age, in 1939). Presumably, Emily Vermeule's excavations at Toumba tou Skourou in Morphou (1971–1974) and the appointment of Anita Walker as co-director of field excavations at Idalion (1971) occurred too late for inclusion in this volume.

Thus, the initial entry of women into the upper echelons of archaeological research occurred a full generation later in Cyprus than in Greece, a factor that may help account for the exceedingly slow pace with which the field has moved toward gender parity. Before turning to equity issues in Cyprus, however, it will be useful to outline the situation in classical archaeology generally in America today, since the latter can serve as a barometer for evaluating the differential levels of male and female participation in the field of Cypriot archaeology over the last thirty years.

Equity Issues in Classical Archaeology: Recent Evidence

Recent reports on issues of gender equity in classical archaeology in the United States have estimated that women constitute between 40 and 50 percent of the population in the discipline (Cullen 2002). This means that more women are earning advanced degrees and obtaining academic positions than was previously the case. In spite of this positive trend, however, publication rates remain higher for men than women. For example, the leading journal for classical archaeology in the United States, the *American Journal of Archaeology* (*AJA*), averaged 38 percent acceptance for articles submitted by women and 62 percent acceptance rate for men during the period 1986–1995 (Cullen 2002). Cullen notes that these figures coincided with submission rates during those years (again, 38 percent women, 62 percent men), so in this case publication rates do not appear to have been the result of bias by academic peer reviewers or editorial staff. In recent years (1996–1997), women have begun to achieve parity with men in *AJA* in numbers of submissions and acceptances of articles, but Cullen asserts that it is probably too early to tell whether these statistics constitute a temporary blip or a long-term trend. It would be useful to compare these figures with those from other prominent archaeological journals to see if similar changes are taking place.

Men still appear to fare better than women in situations where participation is invited; twice as many book reviews in *AJA*, for example, are written by men than women, and only 25 percent of speakers in *AJA* invited lecture series for 1995–1997 were female. This suggests that men are more successful at networking than women and/or that existing power structures in academia, which have always been dominated by males, continue to more vigorously promote the careers of males. Women, in turn, may be less likely to network successfully in environments that are less willing to accommodate them. It seems clear that the attainment of true parity for men and women within the field of classical archaeology would have to involve the restructuring of traditional bases of power along more egalitarian lines.

Gender Inequities in Cypriot Archaeology

Webb and Frankel have noted trends similar to those noted for classical archaeology in the United States for archaeologists working in Cyprus (Webb and Frankel 1995). After examining in detail publication lists, conference proceedings, journal articles, and other sources relevant to Cypriot archaeology, they came to the following conclusions regarding the gender structures within the field:

1. Statistical analysis of publication lists from *Who's Who in Cypriot Archaeology*, totaling more than 1,000 references, concluded that females authored less than 20 percent of scholarly publications before 1970; this low proportion can be attributed to the lack of women in archaeological positions in the early years of the discipline rather than to overt discrimination by editors of books and journals (Webb and Frankel 1995:95–96).

2. Examination of papers presented at sixteen major international conferences on Cypriot archaeology shows an increase over time, doubling during the 1980s (Webb and Frankel 1995:96–97). Women's participation in this aspect of publication appears to be significantly higher than in journals. Reasons for higher female visibility in conference volumes is not easy to explain but may be tied to the more flexible structures of conference organization that tend often to accommodate as many participants as possible. This contrasts with more highly structured and elitist peer-review processes characteristic of most high-end journals.

3. Gender inequities in the direction of fieldwork were determined by looking at the annual reports in *Bulletin de Correspondance Hellénique* (*BCH*), which summarize

results of excavations conducted in Cyprus each year (Webb and Frankel 1995:98 and fig. 6). During the 1970s and 1980s, women accounted for fewer than 20 percent of directors or co-directors of fieldwork projects. In contrast, by 1992 more than 40 percent of field projects were being directed by women, and this trend continues today. Given the great prestige attached to direction of fieldwork projects, this may be the single most important achievement by women in Cypriot archaeology over the last ten years.

The results of Webb and Frankel's study point to the increasing visibility of women within the field of Cypriot archaeology over the last fifty years. While disparities still exist, particularly in the direction of field projects, the publication of theoretical and methodological contributions, and the attainment of tenured academic positions, the situation is rapidly changing, and there is good reason to expect that women's visibility in these key areas will continue to increase in the coming years. This optimistic attitude seems to be shared by younger scholars polled by Webb at a workshop of international scholars in Nicosia in 1994. About than half of the women who returned the questionnaire (most were undergraduate and graduate students) expressed a belief that, despite the difficulties they would undoubtedly face, they would ultimately succeed in attaining a senior academic post. In contrast, 90 percent of males interviewed had the same attitude, suggesting that women still face (or perceive that they face) greater obstacles than men in the pursuit of careers in archaeology (Webb and Frankel 1995:99–100). Men's greater confidence in attaining their career goals, coupled with their belief that women face no more difficulty than men in getting jobs, is likely to reflect the present gendered structures within the field, which are still dominated by males, despite recent inroads made by women.

Gender and Publication in Cyprus: Evidence from the
Report of the Department of Antiquities, Cyprus

One of the most important gauges for gender equity in archaeological research is research output in scholarly journals. For Cyprus, the main academic journal for archaeological reporting is the *Report of the Department of Antiquities, Cyprus* (*RDAC*), an annual volume that, since 1970, has published articles by Cypriot and foreign scholars on a wide range of topics, including preliminary excavation reports, survey results, specialist reports, inscriptions, and studies of Cypriot material in museum collections. Although some archaeologists choose to publish elsewhere, particularly if they are presenting issues of theoretical or methodological interest, they are strongly encouraged to use the journal as a regular vehicle for the presentation of basic archaeological data and interpretation.

Articles submitted to *RDAC* are not subject to peer review. In principal, the decision to accept or reject them rests with the director of antiquities, but, in fact, there have probably been few rejections over the years. Most articles submitted to the journal are accepted for publication without revision, provided that authors are bona fide archaeologists working in Cyprus or on Cypriot collections abroad who have obtained legal permission to excavate, survey, or study their material. While this egalitarian acceptance policy is highly commendable in some respects since it encourages everyone in the field to publish, it has resulted in a product of uneven quality: without peer review, quality control is left to the authors themselves, and there is no pressure or requirement to revise or rewrite a submission.

As we might expect under such circumstances, some articles are of exceptionally high standards; others are fairly weak. Because there are no theoretical or methodological criteria for acceptance, many articles are straightforward accounts of annual field campaigns consisting of descriptive reports of excavation procedures, architectural remains, mortuary features, and various classes of artifacts. Some articles present descriptive reports about single artifacts or groups of artifacts in private collections and public museums of Cyprus, Europe, Australia, and America, while others address issues of chronology or foreign relations. Few introduce innovative methodological or theoretical perspectives, and those archaeologists wishing to disseminate more specialized research usually choose an alternative publishing venue.

Despite these drawbacks, the *RDAC*'s open acceptance policy means that the opportunity to publish is open to all academically minded individuals participating in programs of archaeological research on the island. For present purposes, this allows us to look at gendered patterns of scholarly publication in Cypriot archaeology without the "background noise" of biases frequently associated with the decision-making processes of peer reviewers and editorial committees. An analysis of articles from *RDAC* is thus important not only for detecting gender-related patterns in publishing but also for gaining insights into differential patterns of participation by men and women in fieldwork and research generally. By tracking gender-related changes in the contents of the journal since its inception, we can gain a fairly accurate idea of the degree to which gender constructs within Cypriot archaeology have actually changed over the last thirty years and where the differences between men and women still lie. In addition, they furnish important evidence for speculating on the possibilities of gender equity in the future.

The article by Webb and Frankel discussed earlier in this chapter, which examined proportional representation of male and female authors in *RDAC* from 1970 to 1992 (Webb and Frankel 1995:98), revealed that an average of 36 percent of articles were written by women during that period. All authors were counted equally, regardless of whether they were single authors or formed part of a joint or collaborative team. In the present investigation, I have taken a somewhat different approach. Single-authored articles published between 1970 and 2001 (638 total) were entered into a database listing the author's name, sex, and year of publication. Each article was then classified into one of five subject types based on its primary content, construed either from the title or, in some instances, by skimming the article itself. These categories are described and abbreviated as follows:

1. Artifact Reports (AR) (reports, other than scientific analyses, of material remains such as pottery, sculpture, figurines, coins, etc.)
2. General Reports (GR) (thematic overviews, discussions of chronology or topography, foreign relations, etc., not based on current fieldwork)
3. Scientific Analyses (SCA) (metallurgical studies, chemical or molecular analyses of pottery, discussion of radiocarbon dates and probabilities, etc.)
4. Site Reports (SR) (preliminary reports on survey or excavation of sites or regions)
5. Textual/linguistic reports (TXT) (reports/translations of texts or inscriptions)

Finally, a brief description was entered concerning the specific content of the article (e.g., under AR, whether the focus was pottery, sculpture, or metal objects). This was intended to provide potential information on correlations between gender and research objectives.

A second table includes data for jointly authored articles. The latter were divided into two groups: articles by two individuals (referred to throughout this chapter as "coauthored" articles) and articles authored by three or more individuals (referred to as "collaborative" articles). Co-authored articles were further subdivided into four groups: articles by two females (female co-authors); articles by two males (male co-authors); articles jointly authored by a male and a female in which the first author listed was female (female/male co-authors); and articles by a male and a female in which the first author listed was male (male/female co-authors). These were recorded chronologically according to year of publication, and contents were skimmed for classification into one of the five types listed above. In the case of collaborative articles, each article was listed chronologically according to the principal author's name and sex, and each article was classified into one of the five types just described. In addition, the total number of authors was recorded, along with information regarding the total number of male and female collaborators; if this information was not clear from the table of contents, names were gleaned from the text itself. In several cases, it was not possible to determine the sex of some of the participants, but the number of such cases was low and had no significant bearing on the statistical results presented in the tables below.

Single-Authored Articles

A total of 638 single-authored articles appeared in the *RDAC* between 1970 and 2001, 390 (62 percent) of which were written by males and 236 (38 percent) by females; the remaining twelve authors were not known to me, and their sexes could not

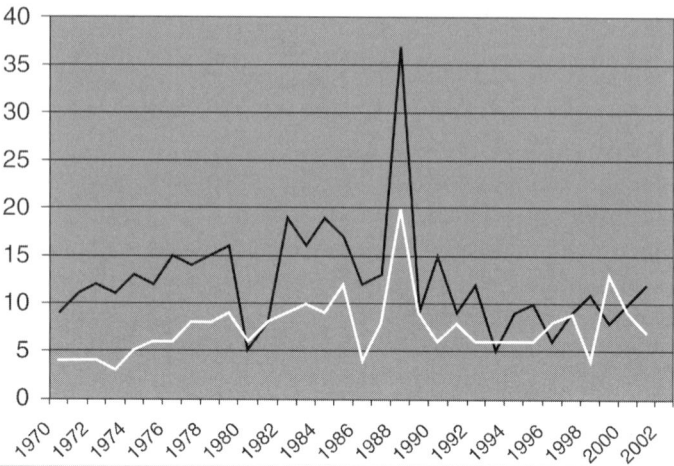

Figure 8.1.   Numbers of male and female single authors in *RDAC* 1970–2001, by year (black=male; white=female).

be determined from their names. These figures correspond closely with those cited by Webb and Frankel above for the years 1971–1992 in which authorship by women averaged 36 percent (Webb and Frankel 1995:98). Figure 8.1 provides percentages of male- and female-authored articles from 1970 to 2001; the sharp increase in contributors for the 1988 volume was due to the publication of a special two-volume issue coinciding with the retirement of a former director of antiquities. In table 8.1, percentages of male and female authors are averaged according to decades (1970–1980, 1981–1990, 1991–2001) in order to track diachronic changes. The results show a steady increase over time in proportions of female-authored articles, with percentages rising from 32 percent in the first decade to 37 percent in the second decade and to 45 percent in the final decade. During this thirty-year period, male participation declined proportionally from a high of 68 percent (1970–1980), to 63 percent (1981–1990), and then to 55 percent (1991–2001).

In addition to rates of publication, gender differences can be observed in the selection of research topics within the general categories listed above, although some categories showed greater differences than others (tabs. 8.2 and 8.3). Within AR studies,

Table 8.1.   Percentages of Male and Female Single Authors in *RDAC* by Decade

	%M	%F
All Years	62	38
1970–80	68	32
1981–90	63	37
1991–2001	55	45

Table 8.2.   Distribution of *RDAC* Article Types by Sex

Type	Number	%M	%F
AR	279	58	42
GR	155	69	31
SCA	11	82	18
SR	127	75	25
TXT	53	30	70

females authored 118 (42 percent) of a total of 279 articles, while males authored 161 (58 percent). This amounts to a slightly higher rate for women than the overall female average (38 percent). In fact, artifact reports accounted for precisely 50 percent of all single-authored articles by women, whereas they comprised only 41 percent of single-authored articles by males.

Topics occurring five or more times among female-authored entries were pottery, figurines, stone sculptures, coins, and seals; topics occurring five times or more among male-authored entries were pottery, figurines, stone sculpture, coins, metal objects, and architecture. In an interesting departure from standard gender stereotypes, five females and only one male wrote articles on stone tool assemblages. It should be noted, however, that the five female-authored articles were written by three members of the same British-based project and thus not indicative of general trends.

There were 155 GRs; 31 percent were authored by females and 69 percent by males. Here, the proportion of females is far below that of males and also well below the overall average for females (38 percent). GRs account for only 20 percent of single-authored reports by females, while they constituted 27 percent of male reports. Common examples of general topics by females included ceramic typology and relative chronology, foreign relations, mythology, religion, temples, and sanctuaries. General topics frequently covered by males included stratigraphy, topography, metallurgy, chronology, religion, general interpretive reports, and critical reviews of others' work.

SCA reports formed only a small proportion of single-authored articles in *RDAC* (presumably these more specialized reports were published as joint articles and/or in other journals); nevertheless, there was a significant gender gap. Of the eleven reports in this category, only two (18 percent) were by female authors, whereas nine (82 percent) were by males. Scientific analyses thus account for less than 1 percent of total single-

Table 8.3.   *RDAC* Article Types as Percentages of Total Male and Female Contributions

Type	Number M	%Total M	Number F	%Total F
AR	161	41	118	50
GR	107	27	48	20
SCA	9	2	2	1
SR	95	24	32	13
TXT	16	4	37	16

authored articles by females and just over 2 percent of single-authored articles by males. The topics covered by the female-authored reports were factor analysis of cemeteries and a neutron activation analysis of ceramics; reports by men included metallurgical analysis of slag; spectrographic, x-ray diffraction, and chemical analysis of pottery; osteological studies; and radiocarbon analyses. Again, this indicates a wider range of topics among male authors.

Apart from scientific analyses, the most pronounced differences in subject selection occurred in the authorship of preliminary SRs. Of the 127 articles in this category, only 32 (25 percent) were written by women whereas 95 (75 percent) were written by men. Among the total range of topics in single-authored articles, moreover, SRs formed less than 14 percent of female articles, while they accounted for nearly 25 percent of articles by males. These figures undoubtedly reflect the greater participation by men than women in field research, a topic that will be taken up in the discussion of collaborative articles (see below). Nevertheless, a breakdown of percentages by decades shows important changes over time. For the years 1970–1980, thirty-three SRs were authored by men and only three by women (a 10 x 1 ratio of M:F); between 1981 and 1990, thirty-five SRs were written by men, while only six were written by women (about a 6 x 1 ratio of M:F); however, in 1991–2002, twenty-seven were written by men and twenty-three by women (just over a 1 x 1 ratio M:F). This indicates that many more women began directing field projects during the 1990s. If this trend continues, women will soon achieve parity with men in this prestigious area of archaeological research.

The final category of topics, articles on ancient texts and inscriptions (TXT) is the only category in which women outdistanced men. Of fifty-three total TXT reports, thirty-seven (70 percent) were by females, and sixteen (30 percent) by males. TXT topics formed 16 percent of single authored articles by females and only 4 percent of those by men. This is the least "archaeological" of all the subject areas, with closer connections to languages and linguistics than archaeology proper. The high proportions of female authors may be due to the fact that this type of research can be carried out independently, at home, or in a library rather than as part of an excavation team demanding long periods of time in the field. The study of texts and inscriptions provides a good publication opportunity for women who either are not interested in a career involving fieldwork, lack the necessary experience and training, or, for various reasons, do not have the time to participate in lengthy excavating seasons far from home.

Co-Authored Articles

Ninety-nine co-authored articles were published in *RDAC* between 1970 and 2001. Of these, nine were written by female co-authors, twenty-five by male co-authors, and sixty-five by male/female co-authors. Taking all of these together, 83 women (42 percent) and 115 men (58 percent) have engaged in jointly authored research over the thirty years of the journal's publication, indicating a slightly higher rate of female participation than for single authored articles (see above).

Within each general category of co-authorship, counts were made of the numbers of instances in which a male's name or a female's name appeared first, with a view to determining patterns of senior and junior authorship (see tab. 8.4). For female/female co-authors, seven out of nine articles listed authors' names in alphabetical order, a pattern that suggests a high degree of egalitarian partnership. Patterns among male/male co-authors were somewhat different. Of the twenty-five articles in this category, twelve were in reverse alphabetical order, clearly designating one of the two males as the senior author. This suggests that male collaboration takes place on a different basis from that of females, with a senior male scholar promoting the work and career of a younger or more junior male; such collaborative strategies for publication do not appear to have been adopted among women archaeologists working in Cyprus, at least as far as I can judge from entries in the *RDAC*.

In the case of the sixty-five articles by male and female co-authors, forty-one (approximately two-thirds) listed men as first authors (these are designated in tab. 8.4 as male/female co-authors), and twenty-four (approximately one-third) listed females as first author (designated in tab. 8.4 as female/male co-authors). While the position of names in jointly authored research may simply reflect the alphabetical order of authors' last names, it is significant that about half of both the male/female co-authored submissions and half of the female/male co-authored submissions were in reverse alphabetical order. This suggests that roughly equivalent numbers of women and men were first authors in joint submissions to *RDAC*. Although this ratio may at first seem surprising, many of the authors in question are senior members of excavation teams in which males normally hold the position of director, and females are recognized specialists who are highly regarded as academics in their own right.

Gender differences were observed in the types of topics addressed in co-authored articles. Although both female co-authors and male co-authors contributed general reports (GR) and reports on artifact assemblages (AR), females co-authored only a single excavation report (SR) and no scientific analyses (SCA). Males, in contrast, co-authored two scientific reports and thirteen excavation reports, statistics that again attest to men's greater level of participation in fieldwork. These figures change dramatically when we

Table 8.4.   Numbers of Males and Females in Coauthored Articles in *RDAC*, 1970–2001, by Article Type

Article Type	F/F co-auth	M/M co-auth	F/M co-auth	M/F co-auth	Totals
AR	5	6	14	13	38
GR	3	4	2	8	17
SCA	0	2	2	1	5
SR	1	13	6	19	39
Totals	9	25	24	41	99

look at cross-gender co-authorship: among the twenty-four female/male co-authored articles, for example, there were six site reports (SR) and two scientific analyses (SCA); and among the forty-one male/female co-authored articles, there were nineteen site reports (SR) and one SCA. Although ARs still account for the greatest single article type among male/female and female/male co-authors, the greater percentage of women authors of site reports in this category contrasts sharply with women as single authors or women co-authoring with other women. One strategy that helps women gain entry into the prestigious arena of excavation reporting, then, is academic partnership with a high-ranking male. However, this is more likely to happen when the male is senior author of the report.

Collaborative Articles

The greatest degree of gender inequity in Cypriot archaeological publication occurs in the area of collaborative research, which is defined here as an article jointly authored by three or more individuals (tabs. 8.5 and 8.6). Only eleven articles, or 15 percent of all collaborative articles, had women as their principal authors, and there were none before 1984. During the 1980s, thirteen females and thirteen males were involved in collaborative projects led by females; in the 1990s, these numbers were reduced to three females and five males, and, at the same time, the overall number of female-led collaborative projects declined. This suggests that it may be some time before the effects of greater female participation in fieldwork direction are felt in publication output.

Finally, the breakdown of participants in collaborative articles led by females shows a relatively equal level of male and female participation, with females totaling 47 percent of contributors and males 53 percent. In contrast, men have been senior authors in 85 percent of the collaborative work in *RDAC* and have been doing so for more than a decade longer than women. The difference can probably be attributed to men's traditional roles as dig directors and to their greater success at obtaining the necessary funding for excavations and other types of collaborative research (two-thirds of the collaborative articles with a male as senior author were preliminary survey or excavations reports).

Table 8.5.   Numbers of Males and Females as Principal Authors of Collaborative Articles in *RDAC*, 1970–2001

	Principal F	% Principal F	Principal M	% Principal M	Total no.	Total %
Article Type						
AR	3	4	3	4	6	8
GR	0	0	9	13	9	13
SCA	3	4	8	11	11	15
SR	5	7	41	57	46	64
Totals	11	15%	61	85%	72	100%

Table 8.6.   Numbers of Male and Female Contributors to Collaborative Articles in *RDAC*, 1970–2001

	Total F in F-led works	Total M in F-led works	Total F in M-led works	Total M in M-led works	Totals
1970–1980	0	0	10	24	34
1981–1990	13	13	35	49	110
1991–2001	3	5	44	78	130
Totals	16	18	89	151	274

On the one hand, the statistics suggest that women have benefited from collaborative authorship with men in recent years. During the 1970s, only ten females and twenty-four males were involved in authoring collaborative articles, but numbers in both sexes increased dramatically during the 1980s, when thirty-five female and forty-nine male participants did so. While males doubled their numbers during those years, female participation increased 3.5 times. And, whereas female participation continued to increase during the 1990s, the increase was not as dramatic (forty-four females and seventy-eight males), and collaborative teams, which currently generate the overwhelming majority of archaeological reports in Cyprus, continue to be made up of many more males than females. Since one of the strategies for "getting ahead" in an archaeological career is association with a well-established team connected to a university or other academic institution, these numbers are meaningful indications that gender parity has not yet been truly attained.

Archaeological Practice in Cyprus: Problems and Prospects

The various statistics referred to above show, on the one hand, that male-dominated traditions in the practice and administration of archaeology in Cyprus have been slow to change. At the same time, however, we can begin to see significant changes in the archaeological workplace that are likely to have positive effects for women in the coming years. Key to these changes is the marked increase in recent years of women's involvement in fieldwork, especially the greater numbers of women now directing excavations (survey projects on the island continue to be a male-dominated precinct).

Today's academic market often requires that candidates wishing to be hired or promoted in the field be directors or managers of field projects; further, recent Ph.D.s who work primarily in the lab and are not in the position to organize and direct a field project are finding it more difficult to obtain an academic position. Similar trends can be noted outside the academic sphere. Important changes regarding the administration and excavation of archaeological sites, for example, are currently underway in the Department of Antiquities of Cyprus (Pilides 2002). In recent years, greater numbers of women have been hired into positions as archaeological officers, and all are required to direct and publish excavations (whether rescue excavations, longer-term projects, or both) as part of their job remit. Since the Department of Antiquities is a branch of the civil service in Cyprus, these junior officers can expect to be promoted and gradually move into the senior administrative ranks, and it will not be long before the department will appoint its first woman director. Whoever she is, she will serve as an important symbol of the move toward gender parity now being felt in all areas of archaeological research and publication on the island.

In conclusion, women's greater participation in excavation and administration of archaeological sites should ultimately work to overcome the traditional "glass ceiling" for their promotion within established research hierarchies. However, this is not the only factor involved in the move toward gender equity in the field. As we have seen elsewhere in this book, post-processualism has fostered a diversification of research agendas in recent years, even among archaeologists working in Cyprus.

Emphasis on theory and methodology, on interpreting evidence rather than unearthing new finds, means that innovative approaches to material culture can be undertaken that do not necessarily depend on the continual unearthing of excavated finds. These developments coincide with radically new perspectives in cultural heritage and cultural resource management that no longer endorse long-term excavation of archaeological sites as a primary research objective. As excavation increasingly comes to be regarded as a destructive process, promoting the exploitation of a valuable and nonrenewable cultural resource, measures are being taken by governments to limit the number and scale of excavations and to encourage archaeologists to shift their attention to the publication of excavations that have already taken place.

The theme of cultural resource management formed the topic of a lively plenary discussion at a recent conference on archaeological survey organized by the University of Cyprus in Nicosia in which the survey and rescue excavation of areas threatened by rapid tourist development were explicitly targeted as important focal points for future activity. If continued discussion along these lines proves successful in generating greater respect for the environment and more stringent enforcement of the antiquities laws, it may ultimately help redefine and reprioritize current research agendas. Within this newly constructed framework, the stereotypical "cowboy" image of the archaeologist, which already appears ridiculously anachronistic in most academic circles, may one day be put to rest entirely, resulting in new structures for research and publication that grant a more central role to gender issues. Such programs would serve to promote principles of equity for women and men in the archaeological workplace while helping us overcome many of the long-held stereotypical views about gender that have long distorted our understanding of the past.

Cypriot Prehistory: A Brief Overview

A RCHAEOLOGICAL ACTIVITY IN CYPRUS began in earnest during the middle of the nineteenth century when Cyprus was part of the Ottoman Empire and archaeological research was still in its infancy. Much of this work was illicit and unprofessional and it was undertaken for profit rather than for the advancement of science (see Goring 1988). Scientific work began only later in the century, and the classification of the various phases of Cypriot prehistory into technologically based periods of stone, bronze, and iron represented a local adaptation by early archaeologists in Cyprus of the Three Age system of Thomsen, Worsaae, and Montelius (tab. app. I.I).

The application of this system to Cypriot material, and in particular the classification of material remains into typological groupings that could be ordered chronologically, was among the chief contributions of Sandwith, Myers, Ohnefalsch-Richer, Gjerstad, and their successors. Also of fundamental importance for the establishment of a relative chronological framework for Cypriot prehistory was the work of the Swedish Cyprus Expedition during the second quarter of the twentieth century, who were responsible for the excavation of numerous sites across the island and produced a monumental series of publications still used extensively by archaeologists today (e.g., Gjerstad et al. 1934).

With the exception of a single site (Akrokiti-*Aetokremnos*), which has been classified as Epipaleolithic, all of the stone-age sites on the island can be assigned to the new stone-age or Neolithic period, with evidence for occupation during three distinct chronological and cultural phases: the Early Aceramic Neolithic (or Cypro-PPNB), Late Aceramic Neolithic (Khirokitian culture), and Late Neolithic (also known as the Ceramic Neolithic period or Sotira culture). In addition, as the result of the discovery of copper artifacts made by Dikaios during his sounding at Erimi, a fourth age or era of prehistory known as the Chalcolithic, or Copper Age, was introduced. Meanwhile, Bronze Age sequence labels (Early, Middle, or Late Cypriot) were widely

Table App. 1.1.   Traditional and Revised Chronologies for Cypriot Prehistory

Traditional Chronology and Periodization

Chronological Period	Cultural Designation	Years B.C.
Epipaleolithic	Akrotiri phase	10,000–9500?
Early Aceramic Neolithic	Cypro-PPNB	8500–7000
Late Aceramic Neolithic	Khirokitian	7000–5500
Ceramic (Late) Neolithic	Sotira culture	4500–3900
Early Chalcolithic	Early Erimi culture	3900–3400
Middle Chalcolithic	Middle Erimi culture	3400–2800
Late Chalcolithic	Late Erimi culture	2800–2400
Chalco/Bronze Age transition	Philia culture	2500–2300
Early Bronze Age	Early Cypriot	2300–2000
Middle Bronze Age	Middle Cypriot	2000–1650
Late Bronze Age	Late Cypriot I	1650–1450
	Late Cypriot II	1450–1225
	Late Cypriot III	1225–1050

Revised Chronology for Bronze Age Cyprus (Knapp 1994)

Chronological Period	Subdivisions	Years B.C.
Prehistoric Bronze Age	Philia culture-Early Cypriot	2400–2000
	EC-MC II	2000–1700
Protohistoric Bronze Age	MC III-LC I	1700–1400
	LC II	1400–1200
	LC III	1200–1000

Note: Dates through third millennium B.C. based on 2002 Oxcal determinations; revised chronology after Knapp 1994.

adopted to facilitate cross-cultural comparisons with Bronze Age sequences outside of Cyprus and to distinguish indigenous cultural attributes from those to the east and west, such as the Helladic sequences of mainland Greece; the Minoan sequences of Crete; the sequence of Old, Middle, and New Kingdom Egypt; and various numbered phases of Bronze Age Anatolia and the Levant.

The prehistoric period ends literally with the introduction of writing, a development first attested to during the fourteenth–thirteenth centuries B.C. in the form of an enigmatic script known as Cypro-Minoan, which remains undeciphered. The existence of writing in Egypt and Mesopotamia was undoubtedly familiar to some Cypriots, and it is now widely accepted that Cyprus (*Alashiya*) is mentioned in a number of important New Kingdom texts; the label "protohistoric" rather than "prehistoric" is therefore used by some archaeologists to characterize the later phases of the Cypriot Brone Age (see, for example, the entry from Knapp 1994 in tab. app. I.I) At around the same time, as the result of extensive trade between Cyprus and mainland ports to the east and west (as exemplified by the Ulu Burun shipwreck) and the island's growing exploitation of copper and manufacture of bronze, indigenous cultural traditions begin to undergo extensive social and political change; acculturation is further advanced by the colonization of the island by foreign populations from the twelfth century B.C. onward, following the destruction of polities on the Greek mainland and the subsequent movements across the Mediterranean of the so-called Sea Peoples (see Oren 2000 for recent perspectives). While such event-driven narratives of social change are limited in scope, it is clear that processes of widespread acculturation were underway well before the close of the Bronze Age. For this reason, in the present work I have chosen to address issues of gender and society in Cyprus only through the LCIIC period to obviate the more intensive "background noise" of intensive cultural influxes to the island after that time.

This appendix aims to provide a broad overview of major socioeconomic developments in Cyprus from its earliest known settlements of the pre-Neolithic Akrotiri phase through to the end of LCII (c. 1200 B.C.). It is intended primarily as background information for readers unfamiliar with the island's major cultural phases and archaeological sites, a "genderless" narrative that lays the groundwork for the gender-based investigations that form the core of this book.

Epipaleolithic and Neolithic Periods

Akrotiri Phase

Since only a single site in Cyprus, Akrotiri-*Aetokremnos*, is known to antedate the Neolithic period, the island's pre-Neolithic inhabitation is commonly referred to as the "Akrotiri phase." Radiocarbon dates place it early within the tenth millenium B.C., making it the oldest-known human occupation on Cyprus and one of the earliest well-documented sites on any Mediterranean island. The site consisted of a collapsed rock shelter 40 m above the sea on the south coast of the Akrotiri peninsula near Limassol (Simmons et al. 1999:fig. 3.1). It was probably occupied on a seasonal basis, as there were no permanent architectural features or evidence of sedentary farming activities. Hunting focused primarily on the pursuit of pygmy hippopotami (*Phanourious minutus*), an endemic species unique to Cyprus.

Other faunal remains, including small amounts of deer, pig, and pygmy elephant, were found, although it is possible that these were brought to the island as articles of clothing rather than as living animals. A variety of marine shells and small collection of chipped stone tools and picrolite artifacts constitute the remainder of the cultural assemblage. Evidence suggests that intensive hunting of the pygmy hippo led to its extinction, which would help explain the site's short span of occupation, estimated at less than a few hundred years, as well as its ultimate abandonment. Excavation at Akrotiri has caused archaeologists to reassess established models of early island colonization in the Mediterranean and to revise earlier views on Pleistocene faunal extinctions (Held 1990; Swiny 2001).

Early Aceramic (Cypro-PPNB)

Following the abandonment of Akrotiri, there is no known human presence attested on the island for more than a millennium, and the subsequent phase of human occupation, referred to as the Early Aceramic or Cypro-PPNB, has only been recognized during the last ten years. Two principal sites of this period, Parekklisha-*Shillourokambos* near Limassol and Kissonerga-*Mylouthkia* near Paphos, are still being investigated and have not yet reached final publication, so we must rely for the time being on preliminary reports (Guilaine and Briois 2001; Guilaine et al. 1995, 1998, 1999; Peltenburg et al. 2000, 2001a, 2001b; for a list of radiocarbon dates of this and other Cypro-PPNB sites, see Peltenburg et al. 2001b:62–65).

Evidence from both sites points to initial occupation during the second half of the ninth millennium B.C. (Early PPNB). The Cypro-Middle PPNB, dating to approximately 8000–7500 B.C., has been attested only at *Shillourokambos*, while both it and *Mylouthkia* have material remains of the Cypro-Late PPNB (c. 7500–7000 B.C.). Although not all scholars have adopted the terminology proposed by Peltenburg and colleagues (see tab. app. I.1), the term "Cypro-PPNB" has been assigned on the basis of careful analysis of cultural links between Cyprus and the Levantine mainland at this time, in particular their respective chipped stone tool assemblages (Bar Josef 2001). Other scholars, however, prefer the more general terms "Early Aceramic" and "Late Aceramic" to distinguish between the phases of the Neolithic represented at *Mylouthkia*/*Shillourokambos* and Khirokitia. At *Mylouthkia*, a series of water wells, the world's oldest-known examples, were constructed during the ninth millennium B.C. These were ultimately abandoned and filled with refuse, including stone tools, disarticulated human remains, artificially deformed human skulls, and entire animal carcasses, providing intriguing insights into economic and ritual practices of these new settlers (see Peltenburg et al. 2000, 2001a, 2001b for substantial preliminary reports).

Shillourokambos has yielded a greater variety of features, including a negative feature of triangular plan provisionally interpreted as the foundation of a stockade. The presence of cattle bones, the earliest recorded in Cyprus, lends support to this hypothesis. The exploitation of cattle is unattested in the earlier Akrotiri phase and entirely absent from the later Aceramic and Chalcolithic periods as well. Since cattle were not endemic to the island, their presence at this early date can only be accounted for by the transport of live animals across the sea from the mainland. Evidence indicates that other species of domesticates were also introduced to the island at this time, as were a number of cultivated species of plants. In addition, the discovery of thousands of limpet shells and a fishhook made of a pig's tusk from one of the *Mylouthkia* wells points to extensive marine activities. Additional finds from Cypro-PPNB sites include lithic assemblages (ground stone vessels and chipped stone tools of chert and obsidian) and even rudimentary artwork (a plaster figurine and sculpted animal head from *Shillourokambos*).

Architectural traditions at *Mylouthkia* are not well attested to and remain to be published for *Shillourokambos*. However, the recently proposed re-dating of Kalavasos-*Tenta* Periods 4–5 to the Cypro-PPNB suggests a circular architectural tradition with roots in the mainland

PPNB (see Peltenburg in press and Peltenburg et al. 2001a, 2001b). While the impact of these recent discoveries needs to be assessed in detail, both for Cypriot prehistory and Mediterranean archaeology as a whole, it is now certain that the island did not remain in total isolation during the almost three millennium gap between Akrotiri and Khirokitia. Yet there is still a gap of about a thousand years between the Akrotiri phase and the initial phase of the Cypro-PPNB. One can only hope that the gap will be narrowed by future archaeological investigations.

Late Aceramic (Khirokitian)

Until recently, sites of the later Aceramic period, most notably the large and impressive settlement at Khirokitia, were believed to represent the earliest human habitation on the island. The initial colonization of the island was accordingly though to occur at around the end of the seventh millennium B.C. As we have seen above, however, this view has had to be revised with discoveries at Akrotiri and at sites of the Cypro-PPNB. The Khirokitian now stands at the end of the Aceramic Neolithic sequence rather than at its inception (Le Brun 2001). About twenty sites have been identified; they have been explored to varying degrees, with distribution island-wide, although occupation occurs more sparsely in the west. In addition to Khirokitia itself, the sites that have received the most extensive excavation and comprehensive study are Cape Andreas-*Kastros*, located in the island's panhandle, Kalavasos-*Tenta*, several kilometers due west of Khirokitia, and Kholetria-*Ortos* in the Paphos district. It should be noted that excavations at *Ortos* yielded extensive numbers of artifacts but unfortunately no architectural remains (Simmons 1996).

Khirokitia and several other contemporary sites provide the first substantial evidence on the island for domestic architecture (Dikaios 1953). Buildings were circular in plan and constructed of pise (or less frequently, mud brick) on stone foundations. The presence of hearths and other evidence for domestic activities outside structures, especially at *Tenta* and Cape Andreas, suggests that work often took place outside the structures, but at Khirokitia, where these features occur regularly inside buildings, buildings play an increasingly central role as focal points of domestic activities. Burials, too, while sometimes out of doors, occurred more frequently underneath the floors. The presence of a substantial circuit wall with a gate at Khirokitia provides further evidence of advances in building technology and implies a need, whether real or imagined, for security (see fig. 2.1).

The economy of the late Aceramic period in Cyprus was based on domesticated sheep, goat, and pig; the hunting of wild fallow deer, *Dama mesopotamica*; and limited fishing of several marine species. Cattle, which were present at some earlier Aceramic Neolithic sites, were apparently not exploited at this time and were not reintroduced to the island until the EBA. Plant remains include a variety of cultivated of cereals, such as einkorn, emmer, and barley, harvested with sickles made of flint and chert. These were supplemented with legumes such as lentils and pistachios, figs, olives, and plums gathered from wild trees.

In addition to the standard repertoire of ground and chipped stone tools, excavations have provided some evidence of a less mundane nature. Khirokitia has produced numerous ground stone vessels carved with elaborate geometric designs, a number of schematic anthropomorphic figurines carved in stone, and fragments of painted plaster on the walls of some of the buildings. It is at Kalavasos-*Tenta*, however, that the most important and intriguing find of the Aceramic Neolithic period has been made. It is a wall painting on the east face of an internal pier of one of the circular structures representing at least two human figures, made by applying red ochre-based paint onto the plastered wall surface; the best preserved of the figures has raised arms (see fig. 4.2).

Taken together, the evidence of architecture, artifacts, and non-artifactual remains from a number of sites attests to increasing sedentarization within the island's Neolithic populations during the seventh millennium B.C. It is likely that these developments were accompanied by changes in social structures, which were undoubtedly more complex than those of the Cypro-PPNB. The cultural differences between this late phase of the Aceramic Neolithic and earlier phases are striking and need to be accounted for, however, as does the decline of the island's early collective socioeconomic tradition, illustrated most dramatically by the collapse and abandonment of Khirokitia, its largest-known site, at about the middle of the sixth millennium B.C.

Late Neolithic (Sotira Culture)

The latest radiocarbon determinations indicate a 500+ year gap between the Khirokitian and the Sotira cultures (or LNeo). Whether there was continuity between these two phases of the Neolithic, or whether LNeo occupation represents a new episode of colonization remains cannot be determined on the basis of evidence currently available. In addition to the settlement of Sotira-*Teppes*, which was excavated by Dikaios in the 1940s–1950s (Dikaios 1961), principal LNeo sites include Ayios Epiktitos-*Vrysi* (Peltenburg 1982a), Philia-*Drakos* A in the north of the island, Paralimni-*Nissia* on the east coast (Flourentzos 1997), and Kandou near Limassol (Mantzourani 1994). Buildings at these sites diverge somewhat from the standard circular plans of the Khirokitian to include sub-rectangular forms with rounded edges. More unorthodox still are the extensive subterranean features (tunnels, shafts, chambers) beneath the settlement at Philia-*Drakos*; some of these were contemporary with the settlement, but the function of these features is unknown, and in the absence of a final report on the site, it is not clear whether they represent functional or social differentiation (Watkins 1973).

Economic patterns centering on the domestication of sheep, goat, and pig, the hunting of wild deer, and the cultivation of cereals apparently continued along the same lines as noted for the late Aceramic Neolithic, but there is considerable technological innovation in other areas. Chief among these was the introduction of ceramics. While the discovery of several clay receptacles at Khirokitia suggests that ceramic technology was not unknown in earlier periods, the ubiquitous occurrence at Sotira culture sites of a range of small- to medium-sized vessels in painted and monochrome styles attests to its production and use on a much wider scale. An initial short-lived monochrome tradition, attested to at a few sites (e.g., Philia-*Drakos* A), was subsequently replaced by vessels with combed and RW painted decoration, and the spatial distribution of these new wares points to the emergence of regional styles: Combed ware, executed with a multiple pronged tool, was found in great abundance at sites in the south of the island, while a lively RW painted tradition dominated in the north.

Mortuary evidence for the LNeo is limited in comparison to the rich mortuary record of the Khirokitian, but where burials exists, as at Sotira, they tend to occur in separate spaces relatively close to, but outside buildings (Dikaios 1961). This contrasts with the practice of intramural burials at Khirokitia and other sites where the deceased were buried intramurally, below the floors of domestic structures. Sites such as Sotira and Philia-*Drakos* seem to have had fairly egalitarian social structures with few discernible differences between building sizes or number of finds among excavated areas, but this was not the case elsewhere. At *Vrysi*, for example, Peltenburg has observed socioeconomic disparities between the two main (north/south) sectors of the site, which were physically divided by an intervening ridge and were associated with different types and concentrations of artifacts (Peltenburg 1982a). In addition, LNeo sites appear to be more standard in size than those of the Khirokitian, perhaps as the result of deliberate resistance to the adoption of more hierarchical social structures (Peltenburg 1993). Similar trends involving non-unlinear trajectories of social change are also attested to in the succeeding period known as the Chalcolithic.

The Chalcolithic Period (Erimi Culture)

The Chalcolithic of Cyprus is also known as Erimi culture, again after the first known site of the period, which was discovered and excavated by Dikaios from 1933 to 1935 (Dikaios 1936). More recently, excavations in the west of the island by the Lemba Archaeological Project have focused on a cluster of Chalcolithic sites in the Paphos district; the results of this work have led to the division of the Chalcolithic into early, middle, and late phases (Peltenburg et al. 1985, 1991, 1998).

Although Chalcolithic occupation has been attested to in most regions of the island, settlement expanded significantly in the west, and it is there that most sites have been found. Survey work by the Lemba Project, the Canadian Palaepaphos Survey Project, and several other teams have succeeded in identifying more than one hundred sites in the west of the island with characteristic Erimi culture artifacts (Bolger, McCartney, and Peltenburg in press). Elsewhere, important Chalcolithic remains have been identified at several localities at Kalavasos, in particular at locality *Ayious* (South 1985; Todd 1991; Todd and Croft in press). In material terms, the hallmarks of the early phase are the development of a bold and intricate style of RW pottery, the extensive use of a soft green stone known as picrolite for the manufacture of beads and pendants, and the production of a wide range of anthropomorphic figurines in pottery and stone, many of which represent females.

Early Chalcolithic

This earliest phase of the Chalcolithic dates between 3900 and 3400 B.C. The majority of EChal sites are found in the west and include sites of the Lemba cluster (*Mylouthkia*, Kissonerga, and Lemba) as well as Maa-*Paleokastro*, where Chalcolithic remains were found beneath the fortified settlement of the LBA (Bolger 1988; Thomas 1988). Despite this demographic shift in settlement concentration to western precincts, cultural developments do not appear to have diverged sharply from those of the LNeo. The absence of a chronological gap between the LNeo and Chalco, as well as a general similarity in ceramic styles and stone tool technology, attest to overall continuity in cultural developments during the fourth millennium B.C.; however, this contrasts with the abandonment of earlier building types with stone foundations and the evidence for activity in pits and flimsy timber-framed structures. As we shall see, these features point to recursive modes of culture change rather than steady, incremental stages of cultural development.

The only site outside of the west where substantial Chalcolithic remains have been investigated is at Kalavasos in the Larnaca district. Dikaios identified two sites here, which he termed Kalavaos "A" and "B," and which he believed overlapped with the LNeo as represented at Sotira (Dikaios 1936). These sites are now identified by their toponyms *Kokkinoyia* and *Pamboules*, respectively. While extensive survey has been made at these sites (Clarke and Todd 1993), excavations by the University of East Anglia had not commenced at the time of this writing (Clarke, personal communication). Earlier excavations were undertaken by Todd, however, at the nearby EChal of *Ayious*, where a network of subterranean features linked with tunnels is reminiscent of Philia-*Drakos* (Todd 1991; Todd and Croft in press).

Similar features have been recorded at the EChal site of *Mylouthkia* in the Paphos district, consisting of more than thirty shallow scoop-shaped hollows situated on slopes overlooking a small river and bay, some of which have been excavated by the Lemba Project (Peltenburg 2003). The discovery of a hearth in one of the hollows indicates that some of these features functioned as work or living spaces; other evidence points to different functions for the various pits. In general, there is little or no evidence in the EChal of solid stone-built architecture, although Maa, Kalavasos, Kissonerga, and *Mylouthkia* furnish evidence of a variety of circular timber-framed structures with external postholes that may have anticipated the well-known roundhouse tradition in stone known so well from subsequent phases of the period.

The tentative character of settlement implied by these building practices does not appear to be paralleled by developments in EChal material culture. Ceramic traditions were robust, involving the production of GBW in great numbers at Lemba cluster sites and the manufacture in smaller proportions of RW painted pottery executed in finer linear-based motifs (Bolger 1991). The latter occur on a diversity of shapes that include new forms, such as flasks with pointed bases and tubular spouted vessels. More important for economic considerations, perhaps, are the earliest recorded examples of metalworking on the island (*Mylouthkia* and *Ayious*); although small in scale, these activities represent the first known exploitation of native copper supplies. Finally, the EChal marks the start of a long creative tradition of anthropomorphic figurines and pendants in stone and pottery linked to birthing rituals. This tradition was to reach its florescence in the subsequent MChal.

Middle Chalcolithic

The transition from EChal–MChal occurs at Erimi, the site that gave its name to the culture of the Chalcolithic of Cyprus following Dikaios's excavations of the 1930s; dates for this phase of the period are now established at between 3400 and 2800 B.C. While the sounding at Erimi was about 5.5 m deep, it was not extensive, and developmental sequences are somewhat obscured by Dikaios's excavation in artificial rather than natural levels. However, there is some evidence for a shift in the lower levels of excavation from timber frame structures to buildings with stone foundations. Dikaios's sounding revealed twelve buildings, as well as a wealth of pottery, flint, stone tools, and fragmentary figurines and thus provided a firm basis on which to reconstruct many of the salient aspects of Chalcolithic society.

Recent excavations of MChal sites elsewhere on the island have greatly increased our understanding of the MChal; this is particularly true of the work of the Lemba Project at the sites of Lemba, Kissonerga, and *Mylouthkia* in the Paphos district. Some sites, such as Kissonerga, were much larger than those of earlier periods, an occurrence that, together with the construction of buildings in more permanent materials, may indicate increasing levels of sedentarization. Population growth and increasing social complexity are further attested to by an increase in building size and inter-building variability, probably attributable to functional differentiation and the emergence of incipient social hierarchies. Experimental work at the Lemba Experimental Village has calculated that considerable investments of time and resources were put into the construction of these buildings and further emphasizes the contrast with the temporary, makeshift timber-framed structures of the EChal.

While burial customs during the MChal appear to largely represent a continuation from earlier prehistoric traditions, the discovery in the 1950s at Souskiou of a cemetery separate from a settlement signals important changes as well. The unusual and rich finds from its rock-cut tombs, which include a varied assemblage of standard and non-standard pottery shapes and an unusual array of pottery, stone figurines, pendants, and several anthropomorphic and zoomorphic vessels, further underscore the complexities of mortuary ritual at this time. Some of the vessels and most of the figurines represent pregnant women or women seated in birthing postures. Unfortunately, the extensive looting of the site during the 1970s has limited the amount of contextual evidence available for the interpretation of this material. However, the discovery of a ritual deposit of figurines in and around a ceramic model of a MChal building at Kissonerga (see fig. 2.4) provides a contextual framework with which to interpret these objects within a larger social framework. Although there are still many questions, it is now clear that many of the pieces of figurative art known from the period involved rituals of fertility and birth and that these rituals were also carried out in public ceremonies of a non-funerary nature.

Late Chalcolithic

The only substantial LChal remains from Cyprus come from the sites of Lemba and Kissonerga in the west of the island. Stratified building deposits at Kissonerga suggest a gap of about two hundred years between the end of the MChal and the start of LChal, and this is corroborated by associated ceramics that show a radically new tradition already well underway at the start of Kissonerga 4 at c. 2700 B.C. and continuing until about 2400 B.C.

While Lemba and Kissonerga both yielded large numbers of RW sherdage, *in situ* finds on the floors of LChal buildings indicate that new pottery types were in use, in particular a monochrome type known as Red and Black Stroke Burnished pottery. While not as aesthetically pleasing as RW , this new ceramic type offered considerable technological improvements, including higher firing temperatures, more regularly standardized vessel sizes, and an increased volume of production. In addition, storage vessels, which rarely occurred in earlier phases of the Chalcolithic, were found in significant quantities in LChal buildings, suggesting the development of surplus production and perhaps redistributive exchange mechanisms. Economic intensification is further indicated by the appearance of more specialized crop-processing equipment and larger stone tools.

Arguably the most important social development during the LChal was contacts between Cyprus and cultures of the Anatolian mainland. Signs of such contact appear in the adoption during the LChal of non-indigenous pottery forms, new burial customs (chamber tombs with multiple burials, pithos burials), new technologies involving textile manufacture (RP spindle whorl at Kissonerga); new types or ornament (shell pendants, gold earrings); and imported materials such as faience. Many of these developments may be attributable to local imitation or emulation of mainland traditions, but there is also increasing evidence that foreigners were present on the island prior to the start of the EBA. Clearly this is a period of contact, acculturation, and upheaval, and these dynamic developments were instrumental for the marked cultural changes on the island during the transition to the Bronze Age.

The Cypriot Bronze Age

Cultural contacts between Cyprus and mainland Anatolia intensified during the Bronze Age and may have involved influxes of foreign groups to the island during the second half of the third millennium B.C. who brought with them new economic practices, most notably the introduction of the plow and traction animals. These developments can be linked to what has been termed the Secondary Products Revolution, as can the introduction of new technologies such as spindle whorls for textile manufacture and a new range of vessel shapes for the processing of food (Sherratt 1983). In addition, traditional roundhouse construction was abandoned and replaced by settlement plans comprising agglomerative networks of rectangular buildings, and group burials in large communal cemeteries replaced the individual pit graves of the Neolithic and Chalcolithic periods. Increasing socioeconomic complexity later in the Bronze Age fostered the rise of larger settlements and administrative centers as the island emerged from a state of relative isolation into an ever widening economic and political sphere. Mining and manufacture of bronze, involving increasingly intensive exploitation of the island's rich copper resources, were central to these processes, as was the island's growing engagement in international trade.

Early and Middle Bronze Ages

The introduction of cattle, plowing technology, and a host of other innovations at around the middle of the third millennium B.C. belongs to a cultural phase or facies known as the Philia culture, whose chronological parameters have not yet been sharply defined. Until recently, this culture was primarily from burial evidence (e.g., Philia-*Vasiliko*, Khrisiliou-*Ammos*, Nicosia-*Ayia Paraskevi*, Sotira-*Kaminoudhia*) and certain artifact types, but recently Philia culture remains have been located in settlement contexts, postdating the LChal occupation at Kissonerga and antedating the EC/MC settlement at Marki. Marki has yielded the most substantial evidence in this regard, but stratified evidence for the Philia horizon at the site is fairly limited, based largely on artifact types (Philia RP and Black Slip and combed pottery, spindle whorls, annular pendants) and nontraditional mortuary features such as a pithos burial (Frankel and Webb 2001).

In succeeding EB–MB levels, however, there is well-documented evidence of radical departures from earlier Chalcolithic traditions (Frankel and Webb 1996a). The excavators ascribe these changes to several waves of migration to Cyprus from Anatolian mainland beginning late in the third millennium B.C. and resulting from upheavals on the mainland during EBII (Frankel, Webb, and Eslick 1995). Processes of acculturation ensued, and the impact on traditional Cypriot society was considerable and included the adoption of an innovative economic package involving cattle, the plow, and traction animals as well as new pottery forms and domestic installations such as plaster bins and hobs for cooking. Similar developments can be observed at sites of a contemporary or slightly later date, such as Alambra-*Mouttes* to the southeast and Sotira-*Kaminoudhia* near

Limassol. Cemeteries associated with the settlement at Marki have been severely looted, but elsewhere, at sites like Vounous and Lapithos along the north coast, there is substantial evidence of changing mortuary practices that began during the EBA and continued into the MBA. Moreover, the construction of large communal rock-cut tombs, accessed from long entry corridors (*dromoi*) and used repeatedly over many generations, are likely to be associated with the emergence of corporate kinship groups.

Finally, mention must be made of the foundation at the end of the MC of the site of Enkomi, an important settlement located along on the east coast near Famagusta that was to become a crucial center of economic developments during the LBA. The construction of a large and imposing building (termed a "fortress" by its excavator, Dikaios) at around 1600 B.C. marked the start of a new architectural tradition that served public rather than exclusively domestic functions and points to the adoption of more hierarchical and bureaucratic modes of political organization at this time, as well as to increasing levels of socioeconomic complexity.

The Late Bronze Age

Sites of the LBA period (c. 1600–1200 B.C.) are too numerous to discuss here on a site-by-site basis, since this period has long been the subject of intensive scholarly investigation among archaeologists concerned with the island's prehistory and protohistory. The LBA was undoubtedly a crucial period of social development in Cyprus, particularly with regard to the political, social, and economic transformations associated with the proposed emergence of urban polities around 1400 B.C. Instabilities and upheavals before 1400 B.C. were accompanied by a gradual demographic shift away from the northern and central regions to the southern and eastern coasts (Peltenburg 1996:28); this occurred as part of the expansion of metallurgical production on the island and the increasing ability of local groups to exploit international markets for purposes of trade. Equally important in terms of emerging centralization and bureaucracy was the advent of literacy on the island, first attested to at the Enkomi Late Cypriot IB fortress on tablets inscribed in a syllabic script known as Cypro-Minoan. It appears to be closely related to the Linear A script and, like Linear A, has not yet been deciphered.

Unfortunately for our understanding of the processes by which the more advanced stages of social complexity developed in Cyprus, archaeological evidence for the MC–LC transition is limited due to a dearth of excavated and adequately published settlement evidence and tomb material (Keswani 1989:516). For the earlier phases of the LBA, the site of Maroni-*Vournes* on the south coast provides stratified evidence of cultural developments from LC I–II that immediately preceded the construction of an imposing building of dressed ashlar masonry (Cadogan and Domurad 1989). In addition, specialized sites like the small copper smelting site of Politiko-*Phorades* (LCI), located in the copper belt, were probably occupied seasonally by portions of the community and underscore the economic importance, even during the early phases of the LBA, of the mining and metallurgy industries (Knapp, Donnelly, and Kassianidou 1998). By LCII, a number of sites have buildings of a non-domestic character.

Although a few sites such as Alassa are located inland, most are situated on or near the coast (see fig. app. 2.1). Apart from Enkomi, the most impressive testament to the new economic and political order is the large public structure (Building X) at Kalavasos-*Ayios Dhimitrios* that, with its olive press and numerous pithoi for storing oil, attests to intensified production and organization of economic activities at this time (South 1992, 1997). The location of *Ayios Dhimitrios* in proximity to the Kalavasos copper mines undoubtedly contributed to the site's importance and wealth in LCII when international demand for bronze had reached unprecedented levels (South 1989).

Mortuary evidence also attests to the emergence of elite groups from about 1400 B.C. onward, when metal objects of local manufacture and imported prestige items such as Mycenaean kraters, gold and silver jewelry, and Egyptian faience began to be deposited in great quantities in selected tombs (Keswani 1989). As demand for luxury items increased, efforts were undertaken to establish and secure the infrastructure of copper production on a much more massive basis. The construction of a number of fortresses between the copper mining regions and the large coastal trading centers of the island may be connected to these activities (Peltenburg 1996).

Increasing involvement in external trade and the wealth it generated was accompanied by advancing levels of hierarchy and the need for management, organization, and bureaucracy. Monumental buildings such as Building X at *Ayios Dhimitrios* and the Enkomi fortress with its various industrial quarters are powerful indicators of these socioeconomic developments, and efforts to legitimize and sanctify the power of emerging elites can be construed from representations of deities standing on copper ingots at major political centers such as Enkomi and Kition (Knapp 1986).

Although state society in Cyprus in the LBA was probably never fully centralized, the island's traditional social structures, which had remained relatively egalitarian throughout the EB and MBA, were thoroughly and permanently transformed (Keswani 1996b; Webb 1999). At the same time, Cyprus was thrust into the full gamut of international relations, a phenomenon that can best be gauged not by sites within Cyprus itself, but by the well-known correspondence in palatial archives of Egypt and Syria between local leaders and the king of "Alashiya," a place now commonly identified with Cyprus. Equally compelling in terms of the island's increasing involvement in international trade is the evidence of the Ulu Burun shipwreck, which contained numerous Cypriot pottery vessels and over ten tons of Cypriot copper ingots stacked in its hull (Pulak 2001).

Gazetteer of Major Prehistoric Sites in Cyprus

THIS APPENDIX PROVIDES BASIC INFORMATION on principal archaeological sites discussed in the text. Site entries are listed alphabetically by the names they are most commonly referred to in the text, with cross-references provided for alternative designations. Main entries include the complete site name (which, according to Cypriot archaeological conventions, consists of the village name followed by the site locality or toponym); the name(s) of the excavator(s); the general location of the site; the main period(s) represented; and references to published reports. The locations of most of these sites are shown on the accompanying map (fig. app. 2.1). For more detailed information on settlement patterns in Cypriot prehistory, you may wish to consult Catling (1963, 1966) and Stanley Price (1979b).

Akrotiri
Complete name: Akrotiri-*Aetokremnos*
Excavator: Alan Simmons, University of Nevada at Las Vegas
Location: Akrotiri Peninsula, Limassol District
Main period: Epipaleolithic
Final report: Simmons et al. 1999

Alambra
Complete name: Alambra-*Mouttes*
Excavator: John Coleman, Cornell University
Location: Nicosia District
Main period: Middle Cypriot
Final report: Coleman et al. 1996

Alassa
Complete names: Alassa-*Pano Mandilares*, Alassa-*Paliotaverna*
Excavator: Sophocles Hadjisavvas, Department of Antiquities of Cyprus

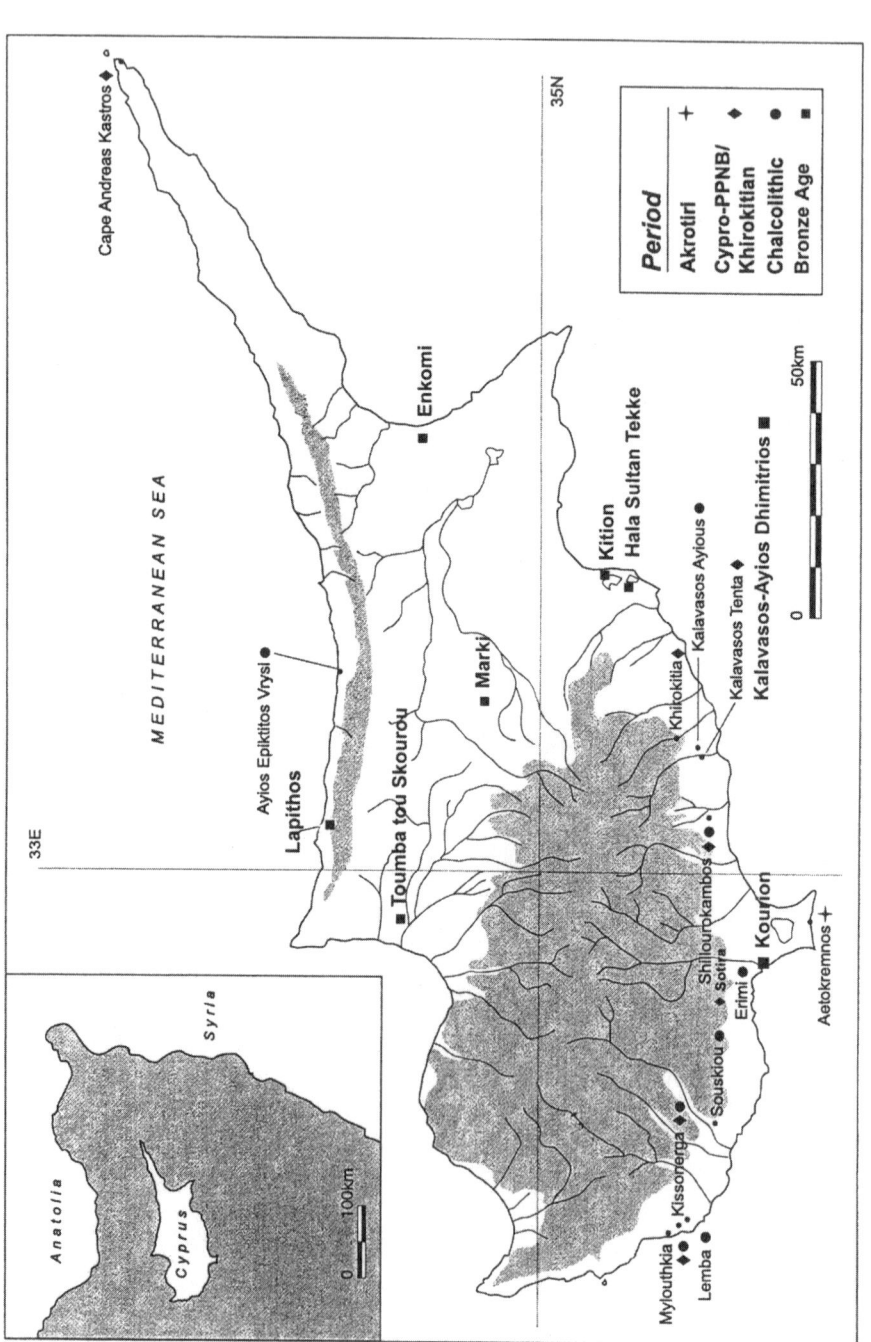

Figure App. 2.1. Map of Cyprus showing locations of major sites discussed in text.

Location: Limassol District
Main period: Late Cypriot II
Preliminary reports: Hadjisavvas 1986, 1989
Final report: in preparation

Ayios Dhimitrios

Complete name: Kalavasos-*Ayios Dhimitrios*
Excavator: Alison South, Cyprus American Archaeological Research Institute, Nicosia
   (CAARI)
Location: Larnaca District
Main period: Late Cypriot II
Preliminary reports: South 1983, 1984, 1985, 1989, 1992, 1997
First final report: South et al. 1989

Ayios Epiktitos-Vrysi

(see Vrysi)

Ayious

Complete name: Kalavasos-*Ayious*
Excavator: Ian Todd, Cyprus American Archaeological Research Institute, Nicosia
   (CAARI)
Location: Larnaca District
Main period: Early Chalcolithic (Erimi culture)
Preliminary reports: South 1985; Todd 1991
Final report: Todd and Croft in press (*Studies in Mediterranean Archaeology* 71).

Cape Andreas

Complete name: Cape Andreas-*Kastros*
Excavator: Alain Le Brun, Centre Nationale Recherche Scientifique (CNRS)
Location: Karpass peninsula, Famagusta District
Main period: Late Aceramic Neolithic (Khirokitian)
Final report: Le Brun 1981

Enkomi

Complete name: Enkomi-*Ayios Iakovos*
Excavators: Porphyrios Dikaios, Claude Schaeffer, Swedish Cyprus Expedition
Location: Famagusta District
Main periods: Middle Cypriot III–Late Cypriot III
Final reports: Dikaios 1969; Gjerstad et al. 1934; Schaeffer 1952

Erimi

Complete name: Erimi-*Pamboula*
Excavator: Porphyrios Dikaios
Location: Limassol District
Main period: Middle Chalcolithic (Erimi culture)
Final reports: Bolger 1988; Dikaios 1936

Hala Sultan Tekke

Complete name: Hala Sultan Tekke-*Vyzakia* (or Dromolaxia-*Vyzakia*)
Excavator: Paul Åström
Location: Larnaca District, near Larnaca salt lake
Main periods: Late Cypriot II–III
Most recent final report: Åström 1998 (with references to earlier volumes).

Kalavasos-Ayios Dhimitrios

(see Ayios Dhimitrios)

Kalavasos-Ayious

(see Ayious)

Kalavasos-Tenta

(see Tenta)

Kaminoudhia

Complete name: Sotira-*Kaminoudhia*
Excavator: Stuart Swiny, State University of New York at Albany
Location: Limassol District
Main periods: Philia culture; Early Cypriot
Preliminary reports: Swiny 1985, 1989
Final report: Swiny, Rapp, and Herscher 2002

Khirokitia

Complete name: Khirokitia-*Vounoi*
Excavators: Porphyrios Dikaios, Alain Le Brun, Centre Nationale Recherche Scientifique
    (CNRS)
Location: Larnaca District
Main period: Late Aceramic Neolithic (Khirokitian)
Final reports: Le Brun 1984, 1989, 1994; Dikaios 1953

Kissonerga

Complete name: Kissonerga-*Mosphilia*
Excavator: Edgar Peltenburg, University of Edinburgh
Location: Paphos District
Main periods: Late Aceramic Neolithic; Late Neolithic; Early, Middle, Late Chalcolithic;
    Philia culture
Final reports: Peltenburg et al. 1991, 1998

Kissonerga-Mylouthkia

(see Mylouthkia)

Kition

Complete name: Kition-*Kathari*
Excavator: Vassos Karageorghis, A., G. Leventis Foundation
Location: Larnaca District, in Larnaca town
Main periods: Late Cypriot IIC–III
Final reports: Karageorghis 1976b; Karageorghis and Demas 1985

Kourion

Complete name: Kourion-*Bamboula*
Excavator: J. F. Daniel
Location: Limassol District
Main periods: Late Cypriot I–III
Final reports: Benson 1972; Weinberg 1983

Lapithos

Complete name: Lapithos-*Vrysi tou Barba*
Excavator: Bert Hodge Hill
Location: Kyrenia District
Main periods: Early–Middle Cypriot
Final report: Herscher 1978

Lemba

Complete name: Lemba-*Lakkous*
Excavator: Edgar Peltenburg, University of Edinburgh
Location: Paphos District
Main periods: Middle–Late Chalcolithic (Erimi culture)
Final report: Peltenburg et al. 1985.

Maa

Complete name: Maa-*Paleokastro*
Excavators: Vassos Karageorghis, A.G. Leventis Foundation and Martha Demas, J. Paul Getty
    Conservation Institute
Location: Paphos District
Main periods: Late Cypriot III, Early Chalcolithic (Erimi culture)
Final report: Karageorghis and Demas 1988

Marki

Complete name: Marki-*Alonia*
Excavators: David Frankel, La Trobe University and Jennifer Webb, La Trobe University
Location: Nicosia District
Main periods: Philia culture; Early–Middle Cypriot
First final report: Frankel and Webb 1996a; second report in preparation

Maroni

Complete names: Maroni-*Vournes*, Maroni-*Tsaroukas*, Maroni-*Kapsaloudhia*
Excavators: British Museum, Gerald Cadogan, independent scholar, and Sturt Manning, Uni-
    versity of Reading
Location: Larnaca District
Main periods: Late Cypriot I–II
Preliminary reports: Cadogan 1983, 1986, 1987, 1988, 1992; Cadogan and Domurad 1989;
    Johnson 1980; Manning 1998a; Manning et al. 1994.

Mosphilia

(see Kissonerga)

Mylouthkia

Complete name: Kissonerga-*Mylouthkia*
Excavator: Edgar Peltenburg, University of Edinburgh
Location: Paphos District
Main periods: Early Aceramic Neolithic (Cypro-PPNB); Early–Middle Chalcolithic
Final report: Peltenburg 2003

Paralimni

Complete name: Paralimni-*Nissia*
Excavator: Pavlos Flourentzos, Department of Antiquities of Cyprus
Location: Famagusta District

Main period: Late Neolithic (Sotira culture)
Preliminary report: Flourentzos 1997

Phaneromeni

Complete name: Episkopi-*Phaneromeni*
Excavator: James Carpenter
Location: Limassol District
Main period: Late Cypriot I
Preliminary report: Carpenter 1981
Final report (lithics and terracottas only): Swiny 1986

Philia

Complete name: Philia-*Laksia tou Kasinou* (also referred to as Philia-*Vasiliko*)
Excavator: Porphyrios Dikaios
Location: Kyrenia District
Main period: Philia culture
Final report: Dikaios 1962

Shillourokambos

Complete name: Parekklisha-*Shillourokambos*
Excavator: Jean Guilaine, Centre Nationale Recherche Scientifique (CNRS)
Location: Limassol District
Main period: Early Aceramic Neolithic (Cypro-PPNB)
Preliminary reports: Guilaine and Briois 2001; Guilaine et al. 1995, 1998, 1999

Sotira

Complete name: Sotira-*Teppes*
Excavator: Porphyrios Dikaios
Location: Limassol District
Main period: Late Neolithic (Sotira culture)
Final report: Dikaios 1961

Sotira-Kaminoudhia

(see Kaminoudhia)

Souskiou

Complete name: Souskiou-*Vathyrkakas*
Excavators: Demos Christou, J. H. Iliffe and Terrence Mitford, Franz Georg Maier

Location: Paphos District, near Kouklia village
Main period: Middle Chalcolithic (Erimi culture)
Preliminary reports: Christou 1989; Lunt 1994; Maier 1973; Vagnetti 1980

Tenta

Complete name: Kalavasos-*Tenta*
Excavator: Ian Todd, CAARI
Location: Larnaca District
Main period: Aceramic Neolithic (PPNB/Khirokitian)
First final report: Todd 1986; second report in preparation.

Teppes

(see Sotira)

Toumba tou Skourou

Complete name: Morphou-*Toumba tou Skourou*
Excavator: Emily Vermeule
Location: Nicosia District, near Bay of Morphou
Main period: Late Cypriot III
Final report: Vermeule and Wolsky 1990

Vounous

Complete name: Bellapais-*Vounous*
Excavators: Porphyrios Dikaios, James Stewart
Location: Kyrenia District, Bellapais village
Main period: Early Cypriot
Final reports: Dikaios 1940; Stewart 1962; Stewart and Stewart 1950

Vrysi

Complete name: Ayios Epiktitos-*Vrysi*
Excavator: Edgar Peltenburg, University of Edinburgh
Location: Kyrenia District
Main period: Late Neolithic (Sotira culture)
Final report: Peltenburg 1982a

References

NOTE: The following abbreviations are used in the references:
ASOR (American Schools of Oriental Research)
BAR (British Archaeological Reports)
BCH (*Bulletin de Correspondance Hellénique*)
CAARI (Cyprus American Archaeological Research Institute)
RDAC (*Report of the Department of Antiquities, Cyprus*)
SIMA (Studies in Mediterranean Archaeology)

a Campo, A. L.
  1994   *Anthropomorphic representations in prehistoric Cyprus: A formal and symbolic analysis of figurines, c. 3500–1800 B.C.* SIMA Pocketbook 109. Jonsered, Sweden: Åströms.
Angel, L.
  1953   The human remains from Khirokitia. Pp. 416–30 (Appendix 2) in *Khirokitia*, by P. Dikaios. Oxford: Oxford University Press.
  1961   Neolithic crania from Sotira. Pp. 223–29 (Appendix I) in *Sotira*, by P. Dikaios. Philadelphia: University Museum.
  1972   Late Bronze Age Cypriotes from Bamboula: The skeletal remains. Pp. 148–58 (Appendix B) in *Bamboula at Kourion*, by J. L. Benson. Philadelphia: University Museum.
Ardener, S., ed.
  1993   *Women and space: Ground rules and social maps.* Oxford: Berg.
Ariès, P.
  1962   *Centuries of childhood.* London: Cape.
Arnold, B.
  1991   The deposed princess of Vix: The need for an engendered European prehistory. Pp. 366–74 in *Proceedings of the twenty-second annual Chacmool conference of the Archaeological Association of the University of Calgary*, eds. D. Walde and N. Willows. Calgary, Canada: University of Calgary Press.
  2002   "Sein und Werden": Gender as process in mortuary ritual. Pp. 239–56 in *In pursuit of gender: Worldwide archaeological approaches*, eds. S. M. Nelson and M. Rosen-Ayalon. Walnut Creek, CA: AltaMira.
Arnold, B., and N. L. Wicker, eds.
  2001   *Gender and the archaeology of death.* Walnut Creek, CA: AltaMira.
Arnold, D.
  1985   *Ceramic theory and culture process.* Cambridge: Cambridge University Press.

Åström, L., and P. Åström
　　1972　　*The Late Cypriote Bronze Age.* Swedish Cyprus Expedition IV.1D. Lund, Sweden: Swedish Cyprus Expedition.

Åström, P.
　　1966　　*Excavations at Kalopsidha and Ayios Iakovos in Cyprus.* SIMA 2. Lund, Sweden: Åströms.
　　1972　　*The Middle Cypriote Bronze Age.* SCE IV.1B. Lund, Sweden: Swedish Cyprus Expedition.
　　1992　　Approaches to the study of women in ancient Cyprus. Pp. 5–8 in *Acta Cypria: Acts of an international congress on Cypriote archaeology held in Göteborg on 22–24 August 1991,* Part 2, ed. P. Åström. SIMA Pocketbook 117. Jonsered, Sweden: Åströms.
　　1998　　*Hala Sultan Tekke 10: The wells.* SIMA 45: 10. Jonsered, Sweden: Åströms.

Åström P., ed.
　　1971　　*Who's who in Cypriote archaeology.* SIMA 23. Göteborg, Sweden: Åströms.

Åström, P. et al.
　　1983　　*Hala Sultan Tekke 8: Excavations1971–79.* SIMA 45: 8. Göteborg, Sweden: Åströms.

Bailey, D. W.
　　1994　　Reading prehistoric figurines as individuals. *World Archaeology* 25: 321–31.

Baker, M.
　　1997　　Invisibility as a symptom of gender categories in archaeology. Pp. 183–91 in *Invisible people and processes: Writing gender and childhood into European archaeology,* eds. J. Moore and E. Scott. London and New York: Leicester University Press.

Balthazar, J. W.
　　1990　　*Copper and bronze working in Early through Middle Bronze Age Cyprus.* SIMA Pocketbook 84. Jonsered, Sweden: Åströms.

Banning, E. B.
　　1996　　Houses, compounds and mansions in the prehistoric Near East. Pp. 165–85 in *People who lived in big houses,* eds. G. Coupland and E. B. Banning. Madison: Prehistory Press.

Banning, E. B., and B. F. Byrd
　　1987　　Houses and the changing residential unit: Domestic architecture at PPNB 'Ain Ghazal, Jordan. *Proceedings of the Prehistoric Society* 53: 309–25.

Bar Josef, O.
　　2001　　The world around Cyprus: From Epi-Paleolithic foragers to the collapse of the PPNB civilization. Pp. 129–64 in *The earliest prehistory of Cyprus,* ed. S. Swiny. CAARI Monographs, vol. 2. Boston: ASOR.

Barber, E. J. W.
　　1991　　*Prehistoric textiles: The development of cloth in the Neolithic and Bronze Ages with special reference to the Aegean.* Princeton: Princeton University Press.
　　1994　　*Women's work: The first 20,000 years. Women, cloth, and society in early times.* New York and London: W. W. Norton.

Barlow, J. A.
　　1985　　Middle Cypriote settlement evidence. A perspective on the chronological foundations. *RDAC*: 47–54.

Barnes, R., and J. B. Eicher
　　1992　　*Dressing gender: Making and meaning in cultural contexts.* Oxford: Berg.

Barrett, J. C.
　　1989　　Food, gender and metal: Questions of social reproduction. Pp. 304–20 in *The Bronze Age-Iron Age transition in Europe,* eds. M. L. S. Sorensen and R. Thomas. BAR International Series 483. Oxford: BAR.
　　2001　　Agency, the duality of structure, and the problem of the archaeological record. Pp. 141–64 in *Archaeological theory today,* ed. I. Hodder. Cambridge: Polity.

Barthes, R.
　　1967　　*Elements of semiology.* Translated by A. Lavers and C. Smith. London: Cape.

Baxevani, P. A.
　　1994　　*The evolution of social complexity in the Early Bronze Age east Mediterranean: A cross-cultural analysis of*

tomb groups from the southern Levant, Cyprus and Crete. Unpublished Ph.D. dissertation, University of Edinburgh.

Begg, P.
1991   *Late Cypriot terracotta figurines: A study in context.* SIMA Pocketbook 101. Jonsered, Sweden: Åströms.

Bem, S.
1993   *The lenses of gender: Transforming the debate on sexual inequality.* New Haven, CT: Yale University Press.

Bender, B.
2000   The roots of inequality. Pp. 201–10 in *Interpretive archaeology: A reader,* ed. J. Thomas. London and New York: Leicester University Press.

Bender, D. R.
1967   A refinement of the concept of household: Families, co-residence and domestic functions. *American Anthropologist* 69: 493–504.

Benson, J. L.
1972   *Bamboula at Kourion.* Philadelphia: University of Pennsylvania Press.

Bintliff, J., ed.
1991   *The Annales school and archaeology.* London and New York: Leicester University Press.

Blanton, R. E.
1994   *Houses and households.* New York: Plenum.

Bolger, D.
n.d.   Writing children into Cypriot archaeology. Unpublished lecture delivered at CAARI, Nicosia, December 1998. Manuscript with author.

1988   Chalcolithic Maa: The pottery. Pp. 290–300 in *Excavations at Maa-Paleokastro, 1979–1986,* by V. Karageorghis and M. Demas. Nicosia: Department of Antiquities.

1991   The evolution of the Chalcolithic painted style. *Bulletin of the American Schools of Oriental Research* 282/283: 81–93.

1992   The archaeology of fertility and birth: A ritual deposit from Chalcolithic Cyprus. *Journal of Anthropological Research* 48(2): 145–54.

1993   The feminine mystique: Gender and society in prehistoric Cypriot studies. *RDAC*: 29–42.

1994a   Engendering Cypriot archaeology: Women's roles and statuses before the Bronze Age. *Opuscula Atheniensia* 20(1): 9–17.

1994b   Ladies of the expedition: Harriet Boyd Hawes and Edith Hall at work in Cypriot archaeology. Pp. 41–50 in *Women in archaeology,* ed. C. Claassen. Philadelphia: University of Pennsylvania Press.

1996   Figurines, fertility and the emergence of complex society in prehistoric Cyprus. *Current Anthropology* 37(2). 365–73.

1998   The Pottery. Pp. 93–131 in *Lemba Archaeological Project II.1A: Excavations at Kissonerga-Mosphilia, 1979–1992,* by E. Peltenburg et al. SIMA 70(2). Jonsered, Sweden: Åströms.

2002   Gender and mortuary ritual in Chalcolithic Cyprus. Pp. 67–86 in *Engendering Aphrodite: Women and society in ancient Cyprus,* eds. D. Bolger and N. Serwint. CAARI Monographs, vol. 3. Boston: ASOR.

2003   The Pottery. Pp. 133–62 in *Lemba Archaeological Project III.1: The colonisation and settlement of Cyprus. Investigations at Kissonerga-Mylouthkia, 1976–1996,* ed. E. Peltenburg. SIMA 70(4). Sävedalen, Sweden: Åströms.

Bolger, D., C. McCartney, and E. Peltenburg
In press   Regional interaction in the prehistoric west: Lemba Archaeological Project western Cyprus survey. Forthcoming in *Archaeological field survey in Cyprus: Past history, future potentials,* ed. M. Iacovou. Athens: British School of Archaeology.

Bolger, D., and N. Serwint, eds.
2002   *Engendering Aphrodite: Women and society in ancient Cyprus.* CAARI Monographs, vol. 3. Boston: ASOR.

Bordieu, P.
1977   *Outline of a theory of practice.* Cambridge: Cambridge University Press.

1990   *The logic of practice.* Cambridge: Polity.

Boserup, E.

1970   *Woman's role in economic development.* New York: St. Martin's.

Boyden, J., and W. Myres

1994   *Exploring alternative approaches to combating child labour: Case studies from developing countries.* Child Rights Series 8. Florence, Italy: Innocenti Occasional Papers.

Brown, J. K.

1963   A cross-cultural study of female initiation rites. *American Anthropologist* 65: 837–53.

Browne, K.

1998   *Divided labours: An evolutionary view of women at work.* London: Weidenfeld and Nicolson.

Brumfiel, E. M.

1991   Weaving and cooking: Women's production in Aztec Mexico. Pp. 224–51 in *Engendering archaeology: Women and prehistory,* eds. J. M. Gero and M. W. Conkey. Oxford: Blackwell.

1992   Distinguished lecture in archaeology: Breaking and entering the ecosystem— gender, class and faction steal the show. *American Anthropologist* 94(3): 551–67.

Brumfiel, E. M., and T. K. Earle

1987   Specialization, exchange and complex societies: An introduction. Pp. 1–9 in *Specialization, exchange and complex societies,* eds. E. M. Brumfiel and T. K. Earle. Cambridge: Cambridge University Press.

Budin, S.

2002   Creating a goddess of sex. In *Engendering Aphrodite: Women and society in ancient Cyprus,* eds. D. Bolger and N. Serwint. CAARI Monographs, vol. 3. Boston: ASOR.

Bunimowitz, S., and R. Barkai

1996   Ancient bones and modern myths: Ninth millennium B.C. hippopotamus hunters at Akrotiri-*Aetokremnos,* Cyprus? *Journal of Mediterranean Archaeology* 9: 85–96.

Butler, J.

1990   *Gender trouble: Feminism and the subversion of identity.* New York: Routledge.

1993   *Bodies that matter: On the discursive limits of 'sex.'* London: Routledge.

Buxton, L. H. D.

1931   Künstlich deformierte Schädel von Cypern. *Anthropologischer Anzeiger* 7: 236–40.

Byrd, B. F.

1994   Public and private, domestic and corporate: The emergence of the southwest Asian village. *American Antiquity* 59(4): 639–66.

Cadogan, G.

1983   Maroni I. *RDAC*: 53–62.

1986   Maroni II. *RDAC*: 40–44.

1987   Maroni and the monuments. Pp. 43–51 in *Early society in Cyprus,* ed. E. Peltenburg. Edinburgh: Edinburgh University Press.

1998   Maroni IV. *RDAC*: 229–31.

1992   Maroni VI. *RDAC*: 51–58.

Cadogan, G., and M. Domurad.

1989   Maroni V. *RDAC*: 77–81.

Campbell, S., and A. Green, eds.

1995   *The archaeology of death in the ancient Near East.* Oxbow Monograph 51. Oxford: Oxbow.

Carpenter, J. R.

1981   Excavations at Phaneromeni, 1975–78. Pp. 59–78 in *Studies in Cypriote archaeology,* eds. J. C. Biers and D. Soren. Institute of Archaeology, University of California, Los Angeles Monograph 18. Los Angeles: Institute of Archaeology, UCLA.

Catling, H. W.

1963   Patterns of settlement in Bronze Age Cyprus. *Opuscula Atheniensia* 4: 241–54.

1966   Cyprus in the Neolithic and Bronze Age periods. *Cambridge Ancient History,* fasc. 43. Revised ed. of vols. I & II. Cambridge: Cambridge University Press.

1971   A Cypriot bronze statuette in the Bomford Collection. Pp. 15–32 in *Alasia* I, ed. C. Schaeffer. Paris: Klincksieck.

Chapman, J.
1998   The impact of modern invasions and migrations on archaeological explanation:
A biographical sketch of Marija Gimbutas. Pp. 295–314 in *Excavating women*, eds.
M. Diaz-Andreu and M. L. Stig Sorensen. London: Routledge.

Christensen, P.
1993   The social construction of help among Danish children. *Sociology of Health and Illness* 15(4):
488–502.

Christou, D.
1989   The Chalcolithic cemetery I at Souskiou-Vathyrkakas. Pp. 82–94 in *Early society in Cyprus*,
ed. E. Peltenburg. Edinburgh: Edinburgh University Press.

Claassen, C., ed.
1994   *Women in archaeology*. Philadelphia: University of Pennsylvania Press.

Claassen, C., and R. A. Joyce, eds.
1997   *Women in prehistory: North America and Mesoamerica*. Philadelphia: University of Pennsylvania Press.

Clarke, J.
2002   Gender, economy and ceramic production in Neolithic Cyprus. Pp. 251–63 in *Engendering Aphrodite: Women and society in ancient Cyprus*, eds. D. Bolger and N. Serwint. CAARI
Monographs, vol. 3. Boston: ASOR.

Clarke, J., and I. A. Todd
1993   The field survey of Kalavasos-*Pamboules*. *RDAC*: 11–28.

Coleman, J. E. et al.
1996   *Alambra: A Middle Bronze Age site in Cyprus. Archaeological investigations by Cornell University
1974–1985.* SIMA 118. Jonsered, Sweden: Åströms.

Conkey, M.
1991   Contexts of action, contexts for power: Material culture and gender in the Magdalenian.
Pp. 57–92 in *Engendering archaeology: Women and prehistory*, eds. J. M. Gero and M. W. Conkey.
Oxford: Blackwell.
1997   Mobilizing ideologies: Paleolithic "art," gender trouble, and thinking about alternatives. Pp.
172–202 in *Women in human evolution*, ed. L. D. Hager. London and New York: Routledge.

Conkey, M., and J. Spector.
1984   Archaeology and the study of gender. Pp. 1–38 in *Advances in archaeological theory and methods*,
ed. M. Schiffer, vol. 7. New York: Academic Press.

Conkey, M., and R. Tringham
1996   Cultivating thinking/challenging authority: Some experiments in feminist pedagogy in archaeology. Pp. 224–50 in *Gender and archaeology*, ed. R. P. Wright. Philadelphia: University
of Pennsylvania Press.

Costin, C. L.
1996   Exploring the relationship between gender and craft in complex societies: Methodological and theoretical issues of gender attribution. Pp. 111–40 in *Gender and archaeology*, ed. R.
P. Wright. Philadelphia: University of Pennsylvania Press.

Crewe, L.
1998   *Spindle whorls: A study of form, function and decoration in prehistoric Bronze Age Cyprus*. SIMA Pocketbook 149. Jonsered, Sweden: Åströms.

Crumley, C. L.
1987   A dialectical critique of hierarchy. Pp. 155–69 in *Power relations and state formation*, eds. T. C.
Patterson and C. W. Gailey. Washington, DC: Archeology Division, American Anthropological Association.

Cullen, T.
2002   Research and publication in classical archaeology in the United States. Pp. 434–36 in *Engendering Aphrodite: Women and society in ancient Cyprus*, eds. D. Bolger and N. Serwint. CAARI
Monographs, vol. 3. Boston: ASOR.

Dahlberg, F., ed.
1981   *Woman the Gatherer.* New Haven: Yale University Press.

Davenport, W.
1986   Two kinds of value in the eastern Solomon Islands. Pp. 95–109 in *The social life of things,* ed. A. Appadurai. New York: Cambridge University Press.

Davies, P.
1997   Mortuary practice in prehistoric Bronze Age Cyprus. Problems and potential. *RDAC*: 11–26.

de Beauvoir, S.
1974   *The second sex.* Translated by H. M. Parshley. New York: Vintage.

Deverenski, J. S.
1997   Engendering children, engendering archaeology. Pp. 192–202 in *Invisible people and processes: Writing gender and childhood into European archaeology,* eds. J. Moore and E. Scott. London and New York: Leicester University Press.

Dikaios, P.
1936   The excavations at Erimi, 1933–35: Final report. *RDAC*: 1–81. *Excavations at Vounous-Bellapais in Cyprus, 1931–2.* Oxford: Oxford University Press.
1953   *Khirokitia.* Oxford: Oxford University Press.
1961   *Sotira.* Philadelphia: University of Pennsylvania Press.
1962   The Stone Age and Early Bronze Age in Cyprus. Pp. 1–204 in *The Swedish Cyprus Expedition* IV:IA. Lund, Sweden: Swedish Cyprus Expedition.
1969   *Enkomi: Excavations 1948–1958* (3 vols.). Mainz-am-Rhein, Germany: Philip von Zabern.

Diprose, R.
1994   *The bodies of women: Ethics, embodiment and sexual difference.* London and New York: Routledge.

Dobres, M-A., and J. Robb, eds.
2000   *Agency in archaeology.* London: Routledge.

Domurad, M.
1986   *The populations of ancient Cyprus.* Unpublished Ph.D. dissertation, University of Cincinnati. Ann Arbor: University Microfilms.

Douglas, M.
1966   *Purity and danger.* London: Routledge & Kegan Paul.

Downs, J., and T. Pollard, eds.
1999   *The loved body's corruption: Archaeological contributions to the study of human mortality.* Glasgow: Cruithne.

Draper, P.
1997   Institutional, evolutionary and demographic contexts on gender roles: A case study of !Kung bushmen. Pp. 220–32 in *The evolving female,* eds. M. E. Morbeck, et al. Princeton: Princeton University Press.

du Cros, H., and L. Smith
1993   *Women in archaeology: A feminist critique.* Occasional Papers in Archaeology, No. 23. Canberra: Department of Prehistory, Research School of Pacific Studies, Australian National University.

Durkheim, E.
1912   *Les formes élémentaires de la vie religieuse.* Paris: Alcan.

Dyson, S.
1998   *Ancient marbles to American shores: Classical archaeology in the United States.* Philadelphia: University of Pennsylvania Press.

Earle, T. K.
1991   The evolution of chiefdoms. Pp. 1–15 in *Chiefdoms: Power, economy and ideology,* ed. T. K. Earle. Cambridge: Cambridge University Press.

Ehrenberg, M.
1989   *Women in prehistory.* London: British Museum.

Ember, C.
    1983   The relative decline in women's contribution to agriculture with intensification. *American Anthropologist* 85: 285–304.
Fasnacht, W., C. Peege, and I. Hedley
    2000   Agia Varvara-*Almyras*. Final excavation report. *RDAC*: 101–16.
Fausto-Sterling, A.
    2000   *Sexing the body: Gender politics and the contsruction of sexuality.* New York: Basic Books.
Fedigan, L.
    1997   Changing views of female life histories. Pp. 15–26 in *The evolving female: A life-history perspective*, eds. M. E. Morbeck et al. Princeton: Princeton University Press.
Finlay, N.
    1997   Kid knapping: The missing children in lithic analysis. Pp. 203–12 in *Invisible people and processes: Writing gender and childhood into European archaeology*, eds. J. Moore and E. Scott. London and New York: Leicester University Press.
Fischer, P.
    1986   *Prehistoric Cypriot skulls.* SIMA 75. Göteborg, Sweden: Åströms.
Flourentzos, P.
    1997   Excavations at the Neolithic site of Paralimni. A preliminary report. *RDAC*: 1–10.
Foucault, M.
    1979   *The history of sexuality; Volume 1: An introduction.* London: Allen Lane.
    1980   The eye of power. Pp. 146–65 in *Power/knowledge: Selected interviews and other writings 1972–77*, ed. C. Gordon. Translated by C. Gordon et al. New York and London: Harvester Wheatsheaf.
Foxhall, L.
    2000   The running sands of time: Archaeology and the short term. *World Archaeology* 31(3): 484–98.
Frankel, D.
    1974   *Middle Cypriot White Painted pottery: An analytical study of the decoration.* SIMA 42. Göteborg, Sweden: Åströms.
    1978   Pottery decoration as an indicator of social relationships. Pp. 147–60 in *Art in Society*, eds. M. Greenhalgh and J. V. S. Megaw. London: Duckworth.
    1993a   Inter- and intrasite variability and social interaction in prehistoric Bronze Age Cyprus: Types, ranges, and trends. *Bulletin of the American Schools of Oriental Research* 292: 59–72.
    1993b   Is this a trivial observation? Gender in prehistoric Bronze Age Cyprus. Pp. 138–42 in *Women in archaeology: A feminist critique*, eds. H. du Cros and L. Smith. Occasional Papers in Prehistory 23. Canberra: Australian National University.
    2000   Migration and ethnicity in prehistoric Cyprus: Technology as habitus. *European Journal of Archaeology* 3(2): 167–87.
    2002   Social stratification, gender and ethnicity in third millennium Cyprus. Pp. 171–79 in *Engendering Aphrodite: Women and society in ancient Cyprus*, eds. D. Bolger and N. Serwint. CAARI Monographs, vol. 3. Boston: ASOR.
Frankel, D., and A. Tamkavi
    1973   Cypriot shrine models and decorated tombs. *Australian Journal of Biblical Archaeology* 2(2): 39–44.
Frankel, D., and J. M. Webb
    1993   Excavations at Marki-*Alonia*, 1992–3. *RDAC*: 43–68.
    1994   Excavations at Marki-*Alonia*, 1993–4. *RDAC*: 51–72.
    1996a   *Marki-Alonia: An Early and Middle Bronze Age town in Cyprus. Excavations 1990–1994.* Jonsered, Sweden: Åströms.
    1996b   Excavations at Marki-*Alonia*, 1995–6. *RDAC*: 51–68.
    1997   Excavations at Marki-*Alonia*, 1996–7. *RDAC*: 85–109.
    1999   Excavations at Marki-*Alonia*, 1998–9. *RDAC*: 87–110.

2000   Excavations at Marki-*Alonia*, 1999–2000. *RDAC*: 65–94.

2001   Excavations at Marki-*Alonia*, 2000. *RDAC*: 15–43.

In press   Population, households and ceramic consumption in a prehistoric village. Forthcoming in *Journal of Field Archaeology*.

Frankel, D., J. Webb, and C. Eslick

1995   Anatolia and Cyprus in the third millennium BCE: A speculative model of interaction. *Abr Nahrain Supplement* 5: 37–50.

Fürst, C. M.

1933   *Zur Kenntnis der Anthropologie der praehistorischen Bevoelkerung der Insel Cypern*. Lunds Universitet Arsskrift, vol. 9, no. 6. Lund, Sweden: University of Lund.

Gailey, C. W.

1987   *Kinship to kingship: Gender hierarchy and state formation in the Tongan Islands*. Austin: University of Texas Press.

Gardiner, J. K.

1995   *Provoking agents: Gender and agency in theory and practice*. Urbana: University of Illinois Press.

Gatens, M.

1996   *Imaginary bodies: Ethics, power and corporeality*. London and New York: Routledge.

Gero, J.

1985   Socio-politics of archaeology and the woman-at-home ideology. *American Antiquity* 50(2): 342–50.

1991   Genderlithics: Women's roles in stone tool production. Pp. 163–93 in *Engendering archaeology: Women and prehistory*, eds. J. M. Gero and M. W. Conkey. Oxford: Blackwell.

1996   Archaeological practice and gendered encounters with field data. Pp. 251–80 in *Gender and archaeology*, ed. R. P. Wright. Philadelphia: University of Pennsylvania Press.

2000   Troubled travels in agency and feminism. Pp. 40–50 in *Agency in archaeology*, eds. M.-A. Dobres and J. Robb. London and New York: Routledge.

Gero, J. M., and M.W. Conkey

1991   Tensions, pluralities, and engendering archaeology: An introduction to women and prehistory. Pp. 3–30 in *Engendering archaeology: Women and prehistory*, eds. J. M. Gero and M.W. Conkey. Oxford: Blackwell.

Gero, J. M., and M. W. Conkey, eds.

1991   *Engendering archaeology: Women and prehistory*. Oxford: Blackwell.

Giddens, A.

1984   *The constitution of society: Outline of the theory of structuration*. Cambridge: Polity.

Gilchrist, R.

1999   *Gender and archaeology: Contesting the past*. New York: Routledge

2000   Archaeological biographies: Realizing human lifecycles, -courses and -histories. *World Archaeology* 31(3): 325–28.

Gimbutas, M.

1974   *Gods and goddesses of old Europe*. London: Thames and Hudson.

1989   *The language of the goddess: Unearthing hidden symbols of Western civilization*. London: Thames and Hudson.

1991   *The civilization of the goddess: The world of old Europe*. San Francisco: Harpers.

Gjerstad, E.

1926   *Studies on prehistoric Cyprus*. Uppsala, Sweden: Uppsala Universitet.

Gjerstad, E. et al.

1934   *The Swedish Cyprus Expedition. Finds and results of the excavations in Cyprus 1927–1931*. Stockholm: The Swedish Cyprus Expedition.

Goodison, L., and C. Morris, eds.

1998   *Ancient goddesses*. London: British Museum.

Goring, E.

1988   *A mischievous pastime: Digging in Cyprus in the nineteenth century*. Edinburgh: National Museums of Scotland.

1989   Death in everyday life: Aspects of burial practice in the Late Bronze Age. Pp. 95–105 in *Early society in Cyprus*, ed. E. Peltenburg. Edinburgh: Edinburgh University Press.

1991a   The anthropomorphic figurines. Pp. 39–60 in *Lemba Archaeological Project II.2 A ceremonial area at Kissonerga*, by E. Peltenburg et al. SIMA 70: 3. Göteborg, Sweden: Åströms.

1991b   Pottery figurines: The development of a coroplastic art in Cyprus. *Bulletin of the American Schools of Oriental Research* 282/283: 153–61.

1998   Figurines, figurine fragments, phalli, possibly figurative worked and unworked stones, unidentifiable worked stone and pottery fragments. Pp. 148–67 in *Lemba Archaeological Project II.1A: Excavations at Kissonerga-Mosphilia, 1979–1992*, by E. Peltenburg et al. SIMA 70(2). Jonsered, Sweden: Åströms.

2003   Figurines, figurine fragments, unidentifiable worked stone and pottery fragments. Pp. 169–76 in *Lemba Archaeological Project III.1: The colonization and settlement of Cyprus. Excavations at Kissonerga-Mylouthkia, 1976–1996*, ed. E. Peltenburg. SIMA 70(4). Sävedalen, Sweden: Åströms.

Goring-Morris et al.
1998   The 1997 season of excavations at the mortuary site of Kfar Hahoresh, Galilee, Israel. *Neo-lithics* 98: 1–4.

Gosden, C.
1994   *Social being and time*. Oxford: Blackwell.

Gould, S. J.
1977   Biological potentiality vs. biological determinism. Pp. 251–59 in *Ever since Darwin*, by S. J. Gould. New York: Norton.

Grosz, E.
1994   *Volatile bodies: Towards a corporeal feminism*. Bloomington: Indiana University Press.

Guilaine, J., and F. Briois
2001   Parekklisha-*Shillourokambos*: An early Neolithic site in Cyprus. Pp. 37–53 in *The earliest prehistory of Cyprus: From colonization to exploitation*, ed. S. Swiny. CAARI Monographs, vol. 2. Boston: ASOR.

Guilaine, J. et al.
1995   L'etablissement neolithique de Shillourokambos (Parekklisha, Chypre). Premiers resultants. *RDAC*: 11–32.

1998   La site neolithique preceramique de Shillourokambos (Parekklisha, Chypre). *BCH* 122: 603–10.

1999   Tête sculptée en pierre dans le neolithique pré-céramique de Shillourokampos (Parekklisia, Chypre). *RDAC*: 1–12.

Hadjisavvas, S.
1986   Alassa: A new Late Cypriot site. *RDAC*. 62–67.

1989   A Late Cypriot community at Alassa. Pp. 32–42 in *Early society in Cyprus*, ed. E. Peltenburg. Edinburgh: Edinburgh University Press.

Hager, L. D., ed.
1997   *Women in human evolution*. London and New York: Routledge.

Halstead, P.
1989   The economy as a normal surplus: Economic stability and social change among early farming communities of Thessaly, Greece. Pp. 68–80 in *Bad year economics: Cultural responses to risk and uncertainty*, eds. P. Halstead and J. O'Shea. Cambridge: Cambridge University Press.

Hamilton, N.
1994   A fresh look at the 'seated gentleman' in the Pierides Foundation Museum, Republic of Cyprus. *Cambridge Archaeological Journal* 4(2): 302–12.

2000   Ungendering archaeology: Concepts of sex and gender in figurine studies. Pp. 17–30 in *Representations of gender from prehistory to the present. Proceedings of the Conference on Gender and Material Culture held at Exeter University, July 1994*, eds. M. Donald and L. Hurcombe. Studies in Gender and Material Culture. New York: MacMillan.

Harris, M.
1971   *Culture, man and nature: An introduction to general anthropology*. New York: Thomas W. Crowell.

Hastorf, C.
1991   Gender, space and food in prehistory. Pp. 132–59 in *Engendering archaeology: Women and prehistory*, eds. J. M. Gero and M. W. Conkey. Oxford: Blackwell.
1998   Women and children first. Review of *Invisible people and processes: Writing gender and childhood into European archaeology*, eds. J. Moore and E. Scott. *Cambridge Archaeological Journal* 8(1): 126–28.
Hawes, H. B.
1908   *Gournia, Vasiliki, and other prehistoric sites on the isthmus of Ierapetra, Crete.* Philadelphia: American Exploration Society.
Hays-Gilpin, K., and D. S. Whitley, eds.
1998   *Reader in gender archaeology.* London and New York: Routledge.
Hekman, S.
1995   Subjects and agents: The question for feminism. Pp. 194–207 in *Provoking agents: Gender and agency in theory and practice*, ed. J. K. Gardiner. Urbana: University of Illinois.
Held, S.
1990   Back to what future? New directions for Cypriot early prehistoric research in the 1990s. *RDAC*: 1–43.
Hennessy, J. B.
1963   *Stephania: A Middle and Late Bronze Age cemetery in Cyprus.* London: Bernard Quaritch.
Herscher, E.
1978   *The Bronze Age cemetery at Lapithos, Vrysi tou Barba, Cyprus. Results of the University of Pennsylvania Museum excavation, 1931.* Unpublished Ph. D. dissertation, University of Pennsylvania. Ann Arbor: University Microfilms.
Hillier, B., and J. Hanson
1984   *The social logic of space.* Cambridge: Cambridge University Press.
Hjortsjö, C-H.
1947   *To the knowledge of the prehistoric craniology of Cyprus.* Lund, Sweden: Särtryck ur Kungl. Hum. Vetenskapssamfundetz i Lund.
Hodder, I.
1982   Theoretical archaeology: A reactionary view. Pp. 1–16 in *Symbolic and structural archaeology*, ed. I. Hodder. Cambridge: Cambridge University Press.
1990   *The domestication of Europe.* Oxford: Blackwell.
Holy, L.
1996   *Anthropological perspectives on kinship.* Chicago: Pluto.
Hulin, L. C.
1989   The identification of Cypriot cult figures through cross-cultural interpretation: Some problems. Pp. 127–39 in *Early society in Cyprus*, ed. E. Peltenburg. Edinburgh: Edinburgh University Press.
Hurcombe, L.
1997   A viable past in the pictorial present? Pp. 15–24 in *Invisible people and processes: Writing gender and childhood into European archaeology*, eds. J. Moore and E. Scott. London and New York: Leicester University Press.
Hurcombe, L., and M. Donald, eds.
2000   *Representations of gender from prehistory to the present. Proceedings of the Conference on Gender and Material Culture held at Exeter University, July 1994.* Studies in Gender and Material Culture. New York: MacMillan.
Isaac, G.
1978   The food sharing behavior of protohuman hominids. *Scientific American* 238: 90–108.
James, A., C. Jenks, and A. Prout
1998   *Theorizing childhood.* Cambridge: Polity.
Johnson, J.
1980   *Maroni de Chypre.* SIMA 59. Göteborg, Sweden: Åströms.
Johnson, M.
2000   Conceptions of agency in archaeological interpretation. Pp. 211–27 in *Interpretive archaeology: A reader*, ed. J. Thomas. London and New York: Leicester University Press.

Joyce, R.
    2000   Girling the girl and boying the boy: The production of adulthood in ancient Mesoamerica. *World Archaeology* 31(3): 473–83.

Karageorghis, J.
    1977   *La grande déesse de Chypre et son culte.* Lyon, France: Maison de l'Orient.

Karageorghis, V.
    1974   *Excavations at Kition I: The tombs* (text). Nicosia: Department of Antiquities.
    1976a   *The civilization of prehistoric Cyprus.* Athens: Ekdotike Athenon.
    1976b   *Kition: Mycenaean and Phoenician discoveries in Cyprus.* London: Thames and Hudson.
    1991   *The coroplastic art of ancient Cyprus I: Chalcolithic—Late Cypriot I.* Nicosia: A. G. Leventis Foundation.
    1993   *The coroplastic art of ancient Cyprus II: Late Cypriot II—Cypro-Geometric III.* Nicosia:, A. Cyprus G. Leventis Foundation.
    1998   *Cypriot archaeology today: Achievements and perspectives.* Glasgow: Glasgow University Press.

Karageorghis, V., and M. Demas
    1985   *Excavations at Kition, vol. V, The pre-Phoenician levels* (Parts I and II). Nicosia: Department of Antiquities.

Karageorghis, V., and D. Michaelides, eds.
    1996   *The development of the Cypriot economy: From the prehistoric period to the present day.* Nicosia: University of Cyprus and Bank of Cyprus.

Karageorghis, V., and L. Vagnetti
    1981   A Chalcolithic terracotta figure in the Pierides Foundation Museum, Cyprus. Pp. 53–56 in *Chalcolithic Cyprus and western Asia*, ed. J. Reade. British Museum Occasional Paper 26. London: British Museum.

Keesing, R. M., and A. J. Strathern
    1998   *Cultural anthropology: A contemporary perspective.* 3rd ed. Orlando, FL: Harcourt, Brace.

Kent, S.
    1990   A cross-cultural study of segmentation, architecture, and the use of space. Pp. 127–52 in *Domestic architecture and the use of space*, ed. S. Kent. New Directions in Archaeology. Cambridge: Cambridge University Press.
    1995   Does sedentarization promote gender inequality? A case study from the Kalahari. *Journal of the Royal Anthropological Institute* (N.S.) 1: 513–36.

Keswani, P. S.
    1989   *Mortuary ritual and social hierarchy in Bronze Age Cyprus.* Unpublished Ph. D. dissertation, University of Michigan. Ann Arbor: University Microfilms.
    1991   Mortuary celebrations in Bronze Age Cyprus. Unpublished paper presented at the Cyprus American Archaeological Research Institute, Nicosia, Cyprus, February 21.
    1993   Models of local exchange in Late Bronze Age Cyprus. *Bulletin of the American Schools of Oriental Research* 292: 73–83.
    1996a   Death in Cyprus: Mortuary rituals and social transformations in the Early and Middle Bronze Age. Unpublished paper presented at the American Anthropological Association Annual Meeting, November, San Francisco.
    1996b   Hierarchies, heterarchies, and urbanization processes: The view from Bronze Age Cyprus. *Journal of Mediterranean Archaeology* 9(2): 211–50.

Killen, J.
    2003   The subjects of a Mycenaean/*wanax*/: Aspects of Mycenaean social structure. Paper delivered at the international conference "From *wanax* to basileus," Department of Classics, University of Edinburgh, January 23.

Kingsnorth, A.
    1993   Complexities of complexity: An anthropological concern. *Bulletin of the American Schools of Oriental Research* 292: 107–20.

Kling, B.
    1989   *Mycenaean IIIC:1b and related pottery in Cyprus.* SIMA 87. Göteborg, Sweden: Åströms.

Knapp. A. B.
   1986   *Copper production and divine protection: Archaeology, ideology and social complexity on Bronze Age Cyprus.*
             Göteborg, Sweden: Åströms.
   1988   Hoards d'oeuvres: Of metals & men on Bronze Age Cyprus. *Oxford Journal of Archaeology* 8:
             147–76.
   1990   Production, location and integration in Bronze Age Cyprus. *Current Anthropology* 31: 147–76.
   1993   Social complexity: Incipience, emergence and development on prehistoric Cyprus. *Bulletin
             of the American Schools of Oriental Research* 292: 85–106.
   1994   Emergence, development and decline on Bronze Age Cyprus. Pp. 271–304 in *Development
             and decline in the Mediterranean Bronze Age*, eds. C. Mathers and S. Stoddard. Sheffield Archae-
             ological Monograph 8. Sheffield, U.K.: John Collis.
   1996   The Bronze Age economy of Cyprus. Pp. 71–106 in *The development of the Cypriot economy: From
             the prehistoric period to the present day*, eds. V. Karageoghis and D. Michaelides. Nicosia: University
             of Cyprus and Bank of Cyprus.
Knapp, A. B., and J. F. Cherry
   1994   *Provenience studies and Bronze Age Cyprus: Production, exchange and politico-economic change.* Mono-
             graphs in World Archaeology 21. Madison: Prehistory Press.
Knapp, A. B., M. Donnelly, and V. Kassianidou
   1998   Excavations at Politico-Phorades 1997. *RDAC*: 247–68.
Knapp, A. B., and L. Meskell
   1997   Bodies of evidence on prehistoric Cyprus. *Cambridge Archaeological Journal* 7(2): 183–204.
Kohlberg, L.
   1966   A cognitive-developmental analysis of children's sex-role concepts and attitudes. Pp.
             82–173 in *The development of sex differences*, ed. E. E. Macoby. London: Tavistock.
Lancaster, R. N., and M. di Leonardo, eds.
   1997   *The gender sexuality reader.* New York: Routledge.
Leacock, E. B.
   1983   Interpreting the origins of gender inequality: Conceptual and historical problems. *Dialec-
             tical Anthropology* 7(4): 263–84.
Le Brun, A.
   1981   *Cap Andreas-Kastros: Un site neolithique preceramique en Chypre.* Paris: Éditions A.D.P.F.
   1984   *Fouilles recentes a Khirokitia (Chypre) 1977–1981.* Paris: Éditions Recherche sur les Civilisa-
             tions.
   1989   *Fouilles recentes a Khirokitia (Chypre) 1983–86.* Paris: Éditions Recherche sur les Civilisa-
             tions.
   1994   *Fouilles recentes a Khirokitia (Chypre) 1988–1991.* Paris: Éditions Recherche sur les Civilisations.
   2001   At the other end of the sequence: The Cypriot Aceramic Neolithic as seen from Khi-
             rokitia. Pp. 109–18 in *The earliest prehistory of Cyprus: From colonization to exploitation*, ed.
             S. Swiny. CAARI Monographs, vol. 2. Boston: ASOR.
   2002   Neolithic society in Cyprus: A tentative analysis. Pp. 23–31 in *Engendering Aphrodite: Women
             and society in ancient Cyprus*, eds. D. Bolger and N. Serwint. CAARI Monographs, vol. 3.
             Boston: ASOR.
Lee, M. M.
   2000   Deciphering gender in Minoan dress. Pp. 111–23 in *Reading the body: Representations and re-
             mains in the archaeological record*, ed. A. E. Rautman. Philadelphia: University of Pennsylvania
             Press.
Lee, R. B., and I. DeVore, eds.
   1968   *Man the hunter.* Chicago: Aldine.
Le Mort, F.
   1994   Les sépultures. Pp. 157–98 in *Fouilles recentes a Khirokitia (Chypre) 1988–1991, ed.* A. Le
             Brun, Paris: Éditions Recherche sur les Civilisations.
   2000   The Neolithic subadult skeletons from Khirokitia (Cyprus): Taphonomy and infant mor-
             tality. *Anthropologie* 38(1): 63–70.

Lerner, G.
1986   *The creation of patriarchy.* Oxford: Oxford University Press.
Lesure, R. G.
2002   The goddess diffracted: Thinking about the figurines of early villages. *Current Anthropology* 43(4): 587–610.
Lillehammer, G.
1989   A child is born: The child's world in an archaeological perspective. *Norwegian Archaeological Review* 22: 89–105.
Lindsey, L. L.
1997   *Gender roles. A sociological perspective.* Upper Saddle River, NJ: Prentice Hall.
London, G. A.
2002   Women potters and craft specialization in a pre-market Cypriot economy. Pp. 265–80 in *Engendering Aphrodite: Women and society in ancient Cyprus*, eds. D. Bolger and N. Serwint. CAARI Monographs, vol. 3. Boston: ASOR.
Lorentz, K.
1998   *Infant archaeology: Activities and attitudes related to children in Cyprus from the Aceramic Neolithic to the Late Bronze Age.* Unpublished M.A. dissertation, University of Edinburgh.
Lunt, D.
1994   Report on human dentitions from Souskiou-*Vathyrkakas* 1972. Pp. 120–29 in *Excavations at Kouklia (Palaipaphos)*. Seventeenth preliminary report: Seasons 1991 and 1992, by F. G. Maier and M.-L. von Wartburg. *RDAC*: 115–28.
Maier, F. G.
1973   *Excavations at Kouklia (Palaepaphos)*. Sixth preliminary report: Seasons 1971 and 1972. *RDAC*: 186–201.
Manning, S. W.
1993   Prestige, distinction and competition: The anatomy of socioeconomic complexity in fourth to second millennium B.C.E. Cyprus. *Bulletin of the American Schools of Oriental Research* 292: 35–58.
1998a   *Tsaroukkas*, Mycenaeans and trade project: Preliminary report on the 1996–1997 seasons. *RDAC*: 39–54.
1998b   Changing pasts and socio-political cognition in Late Bronze Age Cyprus. *World Archaeology* 30(1): 39–58.
Manning, S.W. et al.
1994   *Tsaroukkas*, Mycenaeans and trade project: Preliminary report on the 1993 season. *RDAC*: 83–106.
Mantzourani, E.
1994   Ekthesi apotelesmaton tis anaskaphis sti thesi Kantou-Kouphovounos. *RDAC*: 1–29.
Maradi, T.
1996   Copper mineworkers from Alambra village: An oral history supplement to the Sia-Mathiatis-Ayia Varvara survey project. Pp. 118–24 in *Excavations at Agia Varvara-Almyras*. Fifth preliminary report, by W.A. Fasnacht et al. *RDAC*: 95–125.
Marks, E., and I. de Courtivron
1980   *New French feminisms.* New York: Schocken.
Massey, D.
1994   *Space, place and gender.* Minneapolis: University of Minnesota Press.
Masson, O.
1973   Remarques sur les cultes Chypriotes à l'époque du Bronze Récent. Pp. 110–21 in *Acts of the international archaeological symposium 'The Mycenaeans in the eastern Mediterranean'*. Nicosia: Department of Antiquities, Cyprus.
Matthäus, H.
1982   Die zyprische Metallindustrie in der ausgehenden Bronzezeit: Einheimische, ägäische und nahöstliche Elemente. Pp. 185–201 in *Early metallurgy in Cyprus, 4000–500 BC*, eds. J. D. Muhly, R. Maddin, and V. Karageorghis. Nicosia: Pierides Foundation.

Mays, S.
    1993   Infanticide in Roman Britain. *Antiquity* 67: 883–888.
    1995   Killing the unwanted child. *British Archaeology* 2: 8–9.
McCartney, C.
    2002   Women's knives. Pp. 237–49 in *Engendering Aphrodite: Women and society in ancient Cyprus*, eds.
               D. Bolger and N. Serwint. CAARI Monographs, vol. 3. Boston: ASOR.
McLeod, B.
    1997   Life history, females and evolution: A commentary. Pp. 270–75 in *The Evolving female*,
               eds. M. E. Morbeck, A. Galloway, and A. L. Zilhman. Princeton: Princeton University
               Press.
McNay, L.
    1992   *Foucault and feminism*. Cambridge: Polity.
Mead, M.
    1928   *Coming of age in Samoa*. New York: Museum of Natural History.
    1939   *Sex and temperament in three primitive societies*. New York: William Morrow.
    1949   *Male and female*. New York: William Morrow.
Merleau-Ponty, M.
    1962   *The phenomenology of perception*. Translated by C. Smith. London: Routledge & Kegan Paul..
Merrillees, R.
    1968   *The Cypriote Bronze Age pottery found in Egypt*. SIMA 18. Lund, Sweden: Åströms.
    1980   Representation of the human form in prehistoric Cyprus. *Opuscula Atheniensia* 12: 171–84.
    1992   The government of Cyprus in the Late Bronze Age. Pp. 310–28 in *Acta Cypria. Acts of an
               international congress on Cypriote archaeology held in Göteborg on 22–24 August 1991*, Part 3, ed.
               P. Åström. SIMA Pocketbook 120. Jonsered, Sweden: Åströms.
Meskell, L.
    1995   Goddesses, Gimbutas and "new age" archaeology. *Antiquity* 69: 74–86.
    1998   The irresistible body and the seduction of archaeology. Pp. 139–61 in *Changing bodies,
               changing meanings: Studies on the human body in antiquity*, ed. D. Montserrat. London: Rout-
               ledge.
    1999   *Archaeologies of social life: Age, sex and class in ancient Egypt*. Oxford: Blackwell.
    2000   Writing the body in archaeology. Pp. 13–21 in *Reading the body: Representations and remains
               in the archaeological record*, ed. A. E. Rautman. Philadelphia: University of Pennsylvania
               Press.
    2001   Archaeologies of identity. Pp. 187–213 in *Archaeological theory today*, ed. I. Hodder. Oxford:
               Polity.
Minge-Klevana, W.
    1980   Does labor time decrease with industrialization? A survey of time allocation studies. *Cur-
               rent Anthropology* 21: 279–87.
Mogelonsky, M. K.
    1988   *Early and Middle Cypriot terracotta figurines*. Unpublished Ph.D. dissertation, Cornell Univer-
               sity. Ann Arbor: University Microfilms.
    1991   A typological system for Early and Middle Cypriot anthropomorphic terracotta figurines.
               RDAC: 19–36.
    1996   Anthropomorphic figurines. Pp. 202–3 in *Alambra: A Middle Bronze Age site in Cyprus. Archae-
               ological investigations by Cornell University 1974–1985*, by J. Coleman et al. SIMA 118. Jon-
               sered, Sweden: Åströms.
Montserrat, D., ed.
    1998   *Changing bodies, changing meanings: Studies on the human body in antiquity*. London: Routledge.
Moore, H. L.
    1986   *Space, text and gender: An anthropological study of the Marakwet of Kenya*. Cambridge: Cambridge
               University Press.
    1994   *A passion for difference: Essays in anthropology and gender*. Bloomington: Indiana University
               Press.

Moore, J., and E. Scott, eds.
    1997   *Invisible people and processes: Writing gender and childhood into European archaeology.* London: Leicester
            University Press.
Morbeck, M. E., A. Galloway, and A. L. Zihlman, eds.
    1997   *The evolving female: A life-history perspective.* Princeton: Princeton University Press.
Morgen, S., ed.
    1989   *Gender and anthropology: Critical reviews for research and teaching.* Washington, DC: American An-
            thropological Association.
Morris, D.
    1985   *The art of ancient Cyprus.* Oxford: Phaidon.
Moyer, J.
    1989   Human skeletal remains. Pp. 58–69 in *Vasilikos Valley Project 3: Kalavasos-Ayios Dhimitrios II.
            Ceramics, objects, tombs, specialist studies,* by A. South, P. Russell, and P. S. Keswani. SIMA 71:
            3. Göteborg, Sweden: Åströms.
Muhly, J. D.
    1982   The nature of trade in the LBA eastern Mediterranean: The organization of the
            metals' trade and the role of Cyprus. Pp. 251–69 in *Early metallurgy in Cyprus, 4000–500
            BC,* eds. J. D. Muhly, R. Maddin, and V. Karageorghis. Nicosia: Pierides Foundation.
    1985   The Late Bronze Age in Cyprus: A 25 year retrospect. Pp. 20–46 in *Archaeology in Cyprus
            1960–1985,* ed. V. Karageorghis. Nicosia: A. G. Leventis Foundation.
    1996   The significance of metals in the Late Bronze Age economy of Cyprus. Pp. 45–60 in *The
            development of the Cypriot economy: From the prehistoric period to the present day,* eds. V. Karageorghis
            and D. Michaelides. Nicosia: University of Cyprus and Bank of Cyprus.
Muhly, J. D., R. Maddin, and V. Karageorghis, eds.
    1982   *Early metallurgy in Cyprus, 4000–500 B.C.* Nicosia: Pierides Foundation and Department of
            Antiquities.
Myres, J. L.
    1946   Excavations in Cyprus, 1913. *Annual of the British School at Athens* 41: 53–96.
Nelson, M. C., S. M. Nelson, and A. Wylie, eds.
    1994   *Equity issues for women in archeology.* Archeological Papers of the American Anthropological
            Association 5. Arlington, VA: American Anthropological Association.
Nelson, S. M.
    1997   *Gender in archaeology: Analyzing power and prestige.* Walnut Creek, CA: AltaMira.
Niklasson, K.
    1983   Tomb 23: A shaft grave of the Late Cypriot III period. Pp. 169–87 in *Hala Sultan
            Tekke 8. Excavations 1971–79,* by P. Åström et al. SIMA 45: 8. Göteborg, Sweden:
            Åströms.
    1991   *Early prehistoric burials in Cyprus.* Jonsered, Sweden: Åströms.
Olsen, B. A.
    1998   Women, children and the family in the Late Aegean Bronze Age: Differences in Minoan
            and Mycenaean constructions of gender. *World Archaeology* 29(3): 380–92.
Oren, E. D., ed.
    1990   The meaning and function of the Bronze Age terracotta anthropomorphic figurines from
            Cyprus. *RDAC*: 45–50.
    2000   *The sea peoples and their world: A reassessment.* Philadelphia: University Museum.
Orphanides, A.
    1990   The meaning and function of the Bronze Age terracotta anthropomorphic figurines from
            Cyprus. *RDAC*: 45–50
Ortner, S.
    1974   Is female to male as nature is to culture? Pp. 67–88 in *Woman, culture and society,* eds. M. Z.
            Rosaldo and L. Lamphere. Stanford: Stanford University Press.
Overbeck, J., and S. Swiny
    1972   *Two Cypriot Bronze Age sites at Kafkallia (Dhali).* SIMA 33. Göteborg, Sweden: Åströms.

Paige, K. E., and J. M. Paige
    1981   *The politics of reproductive ritual.* Berkeley and Los Angeles: University of California Press.
Parker Pearson, M.
    1999   *The archaeology of death and burial.* Gloucestershire, U.K.: Sutton.
Parpola, S., and R. M. Whiting, eds.
    2002   *Sex and gender in the ancient Near East:Proceedings of the 47th Recontre Assyriologique Internationale, Helsinki, July 2–6, 2001.* Winona Lake, IN: Eisenbrauns.
Peletz, M. G.
    1995   Kinship studies in late twentieth-century anthropology. *Annual Review of Anthropology* 24: 343–72.
Peltenburg, E. J.
    1978   The Sotira culture: Regional diversity and cultural unity in Late Neolithic Cyprus. *Levant* 10: 55–74.
    1982a   *Vrysi: A subterranean settlement in Cyprus. Excavations at prehistoric Ayios Epiktitos-Vrysi 1969–73.* Warminster, U.K.: Aris & Phillips.
    1982b   The evolution of the Chalcolithic cruciform figurine. *RDAC:* 12–14.
    1991   Kissonerga-*Mosphilia*: A major Chalcolithic site in Cyprus. *Bulletin of the American Schools of Oriental Research* 282/283: 17–35.
    1992   Birth pendants in life and death: Evidence from Kissonerga grave 563. Pp. 27–36 in *Studies in honour of Vassos Karageorghis,* ed. G. C. Ioannides. Nicosia: Society of Cypriot Studies.
    1993   Settlement continuity and resistance to complexity in Cyprus, ca. 4500–2500 B.C.E. *Bulletin of the American Schools of Oriental Research* 292: 9–23.
    1994   Constructing authority: The Vounous enclosure model. *Opuscula Atheniensia* 20(1): 157–62.
    1996   From isolation to state formation in Cyprus, c. 3500–1500 B.C. Pp. 17–44 in *The development of the Cypriot economy: From the prehistoric period to the present day,* eds. V. Karageorghis and D. Michaelides. Nicosia: University of Cyprus and Bank of Cyprus.
    2002   Gender and social structure in prehistoric Cyprus: A case study from Kissonerga. Pp. 53–66 in *Engendering Aphrodite: Women and society in ancient Cyprus,* eds. D. Bolger and N. Serwint. CAARI Monographs, vol. 3. Boston: ASOR.
    In press   Social space in early sedentary communities of southwest Asia and Cyprus. Forthcoming in *Neolithic revolutions: New perspectives on south-west Asia in light of recent discoveries on Cyprus,* eds. A. Wasse and E. Peltenburg.
Peltenburg, E., ed.
    1989   *Early society in Cyprus.* Edinburgh: Edinburgh University Press.
    2003   *Lemba Archaeological Project III.1: The colonisation and settlement of Cyprus. Investigations at Kissonerga-Mylouthkia, 1976–1996.* SIMA 70(4). Sävedalen, Sweden: Åströms.
Peltenburg, E., et al.
    1985   *Lemba Archaeological Project I: Excavations at Lemba-Lakkous, 1976–1983.* SIMA 70(1). Göteborg, Sweden: Åströms.
    1991   *Lemba Archaeological Project II.2: A ceremonial area at Kissonerga.* SIMA 70(3). Göteborg, Sweden: Åströms.
    1998   *Lemba Archaeological Project II.1A: Excavations at Kissonerga-Mosphilia, 1979–1992.* SIMA 70(2). Jonsered, Sweden: Åströms.
    2000   Agro-pastoralist colonization of Cyprus in the 10th millennium BP: Initial assessments. *Antiquity* 74: 844–853.
    2001a   Neolithic dispersals from the Levantine corridor: A Mediterranean perspective. *Levant* 33: 35–64.
    2001b   Well-established colonists: Mylouthkia I and the Cypro-Pre-Pottery Neolithic B. Pp. 61–93 in *The earliest prehistory of Cyprus: From colonization to exploitation,* ed. S. Swiny. CAARI Monographs, vol. 2. Boston: ASOR.
Peterson, J.
    2002   *Sexual revolutions: Gender and labor at the dawn of agriculture.* Walnut Creek, CA: AltaMira.

Piaget, J.
1929 *The child's conception of the world*. London: Kegan Paul.
1955 *Construction of reality in the child*. Translated by Margaret Cook. London: Routledge & Kegan Paul.

Pickles, S., and E. Peltenburg
1998 Metallurgy, society and the bronze/iron transition in the east Mediterranean and the Near East. *RDAC*: 67–100.

Pilides, D.
2002 Gender and administration in the Department of Antiquities, Cyprus. Pp. 443–45 in *Engendering Aphrodite. Women and society in ancient Cyprus*, eds. D. Bolger and N. Serwint. CAARI Monographs, vol. 3. Boston: ASOR.

Pollock, S.
1991 Women in a men's world: Images of Sumerian women. Pp. 366–87 in *Engendering archaeology: Women and prehistory*, eds. J. M. Gero and M. W. Conkey. Oxford: Blackwell.

Price, B. J.
1978 Secondary state formation: An explanatory model. Pp. 161–86 in *The origins of the state*, eds. R. Cohen and E. R. Service. Philadelphia: Institute for the Study of Human Issues (ISHI).

Price, J., and M. Shildrick, eds.
1999 *Feminist theory and the body: A reader*. Edinburgh: Edinburgh University Press.

Price, M.
1999 All the in family: The impact of gender and family constructs on the study of prehistoric settlement. Pp. 31–51 in *Making places in the prehistoric world: Themes in settlement archaeology*, eds. J. Brueck and M. Goodman. London: University College London.

Pulak, C.
2001 The cargo of the Uluburun ship and evidence for trade with the Aegean and beyond. Pp. 13–60 in *Italy and Cyprus in antiquity, 1500–450 B.C.*, eds. L. Bonfante and V. Karageorghis. Nicosia: Severis Foundation.

Rautman, A. E., ed.
2000 *Reading the body: Representations and remains in the archaeological record*. Philadelphia: University of Pennsylvania Press.

Ribeiro, E. C.
2002 Altering the body: Representations of pre-pubescent gender groups on Early and Middle Cypriot "scenic compositions." Pp. 197–209 in *Engendering Aphrodite: Women and society in ancient Cyprus*, eds. D. Bolger and N. Serwint. CAARI Monographs, vol. 3. Boston: ASOR.

Rice, P. C.
1981 Prehistoric Venuses: Symbols of motherhood or womanhood? *Journal of Anthropological Research* 37: 402–14.
1987 *Pottery analysis: A sourcebook*. Chicago: University of Chicago Press.

Robins, G.
1993 *Women in ancient Egypt*. London: British Museum.

Romanowicz, J. V., and R. P. Wright
1996 Gendered perspectives in the classroom. Pp. 199–223 in *Gender and archaeology*, ed. R. P. Wright. Philadelphia: University of Pennsylvania Press.

Rosaldo, M. Z.
1974 Woman, culture and society: A theoretical overview. Pp. 14–42 in *Woman, culture and society*, eds. M. Z. Rosaldo and L. Lamphere. Stanford, CA: Stanford University Press.

Rossi, A., ed.
1983 *Gender and the life course*. New York: Aldine.

Rupp, D.
1993 Aspects of social complexity in Cyprus: Socioeconomic interaction and integration in the fourth through second millennia B.C.E. *Bulletin of the American Schools of Oriental Research* 292: 1–8.

Russell, P.
    1998   The paleolithic mother-goddess: Fact or fiction? Pp. 261–68 in *Reader in gender archaeology*, eds. K. Hays-Gilpin and D. S. Whitley. London: Routledge.
Sacks, K.
    1979   *Sisters and wives: The past and future of sexual equality*. Westport, CT: Greenwood.
Sanday, P.
    1973   Towards a theory of the status of women. *American Anthropologist* 75: 1682–1700.
Sawicki, J.
    1991   *Disciplining Foucault: Feminism, power and the body*. New York: Routledge.
Schaeffer, C. F. A.
    1936   *Missions en Chypre 1932–1935*. Paris: Klincksieck.
    1952   *Enkomi-Alasia. Nouvelles missions en Chypre 1946–1950*. Paris: Klincksieck.
Schmidt, K.
    1999   Frühe Tier- und Menschenbilder vom Göbekli Tepe-Kampagnen 1995–98: Ein kommentierter Katalog der Grossplastik und der Reliefs. *Istanbuler Mitteilungen* 49: 5–21.
Schulte-Campbell, C.
    1983   A Late Bronze Age Cypriote from Hala Sultan Tekke and another discussion of cranial deformation. Pp. 249–52 (Appendix 5) in *Hala Sultan Tekke 8: Excavations 1971–79*, by P. Åström et al. SIMA 45: 8. Göteborg, Sweden: Åströms.
Schwartz, J.
    1974   The human remains from Kition and Hala Sultan Tekke: A cultural interpretation. Pp. 151–62 (Appendix 4) in *Excavations at Kition I: The tombs*, by V. Karageorghis. Nicosia: Department of Antiquities.
Scott, E.
    2002   Killing the female? Archaeological narratives of infanticide. Pp. 1–21 in *Gender and the archaeology of death*, eds. B. Arnold and N. L. Wicker. Walnut Creek, CA: AltaMira.
Shanks, M., and C. Tilley
    1982   Ideology, symbolic power and ritual communication. Pp. 129–54 in *Symbolic and structural archaeology*, ed. I. Hodder. Cambridge: Cambridge University Press.
    1987   *Re-constructing archaeology*. Cambridge: Cambridge University Press.
Sherratt, A.
    1980   Water, soil and seasonality in early cereal cultivation. *World Archaeology* 11(3): 313–30.
    1983   The secondary exploitation of animals in the Old World. *World Archaeology* 15(1): 90–104.
Sherratt, A., and S. Sherratt
    1991   From luxuries to commodities: The nature of Mediterranean Bronze Age trading systems. Pp. 351–86 in *Bronze Age trade in the Mediterranean*, ed. N. H. Gale. SIMA 90. Jonsered, Sweden: Åströms.
Sherratt, S.
    1994   Commerce, iron and ideology: Metallurgical innovation in 12th–11th century Cyprus. Pp. 59–106 in *Cyprus in the 11th century B.C.*, ed. V. Karageorghis. Nicosia: A. G. Leventis Foundation and University of Cyprus.
Shiels, J.
    2003   The experimental replication of Chalcolithic pottery. Pp. 162–68 in *Lemba Archaeological Project III.1: The colonisation and settlement of Cyprus. Investigations at Kissonerga-Mylouthkia, 1976–1996*, ed. E. Peltenburg. SIMA 70(4). Sävedalen, Sweden: Åströms.
Shilling, C.
    1993   *The body and social theory*. London: Sage.
Silverblatt, I.
    1988   *Women in states. Annual Review of Anthropology* 17: 427–60.
    1991   Interpreting women in states: New feminist ethnohistories. Pp. 140–71 in *Gender at the crossroads of knowledge: Feminist anthropology in the postmodern era*, ed. M. di Leonardo. Berkeley: University of California Press.

Simmons, A. H.
    1996   Preliminary report on multidisciplinary investigations at Neolithic Kholetria-*Ortos*, Paphos District. *RDAC*: 29–44.
    2001   The first humans and last pygmy hippopotami of Cyprus. Pp. 1–18 in *The earliest prehistory of Cyprus: From colonization to exploitation*, ed. S. Swiny. CAARI Monographs, vol. 2. Boston: ASOR.

Simmons, A. H. et al.
    1999   *Faunal extinction in an island society: Pygmy hippopotamus hunters of Cyprus*. New York: Kluwer/Plenum.

Smith, E. A., and S. A. Smith
    1994   Inuit sex-ratio variation: Population control, ethnographic error or sex bias. *Current Anthropology* 35: 595–624.

Smith, J. S.
    2002   Changes in the workplace: Women and textile production on Late Bronze Age Cyprus. Pp. 281–312 in *Engendering Aphrodite: Women and society in ancient Cyprus*, eds. D. Bolger and N. Serwint. CAARI Monographs, vol. 3. Boston: ASOR.

Smith, P., and G. Kahila
    1992   Identification of infanticide in archaeological sites; a case study from the Late Roman–Early Byzantine periods at Askalon, Israel. *Journal of Archaeological Science* 19: 667–75.

Sorensen, M. L. S.
    1996   Women as/and metalworkers. Pp. 45–51 in *Women in industry and technology: From prehistory to the present day*, eds. A. Devonshire and B. Wood. London: Museum of London.
    1997   Reading dress: The construction of social categories and identities in Bronze Age Europe. *Journal of European Archaeology* 5(1): 93–114.
    2000   *Gender archaeology*. Cambridge: Polity.

South, A.
    1983   Kalavasos-*Ayios Dhimitrios* 1982. *RDAC*: 92–116.
    1984   Kalavasos-*Ayios Dhimitrios* 1983. *RDAC*: 14–41.
    1985   Figurines and other objects from Kalavasos-Ayious. *Levant* 17: 65–79.
    1989   From copper to kingship: Aspects of Bronze Age society viewed from the Vasilikos Valley. Pp. 315–24 in *Early society in Cyprus*, ed. E. Peltenburg. Edinburgh: Edinburgh University Press.
    1992   Kalavasos-*Ayios Dhimitrios* 1991. *RDAC*: 133–46.
    1997   Kalavasos-*Ayios Dhimitrios* 1992–96. *RDAC*: 151–76.

South, A., P. Russell, and P. S. Keswani
    1989   *Vasilikos Valley Project 3: Kalavasos-Ayios Dhimitrios II. Ceramics, objects, tombs, specialist studies*, ed. I. A. Todd.. SIMA 71: 3. Göteborg, Sweden: Åströms.

Spain, D.
    1992   *Gendered spaces*. Chapel Hill: University of North Carolina Press.

Spector, J.
    1991   What this awl means: Towards a feminist archaeology. Pp. 388–406 in *Engendering archaeology: Women and prehistory*, eds. J. M. Gero and M. W. Conkey. Oxford: Blackwell.
    1994   *What this awl means: Feminist archaeology at a Wahpeton Dakota village*. St. Paul: Minnesota Historical Society.

Spector, J., and M. K. Whelan
    1989   Incorporating gender into archaeology courses. Pp. 65–94 in *Gender and anthropology: Critical reviews for research and teaching*, ed. S. Morgen. Washington, DC: American Anthropological Association.
    1991   What this awl means: Toward a feminist archaeology. Pp. 388–406 in *Engendering archaeology: Women and prehistory*, eds. J. M. Gero and M. W. Conkey. Oxford: Blackwell.
    1994   *What this awl means: Feminist archaeology at a Wahpeton Dakota village*. St. Paul: Minnesota Historical Society.

Stanley Price, N. P.

    1979a   The structure of settlement at Sotira in Cyprus. *Levant* 11: 46–83.

    1979b   *Early prehistoric settlement in Cyprus, 6500–3000 B.C.* BAR International Series 65. Oxford: British Archaeological Reports.

Steel, L.

    1994   Representations of a shrine on a Mycenaean chariot krater from Kalavasos-Ayios Dhimitrios, Cyprus. *Annual of the British School at Athens* 89: 201–11.

    2002   Wine, women and song: Drinking ritual in Cyprus in the Late Bronze and Early Iron Ages. Pp. 105–19 in *Engendering Aphrodite: Women and society in ancient Cyprus*, eds. D. Bolger and N. Serwint. CAARI Monographs, vol. 3. Boston: ASOR.

Stekelis, M.

    1961   The flint implements. Pp. 230–34 (Appendix 2) in *Sotira*, by P. Dikaios. Oxford: Oxford University Press.

Stewart, E., and J. Stewart

    1950   *Excavations at Vounous 1937–38.* Skrifter Utgivna av Svenska Institutet i Rom. Lund, Sweden: C. W. K. Gleerup.

Stewart, J. R.

    1962   The Early Cypriot Bronze Age. Pp. 205–391 in *The Swedish Cyprus Expedition* IV.IA, by P. Dikaios and J. R. Stewart. Lund, Sweden: Swedish Cyprus Expedition.

Stordeur, D.

    1999   Organization de l'espace construit et organization social dans le Neolithique de Jerf el Ahmar (Syrie, X–IX millénaire av. J.C.). Pp. 131–49 in *Habitat et société*, eds. F. Braemer, S. Cleuziou, and A. Coudart. Antibes, France: Éditions APDCA.

Strathern, M.

    1972   *Women in between; Female roles in a male world: Mount Hagen, New Guinea.* London: Seminar Press.

Sweeley, T. L., ed.

    1999   *Manifesting power: Gender and the interpretation of power in archaeology.* London and New York: Routledge.

Swiny, H., and S. Swiny

    1983   An anthropomorphic figurine from the Sotira area. *RDAC:* 56–59.

Swiny, S.

    1982   Correlations between the composition and function of Bronze Age metal types in Cyprus. Pp. 69–80 in *Early metallurgy in Cyprus, 4000–500 BC*, eds. J. D. Muhly, R. Maddin, and V. Karageorghis. Nicosia: Pierides Foundation.

    1985   Sotira-*Kaminoudhia* and the Chalcolithic/Early Bronze Age transition in Cyprus. Pp. 115–24 in *Archaeology in Cyprus 1960–1985*, ed. V. Karageorghis. Nicosia: A. G. Leventis Foundation.

    1986   *The Kent State University Expedition to Episkopi Phaneromeni. Part 2.* SIMA 74: 2. Nicosia: Åströms. From round house to duplex: A re-assessment of prehistoric Cypriot Bronze Age society. Pp. 14–31 in *Early Society in Cyprus*, ed. E. Peltenburg. Edinburgh: Edinburgh University Press.

    1989   From round house to duplex: a re-assessment of prehistoric Cypriot Bronze Age society. Pp. 14–31 in *Early society in Cyprus*, ed. E. Peltenburg. Edinburgh: Edinburgh University Press.

Swiny, S., ed.

    2001   *The earliest prehistory of Cyprus: From colonization to exploitation.* CAARI Monographs, vol. 2. Boston: ASOR.

Swiny, S., G. Rapp, and E. Herscher, eds.

    2002   *Sotira-Kaminoudhia: An Early Bronze Age site in Cyprus.* ASOR Archaeological Reports, vol. 8. Boston: ASOR.

Talalay, L.

    1987   Rethinking the function of clay figurine legs from Neolithic Greece: An argument by analogy. *American Journal of Archaeology* 91: 161–69.

1993 *Deities, dolls and devices: Neolithic figurines from Francthi Cave, Greece.* Excavations at Francthi Cave, Greece, fasc. 9. Bloomington: Indiana University Press.

2000 Archaeological Ms.conceptions: Contemplating gender and power in the Greek Neolithic. Pp. 3–16 in *Representations of gender from prehistory to the present*, eds. M. Donald and L. Hurcombe. New York: St. Martin's.

Talalay, L., and T. Cullen
2002 Sexual ambiguity in Early-Middle Cypriot plank figures. Pp. 181–95 in *Engendering Aphrodite: Women and society in ancient Cyprus*, eds. D. Bolger and N. Serwint. CAARI Monographs, vol. 3. Boston: ASOR.

Tarlow, S.
1999 *Bereavement and commemoration: An archaeology of mortality.* Malden, MA: Blackwell.

Tatton-Brown, V., ed.
1979 *Cyprus BC: 7000 years of history.* London: British Museum.

Thomas, G.
1988 The Maa Chalcolithic excavations. Pp. 267–89 in *Excavations at Maa-Paleokastro, 1979–1986*, by V. Karageorghis and M. Demas. Nicosia: Department of Antiquities.

Thomas, J.
1996 *Time, culture and identity: An interpretive archaeology.* London: Routledge.

Thorne, B.
1990 Children and gender: Constructions of difference. Pp. 100–13 in *Theoretical perspectives on sexual difference*, ed. D. L. Rhode. New Haven, CT: Yale University Press.

Thornhill, R., and C. T. Palmer
2000 *A natural history of rape: Biological bases of sexual coercion.* Cambridge: Massachusetts Institute of Technology Press.

Todd, I. A.
1981 A Cypriote Neolithic wall painting. *Antiquity* 55: 47–51.

1991 The Vasilikos Valley and the Chalcolithic period in Cyprus. *Bulletin of the Americn Schools of Oriental Research* 282/283: 3–16.

1998 *Kalavasos-Tenta.* Nicosia: Bank of Cyprus Cultural Foundation.

Todd, I. A., ed.
1986 *Vasilikos Valley Project 1: The Bronze Age cemetery in Kalavasos village.* SIMA 71: 1. Göteborg, Sweden: Åströms.

Todd, I.A., and P. Croft
In press *Vasilikos Valley Project 8: Excavations at Kalavasos-Ayious.* SIMA 71: 8. Jonsered: Åströms.

Todd, I. A. et al.
1987 *Vasilikos Valley Project 6: Excavations at Kalavasos-Tenta I.* SIMA 71: 6. Göteborg, Sweden: Åströms.

Toren, C.
1993 Making history: The significance of childhood cognition for a comparative anthropology of mind. *Man* 28(3): 461–78.

Treherne, P.
1995 The warrior's beauty: The masculine body and self identity in Bronze Age Europe. *Journal of European Archaeology* 3(1): 105–44.

Tringham, R. E.
1991 Households with faces: The challenge of gender in prehistoric architectural remains. Pp. 93–131 in *Engendering archaeology: Women and prehistory*, eds. J. M. Gero and M. W. Conkey. Oxford: Blackwell.

1994 Engendered places in prehistory. *Gender, Place and Culture* 1(2): 169–203.

Tringham, R. E., and M. Conkey
1998 Rethinking figurines: A critical view from archaeology of Gimbutas, the "goddess" and popular culture. Pp. 22–45 in *Ancient goddesses*, eds. L. Goodison and C. Morris. London: British Museum.

Turner, V.
1969   *The ritual process: Structure and anti-structure.* Ithaca, NY: Cornell University Press.
Tyldesley, J.
1995   *Daughters of Isis: Women of ancient Egypt.* London: Penguin.
Ucko, P.
1968   *Anthropomorphic figurines of predynastic Egypt and Neolithic Crete with comparative material from the prehistoric Near East and mainland Greece.* London: Andrew Szmidla.
Vagnetti, L.
1974   Preliminary remarks on Cypriote Chalcolithic figurines. *RDAC*: 24–34.
1980   Figurines and minor objects from a Chalcolithic cemetery at Souskiou-Vathyrkakas (Cyprus). *Studi Micenei ed Egeo-Anatolici* 21: 17–72.
van der Leeuw, S.
1977   Toward a study of the economics of pottery making. Pp. 68–76 in *Ex Horreo*, eds. B. L. van Beek, R. W. Brandt, and W. Grueman van Waateringe. Amsterdam: University of Amsterdam.
van Gennep, A.
1960   *Rites of passage.* Chicago: University of Chicago Press.
Vermeule, E. T.
1974   *Toumba tou Skourou, the mound of darkness: A Bronze Age town on Morphou Bay in Cyprus.* Boston: Harvard University Museum of Fine Arts.
Vermeule, E. T., and F. Wolsky
1990   *Toumba tou Skourou: A Bronze Age potter's quarter on Morphou Bay in Cyprus.* Boston: Harvard University Press.
Vitzhum, V. J.
1997   Flexibility and paradox: The evolution of a flexibly responsive reproductive system. Pp. 242–58 in *The evolving female: A life-history perspective*, eds. M. E. Morbeck, A. Galloway, and A. L. Zihlman. Princeton: Princeton University Press.
Walde, D., and N. D. Willows, eds.
1991   *The archaeology of gender. Proceedings of the twenty-second annual Chacmool conference of the Archaeological Association of the University of Calgary.* Calgary, Canada: Archaeological Association, University of Calgary.
Wallace, S.
1995   *Recognising change in systems of prehistoric ceramic production: A statistical approach to identifying standardisation in ceramic attributes, applied at Kissonerga-Mosphilia, Cyprus.* Unpublished M.A. dissertation, University of Edinburgh.
Watkins, T.
1973   *Some problems of the Neolithic and Chalcolithic in Cyprus. RDAC*: 34–61.
Watson, P. J., and M. C. Kennedy
1991   The development of horticulture in the eastern woodlands of North America: Women's role. Pp. 255–75 in *Engendering archaeology: Women and prehistory*, eds. J. M. Gero and M. W. Conkey. Oxford: Blackwell.
Webb, J. M.
1999   *Ritual architecture, iconography and practice in the Late Cypriot Bronze Age.* Jonsered, Sweden: Åströms.
2002   Engendering the built environment: Household and community in prehistoric Bronze Age Cyprus. Pp. 87–101 in *Engendering Aphrodite: Women and society in ancient Cyprus*, eds. D. Bolger and N. Serwint. CAARI Monographs, vol. 3. Boston: ASOR.
Webb, J. M., and D. Frankel
1995   Gender inequity and archaeological practice. A Cypriot case study. *Journal of Mediterranean Archaeology* 8: 93–112.
1999   Characterizing the Philia facies: Material culture, chronology, and the origin of the Bronze Age in Cyprus. *American Journal of Archaeology* 103(1): 3–43.
Weinberg, S.
1983   *Bamboula at Kourion: The architecture.* Philadelphia: University Museum.

Weiss, K. M.
  1972   On systematic bias in skeletal sexing. *American Journal of Physical Anthropology* 37: 239–50.
Wilson, E. O.
  1975   *Sociobiology: The new synthesis.* Cambridge, MA: Harvard University Press.
Wright, K. I.
  2000   The social origins of cooking and dining in early villages of western Asia. *Proceedings of the Prehistoric Society* 66: 89–121.
Wright, R. P.
  1991   Women's labor and pottery production in prehistory. Pp. 194–223 in *Engendering archaeology: Women and prehistory,* eds. J. M. Gero and M. W. Conkey. Oxford: Blackwell.
Wright, R. P., ed.
  1996   *Gender and archaeology.* Philadelphia: University of Pennsylvania Press.
Wyke, M., ed.
  1998   *Gender and the body in the ancient Mediterranean.* Oxford: Blackwell.
Wylie, A.
  1991   Gender theory and the archaeological record: Why is there no archaeology of gender? Pp. 31–54 in *Engendering archaeology: Women and prehistory,* eds. J. M. Gero and M. W. Conkey. Oxford: Blackwell.
  1998   The interplay of evidential constraints and political interests: Recent archaeological research on gender. Pp. 57–84 in *Reader in gender archaeology,* eds. K. Hays-Gilpin and D. S. Whitley. London: Routledge.
Yanagisako, S., and C. Delaney
  1995   *Naturalizing power: Essays in feminist cultural analysis.* New York: Routledge.
Yoffee, N., and G. Cowgill, eds.
  1995   *The collapse of ancient states and civilizations.* Tucson and London: University of Arizona Press.
Yoffee, N., and A. Sherratt, eds.
  1993   *Archaeological theory: Who sets the agenda?* Cambridge: Cambridge University Press.
Zihlman, A.
  1998   Woman the gatherer: The role of women in early hominid evolution. Pp. 91–107 in *Reader in gender archaeology,* eds. K. Hays-Gilpin and D. S. Whitley. London: Routledge.
  1999   Women's bodies, women's lives: An evolutionary perspective. Pp. 185–97 in *The evolving female: A life-history perspective,* eds. M. E. Morbeck et al. Princeton: Princeton University Press.

Index

Figures and tables are indicated by italic.

About the Author

Diane Bolger is a research fellow in archaeology at the University of Edinburgh in Scotland. She received her Ph.D. from the University of Cincinnati in 1985 and was appointed professor at the University of Maryland in 2001. From 1986–2001, she was a member of the faculty of Social Sciences at the European Division of the University of Maryland, based in Heidelberg, Germany. She has been working in Cyprus since 1981, when she began research for a doctoral dissertation on the Chalcolithic site of Erimi, and is a ceramics specialist for University of Edinburgh's projects in Cyprus and Syria.

Dr. Bolger's research interests include ceramic production and craft specialization in the prehistoric Near East and the archaeology of gender. In 1998, she co-organized an international conference on gender in ancient Cyprus at the Cyprus American Archaeological Research Institute (CAARI) in Nicosia, the proceedings of which were published in 2002. In addition to conducting annual fieldwork in Cyprus, Dr. Bolger is currently working in Syria on the publication of Uruk ceramics from the site of Jerablus-Tahtani near Carchemish.